Judith Gautier

Judith Gautier

A Biography

Joanna Richardson

FRANKLIN WATTS
New York 1987

First published in Great Britain in 1986
by Quartet Books Ltd.

First published in the United States in 1987
by Franklin Watts, Inc., 387 Park Avenue South,
New York, New York 10016

Library of Congress Catalog Card Number: 86-50337
ISBN 0-531-15025-9

All rights reserved
Printed in the United States
5   4   3   2   1

For
Elizabeth Dickinson

Indépendante j'ai vécu, indépendante je vieillis,
indépendante je mourrai. Je serai, toute mon
existence, une sorte d'Extrême-Orientale détachée
des choses de son temps et de son milieu.

Judith Gautier to Raoul Aubry,
Le Temps, 25 November 1910

Contents

List of Illustrations

Judith Gautier

Introduction

Some years ago, when I was in Paris, writing my life of Théophile Gautier, Alice Théo Bergerat took me to 30, rue Washington. She was the widow of Gautier's grandson, and she had known Judith Gautier: indeed, for a while she had lived with her at Le Pré des Oiseaux. That afternoon she introduced me to Suzanne Meyer-Zundel, Judith's closest friend and confidante. During our rather formal tea, Mme Meyer-Zundel mentioned that she had some unpublished memoirs. Whether she referred to *Dans l'intimité des dieux*, or to the last, unfinished, volume of *Le Collier des jours*, or whether she meant her own memoirs, I am now not sure; but it was, I think, that afternoon that my interest in Judith Gautier began.

She was the elder daughter of Théophile Gautier: that endearing, brilliant Romantic who wore a pink doublet at *Hernani*, wrote *Mademoiselle de Maupin*, and lived to be the poet of *Émaux et Camées* and Art for Art's Sake. Dramatist, author of *Giselle*, critic of drama, literature and art, and travel writer extraordinary, he was a friend of most of the eminent writers and artists, composers and actors in France. Judith owed more to him than she did to her turbulent Italian mother, Ernesta Grisi; and, through him, she spent her adolescence in a world where Hugo was a familiar god, and Baudelaire and Flaubert were casual visitors. She had an enchanted childhood, surrounded by her father's friends, granted the freedom of his library, enlisted as assistant when he wrote *Le Roman de la momie* and *Spirite*. He called her his 'last hope'. It was he who presented her with a Chinese tutor, Tin-Tun-Ling, and – a privilege which must remain unique in its annals – arranged for her to take home rare Chinese manuscripts from the Bibliothèque Impériale (today the Bibliothèque Nationale). Théophile Gautier was largely responsible for Judith's love of the romantic East, for making her the inspired Sinologist of *Le Livre de Jade* and *Le Dragon impérial*. He set her on the road to the Académie-Goncourt.

He had also, as Baudelaire observed, created her in the image of his dreams. Her beauty was classical and extraordinary. To her it was to be calamitous. It brought her marriage with Catulle Mendès: a marriage so unhappy that it destroyed her father's household, ended in divorce, and made her deeply contemptuous of men. She was, beyond much doubt, the mistress of Victor Hugo; she had a brief flirtation with Richard Wagner, but probably no more, although she remained his essential inspiration while he was writing *Parsifal*. But, however she described passion in her work, she was afraid of it in life. Her experience with Mendès made her keep men at a distance. She enjoyed their company, their admiration, she would do a thousand kindnesses for those who – like Fanelli, the composer – seemed to her deserving recipients; but she would not commit herself again. She did not lose her deep despair until the last years of her life, when she lived with Suzanne Meyer-Zundel. Whether this relationship was maternal or Lesbian one cannot ever know, but one infers that, finally, it found physical expression.

Judith's private life was complex and, at times, tormented. Her literary life was full, and it was distinguished. She was, like her father, a prolific writer. Like him, she was obliged to earn her living, compelled by practical necessity to write unremittingly throughout her adult life. Her first article, on an art exhibition, appeared in 1864, when she was eighteen; her last, on Fanelli, appeared in 1917, when she was seventy-two and on the eve of her death. For more than half a century she wrote under pressure: driven, during marriage, by her husband's financial straits and, after their separation, by the need to keep herself, maintain her pied-à-terre in Paris, her villa at Saint-Enogat, provide for her maid, her social life, and for unspoken charities. Such pressure meant that frequently she was obliged to turn journalist and – like her father – to review indifferent books and pictures and plays. She wrote a publicity book for a *chocolatier*. She wrote, at times, beneath herself and, towards the end of her life, she plagiarized herself, and lent her name to works of small distinction. It has been calculated that her work would fill fifty volumes; it is now impossible to trace all that she wrote, and to verify the statement, but she has many titles to remembrance.

As a music critic she has a quite unusual significance. She was one of the first in France to recognize the power of Wagner, and, despite the violent contention which he aroused, she proclaimed his power for half a century. She was not only his Egeria, the inspiration of his *Parsifal*, she was among his most constant partisans. Her book on Wagner's poetry, the third volume of her memoirs, and her own translation of *Parsifal*, are the most substantial of her tributes to him; but he had spoken to her heart when she was still a girl, and, time and again, she discussed his works with passion.

She did not present intellectual analyses, nor did she comment on questions of technique, but she recognized great music from the first, and perhaps her courage, passion and loyalty served Wagner better than any technical assessment. Posterity may not have seen in Ernest Fanelli what Judith saw in his compositions; but, again, she felt his music on her pulse, and, in her final years, supported him with almost youthful fervour. Her love of music came from her heart rather than her head, but it embraced Beethoven and Richard Strauss. Her love of the classical did not diminish her belief in the music of the future.

Her criticism of art is – like her father's – a transposition of genres. A painter and sculptor herself, she translated pictures into prose, writing in a painterly style. Her tastes were perhaps predictable: she was drawn to the Romantics and the Orientalists, who shared or inspired her own visions; but her judgement was sure: she made no concessions to mediocrity, and she recognized the masters.

Judith Gautier wrote some remarkable fiction: *Le Dragon impérial* and *Iskender* move us still by their verve and dynamism, their sustained invention, their brilliant historical detail. Her European novels were trite and often unfelt; her oriental novellas and short stories burn with the familiar fire. Whether she writes of ancient Egypt, Persia, China or Japan, she moves, now, in a real (though, paradoxically, imagined) world. The Middle East and the Far East are her natural habitat; she lives in legendary ages, the pre-Christian era, the medieval world, with an ease and a clear delight which she does not feel in contemporary Paris. Like Madame de Sévigné, in her *Lettres inédites*, those engaging pastiches in Judith's hand, Judith herself preferred to leave modern Paris for the past. She was happiest in the world which she herself had created, a world which she had faithfully built from book knowledge and pictures, sometimes from the descriptions of travellers who had been there, but a world which she had built according to her own ideals. Some of her writing on the East is prose-poetry; few of her own poems – which are largely intellectual and derivative – touch her translations from the Chinese and Japanese, which seem to mirror her own inmost emotions. *Le Livre de Jade* and *Poèmes de la Libellule* are among her chief claims to remembrance.

In *Le Collier des jours* she escaped not to foreign lands, but to her own past; and the three volumes which she completed are among the most delectable of autobiographies. Judith, for all her intellect, remained an innocent, and she readily recaptured her childhood view of life. It is perhaps pedantic to note her disregard for dates; and perhaps, as in other memoirs, some events have been enlarged and others reduced or forgotten. But the childhood view of the adult world is poignantly recalled. The narrow routine of Montrouge, the oppressive convent, the original, tumultuous life at Neuilly are all recorded in authentic detail. The first two volumes give us, still, a panorama of Second Empire Paris, its vivid and familiar celebrities; the third presents a unique insight into Wagner's life. *Le Collier de jours* reveals, perhaps despite herself, much about its author: passionate, private, shrewd, determined, vulnerable and inescapably charming. It is one of her most engaging contributions to literature, and it is one of the most significant. For Judith was a distinguished orientalist, an undoubted intellectual, but she kept her verve and innocence. She lived in a dream world, like a child; and when she returned, in imagination, at the end of her life, to her childhood, to her father's house at Neuilly, she wrote from her heart.

Poet, translator, dramatist, novelist and critic, she had no personal ambition, but she was the first woman to be an Academician in France. Her circle in the rue Washington, and at her little villa in Brittany, was almost as distinguished as that of her father at Neuilly. She is a touching human being, and she has her place in the history of literature and music and, perhaps, in the history of feminism. She covers a notable span of history. She had been born in the days of Louis-Philippe; she lived to be friends with President Poincaré. She had been a child at the time of the Crimean War; she died at the time of the Battle of Verdun.

I am of course indebted to M. Dita Camacho's doctoral thesis, *Judith Gautier. Sa vie et son oeuvre*. This was published in Paris in 1939, and has, until now, been the only substantial work on the subject. It is, however, incomplete in many respects, and it contains numerous errors. I have also largely relied, in my later chapters, on *Quinze ans auprès de Judith Gautier*, the memoirs of Suzanne Meyer-Zundel. They, too, are not exempt from factual errors, but they remain essential reading. I owe much to my late friends in Paris, M. Pierre Théophile Gautier (great-grandson of Théophile) and Mme Alice Théo Bergerat; they gave me not only the freedom of their archives, but much family information. I am indebted to the Marquise de Chabannes la Palice, who illuminated the career of Augusta Holmès, and to Mme Françoise Dumas, Conservateur-en-chef, Bibliothèque de l'Institut de France, who allowed me to consult the papers of Charles Clermont-Ganneau and Leconte de Lisle. I am grateful to M. Pierre Janin and his colleagues in the Département des Manuscrits at the Bibliothèque Nationale, who enabled me to see the correspondence of Judith Gautier, and the letters of Suzanne Meyer-Zundel. I must also record my gratitude to the staff in the Département des Imprimés, the Département des Périodiques and the Département des Arts du Spectacle. I much appreciate the help I received at the Maison de Victor Hugo and the Bibliothèque de l'Arsenal. I am particularly indebted to Monsieur Jacques Suffel, for his generous encouragement at the Bibliothèque

Spoelberch de Lovenjoul, Chantilly. I am glad, once again, to acknowledge the help which I received from the late Count Lanfranco Campello, who let me consult the Primoli Papers. I am very grateful to Mr Richard Ormond, Director of the National Maritime Museum, and great-nephew of John Singer Sargent, for sending me copies of some of the Sargent papers of the late David McKibbin; and I am much indebted to Mr Michael Pakenham, of the University of Exeter, for many useful references and fruitful suggestions for research. I am, as always, particularly pleased to thank Dr Alan Raitt for his interest and expert advice. I must express my gratitude to the patient staff at the British Library in Bloomsbury and at Colindale, and to Dr Giles Barber, Miss Gillian Hughes and their colleagues at the Taylor Institution, Oxford, for their exemplary kindness and expertise.

JOANNA RICHARDSON

I

Mademoiselle Judith Gautier

Chapter One

The Grisi family of Milan was distinguished in the annals of music and the theatre.[1] Giuditta Grisi, an opera singer acclaimed in the early 1830s, married a nobleman, Count Barni, and died at the age of thiry-five. Her sister, Giulia, whom Parisians called *la jolie Grisi*, was renowned for her voice, her acting and her beauty, and she was the star of the Théâtre des Italiens. She married Gérard de Melcy, and then spent her life in a love affair, which was a virtual marriage, with the tenor Mario de Candia. She finally settled in London, and died in 1869.

Three other Grisis, three sisters who were cousins of Giuditta and Giulia, also had their triumphs on the stage. Marina married, left the theatre, and retired into domesticity. Carlotta was born in 1819 at Visinada, in Upper Istria, where her father had worked in the public surveyor's department. From her earliest childhood it was clear that she was born to dance. At the age of ten she was *première danseuse* in the children's *corps de ballet* at La Scala, in Milan. On her twenty-second birthday, 28 June 1841, she had her first and greatest triumph in Paris, in the first performance of *Giselle*.

The libretto of *Giselle* had been written by Théophile Gautier, and his adoration of Carlotta is evident from that moment. His love was to shine from his ballets and poems, from his novel *Spirite* and from his letters. It was, so he told her a quarter of a century later, 'the true, the only love of my heart'. Carlotta had been the mistress of Jules Perrot, her teacher and partner; she was the mother of his daughter, Marie-Julie, and she had taken his name for the sake of convenience. Perrot had wanted to marry her, but her formidable mother and her cousin, Giulia, had secretly negotiated a contract for her at the Opéra, and the marriage did not suit their plans. Perrot continued to take some part in her career, but their close relationship was over, and by 1842 Carlotta was the mistress of the dancer Lucien Petipa. When in time she took another lover, bore his child, and accepted his handsome villa on the shores of Lake Geneva, she chose a Polish nobleman, Prince Léon Radziwill. She rewarded Gautier for his devotion, for ballets, poems, novel, for creating her career, with lasting but platonic affection.

It was therefore not Carlotta who shared Gautier's daily life. Since the human heart is endlessly complex, it was her elder sister, Ernesta. Sallow and large-eyed, seductive, she watches posterity from Riesener's portrait, and from the painting by Bonnegrâce, now at the Musée Carnavalet. Perhaps it was her likeness to Carlotta that first drew Gautier. Perhaps it was her passionate contralto as she sang at the Théâtre des Italiens. Perhaps he was drawn to her simply by physical attraction. He had known her at least since 1842, when he had gone to London to see Carlotta in *Giselle*.[2] By the winter of 1844 he had become the lover of this fiery singer, this capable housewife who took him in her charge as his mother had taken charge of a spoilt child. Impractical and often weak, he needed a maternal hand to guide him. Ernesta gave him the old domestic security, the pampering he had known as a boy. She was not merely attractive; she made herself domestically essential. That was why the liaison was marriage in all but name, and it lasted for more than two decades.

In the summer of 1845, although Ernesta was heavily pregnant, Gautier set out for Algeria, with empty promises of a travel book. 'Be brave, my darling,' he told her in August, from the depths of Kabylia, 'and remember, in your sufferings, that there is someone beyond the seas, in the deserts of Africa, who feels them and shares them in his soul . . . I shall leave Stora on the 29th, and five or six days later I shall be in Paris and embrace you and someone else . . .'[3] On 24 August, Ernesta gave birth to his daughter.

> I began life with a passion [so Judith later wrote] . . . They tell me I showed a good deal of repugnance at coming into the world. I folded my arm across my face, and stubbornly refused to make my entrance into this life, and, having been compelled to do so, I showed my displeasure with a real burst of anger; I screamed, and seized the doctor's fingers, and clung to them with such desperation that he could not move them. He was obliged to shake me off hard, and he cried in utter stupefaction:
> 'What sort of little monster is this?'. . .
> I often made my mother tell me about this incident. It seemed prophetic to me. It so clearly explained the opinion I was later to have of life.[4]

Early in September 1845, when she was about a fortnight old, Judith was presented to her father. After two months in Africa, he had come home enveloped in a burnous against the autumn chill, and (as Sainte-Beuve remembered, twenty years later), holding a small lioness upon his knee. It was an apt and exotic beginning to Judith's family life.

Gautier was already the author of *Mademoiselle de Maupin,* several volumes of poetry and *Voyage en Espagne.* He had written the librettos for *Giselle* and *La Péri.* However, he was compelled to earn his living on *La Presse* to fulfil his family commitments. He already had a son, Théophile (known as Toto), by his former mistress, Eugénie Fort (whom he addressed as Mme Eugénie Gautier); now he had a second mistress and a second child to support. So it was that he became a critic of art and music, theatre and literature, often travelled abroad, and produced an endless series of articles and novels and short stories. While Gautier continued his busy, peripatetic life, Ernesta still belonged to the company at the Théâtre des Italiens. Their daughter could not be allowed to interfere with their careers. Within a few weeks of her birth, she was sent out to nurse.

She was not, it was true, sent far away: her nurse, a carpenter's wife, lived in the impasse d'Antin, in Les Batignolles. Yet, near as it was to her parents, it was a different world. For Damon, her nurse, Judith conceived the first great passion of her existence. The passion was mutual. Damon not only adored her, and humoured her every whim, she made her the centre of family life; so, indeed, did her husband and children.

> The infant Jesus [Judith wrote], entrusted to a Christian family, would certainly not have been treated with more devotion and love . . . I cannot in the least explain the reason for this infatuation, which never failed. For the father and mother, their children took second place in their affection, and the children themselves did not take umbrage, but became my obedient slaves.[5]

Judith grew up in humble surroundings, but she spent her infancy assured of admiration and boundless love; and when, every fortnight, she was taken to visit her parents in the rue Rougemont, she felt no instinctive surge of sympathy. Her own affections belonged elsewhere. 'For me, the only interest of these visits was the journey there and back; I was with the beloved and that was enough to please me. As for the people we went to see, I paid no attention to them.'[6]

Her passion for Damon was jealous and exclusive, and so intense that, even in early childhood, she became determined to protect her. 'I was hardly aware of my own weakness, because this desire to protect, and the certainty that I could do so, dominated all my infancy.'[7] She was already conscious that Damon led a life much inferior to that in the rue Rougemont; and, with the logic of a child, she determined to redress the balance. Whenever they went to see her parents, she wandered through the apartment, opening drawers and cupboards, collecting whatever took her fancy, and heaping it all in her nurse's basket. 'I stole for Her! And with what pride, what ease of conscience! . . . Unfortunately, before we left, the Beloved would disown me: she would empty the basket, and give everything back. On every visit, I began again, and I always felt the same poignant disappointment when I saw my work destroyed.'[8] As for her mother, theatrical and turbulent, Judith hated her. 'I detested the lady who had such a loud voice. I didn't want to visit her again.'[9]

Safely back in the impasse d'Antin, she cajoled *le père* Damon into making her a carriage. It was a sort of wooden basket, set on four wheels and adorned with little balusters. It was painted green, and drawn by a white goat. Escorted by Damon, she went on expeditions in the direction of Montmartre; here, on the waste land, the goat would graze, and Judith would play.

This idyllic life could not last for ever. The white goat died, and, for the first time, Judith became aware of death; to the end of her days she recalled the moment when she saw the carcass tossed on to a passing knacker's cart. There was to be an even more traumatic experience. One day Damon took her back to the rue Rougemont, and this time she left her with her mother.

> I was overcome [Judith remembered] by one unending sob, which lasted I don't know how many days and nights. I rejected everything they forced into my mouth, I was incapable, anyway, of even swallowing a drop of water, my throat was so constricted and convulsed by this endless grief. I, who detested obscurity, stayed in the dark ante-room, sitting on a bench too high for me, near the front door. The door was locked and bolted, but perhaps it would open once, and let me escape . . .[10]

Even her parents grew anxious at this overwhelming, incessant misery. Dr Aussandon – who had brought the tempestuous child into the world – was summoned once again. He decided that Judith must return to the impasse d'Antin. Once again she felt the delightful security of absolute devotion; 'and I have,' she wrote, 'always kept the impression that my most personal, most intense and happiest time was in those days of my early childhood, when . . . such a wealth of love created a vast and splendid kingdom for me.'[11]

The return to Damon could, of course, be only temporary. Soon afterwards she was despatched to live at Montrouge, on the outskirts of Paris, with her grandfather, Pierre Gautier, a retired receiver of taxes, and her two unmarried aunts, Lili and Zoé.

Route de Châtillon! That was where my grandfather lived, in a little house [no. 63] alongside the pavement, which had only a ground floor and an upper storey. He and his daughters occupied this first and only storey, which consisted of four rooms and a kitchen . . .

At first *le père* Gautier, as he was called, seemed very terrible to me. He was quite tall, and spare, and clean-shaven, with a swarthy complexion and a loud voice, and armed with a big cane with a silver knob which I noticed at once; I understood quite well that life would not be comfortable with him. I was not so worried by the aunts; I felt that they had no wills of their own, they were broken into obedience, and they were timid in their father's presence. At first sight they seemed almost identical, but there were differences between them. Tante Lili had a long nose which was thick at the end, and very small eyes, and her mouth was too big. Tante Zoé, who looked like her father, had a short nose, round eyes, and pursed lips. Both of them had black wavy hair which was drawn back behind the nape in a plain bun.

They were both dressed in plain black dresses, with a frill round the hem.[12]

She slept in her aunts' room, where

they had gathered the best remnants of their former comfort: big pieces of furniture in the Empire style, all in the darkest mahogany, and silk curtains of a red which was almost black, . . . precious mantelpiece ornaments, lapis-lazuli and gold, all the débris which held memories for them . . .

As soon as they had got up and done the room, the wooden shutters were closed, to keep the darkness which helped to preserve all this magnificence.[13]

Half a century later, in *Le Collier des jours*, Judith was to recall the spare, severe old man and the two well-meaning spinsters who were already set – and indeed eccentric – in their ways. 'I saw Judith at Châtillon,' Gautier once reported to Ernesta. 'She is as strong as a multitude of Ponts Neufs and runs round the garden like a hare . . .'[14] At the route de Châtillon, Montrouge, she ran wild in the fields and climbed the trees, but she still missed the affectionate warmth of the impasse d'Antin. Strong-willed, as she had always been, she was already hurt by the world. She withdrew into herself, and became more independent than ever. No one, she decided, had the right to know or to judge her inner self.

There were never tears in my eyes. I shouted but I did not cry; I defended myself, but I had no idea whatever of asking for mercy, or of humiliating myself.

I did not want to be punished, any more than I wanted to be caressed. Since I had fallen from my royal state and I was deprived of my dear nurse, who was still the only person I loved, I became very hard on myself, suffered privations with stoicism, and suffered even physical pain uncomplainingly.[15]

Only one way of escape remained: through her imagination; and her imagination was already strong:

> All I really liked were little articulated wooden dolls . . . You can't find them anywhere today, but you could buy them everywhere, in those days, at grocers' and haberdashers'. They cost a sou, but there were even small ones which cost one sou for two.
>
> I never had enough of them. It was a real mania with me; all the money I could get was spent on articulated dolls. I never asked for other toys, none of them interested me. I dressed this miniature world with scraps of material and even scraps of paper, and I arranged them in all sorts of ways.[16]

This was the first of her puppet theatres. The fascination of marionnettes was not to leave her. And already, it seemed, she had a premonition of her passion for the Orient. One Easter she proudly went to mass, and 'what made me so proud was that, for the first time, I had a sunshade. Perhaps some oriental atavism made me divine the symbolic majesty of the parasol, since this little silken dome, sheltering my head, gave me such pride.'[17] It was at Montrouge that she also received the rudiments of education. She went to Mlle Lavenue's school, the only one in the neighbourhood.

She was very small when her grandfather told her to learn the poems of Théophile Gautier, to honour and admire her famous father. He was a father who constantly gave her surprises, and one of the greatest must have been the discovery that she had a sister. Estelle had been born on 27 November 1848; Judith only knew of her existence when they met before their belated baptism.

Once again she had been taken to the rue Rougemont. 'What immediately concerned me,' she wrote, 'was the discovery of my sister, Estelle. No one had ever mentioned her to me, any more than they mentioned my mother, and I did not know that I had a sister. She probably didn't suspect it any more than I did, and looked at me with an air of extreme surprise.'[18]

The next day Judith was presented to her godfather, the journalist and man of letters Maxime du Camp.

> I had not yet read Goethe's *Faust,* or else I should certainly have taken him for Mephisto: tall, very thin, dark-skinned, fine-featured, a thin beard fined down to a point. He had a sharp look, a sly and disdainful expression. He was charming to his god-daughter . . .
>
> It was of course understood that the only possible godmother was the Star, the fairy, the diva, in short Giselle . . . My mother kept a superstitious faith in her sister, who had been like the good genius of the family, and, from the age of nine, through her precocious talent, had helped her to get out of difficult situations . . . But la Péri, who was travelling the world, did not attend her god-daughter's baptism. As a fairy, no doubt, she was invisibly present . . .

The ceremony took place in the église Bonne-Nouvelle, which the Commune later burnt, with the registers in which this memorable fact was recorded . . . As we were very small, we had been stood up on chairs, and told to answer 'yes' to everything the priest might ask. I felt obliged to add a comment on the quality of the salt which they put on my tongue, and to say I would really like a little more.[19]

She was baptized Louise Judith: Louise because she had been born on the day of Saint Louis, and Judith after her cousin, Giuditta Grisi.

It was Carlotta who now decided that Judith must have a respectable education, and it was she who chose to send her to the convent of Notre-Dame de la Miséricorde. Just as she had once been torn from the impasse d'Antin, and taken against her will to the rue Rougemont, Judith was now snatched from Montrouge and taken to the convent near the Panthéon. 'Whatever they do, you're really a Gautier,' so Tante Zoé reminded her. 'We'll see if they succeed in drawing you over to their side. In the meanwhile, they're taking you by force.'[20] Most of the Gautiers were strict and conservative bourgeois, most of the Grisis were dramatic artists. There could hardly be much sympathy between them. In fact there was open aversion between the womenfolk. It seemed only to grow stronger with the years.

Meanwhile, Tante Zoé deposited Judith at the convent. She was never to forget the sense of grim imprisonment she felt when she was first left to her convent life. She sought with desperation for some means of escape. When she realized that there was none, she decided to starve herself to death — a resolution which lasted half a day. Then she tried to kill herself by eating a poisonous plant from the convent garden. She spent several days in the infirmary, and all the poisonous plants were removed. Her attempted suicide made the nuns more vigilant than ever.

Occasionally, on her brief holidays, she would spend a few days with Carlotta Grisi.

I was least bored at Giselle's.
In the morning she used to work for several hours, in a chemise, in front of her cheval-glass. She practised her steps. She ran, leapt, walked on tiptoe, threw herself back in all sorts of poses, supple, light, enchanting. I watched this spectacle, good as gold in my little corner, with extreme surprise and curiosity.[21]

Giselle's admirers waited patiently to express their admiration; and among them, so it seems, was Léon Radziwill. He did not fail to charm her niece. Half a century later, Judith confessed:

> I have kept the still affectionate memory of a young foreign prince, pale and fair-haired, who was my friend more than the rest. I kept him company in his long periods of waiting in the salon. He talked to me as if I had been grown-up . . . He gave me wonderful presents, and among them . . . was a salon, made out of a pink and gold screen. It was adorned with mirrors alternating with pictures, with delightful furniture, and with two fine ladies who were paying a visit. That was my favourite toy, and I kept it very late in life.[22]

Sometimes, if Carlotta was away, Judith would be sent to stay with her formidable grandmother Grisi in the passage Saulnier. The visits were a penance, and the only creature there which earned her affection was an aged parrot, which taught her all its repertoire — and corrected her when she made mistakes. It was livelier in the rue Rougemont, where she rediscovered Estelle, and there was a constant to-ing and fro-ing of visitors. Some of them were famous: among them Ernest Reyer, the composer, Paul de Saint-Victor, the critic, and Eugène Vivier, who played the horn and contrived the most outrageous jokes. Vivier was noted for his alarming likeness to the Emperor; no doubt he impersonated Napoleon III.

From the rue Rougemont Judith returned to the sombre convent, with its morning mass at seven o'clock, its oppressive disapproval of pleasure.

> As far as I was concerned, there were two camps among the nuns, one of which was much in favour of me, the other very hostile towards me.
> The convent had news of the world through its pupils, in the first instance, the eldest of whom were twenty years old, and the walls were not so high that my father's fame had not crossed them. The author of *Mademoiselle de Maupin* was probably not in the odour of sanctity; and, besides, my mother sang in a theatre, my aunt danced, Giulia Grisi was my cousin. It all cast a special aura around me. For some of them, this had the attraction of forbidden fruit; for others it meant reprobation and horror . . .
> They asked me if it was true that my father had two wives!. . .I answered, without hesitation (I don't know where I had found this peremptory reply), 'that he could certainly have two, if he liked, since he was a Turk'. Turk!. . .So I was a pagan, then? That was obvious from my lack of devotion.
> The idea of being Turkish myself did not hurt me in the least; indeed, I was persuaded that I had been in the East, and I gave them all the details they wanted about this imaginary journey. The extraordinary thing was that they were correct![23]

The monthly report on Judith's conduct invariably bore the words 'Religion. None'. It was strange that mysticism had no hold on her. When she had to confess her sins, she found it a matter of pride to have a great many which were damnable, and, as she could not find them, she invented them. The confessor was often helpless with laughter, and the nuns declared that she was so perverted that she could cause the perdition of a priest. It was, perhaps, about now that she wrote a note, on ruled paper, to her father: 'My dear papa, I think I shall be good if the devil doesn't get in the way, I hug mama and my little sister estelle [*sic*] with all my heart.'[24]

Her favourite among the nuns was Mère Sainte-Trinité. She was as old as the hills and very ugly, but occasionally she was known to give Judith a small glass of cassis, and to fill her pockets with macaroons. When Judith was told of her grandfather Gautier's death, she confided to a friend 'that I had felt more grief when my white goat died, and that Mère Sainte-Trinité had caused me more regret when she passed away'.[25]

She spent nearly two years at the convent; and then, one day, with the suddenness to which she had grown accustomed, her mother and sister arrived to take her home, this time to their new fifth-floor apartment in the rue de la Grange-Batelière. 'I am really delighted that this affair is over,' her father said that evening. 'What about you? Are you glad to be here?'

'I'm not sure yet.'

'Of course. You hardly know us, and there is a great deal to forgive us.'[26]

That evening, Baudelaire chanced to call. He appeared to Judith like a priest without a surplice. She appeared to him the epitome of beauty. 'You have fashioned her according to your dreams,' he said to Gautier. 'She is like a little Greek girl.'[27] Judith was as beautiful as one of her father's poems. She might have stepped down from the frieze on the Parthenon.

Chapter Two

Judith later gave her father the details of convent life which he was to use in his novel *Spirite*. Now, in the autumn of 1856, he was writing *Le Roman de la momie*, and Judith – aged eleven – was entrusted with passing him the pictures which he needed. 'While he was writing, I looked at these astonishing pictures, in which the people had animals' heads, incredible horned headdresses and quite extraordinary poses. I was so fascinated by the appearance of this mysterious world . . . that I was very good, and I was kept in office for several days in succession.'[1] The spell of Egypt had taken hold. She swathed her doll in bandelets, and put a gold mask on its face; she set it in a workbox, surrounded by symbolic treasures, including an ear of wheat which she had purloined from a hat. Her father, touched and enchanted, kept the sarcophagus on his mantelpiece.

Illustrious visitors continued to call at the rue de la Grange-Batelière. Among them was the sculptor Antoine Étex.[2] His bust of Judith in Carrara marble was exhibited at the Salon of 1859. But the visitor she admired the most, from the first, was Gustave Flaubert. His towering height and his broad shoulders, his fine blue eyes and his moustaches – the moustaches of a Gallic chieftain – gave him the majesty of a colossus.[3] One night he read Gautier the episode of the Queen of Sheba from the first version of *La Tentation de Saint-Antoine*. Judith slipped out of bed, barefoot, to listen outside the door. Finally he gave his famous imitation of a drunk. It was too real for comfort. She fled in terror.

Her life with her parents continued to be full of surprises. One day a tall, fair-haired young boy arrived in the uniform of a *collégien*. He was introduced to the girls as their brother. 'Our brother! . . . They had never mentioned him . . . He was our brother, but he was not our mother's son. This puzzled us, but we did not trouble about it further.'[4]

Toto's mother, Eugénie Fort, passed her own comments on Judith. On

7 January 1857 she noted in her diary: 'Judith spent the day with me. I was astonished by the ignorance of this young girl, who will soon be twelve. What bad manners, what an unkempt appearance! . . . There's no doubt she's intelligent, but she has no principles, and no guidance. Poor child!'[5]

It was not surprising that Judith lacked guidance. Gautier was the most indulgent father. Ernesta was a feckless mother, and she had always been concerned with her own career. It had often taken her abroad. Early in 1852 she had found herself in Constantinople. 'Judith is well,' so Gautier had reported to her on 17 February 1852. 'She is becoming nice and sweet. She is reading fluently, and she is beginning to write, and she will be a good little girl. Nothing bad can come from you, my darling.'[6] Ten days later, he had added: 'I saw Judith yesterday. She is a little lazy and fond of playing, but a good girl and as beautiful as an angel. I talked to her about you and about her little sister, and she blushed deeply and hugged me very hard.'[7] Ernesta had stayed on in Turkey. On 7 May, he had sent another note to Constantinople: 'It seems to me that, in your last letter, you announced a Greek cap, and a necklace of silver coins for Judith. I haven't yet received them . . .'[8] Ernesta's repeated absences and her neglect gave her daughters little sense of security. In the spring of 1855, when she was in London, Gautier had reported: 'The children constantly ask when you're coming back, and I ask as often as they do.'[9] In 1858, Ernesta was once again on her travels. 'The whole household, deprived of you, has turned to me, and the round continues,' Gautier wrote, 'with me in the lead. Children, attendants, cats and birds, all follow behind . . . The children are good. Alexandre was quite pleased with their piano.'[10]

Their education remained erratic, but they both took lessons at the Conservatoire de danse, and they often practised at the bar which was set up in the hall at the rue de la Grange-Batelière. A series of governesses was engaged to educate the girls, and chief among them was Mademoiselle Virginie Huet. 'She is taking great care of them,' Gautier assured Ernesta, 'and hasn't been out of the house twice since you left. So your little angels are looked after as if they were little devils, and you needn't worry about them.'[11] Even Ernesta might have worried had she known that Mlle Huet took the children to table-turning sessions. Yet Virginie Huet had her virtues. She recognized Judith's love of puppets, and she decided that the girls would give a puppet show based on their father's novella *Avatar*. She herself wrote the script, and Judith remembered: 'My father, monocle to his eye, listened to the play very patiently, and he was charming enough to be surprised.'[12]

Since 1855 he had been a contributor to *Le Moniteur universel;* and his editors, Julien Turgan and Paul Dalloz, both of whom lived at Neuilly, urged him to move there and enjoy a comparatively rural life. Gautier let himself be persuaded. He and his family moved to 32, rue de Longchamp. The children delighted in the terraced garden, which overlooked the Seine; they swung in the hammock, suspended between two acacia trees. They lost themselves in the vine-covered arbour.

> My father maintained [remembered Judith] that reading is the key to everything . . . And so he left the library at our disposal, and he encouraged us to delve in it often. We had already read an enormous amount. After Walter Scott and Alexandre Dumas, it was Victor Hugo, Balzac, Shakespeare – as François-Victor Hugo's translation continued to appear – and Edgar Allan Poe (through the wonderful style of Baudelaire) who particularly enthralled us.[13]

Gautier insisted that it was better to learn one subject well than to dabble in numerous disciplines. He taught his daughters astronomy, and he presented Judith with a telescope. Alas, she could only use it when she was meant to be asleep. She would take it out on the terrace at dead of night.

> It was always the French window in the dining-room which creaked and gave me away . . . And so I had hardly set up the telescope on its copper stand, on the edge of the terrace, the only place from which you could really see the sky, when my mother would appear in her nightgown, candle in hand, in the doorway:
> 'What are you doing there?'
> 'I am noting the position of Jupiter's satellites . . . '[14]

It was now, in her late teens, that a distinguished scholar made his first appearance in her life. One of Gautier's friends, a young widow, Mme Clermont-Ganneau, called at Neuilly with her son. The boy – who was still a *collégien* – showed Judith how to blow an egg. It was her first encounter with Charles Clermont-Ganneau, one day to be Professor at the Collège de France and a member of the Académie des Inscriptions.[15] He was to be a second brother to her.

She and her sister continued to meet their father's friends – and Gautier seemed to know all the world. Victor Hugo was still in political exile in Guernsey, but occasionally his wife and one of his sons would appear in Paris, and Judith met them dining with Charles Robelin, the eccentric architect who lived nearby in Neuilly.[16] Sometimes Judith went to the rue Frochot, to sit for her portrait to la Présidente, the endearing Mme Sabatier, who had been the inspiration of Baudelaire. Mme Sabatier had been a professional singer, and she was a gifted painter of miniatures. She was beautiful, warm-hearted, a renowned *salonnière*, and an ebullient guest at Gautier's Thursdays at the rue de Longchamp. She announced her entrance with a soprano trill, and Gustave Doré promptly swept her off to the piano to improvise Tyrolean duets. Dalloz and Turgan called on their illustrious contributor. Dalloz was elegant, suave and pale, with a silky moustache and a caressing voice. Turgan had studied medicine, and he affected the manners and the speech of a sawbones. The Dumas, *père et fils*, arrived; the Goncourts sat at table, disconcertingly observant. Baudelaire followed. Nadar made his appearance: tall, red-haired, renowned for his photography and for his exploits as a balloonist. Flaubert borrowed one of Gautier's suits, took off his collar, transformed himself into a formidable caricature of stupidity, and danced his famous dance, l'Idiot des Salons; Gautier, not to be outdone, removed his coat and danced le Pas du Créancier, and the evening ended with Bohemian songs. Every actor, singer or artist, every composer, novelist or poet with aspirations or friendship arrived for entertainment; and every Thursday, remembered Judith,

> my mother cooked risotto milanese, and every time it was a triumph for her.
> The hors-d'oeuvre were usually big mortadellas, Bologna sausages, salami, zamponi and black olives. Then, on a bed of parsley, there appeared the fish, which was served cold; it was nearly always salmon trout, for which my father had a marked predilection. I was entrusted with making the mayonnaise.[17]

The miseries of convent life had long since been forgotten. Judith lived at home, delighting in a constellation of visitors, and, above all, in her famous, original and devoted father. One of his pleasures was to take his daughters to the Jardin d'Acclimatation, where the aquarium enthralled him. Often, when he was obliged to attend a first night in Paris, he would take his family with him; sometimes he would fall asleep during the performance, and rely on his daughters' observation. They were compelled to remember the plots until the following Sunday, when he had to write his article. Sunday was a sombre day; the thought of the article loomed over Neuilly, until Judith and Estelle saw him off on the omnibus, 'and he departed to analyse, in his perfect style, the plot of *Le Serpent à plumes* . . . and other forgotten masterpieces'.[18]

Once he had gone, they were free to set out for the Pasdeloup concert.

In 1861 Jules Pasdeloup, of the Société des Jeunes Artistes, had set out to bring music to the general public. He had made arrangements with the owner of the circus in the boulevard des Filles-du-Calvaire, and he had announced a series of eight popular concerts of classical music. The price of the tickets ranged from 3 francs to 75 centimes. The first of these concerts was held on 27 October. It was so successful that the original series had to be followed by a further series of eight. The last took place on 13 April 1862. 'Every year since then,' wrote Paul Féval in 1867, 'M. Pasdeloup has continued his concerts. They are held every Sunday, at the same circus and at the same prices. They perform only the music of the masters: Beethoven, Mozart, Haydn, Weber, Meyerbeer, Mendelssohn, etc. The attendance is always enormous, and the success is increasing. The Popular Concerts have become a Parisian habit.'[19]

Judith and Estelle used to go to the Pasdeloup concert every Sunday. 'The Pasdeloup concert is their greatest pleasure,' their father told Carlotta. 'They are always overcome with enthusiasm, and when they get home they strum the most arduous Beethoven symphonies on their piano as if they were polkas.'[20] On the way home they had also paid some social visits. Judith recalled how,

> at this time, when he was not at Croisset, Flaubert was living in an entresol in this part of the boulevard [42, boulevard du Temple]. It was on our way, and we never failed to go up and see him as we were passing. Sometimes the windows were open, and one could see him from the street, his massive figure filling the salon, which was too small for him. He had enormously baggy otter-skin trousers, held up by a red sash, and a floating dressing-gown over a silk shirt. We used to burst in like a whirlwind, all excited by the pleasure of the concert, and also by the pleasure of seeing him; but even when I threw my arms round his neck, and hugged him, he still didn't understand all the eager admiration which I felt for his genius.
>
> The room he lived in was hung with bright-coloured chintz with a large floral pattern. Everything, apart from the chintz, gave an impression of the East: red and green leather, pipes and carpets, a low divan, a big table on which there stood a huge copper plate full of goose-quills. These quills had been used; some were very worn, others hardly had an ink stain on the tip of the nib. Flaubert wrote on sheets of blue paper, in a tight hand . . . There were sheets of paper on the table, all covered with crossings-out.
>
> I looked at it all with a feeling of devotion; but the author of *Salammbô* could not know . . . [21]

He knew, and he was touched and delighted. He felt an almost paternal affection for her, and for the rest of his life he kept a note from her:

> Cher Maître,
>   I haven't been very well these last few days. I thought I was better today, but with this cold weather they've forbidden me to go out – indeed they've had to hold me back by force. The other day I rang [your bell] for fifteen minutes! I shall try my luck one of these days, but if I'm not let in I shall break the door down.
>
>   With love from
>   Judith[22]

On 3 August 1861 Eugénie Fort recorded: 'Father and son are off to Moscow for three months.'[23] 'M. Théophile Gautier is returning to Moscow to finish his great work on the arts in Russia,' added *Le Moniteur universel*. 'Our readers may rest assured that his absence will not last long. Besides, some more of his travel impressions will soon come to console them.'[24]

Ernesta had taken their daughters to stay with Carlotta at Saint-Jean.

Dear darling [this from Gautier],

I have still had nothing from you except your nice letter of 6 August from Geneva, which gave me very lively pleasure. It told me that you had been warmly welcomed, and that the children were good. We are at Moscow, ready to leave for Nijni-Novgorod . . . After Nijni-Novgorod we'll come back to Moscow and thence to St Petersburg; then, eagerly, to France . . . It's only sixteen days since we left, and it feels to me like a year. It isn't exactly that I'm bored, but my heart is no longer free enough for me to run gaily about the world. Too many threads bind me to the dear house, to you, the children and the *sacrée boutique*. I should have had to bring the whole lot, and I'm not rich enough for that; but it would have been delightful . . .

Judith, you promised to write to me; Estelle, you promised, too. Where is your literature, you adorable little wretches?[25]

The literature was waiting for him in Moscow on his return; and devotedly he answered his favourite daughter:

My dear Judith,

I give you back the title of 'my last hope,' which I'd taken away from you, because I know, from your mother's letters, that you are faithfully keeping your promise to be good and obedient.

You could not imagine, dear child, the profound satisfaction you give me, and the tranquillity you give my mind, which is troubled by so many cares of every kind. Continue as you are, since you love me, and find in your affection the strength to bear all the little miseries that life is made of, wherever one may be. Your good behaviour shall be rewarded at once: I shan't add a word of moralizing. And that is considerate for a father.

You haven't, you say, had the same impressions as I have of Lake Geneva, and you attribute the difference of effect to the fact that I was 'far from my family, with money in my pocket'. That is true, but not as you think. The interior disposition is everything; the landscape is within ourselves as much as outside, and it is our thoughts that colour it . . . If you had stifled a little rebellious or rancorous thought, you would thoroughly have enjoyed this beautiful landscape, so calm, so gentle and so serene. A drop of gall is enough to turn all the azure of Lake Geneva green, and cover the sun with bigger and blacker spots than the ones you see throught your telescope on the terrace at Neuilly. Be happy with yourself, and you will be happy with your horizon.

But here I am playing the preacher again and beginning to moralize. I promised you a moment ago I wouldn't. I hope you'll soon understand the truth of what I'm telling you.

'The mountains didn't give you the effect of novelty you expected. You felt you had seen them already, like the sea; they seemed to you "small and mean".' That is because reality rarely fulfils the promises of the imagination, and also, perhaps, because you haven't actually seen the mountains. These cabbage-patches and vineyards that you describe are only found on the lowest slopes of all; but when you are at the foot of these kitchen-garden hills, they hide the snowy summits, the glaciers, the pine forests and torrents; just as, in life, the fools prevent you from seeing a man of talent. I think I'll be able to come back soon enough to make you see Alpine nature in all its grandiose and virginal beauty. Be careful not to be too quick to apply the critical faculty to things that are genuinely beautiful: for the sake of a witticism you would deprive yourself, in the long run, of the faculty of enjoying them. Do not kill admiration in yourself. Enthusiasm goes well with youth. You will have time enough later on to find that what had seemed sublime to you at fifteen or sixteen is stupid and ridiculous. Don't follow my example. Alas, I shall soon have reached my half-century, and the need to analyse everything has made me fatally and incurably sad. But, at your age, I shouldn't have joked about the Alps.

Read Walter Scott; I permit it — indeed I recommend it. It's an excellent and instructive occupation. I learn from your good mother that it would be easy enough to divert you, that you have a very pure and true soprano voice. You know how flattering this is from an Italian and a Grisi. I'm delighted; but what has given me particular pleasure is the entire good grace with which you youself have asked to sing, and the docile attention you give to your lessons . . .

Goodbye, dear child of my soul; continue well disposed, and you will see everything smooth out before you as if by enchantment.[26]

Judith replied. In September, still from Moscow, Gautier answered: 'I thank you most affectionately for the charming little letter which you sent me, it's noble to write copy for a father! Go on drawing, but don't neglect the pen for the brush. You are gifted. Now you have the three keys. Open the locks and make yourself worthy of the name you bear — I embrace you with my heart and soul.'[27]

There was no more loving father than the poet who was so often called impassible, no gentler man than the one whom Arsène Houssaye had called the Eagle of *Le Moniteur universel*. Nor did many husbands show their wives more lasting affection than Gautier showed Ernesta. And, having answered his daughter, he turned to his mistress:

I'm very pleased with the nice things you tell me about the children. I'd made them a little speech before I left, and they'd promised to behave. I see that they are keeping their promises. I shan't tell you to be nice to them, because you are, but show a little grace and tenderness. Coddle them and show that you notice their new behaviour. You know we like to be spoilt in our family. It's a fault, but it shows a proud and tender heart; if people snap at us, they get nothing except invincible, mulish resistance . . .

The Emperor will return to St Petersburg about 15 September, and I shall be able to see him, and my mission will be finished. And you can imagine how fast

I shall speed to Geneva, if you're still there, for it seems to me an eternity since I left.[28]

Late in October, by way of Geneva, he returned to Paris.

Chapter Three

In about 1862, Maurice Dreyfous, the man of letters, paid a visit to the rue de Longchamp, and first set eyes on Gautier's elder daughter. Judith was then about seventeen, and he was overwhelmed by her beauty. As he remembered, many years later: 'She was, and long remained, one of the most perfectly beautiful creatures that one could see . . . The first time I saw her, she gave me the impression, which has never changed, of the Goddess of Nonchalance.'[1] The Goncourts recorded the same impression. On 27 March 1862, at a dinner party in Paris, they met Gautier and Ernesta with their daughters.

> Gautier's daughters have a singular charm, a sort of oriental languor, a laziness and rhythm of gestures and movements, which they inherit from their father, but it is all made elegant by feminine grace. They have long, searching gazes, . . . a charm which is not French, but mingled with all sorts of French things. They indulge in rather boyish pranks, masculine words, little sulks and pouts, shruggings of the shoulders, contempts and ironies revealed with the petulant gestures of childhood, which set them apart and make them quite different from young society girls. Very individual, pretty little things, . . . young girls who are no doubt misjudged . . .
>
> One of them [Judith] lacks real respect for her mother, who is trying to stop her from drinking champagne. She tells me about her first convent passion, her first love for a lizard which looked at her with gentle eyes, *friendly to man*, a lizard which was constantly in her and on her, which was always sticking its head out of the opening of her bodice to look at her and disappear again. Poor little lizard, it was wickedly squashed by a jealous schoolfriend . . . And then she said, innocently, that she dug him a little grave, on which she set a little cross, and that she refused to go to Mass or pray any more, since her religion was gone, so unjust did the child feel this death to be.[2]

The innocent child had become the innocent girl, but she was learning more about the world. Late in April, with Dalloz, Gautier left for London to attend the opening of the second Great Exhibition. He was to review the fine arts for *Le Moniteur universel*.[3] A few days after he set out, Ernesta followed with their daughters, accompanied by the new maid, Henriette.

> We had not made a sea crossing before [Judith remembered], and we were very excited at the thought of going to England . . . We were going to embark at Boulogne, and enter London down the Thames. It was May, and the weather was fine, but the sea was rather rough . . . At dawn, I was sprawled out in my cabin, dreadfully ill, and reciting *La Légende des siècles* to myself with feverish speed, unable to stop, when Estelle, who was very brave, and apparently a good sailor, came to find me, on the pretext that the sunrise over the sea was a wonderful sight. She dragged me, almost by force, to the bridge. I could only reach the top of the steps, where I collapsed . . . The splendour of the dawn, with its pinks and emeralds, left me indifferent and did not cure me. A compassionate sailor helped me to a bench and brought me a horsehair pillow and some tea.
> However, the moment that the ship entered the Thames estuary, the sickness disappeared, and I did honour to the breakfast. It was served on the bridge and consisted of bacon and eggs, as only the English can cook them, roast beef and excellent pale ale [*sic*].
> My father was waiting for us in London, on the jetty, and he took us to the Hôtel de France in Leicester Square, where an apartment had been booked for us. That same evening, some visitors arrived. Among them were Gérard, the lion-killer, and a Monsieur S——, who offered to be our guide and interpreter in the English capital. He lived there, and knew it wonderfully well . . .
> We were extremely comfortable in this hotel, but, in these Exhibition days, the price was exorbitant. M. S—— advised us, very wisely, to leave the hotel for a furnished apartment. It was he, again, who found a suitable house in Penton Square [*sic*] . . .[4]

Gautier, writing to his sisters, gave the address as 11, Panton Square.[5] 'England would enchant me,' he said, 'if I didn't need to earn a livelihood at once; that spoils all my travels . . .'[6]

> My dear aunts [this from Judith on 2 May],
> Here we are, landed among our mortal enemies, the English . . .
> London is like a morgue to me, despite the infernal din of carriages. The people have a wooden look and they seem like ghosts . . . But I must see things in a bad light because I'm still upset after my crossing.[7]

Judith, like her father, knew no English, and – again like him – she remained resolutely ignorant of English matters. She tended, so it seems, to invent in order to satisfy a French public. Years later, in her memoirs, she recorded that the owner of the house in 'Penton Square'

> undertook to feed us, but she was very stingy, and we felt almost dying of

hunger. It was therefore decided that we would add a meal to the meagre usual fare of the house; a supper which we would all go out and buy in the little shopping streets, brightly lit by gas . . . We came back laden with gigantic victuals: smoked lobster and salmon, York ham, lambs' tongues, smoked beef, Stilton, Chester [sic], rhubarb tart, plum cake, Dundee marmalade, stout, pale ale, port wine. Henriette had laid the table and lit the lamps. We sat down and did prolonged honour to the meal . . .

London society gave a warm welcome to my father. A great many artists came to visit him. We once saw Thackeray, colossal and superb. We had read *Vanity Fair*, which greatly flattered him. He was very agreeable to my sister and to me; he admired our hairstyles, and asked us for details so that he could teach his daughters to do their hair the same way.[8]

Gautier spent much time at the Exhibition. The first of his ten articles was published on 4 May; the last appeared on 11 June. While he was engaged in his work, Ernesta and the children wandered about London, and it was here that Judith had an encounter which helped to determine the course of her career.

My mother, sister and I were walking down some arcade or other when we saw two very strange characters in front of us, followed by an inquisitive crowd. They were two Japanese in their national dress. They pretended not to see all this procession of gaping boobies, but they were tormented by them none the less, because in order to escape them they went into an elegant shop where they sold all sorts of dressing-table things in tortoiseshell and ivory. We couldn't resist: we went into the shop ourselves, while the crowd collected outside the windows. I was fascinated . . . That was my first encounter with the Far East; and, from that moment, I was conquered by it.

One of the Japanese looked tall in the long flowing folds of his silk robe. His pale face, with a fine arched nose of the most aristocratic kind, . . . had a particular expression which was a mixture of melancholy grace, of sweetness and disdain. He was wearing a hat in the shape of a buckler; it was kept in place by white silk pads which went across his cheeks. Out of the sash of gold brocade tied tightly round his waist, there emerged the delicate carved hilts of two sabres . . . Beside them there appeared a fan. He frequently took it out and opened it with a single movement.

The face of the other Japanese was the colour of deep gold, and a few pock-marks from smallpox gave it the appearance of old bronze which had been somewhat battered by time. He likewise wore two sabres in his velvet belt . . .

These two strangers examined us with great curiosity. They knew a few words of English and French, and we tried to talk. They had only arrived in England a few days earlier, and they were taking their first steps in this Europe which was quite unknown to them. It seemed as if the aroma and indeed the atmosphere of their fabulous country still floated about them, and that none of it had yet evaporated.

What a prophetic meeting for me, what an unforgettable vision! A whole unknown world appeared to me. A sort of intuition (which I have always had in the presence of things which would impassion me) made me glimpse it in its entirety, and revealed its special beauties to me.[9]

An exotic visitor, this time 'an authentic Chinaman', was soon to find his way to the rue de Longchamp. Charles Clermont-Ganneau introduced Tin-Tun-Ling, 'who, as the result of unhappy events, had been stranded on the pavements of Paris'.[10]

There was more than one account of Tin-Tun-Ling and his melancholy past.

> He had a tiny little yellowish, raddled face adorned with a minuscule moustache which one would have sworn was false [wrote Georges Grison in 1917]. His slanting eyes were protected by glasses with huge round lenses, the sort that motorists and aviators wear today. A long thin pigtail flapped against his shoulders and came down as far as his sky-blue silk skirt. He wore a skull-cap with a red button, and white sandals. Under his arm he carried an enormous paper parasol with a floral pattern which he had brought from his native land.
> He was the scholar Tin-Tun-Ling whom – no one knew why – Napoleon III had brought to France after the China war to be assistant teacher of Chinese, attached to the titular professor at the Collège de France, Stanislas Julien.[11]

One day, however, in the course of argument, the assistant teacher had informed Monsieur Julien that he, the titular professor, did not know a word of Chinese. 'It was a scandal, an unheard-of scandal. M. Stanislas Julien was sixty-four years old, and he was an Officier de la Légion-d'honneur. Tin-Tun-Ling was half his age, and his only decoration was the red button displayed on his skull-cap. Tin-Tun-Ling was dismissed.'[12]

According to Judith, however, Tin-Tun-Ling had a different history. He had been brought to France by Monseigneur Callery, Bishop of Macao, who had engaged him to work on a Chinese-French dictionary; but Monseigneur Callery had died, and Tin-Tun-Ling had found himself in Paris, unemployed. Clermont-Ganneau had befriended him and presented him at Neuilly. Tin-Tun-Ling, remembered Judith,

> made us the most respectful gesture, clenching his fists and shaking them on a level with his forehead. We thought it was delightful. He was wearing a blue robe of some soft material, and a figured black silk tunic with little copper buttons. According to etiquette, he kept on his little black satin skull-cap, adorned with a square button made of mother-of-pearl set in gold filigree. His yellow face was witty and delicate . . . He was not more than thirty, but at first sight one could hardly give him any particular age. He looked at one and the same time like a priest, a young she-monkey, and an old woman . . .
> What could be done for him, if he did not want to go away? Keep him and give him shelter, in the oriental fashion: that was my father's conclusion.
> 'Do you want to learn Chinese?' he asked me. 'Do you want to study a country which is still unknown, and seems prodigious?'
> Did I want to? I simply answered by turning a series of somersaults, which the Chinaman watched with his slanting eyes, frowning all over his forehead, but, out of politeness, showing no surprise.
> And that was how Tin-Tun-Ling became Théophile Gautier's Chinaman.[13]

Tin-Tun-Ling was to wander in and out of contemporary memoirs. Armand Silvestre recollected the vagabond from the Far East, 'wearing a robe bedecked with flowers and chimeras.'[14] Émile Bergerat recorded that the Chinaman was light-fingered:

> The moment that one of the sisters looked out of the window, and saw him arriving, in the distance, at the end of the rue de Longchamp, the other sister would rush to the cupboards and, with a turn of the key, ensure the safety of the contents. The Chinaman's arrival was always greeted by the sound of shutting drawers. I have never known a man who borrowed more silently than this celestial gentleman.[15]

Theft was not his only failing. After Gautier's death he was to remain a friend of Judith's; but eventually he quarrelled with her, and he was dismissed. Later on, recorded Grison, 'he had a revival of celebrity. In the modest hotel where he was living, he had a schoolmistress as his neighbour. She seduced him, and he married her. Then she learned that Tin-Tun-Ling already had a wife, in China. She lodged a complaint against him, and he was arrested as a bigamist.'[16] During his imprisonment, he wrote his Chinese novel, *Le Petit Pantoufle*.[17]

Tin-Tun-Ling was acquitted of bigamy. Then he vegetated for some time.

> What did he live on? No one knows. He had replaced his fine silk robe with a printed cotton robe which he had cut out and sewn himself; his parasol with a cotton umbrella. He had replaced his beautiful sandals with elastic-sided boots, in which the elastic existed, now, just as a memory. It is true that, as far as food was concerned, a few handfuls of rice were enough for him. It is also true that from time to time, in an indirect way, Judith Gautier sent him some assistance.[18]

He died in 1886. It was Judith who ensured that he had a respectable funeral.[19]

In 1864, just before she reached her nineteenth birthday, Judith was already establishing herself as a writer. On 15 March, in *L'Artiste*, under the pseudonym Judith Walter – a pseudonym which her father had chosen – she reviewed the exhibition held by the Société Nationale des Beaux-Arts. She warmly praised the collection of Doré's biblical drawings. It was Gautier, no doubt, who encouraged her to write art criticism. Knowing her interest in Poe, he also asked her to review Baudelaire's translation of *Eureka*. On 29 March, the article was published in *Le Moniteur universel*, once again under the pseudonym of Judith

Walter, and Baudelaire sent her his congratulations: 'My first impression was astonishment. Then, when I could no longer doubt, I felt an emotion which is difficult to express, composed half of pleasure at having been so well understood, half of delight at seeing that one of my oldest and dearest friends had a daughter truly worthy of him.'[20]

Le Moniteur universel paid Judith 80 francs and 40 centimes. 'I kept the money in my pocket for a long time,' she remembered, 'and jingled it about continually.'[21] On 15 April, again in *L'Artiste*, Judith discussed M. Negroni's Chinese collection:

> Since that prodigious Chinese Expedition which opened the door of the Celestial Empire, the door which had so long been closed to us, the mystery which enveloped that strange country had partly dissipated. The palace of the Son of Heaven, whose threshold was never to be profaned by foreigners, was invaded and pillaged . . .
> The Emperor's summer palace was most fecund in marvels, if one is to judge by M. Negroni's collection, which is almost entirely taken from it . . . I think that it has been given to few people to contemplate such a profusion of marvels: it is a confusion of porcelain, a mountain of jade, a cascade of precious stones; you emerge from it dazzled, and for a while everything seems ugly and black, as if you had been looking at the sun.[22]

Arsène Houssaye, the editor of *L'Artiste*, was delighted by Judith's work. He marked her début in literature by giving her an emerald and diamond ring. On 15 June he published her account of the Salon of 1864; her manner, like that of her father, was descriptive rather than critical, but it was remarkable for a girl of her age. On 1 June 1865, Houssaye published *Variations sur des thèmes chinois*: eight prose-poems based on Chinese poetry. Melancholy and original, they confirmed her passion for China, and the poetry that lay within her.

> I had hardly begun to stammer Chinese [so she was to write in her latter days] before I undertook the most difficult task, the most impossible task, which made the most informed Sinologists flinch: the task of translating the untranslatable Chinese poets . . . Tin-Tun-Ling had become my tutor. When this noble resolution took root in me, the poor Chinaman lost all peace of mind. No more of those indolent siestas which he loved so well, in deep armchairs, no more daydreaming as he wandered along the paths of the Jardin [d'Acclimatation]; he had to struggle with the 214 keys of the Chinese dictionary.[23]

Her father eagerly encouraged her oriental studies. Not content with giving her a Chinese tutor of her own, he asked Jules Taschereau, the administrator of the Bibliothèque Impériale, if he would let her borrow manuscripts 'so that she might finish her work at home'.[24] It was an unorthodox request, and Taschereau consulted Stanislas Julien, who was not only professor at the Collège de France, but assistant curator of the

Chinese collection. 'M. Théophile Gautier,' Julien answered, 'is so honoured and so celebrated that one could not flatly refuse his request.'[25] 'Sir,' wrote Taschereau to Gautier, 'it will give me real satisfaction to be able to facilitate your daughter's studies.'[26]

And so the extraordinary work began. The Goncourts, calling at Neuilly, found Gautier at dinner with his daughters, 'those pretty Parisian Orientals . . . At times,' wrote the diarists, 'they almost seem to be the daughters of their father's nostalgia for the East . . . The elder one is spelling out a Chinese grammar, and goes off to find her sculpture, after *L'Angélique* by Ingres, carved out of a turnip, which is all shrivelled – one can't see anything of it any more.'[27]

Gautier's daughters were enchanting and original. Mme Adam, the politician's wife, met them at the Théâtre-Lyrique, and reported: 'Judith is wonderfully beautiful, the other one is charming.'[28] Estelle was certainly charming: sallow-skinned, alert, with bright, intelligent eyes. But every spectator reached the same inescapable conclusion: Judith was the more remarkable sister. Both Gautier's daughters were beautiful, recalled Robert de Bonnières,

and beautiful with that beauty of line which they inherited from their father; but only one of them had 'the moon face and the lotus eyes' of the Hindu goddesses, with that pure profile which one sees in the medallions of Agrigento. These comparisons must be taken literally if one wants to form an idea of Mademoiselle Judith's face. It reproduced to perfection that classical beauty which her father had so loved. She also had some indefinable wildness in her strange yellow eyes [*sic*], and, in her attitudes, the fatal abandon of an Eastern slave.[29]

Judith was very beautiful [Fernand Calmettes repeated, in his book on Leconte de Lisle], beautiful with a medallic beauty . . . Intellectually active, she was physically passive, and her apparent nonchalance, which made her splendour more human, left on her person a certain grace of seductive languor and of desirable indifference. She was therefore eagerly, even ardently, desired, and if I chose to set down here the names of all the men who yielded to the imperious wish to pay homage to her, I should cover a good many pages. [Léon] Barracand was among these worshippers, but he was one of the discreet. One day, when he had called on Judith, they had come to talk about electro-biological phenomena, and she said that the contact of her tortoiseshell comb produced sparks in her hair. And as Barracand very naturally requested the honour of witnessing a fact which seemed to him a rare and delightful phenomenon, Judith took him without hesitation into her dressing-room to get the comb, and then into a dark little room which served her as a hanging cupboard. She shut the door, let down her flowing mass of hair, and struck the sparks from it, and shook them off the comb on to Barracand's hand in a rain of minuscule stars. And, much impressed by the scintillating emanation, intoxicated by the fragrance of the hair, Barracand contrived to appear content with what he was given, pretty sparks.[30] ·

Armand Silvestre, the future Parnassian poet, who worked at the Ministère des Finances, was also obliged to admire Judith in silence, though his admiration lasted all his life.

Before she came of age, she had already encountered a more serious suitor. One day, as she herself recalled in *Le Collier des jours*, she captivated a visitor from the East: His Excellency Mohsin-Khan, who had been sent by the Shah of Persia on a special mission to France. He chanced to meet her, fell in love, and begged her to marry him. His proposal was unorthodox. He already had a 'temporary wife' – presumably a mistress – in Persia; however, he insisted that he would leave her. Judith was flattered by his admiration. Gautier was 'furious over the affair of the Persian . . . It has all,' he told Ernesta, 'disturbed me more than I can say.'[31] He firmly discouraged Mohsin-Khan. The envoy returned to Persia. When he came back to Europe, as the Shah's ambassador to London, Judith had already flown the nest.[32]

Sometimes, at the end of her life, she regretted that she had not chosen the destiny of a Persian princess,

> the destiny which Mohsin-Khan, Prime Minister of the Shah of Persia, Nassar-Ed-Din, had offered her when he proposed marriage to her. And then her thoughts seemed to return to the Prince's lovely descriptions of this land of dream and beauty: of a journey by sledge across Russia and Persia, of mysterious castles, royal festivities, raiment constellated with precious stones, of this country of the Arabian Nights of which she had so often dreamed, this country which was, in truth, her native land.[33]

Judith, alas, chose another destiny. She determined to marry Catulle Mendès.

Chapter Four

Catulle Mendès had been born in Bordeaux on 12 May 1841.[1] His mother, the former Suzanne Brun, was a Catholic. His father, Tibulle Mendès, came from an old Sephardic Jewish family. The Mendès had left Portugal in the eighteenth century, and had settled in Bordeaux, where they had established themselves in banking. Abraham Mendès had been a Latin scholar as well as a banker; he had called his son after the elegiac Latin poet. It was from Abraham Mendès, his grandfather, that Catulle inherited his love of literature. As an infant, so the legend goes, Catulle was snatched from his nurse's arms by a Neapolitan priest, plunged into a piscina, and given unexpected baptism. If the story was not true, it was *ben trovato*. He was to have a turbulent and a cosmopolitan life. His parents travelled in Switzerland and Belgium, Italy and Germany, and they took him with them. In 1850, the family returned at last to France. This time they settled in Toulouse, where he was educated. Ten years later, he followed his literary vocation, and set out for Paris.

He arrived in a city where poetry was nobly represented; but Hugo remained in political exile, and Théophile Gautier, wrote Catulle, 'had retired from the struggle, finally triumphant'.[2] Baudelaire had written all his poetry. Leconte de Lisle was in his fifties, a mentor rather than an active poet. It was time for a new generation to arise.

At first Catulle lived in poverty in the rue de Provence; but fame soon came to him. At first it was only the adulation of the students who met in his shabby attic. Then he became the centre of a new group of poets. He was not a master, or the leader of a school, he was an animating spirit, honoured to be the lieutenant of older men.

His family became resigned to his literary career, and sent him an allowance; he moved to a small ground-floor apartment in the rue de Douai.

It was a bachelor apartment [François Coppée was to remember]. Two rooms: a bedroom and a sitting-room, which was turned into a study . . .

The lamp had been lit – the most impoverished poet always had a lamp – and every available candle; and Covielle, the little manservant, had even laid out everything for tea . . . He had wiped the cups, boiled the water, and cut the *baba* up into equal slices; because some poets, friends, were expected.[3]

First among them was Albert Glatigny. 'Without apparent cares,' wrote Mendès, 'he strode across Paris with his seven-league legs. Rain or shine he went, and always, whatever the secret anxiety in his soul, he was the same Albert Glatigny, joyous, familiar, a teller of outrageous tales, . . . mad with passion for his art.'[4] Glatigny, 'as thin and agile as a grasshopper', was followed by José-Maria de Heredia, a handsome Creole from Havana, and Léon Dierx, 'grave and pale of face, Léon Dierx, the poet who deserves to be more famous',[5] by Villiers de l'Isle-Adam and many others. The rue de Douai saw the birth of le Parnasse. The poetic brotherhood met on Wednesdays in the rue de Douai, and on Fridays at the Marquise de Ricard's, at 10, boulevard des Batignolles. They later gathered in the entresol of the publisher Alphonse Lemerre, in the passage Choiseul. Mendès himself was writing poems. They were collected in book form as *Philoméla*, in 1863, and dedicated to Gautier, 'with boundless admiration and profound respect'. Mendès also dedicated some poems to Baudelaire. A number of his early poems were so Baudelairean that they were almost pastiches. Mendès already acknowledged his gods.

Among his gods was Richard Wagner. On more than one occasion Wagner had been drawn to Paris in the hope of making his fortune. He had first arrived there in September 1839; he had been obliged to resort to musical chores, and to suffer a hardship which verged on poverty. When he had eventually left, in April 1842, he had set off with five francs in his pocket, and his eyes had been full of tears.

It was seventeen years before he returned for another long visit. In the autumn of 1859 he had settled with his wife near the Champs-Élysées. Early in 1860 there had been three successful Wagner concerts in Paris. On the intervention of Marshal Magnan and Princess Metternich, Napoleon III gave orders for a performance of *Tannhäuser* at the Opéra. The first performance took place on 13 March 1861. After the third, at which the uproar was nothing short of scandalous, Wagner withdrew his score. He suffered from the contempt of the public, the jealousy of French composers, and from his imperial protection. Mme Adam maintained that the failure of *Tannhäuser* was 'an imperialist defeat'.[6]

A month before the first performance of *Tannhäuser*, the first number of *La Revue Fantaisiste* had appeared. It had been founded by Catulle Mendès. Ardent and audacious, it was the earliest literary review in

France to side with Wagner. Among the contributors were Gautier and
Baudelaire; Mendès had even invited Wagner himself.

> I am not leaving Paris without gratitude [Wagner had told the journalist Victor
> Cochin]. I am moved by a feeling of great thankfulness. Because I have had
> encouraging letters from literary men, especially from a young man whom you
> may have heard of, because he has founded a review, the *Revue Fantastique*, or
> *Fantaisiste*, and he has invited me to contribute. Although he is only sixteen or
> seventeen years old [Mendès was in fact nineteen], he has infinite Parisian grace
> and wit, and I think that M. Mendès may become a fair and generous critic.[7]

Mendès was not only known in literary circles; he was already recognized
as one of the handsomest young men of his time. 'Apollo in person', said
the Parnassian poet Louis Ménard;[8] 'a pretty blond Christ', recorded
J.-H. Rosny.[9] Mendès was beautiful but, even now, disturbing. He was,
said Marcel Fouquier, 'as beautiful as a bad angel'.[10] Anatole France
described him as 'that Apollo of Balzac's'.[11] As a mere youth, recorded
Jules Hoche in 1883, 'he brought from the provinces the beauty of a
modern Christ and a certain flower of perversity which has since remained
the dominant note of his talent.'[12] He had, wrote the journalist Maurice
Talmeyr,

> a kind of mission of immorality and sometimes even of pollution . . . He was a
> sort of Christ, but a false Christ, a suspect Christ, a pot-house Christ. No one,
> however, was more engaging, no one showed more spirit, more verve, more
> gallantry in his work. No one got through so many stories, novels, chronicles
> and dramatic criticisms so brilliantly. But, openly or not, he was always
> pursuing his tireless propaganda of demoralization, the sort of pornographic
> apostolate to which he was dedicated.[13]

The shadow side of his character was already plain. In 1861, in *La
Revue Fantaisiste*, he published his outspoken verse-drama, *Le Roman
d'une nuit*. He was accused of offending public morals, and he was
sentenced to a month's imprisonment at Sainte-Pélagie and to a fine of 500
francs. *La Revue Fantaisiste* collapsed as a result of the scandal. Mendès
left for Germany, where he lived the student life of Heidelberg: a life of
books, beer and duels. He returned to France more devoted than ever to
the music of Wagner. He had clearly not changed his way of life. In 1864,
Glatigny wrote to Armand Gouzien, director of the *Revue des Lettres et des
Arts:* 'If you see Catulle, give him my greetings, and remind him that he
promised to come and see me. The journey costs seven francs. Catulle
often spends a louis on a tart; well, let him replace the tart with the
railway.'[14]

Catulle Mendès had, it seems, entered Judith's life at least as early as 1863. Maurice Dreyfous said that they had met at the Pasdeloup concerts, where Wagner was played, and at the eager discussions which followed them. Many years later, Judith recalled:

> The first time Mendès came to the house at Neuilly, my father used the intimate form of address to him . . . The second time, he refused to receive him on the pretext of a heavy cold. The third time, Mendès had himself accompanied by his friend Barbey d'Aurevilly, whose mission it was to occupy Gautier while Mendès – under cover of a piano duet – was to make me a formal declaration. 'Ask your father,' he said to me, point-blank, 'it's the only favour I ask of you, if he would allow me to marry you.' This was said in a dominant and imperious tone which brooked no refusal. There followed encouragement from my father, a visit from the parents – then, suddenly, a change of opinion. Disturbing information had come to my father's ears, and it had made him change his attitude: 'Come back in a year,' was his reply.[15]

Judith does not indicate the nature of the information which her father found so disturbing. He did not (whatever the Goncourts said) reject Catulle Mendès on account of his Jewish ancestry; he did not reject him because he could not bring himself to lose his favourite daughter, whose understanding warmed him, whose original mind and classical beauty constantly delighted him. It is more likely that he had learned of Mendès' reputation as a philanderer, perhaps that even now he suspected his alcoholic tendencies. He disliked his overt decadence, the viciousness and the obscenity which were already clear in his work. He was aware that Mendès was both charming and corrupt. Gautier might be Bohemian in his own way of life, but he had still inherited much of his family's bourgeois creed. His children were illegitimate, but he still felt a deep concern for his daughter's future.

Mendès was desperate; and he unwisely tried to force the issue. In 1863 he announced his engagement to Judith in the Press. Gautier issued a categorical denial. He also ordered him to deny the statement.

> I dined the other evening with Baudelaire [so a correspondent told Mallarmé in December] . . . He informed me that Catulle's marriage was definitely broken off . . . Although he recognized that Catulle had talent, he hardly seemed to be taken with that sweet angel V . . . Baudelaire said that Gautier had done very well, and that M. Catulle had done very badly in publishing his banns everywhere. Catulle, it seems, had confided his secret to the whole boulevard, which no doubt had confided it to the Champs-Élysées, which in turn had mentioned it to Neuilly. On hearing this, Théo rose up, went straight to Mendès, and ordered him, like a counterfeiter, to publish in several papers of his choice that there had never been any question of marriage between Mlle Gautier and M. Catulle . . . Catulle sent this note to Le Figaro, I think, and to

Le Constitutionnel; and now all Paris is reassured: Mlle Gautier will not have the
V . . .[16]

The 'sweet angel V', which Judith was providentially to escape, was no
doubt venereal disease.

The matter was not so simply settled. Mendès and Judith continued to
meet at the Pasdeloup concerts, they snatched occasional meetings
elsewhere, they met at night, when Mendès haunted the river-bank at
Neuilly. They refused to accept that their engagement was broken, and
Tin-Tun-Ling continued to deliver the notes which they wrote to one
another. The published fragments of Judith's letters (letters no doubt
returned to her when her marriage ended) suggest the fierce intensity of
feeling, the increasing tensions and frustrations. 'Isn't it funny that we are
always quarrelling?' she wrote. 'What an infernal ménage ours will be! We
shall have to be muzzled . . .'[17]

At moments Mendès thought of eloping. 'I think you're horrible,' she
told him, 'with your old ideas of elopements and escalades . . . If you
mention that again, I shall tell my father . . . Darling, it isn't true. I love
you, and I'll do what you want . . . Tin is going to you.'[18]

> Tin is going to you [she wrote, again], and I am going to stay here without you.
> He doesn't seem to understand his good fortune . . . Last night, like the night
> before, I didn't sleep a minute. I re-read all your letters; that went on for two
> hours. Darling, I don't want to tell you how sad I am so as not to make you sad,
> but you know it's terrible to be separated for so long and together for so brief a
> time. Life hurts me when I'm far away from you, I find it all angular and hard.
> Everything's so soft and velvety when you are there, I can't be sad when you are
> there. I almost hope that we shall make my father give in. You ought to want it
> because we have only one will for the two of us.[19]

And again: 'I had the most sombre dreams . . . Then Tin came into my
room with a big book of Chinese poetry; your letters were inside, and the
nightmares vanished.'[20]

Sometimes the messenger returned to Neuilly empty-handed, and
Judith was in despair. 'I have waited all day for your letter. Tin has come
back, and he has no letter. I have a wild urge to go up to the second floor
and jump out of the window. I swear to you that if I had had your bottle of
laudanum, I should have drunk it today. I think I'm going to bed; I'm
afraid of crying in the middle of dinner.'[21]

Mendès, too, was sad. 'I forbid you to cry with eyes like yours, you
wretch,' she admonished him. 'Have you no respect for beauty, then? I
assure you that I have kept a dazzlement in my eyes from seeing you; it

seems to me that I only have snouts and bestial faces round me . . . How
beautiful you are! You would make the moon jealous.'[22] Judith was
overwhelmed by Mendès' beauty: it was enough to conquer a girl who was
so enamoured of art and the ideal. And so she sought him, thought about
him constantly: 'I glimpsed you for a second yesterday, I looked for you all
through the concert, I talked about you for half the journey, on the pretext
of talking literature . . . I forbid you to say that you no longer have
talent.'[23] And again, in 1865: 'I won't have you being sad; you have no
more reason to be sad today than yesterday. I shall not be free for a year;
so, granted that I love you, nothing can happen for a year. I cannot answer
for anything. Why deprive yourself of music? It's so good, music, it's a
consolation for everything.'[24]

Both of them needed consolation. Week after week, the frustrated
courtship continued. Judith forgave him for all his outbursts, and for
haunting the house at Neuilly: 'You're mad, quite mad . . . I'm going to
write to your doctor and tell him that you're mad . . . I'll write to your
mother, too. I'll tell her how you look after yourself, coming to
river-banks at night to drink in the mist and snow.'[25]

Sometimes she herself was obliged to take medical advice:

> How little it needs to go from despair to delight! Yesterday I wanted to die,
> today I'm going to the doctor. I don't know what I'll say to him. I'm not in the
> least ill any more. You are a much better doctor than he is. He will never cure
> me if he doesn't put you on the prescription. How charming you were yesterday
> evening! I love you a hundred times more this morning! If you were always like
> that, I should love you so ardently that I should fall into ashes. It's better to be
> bad occasionally to restore the balance.[26]

And again:

> The doctor told me to avoid emotions. Everyone asks me what's the matter with
> me, and I should like to kill everyone. Is it anything to do with them? I don't
> ask what the matter is with *them*. The matter with me is that I love you in spite
> of myself, and that I am furious about it; every day I say no and, despite myself,
> yes.[27]

Judith loved Catulle with all the theatrical passion of the Grisis, all the
violent, exclusive passion which Giulia had felt for Mario. She loved him
with all the Romantic love that Théophile Gautier could express. She
loved him with all the fervour of youth, and of first love.

> How I love you, my Catulle! I think that I've surpassed you, now. It is
> impossible that you love me as much as I love you. It's horribly sweet, I don't
> know what I'm doing any more. I want to shout out your name all the time . . .

I should like to see you, I should like you to be with me always . . . When you come, it is to make me suffer more. When you go away, I don't want you to go away again, it's too horrible.

Since you left, I haven't said a word that wasn't related to you. It is impossible for me to talk about anything except you. I should like to find someone who loved you as much as I do so that I could talk about you when you are not there; but I should kill that person if they existed. Really, I'm mad, I want to cry, my breast is full of sighs. I should like to have you here all alone with me . . .[28]

And again: 'Do you really love me? . . . If it were not for the fear of making you jealous, I should embrace everyone. I'm leaving for Paris. I don't hope to see you, but I shall look for you everywhere.'[29]

She did not see him in Paris, but she passed his open door and saw a little staircase at the back,

and now, when I think of you [she wrote], I also think of the staircase and the door. I should very much like to go in one day when you aren't there, to explore it all and ask the nooks and crannies and the drawers if it is true that you love me. They must know, but they are also your accomplices, they wouldn't tell me the truth.[30]

The truth was not agreeable. Catulle loved Judith with passion, and at times with cruelty. He was frustrated, desperate, and – since he was sure of her – he constantly attempted to make her jealous and unhappy. 'No more big, red-headed mistresses,' she pleaded, 'it's unhealthy; throw her out of the window!'[31] 'How hard your letter was, my Catulle! Why do you so often have these sudden and useless perversities?'[32] 'How wicked it was, your letter yesterday! I couldn't read it . . . I stroked it in my pocket all through the journey, and it was a little serpent.'[33] Judith was wholehearted in her love for him; she was steadfast and she was innocent. Catulle was incapable of feeling such a love; he was exacting and he was sadistic.

Really [she wrote], I cannot forgive the angry impulse which I felt about you. You did deserve it. I saw that you didn't love me as I had thought. No, you didn't love me, or you didn't love me properly, but love me as you like – provided that you love me I shall always adore you, whatever you do, . . . you wretched monster . . . So you forgot the letters you wrote me, the ones that you destroyed . . . I may see you tomorrow, perhaps, you wicked tyrant. I love you despite myself and in spite of you.[34]

Judith might joke about a 'big red-headed mistress', but Catulle could not now change his ways. He was not prepared to lead a life of chastity while he waited for her. By 1865 another young woman had become central in his life: 'a beautiful woman in a red dress' whom Coppée recorded 'smoking cigarettes, stretched out on the sofa' in the rue de Douai.[35]

Augusta Mary Holmes (she later called herself Holmès to Frenchify her surname) was more than two years younger than Judith.[36] She had been born in Paris on 16 December 1847. She was the only daughter of Charles Dalkeith Holmes, a retired Irish cavalry officer, and of his English wife, Tryphima, who appears to have had some literary talent. Tryphima was doubtless the Mrs Dalkeith Holmes who had published *The Law of Rouen*, a dramatic tale, in 1837, and, five years later, *A Ride on Horseback to Florence through France and Switzerland*. Tryphima was noted for her beauty, and the fact that her only child was born after twenty years of marriage raised questions about Augusta's parentage. Legend says that she was not only the god-daughter, but the daughter, of her parents' friend, Alfred de Vigny.

Mrs Holmes died on 10 May 1858, when the girl was ten. Whoever her father was, Augusta inherited her mother's beauty and a lifelong passion for the arts. Maurice Dreyfous recalled her among the enthusiasts at the Pasdeloup concerts, 'a tall young girl with heavy fair hair the colour of ripe corn, of wonderful beauty, of an unforgettable majesty'.[37] Imbert recorded her, too, at these concerts:

> What particularly attracted public attention was that wonderful golden hair, which took on a still more vivid tint under the fire of the sunlight filtering through the windows of the Circus, and seemed to cast an intense light on all around it. Add to that a charming face, with a rich flesh-tint, a sort of grace which belongs to the women painted by Rubens, and a clear profile, which reflects the liveliest intelligence and the greatest decisiveness . . .[38]

Augusta was not only beautiful, she was already an accomplished musician, and the favourite pupil of César Franck. She composed music, wrote lyrics and sang them in her rich contralto voice. In her late teens she held court at her father's house at Versailles. 'She gathered writers, composers and artists in her salon. Villiers de l'Isle-Adam met Gounod there, in all the brilliance of his recent glory, and Saint-Saëns, who was working at *Samson et Dalila* and enjoyed playing excerpts from *Lohengrin*.'[39] Henri Regnault, the artist, came to the house (now 15, rue de l'Orangerie); so did the painter Georges Clairin, who considered Augusta 'more a goddess than a woman'.[40]

Small wonder that Augusta's name often appeared in social columns. She was said to be courted by Liszt, and, on the death of Wagner's wife, rumour said that she was engaged to Wagner. Everyone was to recognize her as Minerva in the painting which Henri Regnault submitted for the

Prix de Rome in 1866. Augusta was famous among the Parnassians, and before Mendès' marriage she was his mistress.[41]

Judith had loved Mendès single-mindedly, and from the first. Mendès continued, even now, to rouse her jealousy. 'You are really wicked, . . .' she wrote. 'Have apple-green mistresses if that can console you.'[42] And again: 'Where are you? What are you doing? You are certainly busy not loving me, or you are walking down the street so that women look at you, miserable wretch . . .'[43] Mendès took much satisfaction in tormenting her. 'I have never been so sad as I have been recently,' she told him. 'You are very wicked . . . But I do wish you'd come and abuse me more. I sulk at everyone except you. If you loved me the first day you saw me, I was not long in reciprocating; after all, I love you as I have never loved anyone. And I'm quite sure I shall not love anyone else.'[44] 'You wretch, you ask me again if I love you? Have you never looked at yourself? Don't you know how charming you can be? . . . I promise you that when I'd gone, and left you all alone, I was heavy-hearted. I said to myself: he is now the only man I could love, and he doesn't love me.'[45] Mendès continued to torment her; no doubt he talked of other women, threatened to leave her. 'What are you saying?' Judith wrote. 'You're mad. Do you say it out of wickedness, or to make me suffer? You plunged me into an agitation which is very rare for me; I don't know what I said. At table, I knocked over everything near me, I couldn't eat, or go, or stay still. I adore you.'[46] 'No one can stop me loving you, and I love you with all my soul.'[47]

She vacillated between ecstatic happiness and despair:

> How happy I am today, I feel that I have just been born! I don't know what I could have done and thought until now; I was a vegetable – that's all. I've discovered life . . . I am suddenly stupid and delighted about it. It seems to me that it's very bright and that everything I look at is gold. Yet I had no letter this morning. What does it matter? I know that you exist. That happiness is enough for me. I hardly dare believe it . . . And perhaps you don't love me. I am mad to be so happy, I'm afraid of a wicked world.[48]

More than once she doubted his love; and, alas, already she had a valid reason for doing so. Mendès could not tell her about the shadow side of his life.

> Do you love me [she asked]? Now I'm afraid. You were so strange. There was something else . . . Something that you didn't want to say . . . I don't know why, I am sad and anxious, I feel that you don't love me. How one trembles when one is so near to attaining one's dream! It seems that the whole jealous

world is going to oppose it . . . Do you love me? As for me, I love you in spite of your wickedness.[49]

She adored him with a devotion, a single-minded passion which, from the first, he had not deserved:

> You are very strong [she told him] if you can believe for a moment that I shouldn't follow you to Hell if you went there. Don't worry, even if I arrive in pieces, I shall go where you go. I am mad today, and furious. I should like the gendarmes to arrest everyone who is stealing our happiness from us. I shall send myself to sleep all the days when you don't come.
>
> I am going to settle down to your watercolour, it is a way of concerning myself with you. I shall make it all dark, because I am not to see you today. Work, do something for me. A beautiful, very long sonnet [*sic*]. When shall I see you? It's horrible not to know. Is it really true that you will love me for a long while? I am sure, myself, of loving you for ever.[50]

Catulle was cruel, and he was unreasonable:

> I am so happy today [she wrote] to have a letter from you, that I've forgotten yesterday's despair. Poor angel, why did you make me suffer so? Look, darling, let's be serious and reasonable. We have hardly got enough time left to look for a house. Next summer, it must have been found. As for myself, I'm going to work, I've already earned some money, and, with my father's protection, I shall earn it whenever I want. Tell me that you are calm and that you love me; then I shall be calm, too . . . I promise you that my father will say yes, when he no longer has the power to say no.[51]

Catulle was miserable, and he imposed his misery upon her. He appears to have mentioned suicide.

> I cry all night like a goose [she confessed], because I'm afraid you're sad . . . You know, darling, if you were a rag-picker, I'd go and pick rags with you. It's no use, you'll never be able to get rid of me. So much the worse, you wanted it, and now I'm the one who wants it. You have no rights, because you swore to me that you were mine: not even the right to kill yourself. This operation concerns me. No, all the world may stand against us, the stars may fall down on our heads, I shall not move. If you draw back, it is because you don't love me.[52]

Sometimes Judith hoped that her father would relent, and give her his permission to marry; but the hope was brief. The question did not cease to disturb him. Once, when he was away from Paris, he had written to her about the rumours which tormented him. She had answered with a sensible, loving letter.

> My dear Judith [he had replied],
> Thank you for your good, affectionate and reasonable answer. When I

appealed to your heart I was sure that I should not be knocking at a closed door. We who appear impassive are serious about the serious things, we feel them more acutely than people who are called expansive. You know that you are the last hope of my poor life: that life which is so tiring and so tormented. The slightest equivocal word about you sends me into rages which I cannot always control. Understand how much you are worth; a diamond of such price should not be tarnished, even by a breath. So don't expose yourself to malevolent interpretations. It is not enough to be irreproachable, one must also appear so. Especially a woman. Don't neglect your old friends for the sake of new acquaintances. Old friends are the enemies to be most feared, because they know us by heart, and people believe what they say. And, while I am away, don't leave your mother too much out of it, either. But here I am, sermonizing to you. I hope you will take it in good part. I am not preaching drivel. You must feel yourself that it is the real, practical, absolute truth, and that I'm talking not as a father but as an elder brother, as an old friend, or, if you prefer, as a companion whose heart is as young as your own . . .

I embrace you with all my soul.

Your father,

Théophile Gautier.[53]

Once Judith had been swayed by her father, open to persuasion, amenable to the promptings of common sense. Once she had been a girl in her teens; but now, as she approached her majority, Gautier could only dissuade. He was both enraged and terrified: terrified because he knew her seriousness of purpose, perhaps foresaw the disasters which the marriage must bring, the divorce in which it must end; enraged because Ernesta, stubborn, stupid and passionate, persistently encouraged both Mendès and her daughter. Late in 1864 Eugénie Fort recorded in her diary: 'TG complains of Neuilly, in a way which might make one think that there will be an explosion.'[54]

Mendès had in fact set out to ensure Ernesta's sympathy.

My mother [Judith remembered] was in Switzerland with her sister Carlotta, who had a most beautiful house at Saint-Jean, near Geneva. Mendès did not hesitate to go and see her there. There followed an exchange of letters between my mother and father. Ernesta came back. One day, she discovered Mendès wandering round the rue de Longchamp, a step which was as impulsive as it was foolish. She decided at once to go and find him and make him give up his plans. Mendès was most delightful, he used his powers of seduction, his eloquence and charm, and asked at least to be given valid and serious consideration. My mother let herself relent, and came home quite converted. And so Mendès gained a footing in the house again.[55]

Gautier respected Mendès' literary achievements, but he still refused to have him as Judith's husband. He was, wrote Maurice Dreyfous, 'totally opposed to a marriage which he considered fraught with the worst dangers.'[56] He had a horror of Mendès, and christened him Crapule Membête.[57] Maupassant would one day define Catulle as 'a lily in urine'.[58]

Judith's projected marriage cast the household at Neuilly into turmoil. In the summer of 1865, Gautier escaped to find solace with Carlotta at Saint-Jean; but he continued, constantly, to brood.

> My dear Judith [this in July],
>   Your last letter gave me pleasure, like everything you write. It is sensible, good and affectionate towards me. All I regret is a tone of bitterness towards your brother which is unworthy of a soul like yours. The unpleasant adjectives which you shower upon him are excessive. You know me well enough to be sure that I haven't asked anyone to *spy* on you. I am not inquisitive by nature, and I know that the things which hurt me deeply will always reach me. In view of a certain persistence, already observed because of the singularity of the person, Toto, who minds about the honour of the family, was naturally alarmed. He does not deserve what you say about him . . .
>   I entrust you to *yourself* until I come back, and I embrace you very warmly.
>   Your father,
>   Théophile Gautier.[59]

The letter was sent, but Toto continued to take note of Judith's behaviour, and Gautier continued to brood. That August, he wrote to his sisters: 'That idiot Toto has sent me a mass of tittle-tattle about Judith. It has got on my mind and taken away my pleasure in being with my dear, sweet Carlotta. Is there any truth in it? Remember to go to Neuilly and keep a sharp look-out.'[60] The gossip went on. Mme Alphonse Daudet heard 'a lot of talk'; she recorded that Judith and Mendès 'corresponded under pseudonyms through a little poetry magazine. It was amusing and romantic, and it naturally attracted the young girl that I was in those days, all enthusiastic about literary affairs.'[61]

Towards the end of 1865, through Alphonse Lemerre, Xavier de Ricard published a short-lived weekly paper, *L'Art*. It was there that the poetic doctrine of the Parnassians was formulated for the first time. The letters from Olivio to Olivia, also published by *L'Art*, were in fact Mendès' letters to Judith. Nor did Mendès content himself with this public courtship under the very eyes of Gautier. The constant tributes which Ricard's paper paid *le bon Théo* would have been a constant vexation had he known that Mendès was the author.[62] Late in 1865 Mendès himself wrote to a teacher in Tournon, by the name of Stéphane Mallarmé: 'Quick, send me your poems . . . It isn't a question of *L'Art* any more, but of *Le Parnasse contemporain*.'[63] The new periodical, which helped to form the Parnassians into a school, was to be significant in literary history.

Judith remained profoundly in love with this remarkable young man.

Poor darling [this on Christmas Eve, 1865], I assure you that there's nothing to be done about it for the next eight months. My father has said no too often ever to say yes. I don't want to do anything against his will. He is unhappy enough as it is. I shan't give him this final body-blow . . .

As for my majority, count eight months starting from today. But I should like a lock of your hair. Isn't it pretty? You can't help thinking of the sun when you look at it . . .

Don't spend your week from one Sunday to the next. Life is there. We're about twenty concerts away from our happiness. August will very soon be here . . . What are you afraid of? I promise you that in eight months I'll be your wife if that's what you want, and if you are patient. Didn't my father say himself: 'She'll do what she wants?' What I want is [to marry] you; we have almost got there. Are you going to let yourself founder when you have only to row another few strokes to reach the shore?[64]

Chapter Five

Gautier and his family saw in the New Year, 1866, at Neuilly.

We had gathered, Ernesta and the children, my sisters and I, in the downstairs salon [so he told Carlotta], waiting till it was midnight to embrace each other according to the patriarchal and solemn custom. Suddenly there was a violent ring at the bell . . . The box arrived from Saint-Jean . . . We took off the lid, and took out the delightful New Year presents which you had sent us . . . I put on the cap immediately. It is charmingly conceived and in exquisite taste. It suits me to perfection, and makes me look like a Muscovite Tsar . . . The children put on the capes at once; Ernesta donned her ruffles, and we quarrelled over the lamps and candles to look at ourselves in the mirrors . . . I am fairly well, except that I have a heavy cold and I am as bored as a trunk forgotten in a shed in a railway station.[1]

Boredom was soon to be succeeded by desperate anxiety. It was now the year in which Judith was to reach her majority. On 12 January, she wrote happily to Catulle: 'I am going to cross the days off the calendar, like a child.'[2]

On 24 August she would be free to marry whom she chose, with or without her father's consent. Unless he could finally discredit Mendès in her eyes, there was little that Gautier could do. In February he asked his editor, Julien Turgan, to make enquiries about him. There was to be a fortnight's truce while the family awaited Turgan's findings. On 26 February, Gautier left once again for Saint-Jean, to find some peace of mind with Carlotta. 'He is very vexed,' noted Eugénie Fort, 'because of a projected marriage for Judith. The young girl wants it and she is waiting until she comes of age to assert her rights.'[3]

The calm of Saint-Jean was soon disturbed. While Gautier was in

Switzerland, Ernesta announced that she was receiving Mendès at Neuilly.

My dear Ernesta [wrote Gautier],
Your letter gave me pleasure, since it brought me your news, and pain, because of the very serious step you have taken by receiving Monsieur Catulle Mendès in my absence. Judith had waited for two years; she might well have waited for a fortnight. However, it had certainly been agreed, so it seems to me, that I should spend this fortnight on my enquiries about somebody whom none of us knows, that this fortnight should be considered as a truce, and that everyone should hold their peace. The time allowed is not over yet. All passion apart, the information received is unfavourable rather than encouraging, and you invite the would-be son-in-law to the house in this furtive way, like a ladykiller. Should there be some degrading impossibility which would make the marriage unacceptable even in Judith's eyes, you engage the present and the future, if there is still a future for the wretched girl who is compromised by so many errors or, rather, indiscretions. It is not a question of my consent, which you have decided to ignore. In the state of madness in which you all find yourselves, Judith will be lost through her own wish, not through mine. I shall have resisted to the end what I consider an act of lunacy from every point of view. But what position have you created for me by this fatal sign of favour? What will my position be in a house where my authority as head of the family is disregarded by mother and daughters? When I come back, will Monsieur Mendès continue or discontinue his visits? Shall I have to take my hat and go and wait in the street until the gentleman has gone? Will he come when he knows that I am working in Paris? Because, alas, despite all this insanity, I must earn my living and yours, the living of the people who depend on me. I must, by the sweat of my brow, create you the leisure to do these stupid things. Turgan has been good enough to undertake these distasteful enquiries. Does he know that Mendès is coming to the house on the sly? With you as introducer, Estelle as duenna, while I am at Geneva, working night and day, my head and heart full of anxiety, to earn the money I left you and the money I'm sending you? I don't think he knows, because he would certainly have been against such compromising, dangerous behaviour. This good man is my best and most loyal friend. Don't you think you are making him play a perfectly ridiculous role? I am not talking about myself; you don't mind about me. You trample on my heart with terrifying tranquillity. What! He is going round, seeing people and trying to find out if the person who is trying to force an entrance into the family is or is not a young scoundrel, as everyone says he is; and, in the meanwhile, you take advantage of the fact that my back is turned, and you receive Monsieur Catulle Mendès with open arms. Is it right? Is it decent? Is it the most ordinary common sense? You claim that, if you had not made this concession, Judith would have gone out without your knowledge and seen him by herself, which would have been more dangerous. Let me say this: if you didn't sit all day beside a pile of clothes in the corridor where you spend your life, if instead of huddling there from ten in the morning till seven in the evening, you came and went about the house, went up to the studio, took a look out of the window at the garden, you would see if your daughters were having escapades or not, and you would prevent them going out by your supervision.
You have found me very indulgent, indeed too indulgent, about many

things, but where my name and honour are concerned, you will find me inflexible. You really hold it too cheap, and you will force me, to my great regret, to some final and irrevocable decision. I have fulfilled my duties to you all with love, abnegation and devotion. I also have duties to myself, that I must not forget. I wasn't thinking about them. You remind me of them.

I embrace you with a broken heart.
Théophile Gautier.[4]

Monsieur Catulle Mendès continued to earn contempt for his private life and acclaim for his literary achievement. It was he who had suggested to Xavier de Ricard that he turned *L'Art* into a publication devoted to poetry; it was he, it seems, who had suggested the title *Le Parnasse contemporain*. The first of the eighteen numbers of this historic publication appeared on 3 March, and opened, ironically, with poems by Théophile Gautier.

On 16 March, Gautier himself returned from Switzerland. As soon as his train reached Paris, he went to see Eugénie Fort.

This morning, at eight o'clock [she wrote, proudly], TG arrived in the rue de Beaune straight from Geneva. He has quite decided not to return to Neuilly. I am not persuaded that he will keep to this wise resolution, but we shall see. He had breakfast and left at eleven. This is the plan for the moment: Gautier is going to live at 58, rue Jacob. I shall stay in the rue de Beaune. We shall wait for 2 April, the time fixed for the final decision about the marriage. He is more determined than ever not to return to Neuilly. At five he came to spend two hours with me, and of course we only talked of this momentous affair. In the evening I went to the rue Jacob and came back very weary.[5]

'My sisters could have told me a good deal about this domestic disaster, which has been stirred up by Judith's madness,' so Gautier wrote that day to Carlotta. 'But at the moment they are at Neuilly . . . I've struggled to the end, and I don't intend to lose my life or my reason in this battle against idiocy, wickedness and perversity . . .'[6] Next day, at three o'clock, Eugénie had a visit from father and son. 'Toto is superbly calm. He guides and protects his father with noble ease. The father is well. He [says that he] feels glad to be free. I am not convinced.'[7] On 19 March, she continued: 'At three o'clock my two men . . . TG is still in the rue Jacob; he still insists that he doesn't want to go back to Neuilly.'[8]

If I were at Neuilly [Gautier explained to Carlotta], I should hear Ernesta grumbling, swearing, blaspheming, abusing the maids, thumping the furniture, crumpling the papers, slamming the doors. I should see the girls with those sweet little morning sulks which you remember, and I should already be beside myself with rage. Instead of that, I think of you, I cherish the dear recollection of you.[9]

On 20 March, Eugénie recorded: 'TG and T at three o'clock, as
yesterday. Matters are still the same. Gautier has seen his sisters, who
naturally agree with him about everything. They are waiting for the return
of Turgan, who is acting as intermediary. In the evening I went to the rue
Jacob.'[10] Lili and Zoé had at last brought news from Neuilly. 'Catulle isn't
coming while they are staying in the house,' Gautier reported to Carlotta.
'They didn't even learn of his visits except from the maids. Their protests
at the impropriety of this behaviour were greeted with a quite unheard-of
insolence. They were told that no one wanted to remain old maids like
them . . .'[11]

At four o'clock next day, he returned to the rue de Beaune. 'He is still
determined,' noted Eugénie. 'But when he needs to act, we shall see. He's
comfortable in the rue Jacob, but he's thinking of settling down. Where
and how?'[12]

Mendès' friends took a different view of events. 'Catulle's marriage is
almost certain,' Emmanuel des Essarts told Mallarmé. 'Théo has exiled
himself from his house. He is living in a miserable little room.'[13] There
was much cutting gossip about Gautier's animosity against Mendès. Yet
no doubt Turgan had discovered Mendès' constant womanizing, and his
attachment to Augusta Holmès; perhaps he had also discovered that
Mendès was in financial straits.

In the past few years he had more than once changed his address,
presumably when he could not, for a time, afford his rooms in the rue de
Douai. In about 1863 he had written to Hetzel from 23, route de
Versailles, Auteuil; early in 1864 he had written from 1, rue de l'Épinette,
Choisy-le-Roi.[14] Even now, in the spring of 1866, Coppée, who was living
with his family, sometimes gave his friend financial help; and sometimes,
recorded Jean Monval, 'after a week of extravagant lyricism or wild love,
he invited him to a meal at Montmartre with his mother and sister –
which, for a moment, gave Mendès the pleasant illusion of living a family
life.'[15]

Carlotta Grisi, normally so placid in her relations with Gautier, was now
becoming anxious about him.

> Thank you a thousand times, my dear Théophile, for your welcome letter [she
> wrote to him on 25 March] . . . I was waiting for it very impatiently. I am
> amazed that my sister is still unaware of your return. Please God it may remain
> unknown until Turgan comes back; I am afraid of any encounter for you before
> his arrival. Whatever happens, keep completely calm, don't lose your temper,
> and remember that it isn't worth making yourself ill because of this child's
> ingratitude towards you. Please go on keeping me up to date. The whole colony
> – not to mention me – is impatient for your news.[16]

On 29 March she added:'Poor dear, you love company so much that this solitude must be painful for you, and I am very anxious to see Turgan come back so that you can make a decision.'[17]

Gautier was not so alone as she seemed to think. On 31 March Eugénie noted: 'At two o'clock T and then TG. We dine together, all three of us. The father is not very well. This family disaster greatly disturbs him. He is stricken, furious, humiliated. At ten o'clock Toto and I took him home and put him to bed.'[18] Next morning: 'Rue Jacob at eight o'clock. TG is better. He is leaving at nine o'clock for Turgan's, at Auteuil, where he'll spend the day. I am not very well.'[19] Gautier was not, however, concerned with Eugénie's health.

That day, Easter Sunday, 1 April, des Essarts announced to Mallarmé: 'Catulle is going to marry Judith, Judith is going to marry Catulle . . .'[20] In four months' time, she was to come of age. For all her father's opposition, she would then be free to marry Mendès. Now, suddenly, distraught with apprehension, and weary after years of tension, Gautier accepted the inevitable. Turgan's findings were set aside, and he bitterly agreed that his daughter might marry Mendès at once.

> My dear Carlotta,
> Yesterday, in writing, I gave the necessary paternal consent. Although I had decided about this a long time ago, I must admit that my hand was trembling as I signed at the bottom of that paper – with a signature which is not perhaps unknown. I felt as a King must feel as he signs his act of abdication and dethronement. Indeed, I am no longer the head of the family, since I am disobeyed within the clan, and modern customs deprive me of the means of punishment. Yet, thanks to the good and worthy Turgan, the thing is less disastrous than one might have feared. The three thousand francs, which were just an annuity, are assured and, should Catulle die, revertible to Judith, which means that, whatever happens, she will not actually die of hunger. The parents are also giving five thousand francs for setting up house. To this I shall add the small trousseau which we discussed, so that she leaves home with a few dozen pairs of stockings and petticoats and doesn't wear her silk dresses next to her skin, as she would be capable of doing. The contract will be signed next Wednesday. The banns will be published at once and the thing will be concluded as quickly as possible. I shall not attend the ceremony, and I hope, dear Carlotta, that you will grant me, for a few days, the gracious hospitality of Saint-Jean. It is better for me really to be on my travels while these things which I disapprove of are accomplished . . .[21]

> I just want you to have a letter from me before the fatal contract is signed [Carlotta answered on 3 April] . . . I quite understand how you feel, and we know how lonely you must be, you who are made for domestic and family life. I hope that, once this wretched child is settled, you will find the calm you need so much with Estelle. Whatever happens, my dear, you know we are always

delighted to see you at Saint-Jean, and if we cannot give you all that you are
losing, at least you can be sure that we will do our best to give you as much
happiness as possible. So come when you like, we are always ready for you.[22]

The first days of April passed as Eugénie might have expected. She
waited, maternally, every day, to soothe both father and son. On 5 April,
Gautier (who was, that year, vice-president of the jury) visited Eugénie
after a Salon meeting, 'very weary and distraught. T at eight o'clock,' she
noted. 'We have supper. The father bursts into a torrent of insults, he
threatens revenge . . . He is really greatly to be pitied.'[23] On 7 April: 'TG
at six o'clock, more tired than ever . . . He sleeps before supper. T at eight
o'clock. The father eats his supper half asleep and after the meal he sleeps
again . . . At eleven o'clock T takes him home.'[24] On 9 April he returned
to the rue de Beaune. 'He is still obsessed, tormented by this marriage.
The contract should be signed today.'[25]

The contract is signed today [he himself announced to Carlotta]. The
irreparable misfortune will be settled. This marriage, an act of rebellion,
madness and indecency, must take place. For the past week and more, this
wretched Jew has been filling the popular Press, and the odd papers to which he
can have access, with pompous announcements of his alliance with the daughter
of the illustrious poet. He is beginning his publicity, and, all day, every
imbecile I meet feels obliged to offer me nauseating congratulations which
torment me and make me want to box his ears . . .[26]

On 10 April, Carlotta wrote again:

I understand how painful a position like yours must be to you. But you must
remember that you have good, devoted friends who can appreciate you, and
that you must contrive to live for us, and for them, and that together we shall all
manage to make a better life for you, the sort of life which you deserve . . .
    Come when you like. Your room is ready, and all our hearts, especially mine,
rejoice at the thought of embracing you.[27]

That day, in Paris, Eugénie noted: 'Rue Jacob this morning. T, then the
aunts. Great deliberations. We're looking for an apartment. In the evening
T and TG come to supper.'[28] On 11 April: 'This morning rue Jacob . . .
TG leaves at eight o'clock for Geneva.'[29] On 13 April: 'Toto . . . has
written to Geneva. He is busy with the affair at Neuilly.'[30] On 15 April:
'This morning at Toto's at nine o'clock. The marriage is postponed until
Tuesday.'[31]

Mendès himself confirmed to Flaubert: 'My wedding will take place on
Tuesday, 17 April, at the mairie at Neuilly, *at four o'clock very precisely*.
Thank you again for the kindness which you are good enough to show
us.'[32] Flaubert was to be one of Judith's witnesses.

On 16 April, at eight o'clock – presumably thinking that Judith was married— Gautier returned from Geneva.[33] He found that the marriage had been postponed. As he explained to Carlotta:

The marriage, delayed for want of a signature on a document, will take place tomorrow, Tuesday, unless there is a further hitch. Mendès' behaviour is more and more louche. The scoundrel has had it published in *Le Soleil* and *L'Époque* that he would probably replace me as dramatic critic on *Le Moniteur*. Ernesta persists in keeping Estelle, slanders me everywhere and rushes to lawyers to find means of resistance. I am very afraid that it may all end in some judicial scandal. I'm going to consult Chaix d'Est-Ange, the famous advocate, to ascertain my rights. One mustn't risk any step without knowing what one is doing. I wanted to descend on the house and, willy-nilly, remove Estelle; but that might cause furious scenes. Given Ernesta's character, anything is possible. She clearly wants to keep the child as a pawn, or perhaps as a means of conciliation.

On the day which was [originally] fixed for the marriage, Ernesta went out at nine o'clock in the morning, leaving her daughters alone, and didn't come back till five o'clock in the evening. She had, she said, gone out to buy a pound of chocolate. All the witnesses were there: Villiers de l'Isle-Adam with the Order of Jerusalem, the Cross of Malta, and of the [Greek Order of the] Redeemer, not on the famous red suit, but on a superb black suit. He had come in an enormous and magnificent barouche drawn by two superb white horses, like the ones he destined for his Argyraspides in his kingdom of Greece. Only Catulle did not appear, and he arrived about six o'clock, excusing himself on the grounds that his birth certificate was invalid (as I can well imagine). Judith had put sprigs of may-blossom on her head, and remained seated with the vague, wild air of Ophelia, with 'rosemary, for remembrance', as if the thing was completely indifferent to her. One of my sisters was ordered not to leave the house, which Ernesta deserted all day, to run about God knows where.

Tomorrow, at dawn, I shall go to Turgan's and stay at the edge of the Bois so that they know where to find me if my intervention is necessary. Toto will be with me. That, my beloved, is all that I can say to you today. Rest assured that, throughout these horrors and rages, your gentle thought never leaves me, and it sustains me. Although the Mendès tribe proclaim that I am an idiot and are already claiming my inheritance, I have still written the poem on *les marronniers de Saint-Jean*, and perhaps it is not too unsuccessful. I don't have time to write it [here], but you will have it in the next letter . . .[34]

On 17 April, Eugénie noted: 'Judith is married. It all went off in perfect order.'[35]

Perfect order there might be. *La Gazette des Étrangers* duly recorded the marriage of 'M. Mendès, man of letters, of 16, rue de Douai, and Mlle Gautier, of 32, rue de Longchamp, Neuilly'.[36] But Flaubert considered it 'a sad story'.[37] And so did Gautier himself, when he wrote from his sisters' at Montrouge a few days later:

My dear Carlotta,

The marriage took place on Tuesday at the mairie at Neuilly. Turgan and Flaubert were Judith's witnesses, Villiers de l'Isle-Adam and Leconte de Lisle were witnesses for Mendès. The ceremony was as chilling as could be. Mendès was as pale as a corpse, Judith unconcerned and very beautiful, dressed as a bride: a white satin skirt with a train, a little sprig of orange-blossom on her head, a lace veil, but rather less full that if the thing had taken place in church. Alphonse Karr had sent a wonderful bouquet from Nice: a bouquet of orange-blossom, white roses, white carnations and camellias of the same colour. I was touched by this remembrance from an old friend. Naturally Karr did not know how horrified I was by this marriage. Toto and I and my sisters were absent. They dined in a house which was lent by Robelin . . . There were fourteen people at table, but none of my friends was present except Madarasz, the Hungarian . . . The guests were: the bride and groom, Ernesta, father and mother Mendès, Leconte de Lisle, Villiers de l'Isle-Adam, Madarasz, François Coppée, a friend of Mendès', Estelle, etc. The meal was not very gay, although they recited poetry at dessert.[38]

The meal had not, indeed, been gay. Judith was embarking on a marriage which, her father feared, would prove to be an irreparable misfortune. And Gautier the indolent had at last made his 'final and irrevocable decision'.[39] The liaison of some twenty years was broken.

As for Ernesta [he told Carlotta, at the end of April], she will leave Neuilly for Villiers [-sur-Marne] on 1 May. I shall show her every possible indulgence, but my decision is unchangeable. All the details which I have learned about her participation in this lamentable affair are of such a kind that I am loath to put them on paper. The only excuse one could find for them is Judith's madness; all I know is that she has sent some Chinese translations to Houssaye's publication, the *Revue du XIXe siècle*. Talking of China, Tin-Tun-Ling came to see me at Montrouge; he embraced me with real delight and genuine affection. The tears were rolling down his little yellow, wrinkled, marmoset's face . . .[40]

Ernesta duly retired to the house at Villiers-sur-Marne where she was to spend many of the years which remained to her. And here, at last, the Gautiers had triumphed over the Grisis. 'To tell the truth,' wrote Émile Bergerat, who was later to marry Estelle, 'neither of Gautier's daughters could readily forgive their aunts, Lili and Zoé, for the way they had acted against their mother in the family drama in which the poet's happiness had foundered.'[41]

II

Madame Catulle Mendès

Chapter Six

On 18 April, Gautier and his younger daughter had gone to stay with his sisters at Montrouge. He was angry, bitter and unwell. One of his knees, reported Maurice Dreyfous, 'gave him terrible pain. It had turned quite black. The doctor told him that he had had the equivalent of an attack of apoplexy. His athletic constitution had stopped it half way.'[1] Dreyfous exaggerated. Gautier had rheumatism, and he soon recovered. On 24 April he called at the rue de Beaune. 'He is well,' Eugénie wrote, 'the pain has gone. He tells me what youthful memories he recalled in that intimate life with his sisters among the familiar furniture. He has almost decided to return to Neuilly.'[2]

He was always sure of Eugénie's devotion; and so, while he treated her deplorably, he continued to make demands of her. On 28 April he arrived at midnight, when she patiently made up his bed on the divan; next morning she had to suffer a long romantic tirade about revenge and hate. And now that he was in every way free to marry her, now that he could have realized the dreams they had so often spun together, he insisted that he must be free.

He was, of course, as Eugénie must have known, much too impractical, much too dependent, to regain (or even want) his freedom. He was in fact exchanging the rule of Ernesta for the rule of Lili and Zoé: strong-willed, unintelligent spinsters absorbed by lasting hatred of the Grisis and possessive devotion to their famous brother. On 14 May Eugénie reported with resignation: 'He is going back to Neuilly this evening; the Aunts are installed there.'[3] The aunts, explained Émile Bergerat, tartly, 'had rushed up from Montrouge, where they they were fretting at their spinsterhood, and, with their ascendency, they resumed the family domination which the compliant Théo had never wholly shaken off.'[4]

On 24 May, once again, he called at the rue de Beaune. It was

conveniently near his office. 'He is anxious and worried,' Eugénie noted.
'He can't get workmen to do the repairs in the house at Neuilly. And then
he also has vexations from Villiers[-sur-Marne], letters to lawyers, etc.'[5]
On 31 May: 'TG comes early. He is very vexed with Villier[s]. He is in a
pitiful nervous state. He talks with a great deal of bitterness.'[6]

All through June he vacillated between pleasure and depression. One
evening he came in happy with his new domestic arrangements. A few
days later the balance was upset, and he arrived in a fury. He had seen
Judith at the Théâtre-Français, and Ernesta had visited Neuilly.

> On Thursday the ultimate happened [he explained to Carlotta]. Estelle and I
> had gone to the Théâtre-Français to see the first performance of *Gringoire*, and,
> as luck would have it, Judith and Catulle were sitting in the gallery in front of
> our box . . . Imagine the situation. The whole audience had its eyes on us, and
> we did not dare to make the slightest movement. Never was a performance
> more painful . . .[7]

> As far as the Mendès and Ernesta are concerned [Carlotta replied, very
> sensibly], you can't think that, living in the same world, or nearly so, you are
> never going to meet them. All the better that it's already happened. I can
> understand that it's painful, but you will really have to get used to it . . . As for
> Ernesta, I think you're wrong to be afraid; she has certainly assured me that she
> would never set foot in your house again.[8]

> Dinner at Gautier's [so the Goncourts recorded on 29 June] . . . The house is
> still topsy-turvy from the rupture and the moving out. At table, Gautier, his
> two old sisters, his daughter Estelle, prettily oriental, the authentic Chinaman,
> her professor, and Éponine, a black cat with green eyes, which has its own place
> laid beside Estelle.
>   These two sisters, these two old women, seem to have given up being
> women . . . They would be a good type to study, a type which escaped Balzac.[9]

'My sisters are wonderful,' Gautier told Carlotta early in July. 'Estelle is
very sweet, very good, but quite indifferent and vague. She doesn't say
half-a-dozen words a day apart from *yes* and *no*. She isn't exactly ill, but
she is spiritless, languid and apathetic.'[10] It was small wonder. After years
of tension, her sister and her mother had both gone. Her father was bitter
and brooding, her aunts as stubborn and eccentric as ever. She had always
suffered from being Judith's sister; but she, too, existed, and she had her
needs and her emotions. No one considered her, and no one showed her
sympathy. She must have felt abandoned in a selfish, loveless world.

Throughout May and June, as Judith Walter, the pseudonym which her
father had once chosen for her, Judith reviewed the Salon. *La Gazette des*

Étrangers published her comments on a host of now forgotten painters, and on remembered artists, among them Courbet, Monet, and Gustave Moreau. Judith was always to be drawn to Moreau, enthralled by his romanticism and his mystery. 'In all his works, M. Moreau shows an ardent and poetic imagination. His ideas are usually strangely beautiful, but the impression is never complete. One admires what the artist might have done rather than what he has done. One glimpses it and one regrets it . . .'[11]

Some time that summer, Judith and Catulle went to Barbizon, near Fontainebleau. It was famous for its artists' colony. In September, yet again, Gautier returned to Saint-Jean. He spent three weeks on the shores of Lake Geneva. On 19 September Toto Gautier duly reported:

> I have been to Neuilly, where everything seems to me to be in order. Estelle is always nice, and beautifully behaved. One can't say the same of Judith, who is ambling round at Barbizon, among the landscapes and the landscape-painters, in pantaloons and linen smock, astride a donkey and smoking cigars! These eccentricities have been displayed too well by Mme Sand for anyone to attempt to equal them, and all you achieve by trying to is to make yourself grotesque. Mendès' father has gone bankrupt. We have finally gone bankrupt! Perhaps that will settle their affairs.[12]

Late that month, from Geneva, Gautier wrote to Estelle: 'I hope that your room will be finished when I come back, and that my dear little bird, the last of the brood and the only one that remains to me, will have a silky nest, downy and nice and warm.'[13] But the presence of Estelle did not console him for the absence of his favourite daughter. On 3 December, Eugénie recorded: 'We talk about Judith, and I was astonished to see him quite as overcome by anger as he was in the early days of the affair.'[14] 'I have always wondered,' wrote the journalist Maxime Rude, 'what attitude his father-in-law, the great poet Théophile Gautier, took towards that presumptuous half-caste [Catulle Mendès].'[15] Judith's marriage to Catulle was to remain the greatest grief of Gautier's life.

Henri Cazalis, who was born in 1840, divided his existence between medicine and poetry. In 1875 he was finally to earn his doctorate, and he spent much of his career as a medical consultant at Aix-les-Bains. As Maurice Fleury was to write: 'He has a perfect double intellect . . . Unlike the cricket, he can sing superb rhymes for the five months of the winter, and look after his patients diligently in the watering-place where he practises for the seven months of the summer.'[16] Cazalis was an ardent admirer of Augusta Holmès. By 1865 he was also a friend of Mendès and

Mallarmé. 'I spent a delightful evening at Mendès',' he told Mallarmé that November, 'where I was introduced to Dierx, Heredia and Mérat. Dierx and Heredia read some fine poems; I recited my sonnet . . . I shall go back as soon as possible.'[17] His assiduous attendance was to be rewarded. In 1866, at Mendès', he met Villiers and Coppée. In this salon, which was full of *chinoiseries*, he also continued to meet Mme Mendès, who was happily wearing Chinese dress.

In May 1866, within a month of their wedding, Cazalis had reported to Mallarmé: 'I saw Mendès with his wife. They were charming; Judith is adorable. But I don't give them nine months to love each other.'[18] On two occasions Emmanuel des Essarts returned to the subject of the marriage. 'I do not associate myself with the universal ill-will and hostility,' he explained to Mallarmé. 'But I cannot hide from you that Théo was formally opposed to this marriage, that he left the house, and that he was grieved. He predicted that it would end badly.'[19] And again: 'You talk to me about Catulle's marriage. I don't know what to think of it. I believe that Catulle is uncommonly gifted. I like him personally. I don't know him well enough to know if he will make a woman happy – a woman whom I don't know so well . . . I am very much afraid that Catulle is not mature enough to become a proper husband.'[20] That autumn, writing again to Mallarmé, Cazalis gave his ominous impression: 'Love is a kitchen fire which must have money if it is to burn. I saw Mendès at Barbizon all this summer; he is living God knows how. His wife is charming, but ill; and there is also a very sad *change* there.'[21]

The illness was not specified; but, on 6 September, Leconte de Lisle informed Heredia: 'The cholera is going, and Mendès is still at Barbizon – which he can no longer leave, I presume . . .'[22] Mendès and Judith were, it seems, kept in Barbizon both by illness and by poverty. As for the change in Judith which Cazalis had observed, it was perhaps reflected in a photograph by Carjat; yet it is difficult to believe that this flaccid woman, sitting cross-legged, à la Turque, smoking a cigar, is Judith at the age of twenty-one. Perhaps the change was simply a bitter change in her attitude to Mendès.

'The marriage was not happy,' continued Laurent Tailhade. 'Mendès was soon flitting through all sorts of boudoirs, while his wife, who was too proud to complain, kept her husband's name undefiled.'[23] She did not lack admirers. Every evening, month after month, Armand Silvestre sent her a sonnet, so that she might wake to his song of praise.[24] But, despite the love whose flowers he strewed beneath her feet, Judith withdrew into herself; she locked herself up in the hieratic impassibility which soon became her everyday demeanour.[25]

Whatever her unhappiness, her disillusionment with marriage, one secure relationship remained. Gautier detested Catulle, but he was still devoted to his daughter. Literature offered a pretext to keep in touch with her; and, soon after her marriage, they were already writing to each other. Gautier was no doubt anxious about her continued illness. She was ill for several months – perhaps as the result of a difficult and unsuccessful pregnancy. He could at least further her career; and he took the chance to smooth her path in journalism. Late in 1866, or early in the following year, she wrote to him:

Dear Father,
It is impossible for me not to thank you for having kindly arranged for my little story to be passed so quickly, and especially for having approved of it; for, as you know, your opinion is the only one which seriously concerns me. From now on I shall . . . work with more pleasure. I am busy on a long story, Chinese, political and dramatic, and I am taking all the more trouble with it because I think that it will be better than the others; as soon as the manuscript is ready I shall send it to you, because all the writing I do is done for you.
I hope that people aren't maligning me to you any more. I spend my life on a divan, pen in hand, rarely making the journey from one room to another; anyone who says anything else is certainly inventing. Besides, I have recently done two books [sic] which have given me a great deal of trouble – because Tin scented work and fled as fast as his legs would carry him.
Le Livre de Jade was delivered a month ago, and it will appear at the end of February. The volume of short stories will be ready at the same time, and there will even be a third volume in preparation. I see a horizon full of copy, which doesn't alarm me in the least; I hope to do the Salon somewhere, then China at the Exposition Universelle. If I weren't ill, I should do very much more than that, but for three or four months I have been very ill.
I daren't talk to you about anything except literature for fear of making you angry, but you know quite well that I still think about something else, and I embrace you, in spite of yourself, with all my heart.
Judith[26]

The coming Exhibition preoccupied the Press. On 21 February 1867 *La Presse* announced some of the exotic exhibits which would soon arrive in Paris. Morocco was sending the imperial tent and the tents of the Emperor's guards. Tunis was sending the Bey's tent, and building a caravanserai. Turkey was erecting a mosque, and a Mohammedan sarcophagus. Visitors to the Japanese garden would see a kiosk, a bamboo house and the hunting lodge of Prince Stazomy. China was building a café and two bazaars, and a porcelain tower in a garden. On 1 April, Napoleon III duly opened the Exhibition, and throughout the summer Paris was regaled with royal visits. In June, Princess Mathilde embarked at the Exhibition harbour on the King of Egypt's *dahabieh*. Twelve Nubian

oarsmen in State dress rowed her down the Seine to Saint-Cloud, where
they gave her a concert of native music. Until July, when the news arrived
that the Emperor Maximilian had been shot by rebels in Mexico, Paris was
alive with pleasure and with excitement. It was an exotic summer after
Judith's heart.

It saw not only the Exhibition, but the publication, by Alphonse
Lemerre, of *Le Livre de Jade*.

In the last months before her marriage and, presumably, in the months
that followed, Judith had worked intensely on her translations of Chinese
poetry. As she recalled:

> *Le Livre de Jade* was the result of this noble effort, but, though I had gone at it
> fiercely, though it was honest, I was not absolutely sure about the accuracy of
> the poems which made up this little book; and so I did not dare affirm that they
> were exact translations . . . Later on, I took up *Le Livre de Jade* again. I
> enlarged it a great deal and corrected it ruthlessly, and, this time, I could
> guarantee that it was translated from the Chinese.[27]

She could, indeed. As Suzanne Meyer-Zundel, her confidante, later
wrote: 'Judith Gautier knew Chinese at an age when young girls are
learning to pick up their first long dress. The whole of the Orient attracted
her. M. Clermont-Ganneau taught her Persian, and that gave us *Iskender*,
but it was China which remained her favourite and inspired the finest of
her books . . . Judith Gautier was a Chinese scholar. She wrote the
mandarin language, and she spoke the ordinary language.'[28] *Le Livre de
Jade* was, she said herself, the book which she had written with most
pleasure.[29]

Its publication was somewhat delayed. She had expected it to be late in
February 1867, but it was not until 9 May, in a letter to Heredia, that
Leconte de Lisle announced at last:

> *Le Livre de Jade* was put on sale the day before yesterday. Lemerre has made it
> an elegant and original book, and its typographical appearance corresponds,
> though not slavishly, to the pseudo-Chinese poems of Mme Judith Walter, the
> most singular of women and the least comprehensible I know. This little book
> has, moreover, this in its favour, besides the rare merit of a simple, graceful
> language, delicately coloured and naturally feminine, in the best sense of the
> word. It is written from beginning to end with a constant sense of *purity* and
> nobility. It goes without saying that one wouldn't find anything like it in China,
> which is undoubtedly just a stupid, ridiculous, savage country . . .[30]

Heredia read *Le Livre de Jade*, and asked Leconte de Lisle to congratulate its translator. 'I gave your congratulations to Mme Mendès,' came the reply. 'She received them with her usual impassivity.'[31]

One copy of the book was naturally sent, in homage, to Victor Hugo in Guernsey. 'I still haven't received Le Livre de Jade,' Hugo complained to Auguste Vacquerie on 9 June. 'In the meanwhile, thank Mme Catulle Mendès for her gracious and charming gift . . . I am delighted to have such a good name in Chinese.'[32]

Once again, poor Tin-Tun-Ling, who had thought himself at the end of his troubles, had seen his serenity disturbed. As Judith was later to explain:

> She felt that the inscription on the first page must not be commonplace. The Master's name was written in Chinese characters, which seemed to her the most appropriate. Each Chinese character has a meaning of its own and it is expressed by a monosyllable. Her own Christian name had been established by a mandarin who was passing through Paris. It was pronounced *Yu-Ti-Te* and meant: 'gracious and primordial virtue' . . .
> The Master's name, *Hi-Ka-To-Hu-Ko*, formed the prophetic phrase: 'To the triumphant exile who walks with solemnity, saying immortal things.'[33]

The phrase was music to Hugo's ears; a few weeks later, he addressed a graceful letter to the translator:

> Madame,
> I have your book, and, on the first page, I see my name written by you, and become a luminous hieroglyph, as if by the hand of a goddess. *Le Livre de Jade* is an exquisite work, and let me say that I see France in this China, and your alabaster in this porcelain. You are the daughter of a poet and the wife of a poet, daughter of a king and wife of a king, and you are yourself a queen. More than a queen, a Muse.
> Your dawn smiles on my shadows. Thank you, madame, and I kiss your feet.
> Victor Hugo[34]

'The Master,' remembered Judith, 'had written my name in Chinese characters, which he had carefully copied out: *"To Judith"*. I think I am the only person to possess some Chinese in the hand of Victor Hugo.'[35]

François Coppée, who went to see Hugo in Brussels, reported: 'The Master talked to me for a long while about the dedication of *Le Livre de Jade*, which greatly surprised and delighted him.'[36]

Anatole France, who was one of Judith's lifelong admirers, also expressed his delight and astonishment; he was aware that the poems owed much to the translator. 'I doubt,' he wrote, 'whether she found in Tu-Fu, Ché-Tsi or Li-Tai-pei all the details of the delicate pictures contained in *Le Livre de*

Jade.'[37] Whatever their origin, these pictures seemed to him to deserve comparison with the prose-poems of Baudelaire. Armand Silvestre declared that they had 'infinite wit and melancholy grace'.[38] They were melancholy indeed. They spoke of the passing of time and the passing of love. They recalled that happiness was transient:

> I know well where to find it, the blessed plant that brings oblivion . . .
> But I shall not go and gather it, I do not want to forget. I am tortured by despair, and yet I cherish this despair, because it is all that remains to me of the beloved![39]

And again:

> . . . The twilight slowly comes. The darkness falls and falls, drop by drop.
> Now darkest night has fallen, and for me nothing has changed . . .
> Oh, how could one destroy, for all eternity, the word despair?[40]

'Every sentence, every line of this singular collection,' wrote the Orientalist Albert de Pouvourville, 'is imprinted with the gentle, resigned and slightly disdainful philosophy of those magnificent sages of the Celestial Empire, who judge humanity at its true worth – and do not ask much of it – and do not expect more from it.'[41]

> Oh! the tranquil harmony that comes from the union of things which are made to be united!
> But the things which are made to be united rarely unite.[42]

Judith dedicated the book to Tin-Tun-Ling, her professor of Chinese. In *Le Livre de Jade*, at a single stroke, she had shown her literary mastery.

From that moment onwards [so Anatole France was to recall], Judith Gautier had found her form. She had a style of her own, a style that was serene and sure, rich and placid, like that of Théophile Gautier, less robust, less solid, but infinitely fluid and light.

She had her own style, because she had her own world of ideas and dreams. That world was the Far East, not at all as the travellers describe it to us, even when, like Loti, they are poets, but such as it had formed in the young girl's soul, a silent soul, a kind of deep mine, where the diamond takes shape in the darkness . . . Judith Gautier invented a measureless East as a habitation for her dreams. And that indeed is true genius!

She is not highly self-critical, but she has some suspicions of what she has done, if it is true, as people say, that she has always shown the greatest reluctance to travel in the East. She has not seen China and Japan. She has done better: she has dreamed them and she has peopled them with the delightful children of her mind and love.[43]

During the summer of 1867 Mendès and Judith set out for Spain. Coppée was kept in Paris by his work as a clerk at the Ministère de la Guerre; but he undertook to send Mendès money, and to correct the proofs of his articles. Mendès was charmed by Biarritz: 'I should like to spend my life here,' he told Coppée, 'if I didn't need to see you again – I love you so much.'[44] It was a curious confession after a year of marriage. Already, so it seems, Judith's company was not enough for him. The dream was not matched by reality. The unattainable had been attained, and Mendès was disappointed. Possibly he found his wife sexually incompatible . Whatever the cause of disenchantment, he remained disenchanted. Once again he wrote to Coppée:

> My good friend, my real, my only friend (because you *are* my friend, aren't you?), I should give anything in the world to have you with us. How you would love this part of the country, and what good account you would turn it to! Personally, I *cannot* describe what I *see*. I need something *imagined*, what has *happened* doesn't absorb me enough. That's the bad habit of a hypochondriac – but, to be honest, I've got the spleen! I really must admit it to myself . . . I have all the elements of happiness, but I am suffering, and, if I wrote poems on the subject, people would tell me I was like Baudelaire! Yet God knows that nothing is more personal than my sufferings! . . .
>
> If you have some money to send me, send me a postal order, *poste restante, Bayonne*, and a letter of advice, *poste restante, San Sebastián*, because it is dangerous to have money sent to oneself in Spain. So I'll go in search of it at Bayonne.[45]

Coppée duly replied, but he had more serious preoccupations: his mother was now ill. So he explained to Mendès; and on 3 September, from Ernani, Mendès answered in a characteristic mood of self-pity:

> How I envy you your anxieties! You have a mother . . . Your mother is the real classic mother. If I had had one like that, what a man I should have been! Tomorrow I'll be at Pamplona, and the day after at Tolosa, in a week's time I'll be in Saragossa, for the feast of Notre-Dame del Pilar . . . and for the bull fights. Perhaps I shall go as far as Madrid, but my address is still *poste restante*, at San Sebastián.[46]

Coppée remained a perfect friend. He dedicated a poem to Judith, and, on 5 October, he reviewed *Le Livre de Jade* in *Le Moniteur universel*. 'I should not be surprised if by dint of reading Tu-fu and Su-Ton-pu, Mme Judith Walter had become a Chinese poet herself, and if she dreamed of wearing the jade button of the first-class mandarins at a ball . . . The whole of the Celestial Empire passes through this book.'[47]

Mendès remained short of money, and continued his journalism; Judith, too, continued to write. They both contributed to the *Revue des Lettres et des Arts*. It was edited by Villiers de l'Isle-Adam. The short-lived publication first appeared this October, and, under her familiar pseudonym, Judith contributed *Chanson chinoise*, a translation of a poem by Tin-Tun-Ling, and a critical study of Poe's *Eureka*.

Such occasional writing could hardly ensure her livelihood. She and Catulle were in such financial straits that, on 29 October, back in Paris, they called on Sainte-Beuve. The critic, now at the height of his power and influence, was a friend of Gautier, and the friend and counsellor of the Emperor's cousin, Princess Mathilde – often known as Notre Dame des Arts. Sainte-Beuve was instantly and deeply moved by Judith's beauty and intelligence.

> Princess [he wrote next day],
>   Yesterday morning I saw Mme Catulle Mendès, the delightful daughter of Théophile Gautier. She came with her husband to talk to me about your benevolence, and to ask how it might be applied in favour of her husband, himself a poet . . . She certainly deserves interest, she has such a delicate talent, and such personal beauty. I saw her for the first time at quite close quarters and apart from her sister; she enchanted me. Wouldn't there be something possible in the Beaux-Arts? Or perhaps in the Interior, since M. de la Valette is well disposed?. . .
>   I lay at your feet, Princess, the tribute of my affectionate and respectful devotion.[48]

Princess Mathilde was prepared to use her imperial influence; but at this moment, so it seems, Mendès was threatened by his past. *Le Roman d'une nuit*, and his prison sentence, had not been forgotten. Authority now questioned whether he deserved a sinecure. The Princess was angered. Sainte-Beuve, still enchanted by Judith, was outraged.

> Princess [this on 26 November],
>   It is infamous!
>   This condemnation can only be a condemnation for some *doggerel* which seemed too wanton. I seem to have a vague recollection of it . . .
>   What! A whole life shattered because one was young at nineteen!
>   All I see at this moment, Princess, is my hatred for the malicious . . .[49]

The next day he wrote to Marshal Vaillant, Minister of the Fine Arts and of the Imperial Household:

> I am grieved to learn that M. Catulle Mendès is about to be excluded from the Marshal's benevolence for something he did in his youth, six years ago. It is not a moral matter at all, it is a *Press* matter. This young man published a few lines of verse which were too free, and he was wrong, but is that an irremediable crime, and one which should tarnish his life?[50]

The thought of Théophile Gautier, and his daughter, continued to drive Sainte-Beuve. The following day he wrote to Jules Taschereau of the Bibliothèque Impériale:

A place is vacant, a very modest place, in the Beaux-Arts. It has been requested – I request it – for Théophile Gautier's son-in-law, Catulle Mendès, and just as the promised place is about to be obtained, what happens? The Marshal receives a denunciation of Mendès, an allegation that he was condemned on moral grounds, six years ago.[51]

Next day Sainte-Beuve lamented to Princess Mathilde: 'What a lot of wretchedness and mystery about a simple good deed which your kindness suggested to you!'[52]

There was another problem, too: Mathilde, who was well aware of Gautier's family dissensions, had tactfully asked him if she might help his daughter.

All that you do is good, fair and kind [he answered], and, since you want it, I give my entire consent. Besides, Princess, rest assured that I bear no ill will against this young couple, who married in spite of my personal feelings. I should deeply regret it if someone refrained from helping them because they were afraid of hurting me. So continue your kindness to Judith because of her papa and also, a little, because of her. Although she has caused me great sorrow, she has many good points and a talent of the first order.[53]

He himself was delighted with *Le Livre de Jade*. No doubt it was he, and not Judith, who had sent a copy, luxuriously bound, to the Princess.

I hear that Princess Mathilde was pleased with my book [Judith wrote to him], and that she talks of offering us her protection; she could not choose a better moment, for, as the result of circumstances which I need not trouble you with, we do indeed need protection; we have had to have recourse to chores which give us little satisfaction.

As for the work or the position which the Princess's kindness might obtain for us, we should not be demanding. Anything that a man who knows one or two languages and has no commitments can do, we should undertake with pleasure. We have been told that certain appointments as librarian, assistant in the Emperor's Household or the Prince Imperial's, or inspector of provincial museums, would be agreeable . . .

Is it really true that you are prepared to undertake yourself to present our request to the Princess? I have been told so, but I shouldn't have dared to hope so. Yet I believe it and thank you and embrace you.[54]

Sainte-Beuve and Gautier had no doubt of Judith's distinction. Princess Mathilde remained concerned about Mendès' youthful folly. On 10 December Sainte-Beuve sent her his final advice: 'Princess, I can only see one thing to be done: summon the culprit, and make him give a complete confession . . . Let him show Your Highness this bad poetry. Let him prove above all that he was guilty of imitating Alfred de Musset. That is his most serious offence.'[55]

Joseph Primoli, the great-nephew of Princess Mathilde, duly recorded the sequel. 'While the young couple are living on love, they are dying of hunger. Théo had tears in his eyes as he thanked the Princess for the situation which she had had given to Mendès, and for the articles which she had arranged for Judith to write in *Le Moniteur universel*.'[56]

Mendès was given a place in the Beaux-Arts which brought him 1,500 francs. Judith had more need than ever of her imperial protection. She was not only in need of money, she was once again far from well. There is no indication of the nature of her illness; but Judith had, it seems, been a sturdy child. It was only since her marriage that she had been troubled by poor health.

> Dear Father [this to Gautier],
>   I'm going to bother you again. The doctor has ordered me sea and fir trees to restore me completely. I'm going to the South, to Arcachon, for a fortnight or two; I haven't time to finish a rather long novella and a few articles on the Exhibition which I've promised Dalloz; but I have great need of the little money that they're worth, just [as much] as if they'd been done. Let me say that I only have another few days' work to finish everything, and that I shall have delivered the manuscripts within the next fortnight. But for serious reasons I am obliged to leave next Tuesday. So I am asking Dalloz, in a letter which he will receive at the very moment you get this, if he has faith enough in my punctuality to advance me a small sum of money. If he speaks to you, help me, and even – but I dare not ask you – speak to him about it yourself . . .
>   Good-bye, my darling father. I thank you and embrace you.
>   Judith[57]

Soon afterwards, from the Villa Vauban, at Arcachon, she wrote again:

> I am in a very calm and beautiful part of the world. Perhaps it is too beautiful, and it is full of temptations. One would like to do nothing but watch the crashing of the waves and listen to the moaning of the fir trees, but there are healthier occupations: literature is unrelenting, it has never agreed to write itself . . . I am sure that, if you were here, you would not be writing your article, you would be writing poetry as you wandered by the sea. You are writing very little of it, so it seems to me. I am better than you, I'm writing some; it's true that it isn't pretty pretty, but when it's presentable I shall present it to you.
>   I sent Dalloz three long articles on China, Japan and Siam; I think that they will acquit me of the advance that he gave me. It would be very kind of you to use your influence to get them passed; anyway Dalloz is very well disposed.

Would you correct my proofs? I have written to ask that they should be sent to you . . .

I don't want to come back to Paris until I have completely finished my volume of short stories. What are you doing? I don't know anything, I should be glad to get *Le Moniteur* . . .

I embrace you as I love you.

Judith[58]

That November and December, she published four articles on the Chinese, Japanese and Siamese contributions to the International Exhibition. Mendès discussed the Russian and German sectors.[59]

Sainte-Beuve and Princess Mathilde had improved the Mendès' situation, but they had not transformed it. Among the papers of Nadar, the photographer, is a letter from Judith to his wife; it suggests a little of her financial pressure.

Dear Madame,

When I left you yesterday, I learned that between now and *Tuesday* next I must produce a work of fiction of which not a single line is written yet. You understand that I must keep my nose to the grindstone.

Besides, I have a cold, which consoles me for not having my picture taken – I look like a cat which has swallowed some pepper.

I will see you soon, dear Madame. All my good wishes to M. Nadar and to Paul.

Judith Mendès[60]

Judith was driven on by her need for money, her passion for literature and for the East. On 23 March 1868 *La Liberté* announced that it would soon begin to serialize her Chinese novel, *Le Dragon impérial*.

This work is destined to have a very great success . . . One does not know which to admire more: the rare knowledge and the power of divination which enable the author to recreate an unknown society for us, or the art with which she has developed the simple, noble theme of her book. As for the style, . . . it is entirely worthy of the young and excellent writer who signed *Le Livre de Jade*.[61]

On 11 April, *La Liberté* published the first instalment of 'this eminently remarkable book by a young girl of twenty [Judith was in fact twenty-two] who knows Chinese like a mandarin, and already has the style of her father, the great colourist.'[62]

For all his grief and bitterness about his daughter's marriage, Gautier remained intensely proud of her. Four days later, at Princess Mathilde's, in the rue de Courcelles, he took Edmond de Goncourt aside in the smoking-room and talked to him about Judith, and

> about her Chinese novel which is appearing in *La Liberté*. He finds it '*Salammbô* without the heaviness'. He told me [reported Goncourt] that she was the most astonishing creature in the world. She has a wonderful brain, but a brain which is set apart, and has no relation to herself, . . . and leaves her as childlike and as ninnyish as can be. 'She is just an instrument, a tool in front of a sheet of paper.'[63]

'Judith is really a splendid creature,' he added, to Maurice Dreyfous. 'She has never bothered to learn anything, and she writes wonderful books. She is a sponge which has dipped into all my old buckets.'[64]

Gautier still loved his elder daughter with a deep, unchangeable devotion; and no rancour would have marred his appreciation of literature. When, this year, he helped to write the *Rapport sur le progrès des lettres depuis vingt-cinq ans*, even his son-in-law received an honourable mention.

> Monsieur [wrote Mendès on 16 April],
> Let me express my gratitude for the kind words which accompany and honour my name in your report on contemporary poetry. To me it is more precious than all the rest: the encouragement of a master whom we all increasingly admire for his wonderful gifts as a poet, novelist and critic, and, as Charles Baudelaire said, for his impeccability.
> I have the honour to be, with the most humble respect, your enthusiastic disciple,
>
> Catulle Mendès[65]

On 27 May 1868 *La Liberté* published the thirty-third and final instalment of Judith's novel. 'Its success has increased every day,' wrote the editor, 'thanks to the dramatic violence of the action, the audacious strangeness of the characters, the splendour of the descriptions, and the beauty of the style. This novel sets Mme Judith Mendès among our foremost novelists.'[66]

A publisher still had to be found to produce it as a book, and Mendès approached Jules Hetzel:

> Dear Monsieur Hetzel,
> When I had the pleasure of seeing you, you kindly gave me to understand that you could publish a book by Madame Mendès or by myself on condition that this book was a *novel*.
> Have you heard about *Le Dragon impérial*, by Madame Mendès, in *La Liberté?* Thirty instalments or so, and they have had the most brilliant success.

Do you want it? We shall come and see you one morning.
Yours most respectfully,
Catulle Mendès.[67]

It was not Hetzel who set his imprint on Judith's first novel. *Le Dragon impérial* was published by Lemerre in 1869. It is a brilliant, rich and complex epic about ancient China. It is the story of Ta-Kiang, the peasant who is destined to attain supreme political power; of Yo-Men-Li, his faithful fiancée, and Ko-Li-Tsin, the poet. Here, in fantastic detail, for some three hundred pages, Judith re-creates the life of soldiers and peasants, courtiers and priests: a world of pagodas, jewels and multicoloured landscapes, of extravagant adventures. She writes with unremitting verve and ironic humour, and her lyrical descriptions suggest how deeply she is versed in Chinese literature. Her admiration for the Chinese world is reflected, too, in her portrayal of the central characters. Honour means much to them, and they have a simple, quixotic sense of loyalty. *La Dragon impérial* is remarkable for its poetic quality, its vigorous, sustained imagination; it is also notable for its violence. There are a lust for torture, an ardent interest in war, which are curious in a young woman. This savagery – like the poetry – was always to characterize Judith's work.

Villiers de l'Isle-Adam acclaimed the novel in *La Vogue Parisienne* for its prodigious sense of local colour. It was, to him, a literary truffle to delight the artistic gourmets of France.[68] Anatole France was to be still more enthusiastic:

> Her first novel, I should say her first poem (for they are really poems), is *Le Dragon impérial*, a book all embroidered with silk and gold, and of a style which is limpid in its brilliance. I am not talking about the descriptions, which are wonderful. But the principal figure, which stands out from a background of unheard-of richness, the poet Ko-Li-Tsin, already has this character of savage pride, of youthful heroism, of curious chivalry, which Judith Gautier imprints on her principal creations: this character which makes them original. The young woman's imagination is cruel and violent in this first work, but she already has, for ever, that proud chastity, that romantic purity which do her honour.[69]

Mallarmé, writing to Henri Cazalis, pronounced the book to be 'a great marvel'.[70] Years later, Albert de Pouvourville added:

> Perhaps Judith Gautier never wrote anything more subtle and more 'yellow' than this *Dragon impérial* . . . And when one thinks that Judith Gautier never went to the other side of the world, one feels stupefied by the faculty of adaptation and the power of vision – today one would use the word telepathy – with which the author created, in their actual poses and their familiar demeanours, the people and the lands of which she had only heard tell.[71]

Literature, wrote Armand Silvestre, owed Tin-Tun-Ling 'that fine book, *Le Dragon impérial*, which Flaubert considered one of the wonders of the age.'[72]

The author of *Le Dragon impérial* still lived in a less than imperial world. She and Mendès (and Villiers, for a time) were boarding at a *pension de famille* at 25, rue Royale, in Paris. It was run by a Monsieur Garcias, a former banker who had himself fallen on hard times. On 15 July, from Charny, after a five-week visit to Paris, Lefebure wrote to Mallarmé: 'I must tell you a bit of gossip which came my way: it is that Mme Mendès is on the best of terms with a big bearded pantheist poet, S——, I think, who is living at the same hotel, like Villiers. According to Cazalis, Mendès is still the elegant swindler that he always was.'[73] Possibly the poet in question was Armand Silvestre, famous among the Parnassians for his *Sonnets païens*. Yet it is hard to believe that Judith was already unfaithful to Mendès; if indeed she affected any intimacy, it was probably an innocent attempt to hold her husband's interest.

'Whether you want to or not,' he had told her, 'you love me, and I defy you to love anyone else.'

'How,' she had asked him, 'did you know?'[74]

Whatever the strains and disappointments of their private life, the Mendès remained absorbed in literature. Judith was at first amused by the Parnassians.

> I thought them slightly contemptible [she said later] and ridiculous. I secretly laughed at them.
>
> How was it that, in order to compose a quatrain or perfect the slightest page, they seemed to suffer torture, prowled up and down like wild animals in cages, repeated the same sentence twenty times over, consulted one another and never admitted that they were satisfied with their work? 'Why are they so desperate to write,' I wondered, 'since they evidently lack the gift?' . . .
>
> The reaction which they attempted was undertaken against the *élégie larmoyante* which was invading poetry: the sentimental confidences revealing all the weaknesses of the heart . . . As Rémy de Gourmont so well expressed it: 'The Parnassian reaction was a gesture of modesty.'[75]

Whatever her private opinion of them, Judith enjoyed their admiration. Leconte de Lisle himself, their master, could not look upon her without emotion: this woman, whom he considered a feminine power, had a beauty which recalled the Greek ideal.

He held court, every Saturday, at his fifth-floor apartment at 8, boulevard des Invalides. It was hardly luxurious, Mendès remembered, but it was very neat, and always in order, like a well-written stanza. 'How impatiently,' added Mendès, 'as each week went on, we awaited Saturday, our precious Saturday, when we might assemble once again, united in mind and heart, around the man who had all our admiration and affection! It was to this little salon . . . that we went to announce our plans, and brought our new poems, it was there that we eagerly asked the opinion of our comrades and our great friend.'[76] Mendès and Judith did not miss a meeting, recalled Fernard Calmettes, the historian of the salon. 'The evenings were full of heated arguments. They went on late, and in winter, in the cold and snow and rain, it was of course difficult getting home . . . Leconte de Lisle himself seemed to live only for his Saturdays. Henceforward he was recognized as a leader by the young men of letters who surrounded him.'[77]

Among them were Théodore de Banville and Stéphane Mallarmé. Paul Verlaine came to Leconte de Lisle's 'when he was still presentable'.[78] Mendès had been among the first to divine the power of Verlaine. 'There is everything in Poèmes saturniens except mediocrity,' he had announced in 1866. 'A splendid poetic future is assured him.'[79] With the poets, now, at Leconte de Lisle's mingled the novelist Paul Bourget, Judith's admirer Léon Barracand, Baudelaire's friend Charles Asselineau, the learned Parnassian Jean Marras, assistant curator at the Palace of Fontainebleau, and the publisher Alphonse Lemerre.

When the acknowledged master of the Parnassians came himself to visit Lemerre, all conversation stopped. His massive bulk and ponderous movements gave him an almost sacerdotal appearance. Since he frowned to keep his monocle over his right eye, his face had a certain permanent disdain; but his glance changed with surprising rapidity. Just at the moment when he seemed weary and withdrawn, there would be a sudden flash, a blinding flame; he attracted and fascinated his prey. Some people could not bear this gaze, and turned pale, and were put out of countenance.[80]

Chapter Seven

Judith and Catulle had their gods in literature and music, and the god of music remained Richard Wagner. It was not entirely surprising. Although Ernesta Grisi had sung at the Théâtre des Italiens, Gautier had long been one of Wagner's champions. In 1857 he had gone with the composer and critic Ernest Reyer to hear *Tannhäuser* performed in Wiesbaden. 'And I still remember,' wrote Reyer, in 1872, 'how deeply he was moved by this music, which was as new for him as it was for me. From the first moment he appreciated its epic grandeur and its smallest details.'[1]

Judith was not unaware of her father's sympathies. She herself had discovered Wagner by chance, as a girl, in the days of her piano lessons; she, too, had found his music a revelation. Laurent Tailhade recalled that, during Wagner's first concert at the Théâtre des Italiens,

> while she was strolling round in the interval with Théophile Gautier, a little man with thin lips and razor-sharp features had come up to them, and begun to rant wildly against the newcomer. It was Hector Berlioz. 'As far as I can understand,' the young girl said to him, 'you are indignant about a colleague and a work of transcendent importance.' Gautier rebuked her for the sake of appearance, but he was laughing to himself, and, deep down, he was delighted.[2]

Judith had often heard Wagner at the Pasdeloup concerts, and now she and Mendès shared an almost uncritical passion for him.

On 5 September 1868, Leconte de Lisle announced to Heredia: 'M. and Mme Mendès came back two days ago, and they left again yesterday for Baden, where there is going to be a performance of a Wagner opera.'[3] They had in fact gone to hear *Lohengrin*, and on 8 September, in *La Presse*, Judith published an article which was very much in her father's style – and almost an anthem in Wagner's praise:

Genius is a despot to whom one must, sooner or later, submit. To resent obedience, that is to say resent admiration, is only a sterile effort and a waste of time . . . When a man like Richard Wagner arises, he assumes his glory as a sovereign assumes his rightful throne . . .

This time the triumph of Wagner was complete. It was the theatre in Baden which was given the honour of rehabilitating French taste, so gravely compromised by the inopportune defeat of *Tannhäuser;* for the audience at the performance of *Lohengrin* was in fact the first-night audience of Paris. The few Germans who were present that evening had determined not to applaud so as not to influence French opinion, they said. They had tears in their eyes, but they kept their hands in their pockets.[4]

Battle was joined. On 30 September, in the *Journal des Débats*, Reyer criticized *Lohengrin*. On 17 October, in *La Presse*, Judith published three columns on *Richard Wagner et la critique*. She questioned some of Reyer's statements. She maintained that Wagner's operas were not conceived according to the same system as Gluck's, and she explained his innovations. Reyer answered with a courteous open letter, and proved that he knew his Gluck as well as she did, and that the discussion was largely academic.[5] On 20 October, Judith published a second article, this time nearly four columns long. She analysed each of Wagner's works; her analyses were poetic rather than technical, and, as Servières observed, in *Richard Wagner jugé en France*, they were 'absolutely hyperbolical'.[6] The public, she ended, . 'is increasingly learning to understand. Richard Wagner's system and operas, widely admired in Germany and Russia, have already gained the sympathy of the most distinguished minds in France.'[7] She was now an impassioned fighter in a crusade that was to last for the rest of her life. When Félix Régamey published his cartoon, *L'Apothéose de Pasdeloup*, in *Paris-Artiste*, he showed Wagner and Gluck looking on while the Muse crowned Pasdeloup. The Muse was Judith in the guise of a Japanese woman holding *Le Livre de Jade*.[8]

When she goes down the boulevard on her return from one of those concerts at which the valorous young girl defends Wagner against the infidels, she traces a luminous course [wrote Anatole France]. One almost bows before her, in reverence, as if she were Helen of Troy. She has the erudition of a mandarin and the gaiety of a Parisian.[9]

She also had the boldness of youth. Late in 1868, she sent all her articles to Wagner, and she asked him for his corrections. Early in November he answered, from Lucerne:

Madame,
You cannot possibly have the slightest idea of the touching and consoling impression which your articles have made upon me. Thank you for them, and

let me count you among the number of true friends whose far-sighted sympathy is all my glory . . .

I shall probably go to Paris soon, perhaps even this winter, and I rejoice in advance at the real pleasure which I shall have in shaking hands with you, and telling you how much good you have done to

Your most obliged and devoted
Richard Wagner[10]

God had spoken to his worshipper. Judith's passion for Wagner's music could only become more intense. In April 1869 *Rienzi* was performed at the Théâtre-Lyrique.

Dear father [this to Gautier],

I count on you to defend Richard Wagner's splendid cause with all your might. Unfortunately the cause is not yet completely won. With the authority of your genius you could so easily crush all those vermin on *Le Figaro* who dribble their slime on everything that is great and good and so dishonour literature that one is really tempted to abandon it for ever.

I have no doubt that you, who were the first to speak of Wagner in France, and cannot fail to admire absolute beauty, in whatever art it is revealed, have already decided to write a favourable piece. I am simply writing to offer you a few details about the score, and a few facts if you should need them . . .

Thank you in advance, and I embrace you as I love you.

Judith

Would you like to have a box for the third performance, which will be on Sunday?

I shall soon bring you *Le Dragon impérial.*

Judith[11]

On 12 April, Gautier's piece appeared in the *Journal officiel.*

Wagner was not the only hero Judith revered. Since their controversial marriage, she and Mendès had sometimes felt ostracized. They had often been unsure how her father's friends, the older generation, would receive them. They were all the more touched and proud to find that Victor Hugo accepted them. He did not only admire Judith's work, he sent the young couple a copy of his latest novel. On 6 May, from 69, boulevard de Madrid, at Neuilly, Judith answered gratefully:

Monsieur,

Let me thank you with all my heart for the great delight you have given us by sending us *L'Homme qui rit.* You have deigned to think of it, and to write our names on the first page – and with what a charming implication! This hyphen [between our names] seemed to us to show your approbation, and we need not tell you how precious approbation is when it comes from you.

We had already felt your benevolence towards us for some time, and that benevolence consoled us for much malevolence. Today it is affirmed, and we shall be eternally grateful to you for the pride and confidence it gives us.

I dare not say anything to you about your formidable and splendid novel. You alone could explain the incomparable emotion that one feels on reading one of your books. But you yourself do not know this emotion, since your works alone are capable of giving it.

Allow us to offer you our boundless admiration and respect.

Judith-Catulle Mendès[12]

Winter, however, had come and gone, and Richard Wagner had not been to Paris. With the audacity of youth, Judith decided to visit him. Since 1866 he had been living at Tribschen, near Lucerne.

> But how would one be received? There were fantastic legends circulating about Wagner. Someone who was well informed reported that he had a harem of women of every colour and every nationality, clad in magnificent dresses, and that no one crossed the threshold of his house.
>
> Someone else depicted him as an unsociable man, sombre, sullen, living alone in a jealously guarded retreat, alone with a big black dog.[13]

He was, in fact, far from unsociable. Early in July he wrote again to Judith: 'I don't need to tell you how happy I'd be to see you and Monsieur Mendès. All I should like is to ask you to prolong your stay for a little while at Lucerne, so that the pleasure you grant me doesn't disappear too fast.'[14]

On 12 July, Leconte de Lisle reported to Heredia: 'Catulle and Judith came on Saturday to say goodbye to us. They are leaving for Munich with Villiers, very happy to have let their house, and their pockets full of gold.'[15]

In mid-July, with Villiers de l'Isle-Adam, the Mendès duly set off for Lucerne. Officially they were on their way to Munich, to report on an international art exhibition (Mendès duly discussed it in L'Artiste); they were to break their journey in Switzerland. All three of them were in time to leave an account of this momentous journey, but Mendès and Judith – who by then had separated – were to contrive not to mention one another. Mendès simply referred to 'a young woman whom we had the honour of escorting'.[16]

At the station at Lucerne, Wagner was waiting. He was small and thin, remembered Mendès, 'and tightly wrapped up in a brown cloth coat, and his whole skinny body . . . was trembling almost convulsively, as if he had been a neurotic woman. But the upper part of his face kept a splendid expression of pride and serenity . . .'[17] Catulle was writing long after he had grown disillusioned with the man. Judith recalled her first meeting with the warmth of a lifelong admirer.

> Alone, erect, and wearing a broad-brimmed straw hat, Wagner was on the platform waiting for us. We had never seen him, but how could we fail to recognize him? . . .
> He himself had no idea what we looked like, and he counted on us to find him. But, immobile, well in view, he was watching the stream of arrivals with intense attention.
> It was I who rushed towards him, in an effusion of delight which dominated all other emotions. He enveloped us all in that fixed and luminous gaze which searched you to the very soul, and he grasped our hands.
> After a moment of solemn silence, he smiled and offered me his arm.
> 'Come on,' he said. 'If you're not intent on luxury, you will like the Hôtel du Lac. I've booked you rooms there.'[18]

Later that day, the three admirers made their way to Tribschen, where they found no harem, but Cosima von Bülow, the daughter of Liszt. She had left her husband, Hans von Bülow, and for the past year she had been living with Wagner. She was 'a tall, slim young woman with a noble and distinguished face, blue eyes, a kindly smile, and a magnificent head of fair hair. She was standing in the middle of the salon, surrounded by four little girls, one of them very small.'[19] The elder two were her daughters by Bülow. Isolde, who was four, and Eva, who was two, were her daughters by Wagner. Only a month earlier, on 18 June, she had given birth to Siegfried, his son. 'Mme von Bülow is wonderful, gentle, intelligent and delightful,' Villiers reported to Jean Marras. 'She and Judith are good friends.'[20]

From the first moment, the visitors were drawn into Wagner's household. They had supper with him every evening, and drank the champagne which 'his friend Chandon' lavished upon him. They discussed the music of the future. Judith needed to worship; now she worshipped at the feet of the Master. Worship was not too strong a word:

> Certainly [she was to write] I had never known so blue a lake with such verdant hills, and yet I did not see them. The Master's gaze, his shining eyes, in which there melted the most beautiful shades of sapphire: that is what I saw, and I said to Mme Cosima, who thought exactly as I did:
> 'It is only now that I understand the felicity of Paradise, which is so extolled by the faithful: the joy of seeing God face to face!'[21]

They sailed one evening on the lake with Wagner, all of them singing his compositions until at last even he exclaimed: 'We have exhausted my water music.'[22] They climbed Mount Axenstein with him. One day, Judith arrived alone at Tribschen.

The garden door of the *salon* was open wide, and, as I reached the threshold, I heard very gentle chords. They were coming from the little sanctuary where the Master worked . . . I hardly dared to breathe. I sat down on the nearest chair, extremely moved, troubled, and even frightened. Was it not indiscreet, even sacrilegious, to surprise the sacred mystery like this? . . . And yet, what rare happiness! To hear Wagner compose! . . . Motionless, unblinking, I listened in devout silence.

What I heard appeared to me incomparably suave . . . It was a series of chords, very slow, which seemed to escape from a harp rather than a piano: a distant, mysterious, supernatural harmony . . . I discovered, later, that it was the first sketch of Wotan's evocation of Erda, in the third act of *Siegfried*, when the goddess rises up with closed eyes, all covered with dew . . .

After a few moments, there was silence, and soon Wagner appeared between the silken folds of the door-curtains. He was serene, his face was haloed by his silver hair, and his big eyes were even more luminous, more radiant than usual. He caught sight of me, riveted to my chair.

'Ah!' he said. 'So you were there? . . . You were as good as gold, because I didn't hear anything.'

'Oh, Master, think of the terror and the ecstasy! . . . To surprise God in His creation!'

'I've told you already not to be too enthusiastic,' he said, laughing. 'It isn't good for your health.'

'On the contrary, it makes me live twice over!'

'Well, come on . . . I've been as good as gold, too. Come and see how well I work.'

There is a rather strong scent of essence of white roses floating in the sanctuary; the room is lit by a restful light, softened by the verdure outside. The spines of a few books are gleaming on the shelves; the royal friend [Ludwig II of Bavaria], in his golden frame, seems to follow you with the magic gaze of his Polar blue eyes.

No disorder on the piano-desk: a few big sheets of music paper, most of them covered with writing, are lying, here and there, on the sombre rosewood. The passages which the Master has just composed are written down in pencil, in a delicate, very legible hand.

'I recopy in pen and ink,' he says. 'I like it to be very clear. When I make a mistake, I'm furious.'

On top of one re-copied page, I read: '*Siegfried*. Act Three.'

'Exactly,' says Wagner. 'That's where I have to re-write nearly two pages, because I scribbled . . .'

And he shows me three bars crossed out on the right-hand page . . .

'What will happen to that precious sheet of paper?'

'Do you want it?' asks the Master, who has guessed my greed.

'Oh, yes!'

Then he takes his pen and writes Tribschen and the date at the top of the margin.[23]

According to Guichard, Judith had arrived at Lucerne on 16 or 17 July. On 25 July, with her husband and Villiers, she left for Munich.[24]

The three of them settled at 4b, Maximilianstrasse. The moment of euphoria was over, and the problem of money arose again. On 28 July they drafted a joint letter to the editor of *La Vie Parisienne:*

> Sir,
> We shall soon be sending you our first article on Munich. Here, in the meanwhile, are some brief travel notes (prose and sketches). We should be delighted if *La Vie Parisienne* could do something with these scraps of paper . . .[25]

Alas, the travel notes were not published.

From their entresol, Mendès also sent a note to Victor Hugo, a note which showed a singular misjudgement of Hugo's nature. Hugo never found praise unwelcome, let alone excessive, but he disliked admiration of Richard Wagner. Mendès should have known that Hugo wanted to be the solitary star in the sky.

> Monsieur et vénéré Maître [he wrote],
> We are in Munich – where we have come to applaud the great and admirable Richard Wagner. You like him, don't you? I have just received a poem which has recently been published in *La Liberté*. I confess that I am almost satisfied with these few lines, and I venture to send them to you so that the least imperfect of my works does not remain unknown to Him who is the ultimate judge.
>
> > Your humble admirer,
> > Catulle Mendès
>
> Maximilianstrasse 4b
> II eingang, entresol
> Munich
>
> Have you received *Le Dragon impérial* by Mme Mendès?[26]

Mme Mendès herself conscientiously wrote her articles about the exhibition, but she remained absorbed by the thought of Tribschen. She wrote to thank Wagner and Cosima for their hospitality. On 29 July, Cosima answered:

> It is a great deal to have found each other, and, as for me, in recent years I have only had to shield my heart from hate, and I have still hardly recovered from my amazement at being obliged to love with all my heart . . .
> The children were stupefied by your departure, they called you *our lady*, in other words the one who belongs to us and therefore the one who stays here. When you asked me if our servants' little boy was mine I didn't tell you about my fifth because I knew that you felt an antipathy towards very young children.

Now that you are not obliged to ask to see him, I recommend my little *Siegfried* to your benevolence; next year I will introduce him to you . . .[27]

It was remarkably sensitive behaviour from the mother of Wagner's son. Cosima had set aside her pride and her delight (and presumably asked Wagner to do likewise); she had chosen not to talk of the recent birth in order to spare Judith's feelings. Her decision says much about her character; and perhaps it says something, too, about the Mendès marriage. It seems curious that a young woman, only recently married to the man she passionately loved, did not want to bear his children. One wonders if Judith's antipathy to babies was genuine, or if perhaps it disguised her inability to conceive. These few chance words from Cosima, in 1869, may be the first known indication of a marital problem.

For a moment, too, there was a cloud over the new friendship. On 3 August, without warning and without permission, Judith published her impressions of Tribschen: *Richard Wagner chez lui*. The article, in *Le Rappel*, was an unwarranted invasion of his privacy, and he understandably resented it; but, if the gesture was tactless, the admiration was plain, and the admirer was quickly forgiven. On 8 August, Cosima reported to Judith: 'The master is working, Tag [the dog] has recovered, *Siegfried* is blooming on the paper and in his cradle, and everything is flourishing; it's only your friend, my dear Judith, who occasionally sighs, and to whom all this wellbeing sometimes seems like a crystallization of her tears.'[28] Cosima remained profoundly unhappy about her private life. She longed for a divorce from Bülow, so that she could finally marry Wagner, but her father, Liszt – for whom Marie d'Agoult had once left her husband and children – now took an unexpected moral stance. On 25 August, Cosima explained to Judith:

As for my father, . . . he has just given me the most hurtful blow by dissuading Mr von Bülow from the legal separation which we had agreed by common accord. He would rather let me be dragged in the mud by the popular Press and prolong a false situation than see the consecration of an indissoluble union . . . As my father has arranged a meeting in Munich with one of my women friends (the one to whom your father addressed the *Symphonie en Blanc Majeur*), I have had recourse to her and asked her to use her influence on him and persuade him not to ruin a situation which has finally been cleared up after years of tribulation. If you meet Mme Moukhanoff [the former Mme Kalergis], I think you will like her, she is gracious and intelligent. But Mlle Holmès is quite sure to be shown the door [here]; it would not be worth living in retirement if one let in creatures like that . . . My father drags her round everywhere; I should like him to rid you of her because I have great compassion for you in your trouble.[29]

Cosima had hinted at another marital problem. Already, it seems, a shadow lay across Judith's marriage. Augusta Holmès could not be forgotten. In 1869 she found herself in Munich with the Mendès. Servières reported that the dress rehearsal of *Rheingold* was attended by the Mendès, Augusta Holmès and Saint-Saëns.[30]

The Mendès, too, were immersed in Wagnerian politics. Hans Richter, the conductor at the Royal Theatre, was going to conduct *Rheingold*. In the small hours of 27 August, an impassioned Judith wrote to Wagner:

> Master, come yourself or give full powers to someone you can absolutely trust. It is impossible for *Rheingold* to be performed like this; it is all due to malice and stupidity. The orchestra and singers are very good, especially the orchestra, but the décors and machinery are impossible, the most insignificant circus would blush at them . . . The manager and the director are birds of a feather; I think that I am going to die of rage.
>
> In short, if you were here it would all be settled in a week, but with fools like this it would be better to withdraw the work; all you really have for you are Richter and the singers. The King attended the rehearsal. I don't know him well enough to say what he felt. He stayed till the end.[31]

There was a heated exchange of letters and telegrams. Richter resigned, and Mendès claimed that he himself had braved the will of Ludwig II and risked imprisonment. Years later, in 1881, he published a roman à clef, *Le Roi vierge*. The King had it seized, in revenge against the man who had dared to stand against him, in Wagner's interest, and had been triumphant. Mendès replied to the seizure by writing *Épître au Roi de Thuringue*, in which he claimed the credit for the events of 1869.[32]

Meanwhile, on 5 September, Mendès published his eulogy of Wagner in *Le National;* two days later Judith published hers in *Le Rappel*. As for Augusta, she already showed such passionate devotion to Wagner that Cosima mistrusted and disliked her; Wagner himself feared for her musical development, and, perhaps, for his own domestic peace.

> 'Less affection for me, Mademoiselle!' Richard Wagner used to say to Augusta Holmès. 'I do not want to be a manchineel tree for living, creative spirits, a tree which stifles the birds in its shade. One piece of advice: do not belong to any school, especially mine.'
>
> Augusta Holmès [recorded Hugues Imbert, at the turn of the century] admired the beauty of the manchineel tree without forgetting herself beneath its vast branches . . . What she took from Wagner was faith in her art, the constant quest for Beauty and Truth.[33]

However, she was not only a composer and lover of music; as Villiers observed, she was still 'most nobly beautiful'.[34] André Theuriet, the Parnassian poet and future novelist, recalled that 'she had the bearing of a young goddess. I have just [in 1901] re-discovered and re-read the lines I wrote in her honour (we had all written some to her, then, because we had all caught fire at first sight).'[35]

Catulle was overwhelmed by her; and it was, perhaps, in Munich that she became pregnant by him. Rumour said that there would have been a family scandal had her father not died before the child was born.[36] Judith said later that she herself was the last to learn the truth, but she can scarcely have been unaware of her husband's infidelity. Yet if she was vulnerable, she was also proud, and she was determined that her father should not know that his fears about Catulle had been abundantly justified. If she was already aware, three years after marriage, that her husband was unfaithful to her, she chose to maintain a dignified silence.

Whatever Judith's personal anguish in the summer of 1869, she found herself able to help Cosima. In Munich, the visitors attended a reception given by the Countess Schleinitz, wife of the Minister of the Royal Prussian Household; and there, she recorded, 'Liszt came up to me. He talked to me about my father, whom he knew; he had seen me as a child and remembered me, although I no longer remembered him. I thought he had the unctuous manners of a priest; but how was he a priest, and why did all the women seem to be taken with him?'[37] Judith boldly seized her chance, and urged him to support Cosima in her controversial decision. Liszt gave her a message of support for his daughter. He, more than anyone, wanted a legal end to this painful crisis.

The message went at once to Tribschen.

Your letter was a real balm to my soul [answered Cosima], and since it arrived I can breathe again. The master saw the reviving effect which it had on me, and he asks me to say that he blesses you . . . I know that my father and I are united in the regions where the clamours of the world cannot be heard . . . Goodbye, my dear friend. If I sleep tonight, I shall owe it to you. I embrace you with all my heart, and the master kisses your hands.[38]

The travellers returned to Tribschen on 13 September; four days later, they went back to Paris.

We took away some fine memories when we left Lucerne; we also took some ambitious schemes [so Judith was to remember] . . . Franz Servais had come back with us and accepted hospitality for a while in my little house in Neuilly. That was where we made our plans.

Servais was the son of the great cellist whose statue had recently been unveiled at Hal. He was a talented composer who had already had his successes in Brussels. He had a certain notoriety and influence in Belgium, so it was in this direction that we guided our hopes.

Hans Richter was the most unfortunate victim of the *Rheingold* adventure at the theatre in Munich. The noble gesture which had made him throw his conductor's baton at the head of the treacherous manager, Perfall, cast him out of a very fine position, and one which was very rare at his age, into utter destitution. Wagner felt deep regret. Any enterprise which aimed to procure a position for this man who had shown him such devotion could only be greeted with sympathy by the Master. But if we could obtain a result which would also serve as propaganda for the work, we should be doubly fortunate.

The whole grandiose project was decided: a performance of *Lohengrin* in Brussels, with Richter as the conductor.[39]

Soon afterwards, no doubt with Mendès (though she chose again not to mention him in her narrative), Judith went to stay with the Servais, at Hal, near Brussels. It was only a carriage-ride from the field of Waterloo, and one day they went there. She found it sombre, though it was sunlit.

Why? If you didn't know, there is nothing to attract your attention . . . And yet, at the sight of it, oppression overcomes you; this great horizon gives you a kind of vertigo. You say to yourself at once: What a splendid battlefield! . . .

Despite the proud bronze lion set up on a hillside by the victors, it is only the vanquished whom one seeks: he alone survives, it is his name which seems to echo through all that is silent . . .

For a long while I kept a bone, perhaps a hero's bone, but more probably a bone from a casserole, which assumed a curious interest, since it had been picked up from the bottom of a rut on the field of Waterloo.[40]

It was a year for heroes. Encouraged by his signs of approval, Judith had sent a copy of *Le Dragon impérial* to Victor Hugo. He acknowledged it with his own unmistakable grandiloquence:

Madame,
I have read your *Dragon impérial* . . . You have within yourself the soul of this poetry of the Far East, and you put the spirit of it into your books. To go to China is almost to travel to the moon. You make this sidereal journey for us. We follow you with ecstasy, and you escape into the blue depths of dreams, winged and starred.

Please accept my admiration.

Victor Hugo[41]

Victor Hugo [continued Judith] quite often came to stay in Brussels, where his admirers and his political friends came to see him, and brought him the atmosphere of Paris.

One evening [Louis] Brassin [the pianist, and professor at the Brussels

Conservatoire] announced that the great exile had arrived from Guernsey and that he would be spending a few days in Brussels.

I had never seen Victor Hugo, but his name had shone over all my childhood. I had, so to speak, learned to read from *La Légende des siècles*. I was the daughter of one of his dearest disciples. I did not hesitate a moment in my resolve to go and see him, and I wrote to him immediately.[42]

On 1 October he arrived in Brussels to find a request for an audience from Judith. He invited her and Mendès to dine with him next day.

Once again Judith omitted to mention Mendès in her narrative; she implied that she had gone to visit Victor Hugo alone:

> I arrived punctually at the Hôtel du Grand Miroir . . . I was sent up to the first floor, and they opened the door of a room, in the corner of which a table was laid.
>
> Victor Hugo was sitting there beside a lady who . . . looked like a marquise with powdered hair. He came forward eagerly, and talked to me at once about my father, then he introduced me to the lady: Madame Juliette Drouet . . .
>
> I found it hard to feel that it was Victor Hugo who stood before me. This banal setting suited him so badly. The stuffy room, the boat-shaped bed, the mahogany furniture, the green curtains, the hotel waiter, napkin in hand, who moved about and uncorked the bottles: everything thwarted and troubled my admiration.
>
> Victor Hugo gave, first and foremost, the impression of being a sailor. He looked like an old salt, with his short beard, his white hair cut *en brosse*, his robust build. He was very simple and very affable, he had a musical voice and a charming smile . . .
>
> When I had to take leave, Victor Hugo said that he was going out, too, and he offered to take me back to my hotel, which, incidentally, was not far away. As he walked slowly down the street, with me on his arm, he asked me if I had read his poem 'Ce que dit la bouche d'Ombre'. It was not my favourite among the Master's poems; this lofty philosophy rather alarmed me, but I did not dare to say so.[43]

Perhaps, already, at this first meeting, Judith found a charm in Victor Hugo which she was never to find in Richard Wagner; and perhaps this charm was not merely physical attraction. Wagner was a symbol of the Germany to be; Hugo was already, to some, a symbol of France.

Judith and Mendès left Brussels next day. 'They are delightful, these young people,' Juliette Drouet wrote to Hugo, 'but a little too caught up in Wagnerism . . . I'm afraid that in the end they perceived your indifference on the subject.'[44] Hugo was not indifferent, he was irritated. The Mendès' admiration for Wagner remained as vexing to Hugo as their admiration for Hugo was to Wagner.

On her return to Paris, Judith continued her writing. She did so, still, with her father's affectionate encouragement.

> Dear father [goes an undated letter],
>   I should be very glad to have your opinion of an idea which I have been considering for a long time. I think it's rather good . . . It's a question of discussing the various musical publications in France and abroad, on a certain day every week . . .
>   Do you think that *Le Petit Moniteur* would agree? And would you take the trouble to talk about it to Dalloz? I think that a simple recommendation from you could decide it.
>   I embrace you with all my heart.
>   Judith[45]

She confided in him about her work, her plans, and her financial situation. Knowing his kindness, she also asked him to help Damon's family in the impasse d'Antin:

> Dear father,
>   My poor nurse's daughter is overwhelmed with trouble about her young brother. He has turned *thief* and has now begun to work on a large scale. You can imagine what grief that must cause a family which is so completely honest. Could you have this young bandit put in a reformatory? Apparently it is called a settlement; it is less degrading than prison or even an ordinary reformatory. His family is good enough not to want to have him arrested. I should be very grateful if you took some interest in it and gave him some letter of recommendation.
>   I embrace you with all my heart, and thank you for all the good things which you have done for me in the past few days.
>   Judith[46]

She loved and admired her father as much as she had ever done. In spirit, and in style, she remained his daughter. On 1 November, *L'Artiste* published her article on Siamese art. It was written, like so much of her work, in her father's manner and with his verve:

> The general colouring of the picture reveals [she confessed] only a moderate tendency to reproduce the real colour of things. But a little independence is not out of place in painting . . . I don't at all see why the trees should not actually be violet, and why the sky should not be gold. As for the rhinoceros, who would have the right to complain if they were a splendid apple-green?[47]

Judith was aware of Siam. She was very much aware of Persia. On 10 November *La Liberté* began to serialize her new novel, *Iskender*. 'I have read the beginning of *Iskender*,' Villiers told Mendès. 'I think it shows an intelligence and loftiness of mind which are unprecedented in a woman!'[48]

This tale of ancient Persia, clearly written from the heart, was the glittering chronicle of Iskender, King of Roum, conqueror. of India, Touran and Iran, his battles and his courage, his cunning and his beauty. It was also the chronicle of Rustem, his adopted brother. It was written with the erudition, the gusto and colour, the delight in violence, the childlike love of legend, which had marked *Le Dragon impérial*:

> When they saw the Diadem of the World beside the Glory of Iran – Iskender with Rustem at his right hand – ascend the steps of Istakr, an enormous clamour of joy rose up from the city. Suddenly the streets were covered with precious carpets, and the façades of the houses disappeared under the brilliant hangings: stuff of gold and silver, gauze embroidered with pearls, silk calico or Chinese satin. Those who did not possess materials of worth adorned their lodgings with their festival clothes. And when the King passed through the middle of the crowd, the poor cast full-blown roses and narcissi at him, the rich cast jewels and musk . . .[49]

Iskender was heroic, and it was sexually powerful. To Rustem, his adopted brother, Iskender gives the exquisite Indûmatî, who was to have been his own queen; and here the chronicle reaches the intensity of a prose-poem. Rustem is led to a garden

> where the trees had only blossoms, where the soil was a dense flowerbed sprinkled with quivering bees, where the kokilas sang as if they were in the trees of paradise.
> 'There she is!' said the slave to Rustem, who grew pale and slowed his pace.
> And he saw her beside a crystal pool, lying on crushed lotus flowers.
> Oppressed by the heat and by her grief, she cast back her head, closing her eyes, her lashes damp with tears, dangling two of her fingers in the water.
> She looked like a moon saddened by a stormcloud, a bee deprived of honey, a bird ensnared in a golden net.
> Rustem, seeing her like this, sprang towards her with a sob of grief, and fell upon his knees among the flowers. Indûmatî, woken from her melancholy dream, raised herself up and turned towards Rustem. Her eyes shone through her tears like wet diamonds. She saw the young warrior, and suddenly grew splendid, like the sun rising over the horizon. She rested her hands like tilaka flowers upon Rustem's shoulders, and on her lips, like a swarm of butterflies, crowded a thousand words, none of which dared to fly away. Rustem felt his soul rise up towards Indûmatî, like a lake drunk up by the sun . . .[50]

The serial version of *Iskender* ended in *La Liberté* on 17 December 1869. It was gratefully dedicated to the editor, Émile de Girardin. The novel was to appear in book form in 1886, and to be reprinted by Armand Colin in 1894 in their Bibliothèque de Romans Historiques. It was then to bear a still more interesting dedication:

À

SON EXCELLENCE LE MARÉCHAL
MOHSIN KHAN
MOÏNUL MULK, MINISTRE DE LA JUSTICE À TÉHÉRAN
HOMMAGE D'UNE AMITIÉ FIDÈLE

The friendship with Mohsin Khan endured. Early in 1870, less than four
years after their marriage, the Mendès were already reported to be on the
verge of parting. In January, Juliette Adam, wife of the politician Edmond
Adam, was given 'an account of the latest gossip. The separation between
Catulle Mendès and Judith Gautier . . .'[51]

Whatever the gossip, both in private and in the Press, the marriage
continued. On 13 January 1870, from 69, boulevard de Madrid, Catulle
sent a letter of thanks to Victor Hugo, presumably for his New Year
greetings: 'Dear and venerated master, we have had your most indulgent
and heartening letter. We are proud to have a place in your memory.
Thank you with all our soul . . .'[52] At Tribschen, Cosima and Wagner
delighted in a multitude of New Year presents from Judith, among them a
magic lantern with hand-painted slides of scenes from Wagner's operas, a
statuette, and a copy of *Paul et Virginie*. There was also a learned book on
Buddhism, for Judith hoped to persuade the Master to write an oriental
opera.

> Dear friend [scribbled Cosima on 5 January],
>   Yesterday morning we received the box packed with all the wonders, and
> yesterday evening I gave a first performance, to the great delight of the master
> and the admiration of all Tribschen. The wax statuette which the master had
> taken for Minerva and I had guessed to be Brünnhilde (aren't I right?) is set up
> in the gallery not far from Buddha. As for the *Lotus de la bonne nouvelle* [*sic*], the
> master was really touched that you sent it, because it concerns what interests
> him most in the world. We don't know if *Paul et Virginie* is for the children or
> for the grown-ups; if it is for the children, they will have it later, and in the
> meanwhile the grown-ups are enjoying it . . .
>   My little girls all embrace you warmly; they talk about you incessantly . . .
>   Goodbye, my dear, I embrace you with all my heart and thank you a million
> times for the pleasure your box has given everyone in Tribschen. Your
> paintings on glass are stunning, and the apotheosis, and especially the prelude
> to *Lohengrin*, have had a *magical* effect . . .[53]

Judith had perhaps hinted at marital problems, for soon afterwards
Cosima wrote again:

> You have no idea how much we think of you and how much we want you to be
> happy. I do hope you will succeed. Not a day passes but we talk about you,

remembering your expressions, your witticisms, your beauty, Madame, and everything else. *Le Lotus de la bonne loi* gives the master keen pleasure and a certain pride; he maintains that this venerable book is the glory of his library and that he is happy that it comes from you. As for the magic lantern, I am still having fabulous triumphs with it.[54]

The plan which Judith had contrived with Brassin had succeeded. On 22 March, conducted by Hans Richter, *Lohengrin* was first given in French at the Théâtre de la Monnaie, in Brussels. The Mendès attended the performance. Four days later, Judith published an ecstatic analysis in *La Liberté*, and her husband discussed the opera in *Le Diable*.

Mendès himself considered Wagner's music one of the few delights in his life. It had been clear, almost from the first, that his marriage did not satisfy him. He was suffering, too, from financial hardship, and from literary frustration. 'I see a good many things which sadden me,' lamented Emmanuel des Essarts. 'I see Glatigny almost dead and gone, [and I see] Mendès finished . . .'[55] On 27 May, Mendès himself explained to Mallarmé:

> I am suffering greatly. I have been struggling for ten years, and if, outwardly, my courage seems the same, I feel inside myself that it is much diminished . . .
>
> I, whose tormented life, frittered away in a thousand things, may appear so full, feel within myself a void which is almost beyond description . . . One thing revives and consoles me. From this alone come our real joys. Hugo and Leconte de Lisle are our salvation, and they make us live, and, thanks to Richard Wagner, I know infinite delight.[56]

Mallarmé himself was suffering from financial straits, and from the disadvantages of a provincial life. He was working as a teacher in Avignon. 'Will you come back soon?' Mendès enquired. 'I want to offer you something. I am living in Neuilly, in the middle of the Bois de Boulogne . . .' He proposed that the Mallarmés should join him and Judith in the boulevard de Madrid. 'Our wives would love each other, since you and I love one another. We live very simply. You would only need the smallest resources in order to share our life.'[57]

It was a generous suggestion, but for the moment the answer was deferred. The Mendès returned again to Germany. One may follow the stages of their journey through the correspondence which Catulle sent to *Le National*, and more especially to *Le Diable*, under the title of *Le diable en voyage*. On 11 June he wrote from Baden-Baden, on 18 June he wrote from Homburg. On 19 June, in Weimar, Judith reported the Richard Wagner Festival for *Le Rappel*.[58]

The journey, recorded by Mendès, continued through Wiesbaden.

Early in July, once more in company with Villiers, the Mendès set out for Munich, where *Die Walküre* was to be performed; once again they stopped at Lucerne, to visit Wagner at Tribschen. Mendès' letters to *Le Diable* continued from Wilhelmstadt and Frankfurt. From Munich, this year, he wrote to Mallarmé in deep dejection:

> My dear friend, do not try to endure what I endure! I am dying, in order to maintain my wife! I can barely snatch three hours from destiny, once in three months, to write a sonnet! Oh, this misery, this poverty! Would a poet really be criminal if he murdered in order to have the means of work? No, I dare not say to you: share this hell. I have had days without bread, the process-servers at the door – yes, I have!
>
> But if you have a small fixed income, all is well. This money saves everything. Since I have had 1,500 francs at the Beaux-Arts, I live better. Water only flows to the sea: have money, and you will earn it.[59]

The performance of Wagner's opera on 17 July was attended by Saint-Saëns, Henri Duparc, the composer, and the Mendès; but the French Press remained silent about this new Wagnerian triumph. No doubt they did so largely for patriotic reasons. On 15 July France had declared war on Prussia, and embarked on one of the most disastrous conflicts in its history.

Undeterred by the political situation, Villiers and the Mendès returned once again to Lucerne.

> It was clear [wrote Judith] that, with his ardent nature, Wagner could not fail to be deeply impressed by events. The idea of German unity was to impassion him, and I confess that I should have loved him less if he had not felt, like all of us in these moments of crisis, a fanatical love for his country.
>
> It was, however, agreed that we should not touch on the burning question, on which nothing could make us agree. We prudently remained in the realm of art, in which we were so much in sympathy.[60]

For all her patriotic fervour, Judith herself was in no hurry to return to Paris; indeed, she and Mendès and Villiers planned to visit Avignon. On 27 July, Mendès announced to Mallarmé: 'We are coming in ten or twelve days. I should have left at once if Richard Wagner, with whom I am staying at Lucerne, had not announced this morning that he expected to keep us for another week and more . . . Send me all the details about departure and costs . . . Villiers is coming, of course.'[61] In the event, they left Lucerne earlier than they expected. On 30 July, Mendès added: 'We're leaving in ten minutes; unless there is some great disaster, we shall take the packet to Lyons on Tuesday at eight o'clock in the morning. Calculate the time of arrival.'[62]

On 6 August the travellers arrived in Avignon. 'They are all three

Parnassian and impassible,' reported Théodore Aubanel, the Provençal poet, two days later. 'Their theses are not in the least amusing, and their poetry is diabolically nebulous, but Judith is wonderful: tall, dark, pale, with the buxom figure and nonchalance of an Oriental woman. One ought to see her lying on a tiger-skin and smoking a narghile.'[63]

The travellers left that day for Paris; and there, at last, Judith understood the gravity of events. Already, in the first weeks of war, the French had suffered massive reverses, and the Prussians were moving towards the capital. There was every prospect of a siege. She and Mendès wrote in anguish to Wagner. On 12 August, he answered with Teutonic arrogance:

> I have nothing, absolutely nothing to offer you which might seem like a consolation, since I understand that, even if it were possible to persuade you of the perfect justice of my point of view about everything that is happening, you would always remain sad and elegiac souls, and determined to remain so . . . I write to you now: accept fate, as it is ordained, as a judgement of God, and study the deep meaning of this judgement.
>
> I see myself – in your place – on the ramparts of Paris, and then I say to myself: suppose this vast capital were perhaps to fall into ruin! But it is not perhaps. It is certain. The regeneration of the French people will then have its point of departure, for this Paris was the gulf in which the true spirit of a nation was lost.[64]

Wagner had not forgotten his early rejection in Paris; he longed for German unity, for the Empire which Prussian victory must bring.

He was also, at last, about to marry Cosima. On 18 July, after two years of separation, she had finally been divorced by Hans von Bülow. On 25 August she and Wagner were married in Lucerne. That day, with a lack of understanding which was nothing less than monumental, she sent a note to Judith:

> My dear, we were expecting you all the time, and we were very worried; where are you? My first word after the nuptial benediction is for you. We both embrace you with all our hearts, very anxious about you.
>   The baptism is on Sunday.
>   Cosima
> Thursday morning, just out of church.[65]

One result of the marriage was to legitimize Siegfried, who was now fifteen months old. He was in fact baptized on 4 September. Next day Wagner wrote to Judith. 'He told me,' she remembered, 'about the baptism of his son, whose godmother I was – but, alas, at a distance!'[66]

It was a distance which could now no longer be travelled. On 3 September, Paris had learned that Napoleon III had surrendered with his army at Sedan; on 4 September the fall of the Empire, and of the Bonaparte dynasty, were decreed, and the French Republic was proclaimed. The Emperor's defeat had not, however, brought the end of the Franco-Prussian War, and the enemy continued to march on Paris.

Chapter Eight

Victor Hugo had long ago refused an imperial amnesty; he had vowed not to set foot in France while the Second Empire lasted. Now, on the evening of 5 September, at 9.35, accompanied by Juliette Drouet, Charles Hugo and his wife Alice, he returned from exile. Judith went to greet him at the Gare du Nord.

> There was [she recalled] a delirious mob. They gave the great exile a frenzied welcome, and rushed towards him with such fervour that they nearly suffocated him. He offered me his arm, and gripped mine nervously . . . With great difficulty we managed to reach a little café opposite the station and to go up to the first floor. There the Master went into a small room, and I determined to bar the way, whatever the cost. Leaning against the jambs and lintel of the door, I stretched out a leg and buttressed it with my foot . . .
>
> As soon as he had recovered his breath a little, Victor Hugo seemed to be very calm and in control of his emotions. He was delightfully gallant to me, and recited those lines of André Chenier's:
>
> > . . . C'est toi qui, la première,
> > Ma fille, m'as ouvert la porte hospitalière.
>
> I made way for Paul Meurice, who had managed to push through the crowd. It was threatening to make the stairs collapse.
>
> He told the Master that he absolutely must address the people, who were waiting for him to speak, and he opened the window looking on to the square. A vast clamour arose. It was from this window that Victor Hugo delivered his speech to the people of Paris.[1]

'You have repaid me, in an hour,' he told them, 'for nineteen years of exile.'

A battalion of soldiers presented arms as his carriage passed on, down the boulevard. Paul Meurice had offered him shelter in the rue Frochot.

He did not reach the house until midnight. He was sixty-eight. A new and triumphant life had begun for him.[2]

Exactly a fortnight later, on 19 September, the Siège of Paris began.

> Beloved Master [wrote Mendès to Hugo],
>
> I should like to enrol in the company of the Garde Nationale to which you belong, so as to do my duty under your command.
>
> Would you be kind enough to let me know at which *mairie* you are registered?
>
> Thank you, and believe me
>
> Your humble and passionate admirer
Catulle Mendès[3]

The effusive note was sent from the offices of the publisher Lemerre, at 47, passage Choiseul. The family was now widely scattered. Eugénie Fort went to London, to join her son. Gautier, compelled to abandon Neuilly, moved into her familiar lodgings in the rue de Beaune. They were conveniently near the offices of *Le Journal officiel*, on the quai Voltaire. They were too small, however, to house the rest of the family. Judith and Ernesta lived in the rue Richer for part of the Siège, and Judith implied in later life that Mendès was not with them.

> Just before the Siege of Paris, in 1870, a Mme F——, a quite new acquaintance, had invited my mother and me to spend an afternoon with her at Billancourt, in a house which she had recently moved into. But, almost at once, she was terrified by the threat of a siege, and she was irresistibly inspired to make a quick escape. However, she wanted to save her furniture from possible destruction, and she hastily rented a big apartment in the rue Richer in Paris, where she moved it all. She begged us to keep the keys of the apartment, to look after it, and even to live in it so that it would not be requisitioned. Although his lodgings were very cramped, my father wanted to stay in the rue de Beaune. The republican editor of *Le Journal officiel* had been polite and affable. The nearness of the quai Voltaire was more precious to him than ever. In order to disencumber the lodging a little, my mother and I went to the rue Richer. My sister had stayed in Geneva with Aunt Carlotta. My father therefore lived in the rue de Beaune with his two sisters, Lili and Zoé, and Éponine, the cat.[4]

There was another indication that Mendès and Judith sometimes went their separate ways. One evening in January 1871 – apparently Tuesday the 17th – Villiers de l'Isle-Adam visited Augusta Holmès in Paris. Mendès was present, but not his wife.[5] Yet for some of the Siège, at least, the Mendès were living together at 4, Cité Trévise. Leconte de Lisle came to live with them.

Judith's health was to suffer for years from the hardship she had known in that fearful autumn and winter. It was so cold that soldiers were dying in the outposts for want of proper clothes; by Christmas Day all fuel was exhausted, and Parisians were eating rats and mice, sparrows and dogs, even the elephants from the zoo. The hospitals were crowded with dying soldiers and civilians, and the Prussian bombardment continued. Paris finally succumbed: not to the Prussians, but to starvation. On 28 January the Government announced that the Siege was over; it had lasted for four months and twelve days. 'Since 15 January,' recorded *Le Journal officiel*, 'the bread ration has been reduced to 300 grammes; since 15 December, the horsemeat ration has been only 30 grammes. Mortality has more than trebled. Amidst all these disasters, there has not been a single day of discouragement.'[6]

There was discouragement now. On 18 January, one of Wagner's dreams had been realized: King William I of Prussia had been proclaimed Emperor of the new German Empire. The ceremony had been held in the Hall of Mirrors at Versailles. Germany was in the ascendant, France appeared in hopeless decline, and she sued for peace. According to the convention signed by Bismarck and the Minister for Foreign Affairs, the whole French Army were to be prisoners of war, and all the cannon were to be handed over; France was to pay an indemnity of two hundred million francs.

In February, Gautier wrote to Carlotta Grisi: 'After five months in a dungeon they half open our prison door . . . It isn't the famine or the rain of shells that has been most painful in Paris, it has been this sequestration, this horrible isolation.'[7] Paris could at last renew relations with the living world. 'We have not ceased to think of you, or ceased to love you with all our hearts,' Mendès told Mallarmé on 20 February. 'But we are constantly harassed by so many griefs that we have not written.'[8]

One of their anxieties had of course been the desperate lack of food. At the time of the capitulation, so it is said, Judith had gone one day with Ernesta to the Pont de Neuilly, to queue for their meagre rations. A Prussian prince, in the uniform of a general, passed by, and noticed this young woman of surpassing beauty. He stopped and asked her what she wanted. Judith refused to answer. The onlookers were well aware of the prince's reputation for brutality, and they looked at each other with apprehension; but he suddenly bowed, and gave orders to his aide-de-camp to serve this young woman before the rest.

On 1 March the German army was to occupy Paris, and to stay there until the peace terms had been ratified. It was the supreme humiliation. The terms were ratified that day by the National Assembly at Bordeaux. The occupation of Paris lasted a little over forty-eight hours; but the humiliation remained. Wagner had written an *Ode to the German Army before Paris* and the *Kaisersmarsch* to the glory of the Emperor William; he had also written a heavy-handed farce, *Une Capitulation*. He was to publish it in 1873. Many Frenchmen, Mendès among them, were not to forgive him.

Now, on 16 March, Cosima wrote to Judith: 'I am very sorry to see you agree that you are morose and gloomy. If you love me, which I shall begin to doubt, you will fight against these unhappy dispositions, and when M. Catulle comes back in the evening, harassed by his errands and troubles, you will keep your smiling countenance.'[9] It is curious that Cosima, who had once felt 'great compassion' for Judith, did not apparently suspect one probable cause of her unhappiness. At the beginning of the siege, Mendès had been a *garde national* at Vaugirard, then he had joined a mobile platoon. For a while he had also been an inspector of ambulances, and Augusta Holmès had promptly enrolled as a nurse. Judith continued to have her anxieties.

> Tell us about M. Catulle and what he is doing [Cosima continued]. We are very sad to see him rush about like this all day, instead of being able to work at his leisure. Be good, my dear Judith, and lighten the burden of his life for him; he finds it so heavy. Be cheerful and hard working. He really isn't made for so difficult a life! If you are nice the 'something' will come back, I promise you myself, and I have always kept my word.[10]

The 'something' was perhaps the love between husband and wife.

Two days after Cosima wrote, revolution began in Paris. The National Assembly, now meeting at Bordeaux, was largely monarchist. Under the leadership of Adolphe Thiers, they determined to eliminate the danger from the Left, and now this virtually meant Paris. The Assembly was brought back from Bordeaux – not to Paris, but to Versailles. Finally Thiers gave orders that the four hundred guns which were still in the hands of the National Guard in Paris were to be removed on 18 March. Thiers' order has been described as a provocation; but he did not expect his troops from Versailles to fraternize with the Parisians. He did expect the National Guard from the middle-class quarters of Paris to support him.

Thiers' attempted seizure of the guns was the spark which set off revolution in Paris. The troops were fired on in the place Pigalle, and retired to Versailles. On 28 March, the Commune officially installed itself at the Hôtel de Ville.

The day after Gautier returned to the rue de Longchamp, he was forced to move. While Lili stubbornly remained in the cellar at Neuilly, he and Zoé settled in Eugénie Fort's apartment in the avenue de Saint-Cloud, at Versailles. For a moment it seemed that he might lose work for *Le Journal officiel*. Judith was concerned about his livelihood. She was far from wealthy, but she offered to send him money.

> Dear child [he answered],
> I was very touched by your letter. What! You think of the old abandoned Sachem, and you have enough soul to imagine that your father might be short of money and starve a little in his exodus. You are the only person to have thought of it, and I thank you for it; everyone else pretends to believe – it's more convenient – that I am rolling in gold and as solid as the Pont-Neuf. You, a bizarre and original creature, are concerned about my fate. It is true, you remember, that in my troubles I have often called you my last hope. Keep your money, darling, keep it for yourself. I've found a vein of copy which befits the situation – articles on the Versailles of Louis XIV, restoring the former state of the Palace – and in a little while I shall be prosperous once more. Just give your mother something for a day or two, until I can give her her pension again; it won't be long. One must hope that Paris will soon be restored to order, and that we'll be able to go on with human life, because we are living the life of savages. Thank Ernesta for the socks she sent me, they fit me like gloves. The heroic Lili is still in the cellar; she refused to leave the house, because it would be ransacked if it were abandoned. In a few days we'll go and free her. We get news from Neuilly from time to time, and Zoé, escorted by a *sergent de ville*, made the most dangerous journey there with a bravery which few men would have shown . . . Who would have thought it? It all seems unreal and recalls the Chinese siege of Peking in *Le Dragon impérial*. À propos of *Le Dragon impérial*, there is a little society of mandarins and exquisites here who would very much like to read it, surfeited as they are by the war bulletins in *Le Gaulois*. If you could send this book to me, you would please both me and them. If socks can get through, so can the book. I embrace you with all my heart.[11]

In his life of Cosima Wagner, Count Richard du Moulin-Eckart said that Judith 'was keeping her husband in hiding at Orleans, after he had been condemned to death by the Commune. [Mendès] had escaped from these horrors and he had been rescued by his wife.'[12] There seem to be no grounds for this statement. Escholier says that it was a Communard whom Judith concealed. Mendès himself maintained that he had been arrested and released, and Edmond Lepelletier, in his history of the Commune, recorded that Mendès 'was hardly in favour of the Communards, but remained in Paris throughout the conflict.'[13] He was in fact writing *Les 73 Jours de la Commune*. He may not always have been at the Cité Trévise, but he had his reasons for staying in the beleaguered capital.

Cosima still remained anxious about him and his wife. 'Send us a word,' she wrote to Judith. 'It seems that the Angel of the Apocalypse has emptied the seven vials of wrath over poor Paris. Don't send me a long letter, but tell me if you are alive!'[14] She was understandably apprehensive. A second siege of Paris had now begun, more dreadful than the first, for Frenchman was now fighting against Frenchman. Thiers – with the help of the Germans – organized a blockade of food supplies. On 10 May the Treaty of Frankfurt was signed, and the Franco-Prussian War was officially over, but the besieging army of Versaillais was drawing ever closer to the city. At last, on 21 May, near the Point-du-Jour, through an undefended gate, the Versaillais began to pour into the capital. There followed *la semaine sanglante*: a week of savage violence, of desperate and dastardly reprisals. The Communards set fire to Paris. The Tuileries was soon ablaze, the Hôtel de Ville alight, there was even an abortive attempt to destroy Notre-Dame. The Invalides escaped by a miracle. The Communards mined the sewers from the Hôtel de Ville to the Banque de France, intending to blow up the whole *quartier*. They shot the Archbishop of Paris at La Roquette.

On 28 May, Marshal MacMahon announced that Paris was free of the insurgents. What was left of Paris were 'acres of smoking ruins – vistas of shattered and blackened columns belonging to buildings that had once been among the finest in Europe – roofless palaces, devastated churches, houses utterly destroyed, or dinted with shot and shell'.[15] It was a bitter, mutilated and exhausted city.

In June, at last, Mallarmé arrived at the Cité Trévise. No doubt he was entrusted with a secret which was apparently still kept from Judith. Catulle had been unable to abandon Augusta Holmès; for the past year, at least, she had been his mistress. He had no children by Judith. He already had a son, Raphaël, by Augusta, and Augusta was once again pregnant: their daughter, Huguette, was to be born on 1 March 1872. All five of Mendès' children by Augusta were to be recognized by Mendès' father. This may have been partly to spare Judith's feelings; it was more probably to spare Augusta, who was anxious to preserve her reputation as an untouchable goddess.[16]

On 9 August, Mallarmé arrived in London, to write about the International Exhibition at South Kensington. He settled at 1, Alexander Square, off the Fulham Road, where he asked the Mendès to join him.[17] The Mendès were silent. 'Are the sea and air doing you good?' Mallarmé enquired. 'Are you working?'[18] It is not clear when they went to London, but on 14 September, from Fécamp, in Normandy, Judith wrote to Wagner:

Maître! What must you have thought of us? We were in Fécamp, and then in London, while *Siegfried* was at the Cité Trévise. When we came back to Fécamp there was a letter from our concierge telling us, among other things, that she had taken in a *music catalogue* for us. We thought it was a concert programme or something like that, but a few days later it crossed my mind that it was *Siegfried*, and then Catulle left for Paris and at five o'clock this morning he brought me the precious pearl-grey book with the bold black lettering. You can see my radiant face [from Germany]. Oh, that beloved writing on the first page![19]

Wagner had inscribed the piano version of *Siegfried*: 'To my dear friends, Judith and Catulle.'[20]

I kissed the writing with all my heart [Judith continued], as if it had been you. It was more than a year since I had seen that writing! . . .

Nothing has changed in our life, it's still the same. I am working a little, but very little. I seriously believe I've become an idiot. To say 'become' may be pretentious.

The beach is splendid here. There's open sea all round. Catulle is so sunburnt he's gingerbread colour. I look dreadful, myself, although I am quite well, because the bathing has cured me of my throat infection for the time being . . .

No music. No Wagner for such a long while. It's enough to drive one mad. Fish cannot live without water. Thank you for having thought of the poor starving people, and sent them the food they greatly needed.[21]

She and Mendès returned from Fécamp to the Cité Trévise, and, later that autumn, Mallarmé encountered them in Paris. He had at last left the provinces: he had been appointed to teach at the Lycée Fontanes.

Now, come to Leconte de Lisle's tomorrow evening [this to Mendès on 20 October], because he is going to read the first part of his drama [*Les Erinnyes*], so Heredia assures me . . .

I shall spend the day tomorrow at the library. Will Madame Mendès be there? No, I think not. I am afraid it is her fatal day for the article.[22]

Judith continued to earn her living.

Chapter Nine

On 1 January 1872, Judith called on Victor Hugo with her New Year wishes.[1] As the year opened, Gautier lingered on. Though he had long been reconciled with his favourite child, life was little to him, now, but a dim solitude. He continued his reviewing, but he lacked the courage to write poetry. He suffered from a heart condition – and he suffered, still, from the hardships he had known in the Siege.

That spring he attended the wedding of the publisher Georges Charpentier and Marguerite Lemonnier. It took place at Hurepoix. Michel Robida, the great-nephew of Mme Charpentier, recorded that Émile Bergerat, the young journalist and dramatist, 'the indispensable witness of Georges Charpentier, was detailed to go to Bures, in the Chevreuse valley, to meet some of the guests. It was that day that he made the acquaintance of Théophile Gautier and of his two daughters: the elder, Judith, then Mme Catulle Mendès, and the younger, Estelle, whom he was later to marry.'[2] Gautier stretched out his hand to Bergerat, and asked: 'May I introduce my ruin?'

He dreamed, still, of Carlotta; he consoled himself, still, with the thought of Judith. On 7 February, at Princess Mathilde's, Goncourt recorded:

> This evening . . . Gautier takes me aside and talks to me for a long while, lovingly, about *Le Dragon impérial* and about his daughter. I feel that he is proud of having created that mind. The sense of the Far East which the girl possesses, the intuition which she has of the great epochs of history, the *divination* of China, of Japan, of India under Alexander, of Rome under Hadrian, fill him with enchantment . . . 'And,' he adds, 'she created herself, she did it all alone. She was brought up like a puppy which you allow to run over the table; no one, so to speak, taught her to write.'[3]

That month, he called on Hugo and asked him for a seat at the imminent revival of *Ruy Blas*. On 19 February the drama was again performed at the Théâtre de l'Odéon, with Sarah Bernhardt as the Queen of Spain. Hugo wrote simply: 'A triumph like *Hernani*.' The audience that night had included not only Gautier but, it seems, his son-in-law and daughter.[4]

Perhaps there had already been some sign of reconciliation with Mendès, for Hugo asked them all to dinner on 4 March.[5] Gautier was too ill to go, but Hugo recorded the presence of Judith, her husband and Ernesta Grisi. They dined at Mme Drouet's apartment at 55, rue Pigalle. Juliette was now nearly sixty-six. She suffered from gout and from a heart condition; she had been Hugo's mistress for thirty-nine years, and she had long ceased to attract him. Hugo had had many lesser love affairs, and, though he had just turned seventy, he still had urgent sexual desires.

His notebooks record, in code, the extent of his activity. On 4 March 1872, he noted: 'After dinner, I went home with Mme Judith, O, to look for some poems from *L'Année terrible* to read to them.'[6] The O stood for *oscula*, and recorded his first passionate kiss.

He seems to have started, now, to call on Judith at 4, Cité Trévise. On 24 March, the ever-vigilant Goncourt noted Hugo's admiration for her, and made his own sharp comments on the Mendès marriage:

> The other day, on one of those visits when he escapes his domesticity, Victor Hugo said to Judith: 'Suppose we conspired a little to get the Bonapartes restored? Then we'd go back again, wouldn't we? We'd go back to Jersey [sic] and work together.'
>
> An extraordinary ménage, this Mendès ménage, in which the husband, this blond Portuguese Jew, who was once a ragged Bohemian, now puts on proper clothes, the expression of a businessman, the sharp glance of an impresario who is exploiting a *prima donna* and living off her.[7]

Mme Daudet, too, observed a somewhat theatrical husband and wife: 'He was splendid, with a halo of fine silky hair, slightly effeminate, slightly affected; she, like an idol on a screen, or a Japanese kakemono, had her face painted white, her eyes fixed and encircled with kohl.'[8]

Juliette Drouet was soon aware that there was some new woman in Hugo's life. On 5 May, after a restless night, she wrote to him to ask 'why you put the clock forward half an hour yesterday evening, and why you went off in such a hurry: you who usually prolong the evening to the very limit? I suspect that in this sudden change of habit there is some ravishing woman who interests you and was waiting for you.'[9]

Early in May 1872 – very soon, it seems, after their meeting – preparations

were made for Estelle to marry Émile Bergerat. Bergerat was just
twenty-seven. He had been born in Paris on 29 April 1845, and he had
made his début as a dramatist at the age of twenty, when his play *Une amie*
had been performed at the Théâtre-Français. Brisson recorded his tousled
beard and piercing blue eyes, 'the eyes of a dreamer and a fighter'.[10]
Bergerat could hardly have been more different from Mendès. He was a
solid bourgeois, and he did not belong to any literary coterie. He enjoyed
great moral authority.[11]

As the marriage approached, Gautier himself was aware of impending
death; he determined to gather his family round him. Bergerat was to
remember how,

> at the time arranged, poor Catulle Mendès came to the rue de Longchamp to
> resume his place in the family [*sic*]. He was very agitated, and he was afraid of
> the first encounter with the father, who himself was no less agitated. A game of
> battledore and shuttlecock was organized on the terrace, in which the
> shuttlecocks rarely met the racquets. This took us up to the sound of the bell,
> and, at table, [there were] Zoé, Lili, Théophile [Gautier *fils*] and his wife,
> Catulle and his, me and my fiancée, Ernesta and Eugénie on either side of the
> master, a patriarch with two wives surrounded by his family: in other words
> there were twelve of us, counting Éponine [the cat].[12]

Estelle was married on 15 May. At the wedding breakfast, Goncourt felt
the general anxiety at Gautier's condition. His legs and feet were so
swollen that he had to wear slippers; he sat in a dream. On 18 June
Eugénie Fort saw him at Neuilly, 'still in that state of languor which seems
to me much more serious than they appear to realize. He is not suffering,
but life is going!'[13]

Through Judith, whom he did not cease to see, Hugo learned of
Gautier's illness – he had two heart attacks in June – and of his continuing
hardship. On 23 June he noted: 'Mme Judith Mendès. We talked about
her father, who is ill and working for a living. I offered to take Théophile
Gautier to live with me at Hauteville House, and to be his host, sick-nurse
and brother until one of us should die. She told me that his household
would prevent his coming.'[14] The next day Hugo added: 'I wrote to Jules
Simon [the Minister of Public Instruction] about Théophile Gautier. After
dinner, we went to the [Théâtre-]Français. Visits to our box. Mme Judith
Mendès had seen Jules Simon and she had been very hurt. Apparently
Jules Simon does not know who Théophile Gautier is.'[15] On 26 June: 'I
received a letter from Jules Simon telling me that he had given Théophile
Gautier his pension of 3000 francs and that, at my request, he was
immediately granting him an additional 3000 francs. I sent this letter by
Mme Judith Mendès to Théophile Gautier. He was very pleased and said

to his daughter: "Tell Victor Hugo that he has saved me."[16]

Hugo was increasingly drawn to Judith. Edmond de Goncourt, who had once been an admirer, had, it seems, come to mistrust and dislike her. On 7 July, dining at Neuilly, he met her, and wrote in his diary:

> No one is more of a simpleton than this gifted woman. She chatters in an imbecile way about a mass of things which she knows from hearsay . . .
>
> Poor Théo goes to sleep, collapsing on the arm of his chair, in the broken pose of a wooden puppet. We get up from table. There is a ring at the bell. Judith disappears. She has gone to join her husband, whom Théo refuses to have in the house [sic]. The young Bergerats make their entrance.
>
> At the end of the evening, the Bergerats escort me back through the fair at Neuilly. They chat away, and tell me about the little domestic dramas which are being acted out round Théo. They are rather worried about Judith's attempts to have Mendès accepted in the house again. Judith has always been the father's favourite child. According to the Bergerats, she has come to dominate her father, combing his hair and beard, washing his feet, helping him in the cult of his body. She has one aunt on her side, who wants to reconcile the son-in-law with the father-in-law. She has just persuaded her father to come to dinner with her. And the prospect of the return of Judith, whom Estelle detests, and I think rightly, the prospect of the return of Mendès, whom Bergerat considers a crook, give the young couple some ominous thoughts. One feels that in this house, where death is hovering, a curious bourgeois tragedy is about to be performed.[17]

Goncourt tended to be malicious, and perhaps to encourage malice in others. He alone maintained that Estelle detested her sister. He alone implied that she did so with good reason. Possibly Estelle blamed Judith for their mother's departure, the disruption of their family life. More probably she was jealous of Judith's intelligence, her literary success and her all-conquering beauty; she resented Gautier's unchangeable favouritism. Gautier had turned to Estelle after Judith's marriage; now, once again, he showed where his abiding affection lay.

> Dear papa [wrote Judith],
>
> Keep free for Wednesday: Hugo wants to have you to dinner. Are you well enough for that?
>
> I shall come and see you before Wednesday and we'll make arrangements to go there together.
>
> Hugo is leaving very soon for Hauteville House.
>
> See you soon, darling.
>
> Judith[18]

On 10 July, Gautier dragged himself to dinner with Hugo. The author of *Hernani* sometimes had no sense of loyalty, no sense of honour or compassion. According to Escholier, it was probably next day that he became Judith's lover.[19] On 12 July, he set down his impressions of the dying Gautier; he also wrote *Ave, Dea: moriturus te salutat*. It was, it seems, his tribute to his latest mistress:

La mort et la beauté sont deux choses profondes
Qui contiennent tant d'ombre et d'azur qu'on dirait
Deux soeurs également terribles et fécondes
Ayant le même énigme et le même secret;

O femmes, voix, regards, cheveux noirs, tresses blondes,
Brillez, je meurs! ayez l'éclat, l'amour, l'attrait,
O perles que la mer mêle à ses grandes ondes,
O lumineux oiseaux de la sombre forêt!

Judith, nos deux destins sont plus près l'un de l'autre
Qu'on ne croirait, à voir mon visage et le vôtre;
Tout le divin abîme apparaît dans vos yeux,

Et moi, je sens le gouffre étoilé dans mon âme;
Nous sommes tous les deux voisins du ciel, madame,
Puisque vous êtres belle et puisque je suis vieux.[20]

Raymond Escholier maintained, in *Victor Hugo, l'homme*, that, 'for at least five years, this reciprocal love united Théophile Gautier's daughter . . . and the author of *Hernani*'.[21] Escholier is not always reliable. There is no direct documentary evidence that Judith was Hugo's mistress, or that their liaison lasted for this time; most of the evidence is indirect, and lies in the tone of Hugo's poems, the tone of the few surviving letters which he and Judith wrote to one another. This tone, however, seems unmistakable. Hugo, Judith was to say, 'was seriously in love with her, and paid court to her like a schoolboy'.[22] She was overwhelmed by his distinction, passionately drawn to him at a time when her father was dying, her marriage was foundering, and her whole security was threatened. There is an urgency about her letters which suggests a deep emotional involvement. There is a bitterness in some of Juliette Drouet's comments which suggests that she recognized Judith's status. She refers in 1879 to 'a past which I detest'.[23] It would be surprising if there had been no love affair between Victor Hugo and Gautier's elder daughter.

On 7 August 1872, Hugo left Paris for Guernsey, not only to write *Quatrevingt-treize*, but also, as Henri Guillemin acutely observed, 'to escape his demons and try to recover himself'.[24] On the day of his departure, however, he called again on Judith. 'Her father is very ill,' he noted. 'I told Mme Mendès to bring him to me at Hauteville House. He will be at home there; he can live and die there. She accepts, if the sea agrees (because it seems that the crossing might be very hard for Théophile Gautier).'[25]

Hugo made the offer ostensibly to Gautier; but he had dreamed for months of enticing Judith to his island. He had hardly taken possession of Hauteville House before, on 12 August, he wrote to her:

> Here I am in Guernsey, at the price of two storms which did me the honour of waiting for me, one at Granville, the other in Jersey. Our little Family Hotel is still standing opposite, and it is waiting for you. My ground-floor room would be full of glory if my dear Théophile Gautier came to live in it. Say that to your wonderful father, and allow me, as I hope for you, to kiss the stars you have on your heels.[26]

On 24 August, her twenty-seventh birthday, Judith answered:

> Maître, I had foreseen those wicked storms, do you remember? And so I was very anxious . . . But there was no danger; as you said to me, the elements are not as stupid as men.
>
> My father is still ill; he was very happy with your message for him. His greatest wish would be to be beside you. But, alas, he cannot move for the moment.
>
> As for me, if I can leave Paris, it will be for Guernsey, and I shall not need the stars with which you adorn my heels to spur on my impatience to see you again.[27]

At Hauteville House, Victor Hugo, too, became impatient.

> Be as charming as you are beautiful, and as good as you are divine, and come and see the hermit [this on 10 September]. The stars sometimes pay me a visit, and their rays enter my house. Do as they do.
>
> Two years' absence have left my tumbledown hovel in ruins, and I dare not offer you a dreadful corner in it; but opposite Hauteville House there is a little Family Hotel . . . Let yourself be tempted. If you cannot come with your father, come with your husband; if neither of them can come, then come alone. I should be very glad to shake them by the hand, and to kiss your feet, madame.
> V.H.[28]

Gautier remained at Neuilly. The household was overshadowed not only by his grave condition, but by the illness of one of his sisters. Lili had had a stroke. Later that month, Judith replied to Victor Hugo:

> Maître, if I have been so long in answering, it was because of a persistent hope which I find very hard to abandon. Every day we expect to leave, and every day something happens to delay us. But what has prevented us from leaving Paris is a disaster at my father's: one of his sisters has had a stroke, she will probably remain paralysed all down one side. We are very afraid for papa of the emotion that a possible Misfortune would cause him. We are careful to hide the Truth

from him; he thinks that his sister is suffering from rheumatism. He himself is very much better. He is now being very well looked after, and we hope he will completely recover.[29]

He was in fact dying. His sisters, full of hatred for the Grisis, kept Ernesta and Carlotta from his bedside. Bergerat said that Judith 'almost strangled' Zoé for such implacable hostility.[30]

Théophile Gautier died on 23 October. A telegram from Mendès gave the news to Hugo.

> It was foreseen [answered Hugo], and it is terrible. That great poet, that great artist, that wonderful heart – now he has gone!
> I am now the only one of the men of 1830 who survives. Now it is my turn.
> Dear poet, I clasp you in my arms. Lay my affectionate and grievous respects at the feet of Madame Judith Mendès.[31]

Since her childhood at Montrouge, Judith had become increasingly aware of her father's literary distinction. Since the day when she had left the convent for the rue de la Grange-Batelière, she had come to know his charm and zest and originality. He had encouraged her to write, fostered her passion for the East, he had rejoiced in her literary triumphs. He had admired her beauty, shown his love for her, a love which – despite her unhappy marriage – remained inalterable and profound. Father and daughter were alike, not only in their love of art and literature, their thirst for beauty, but in their manner, their appearance, their very tone of voice. They had been exceptionally close to one another; and now, when her marriage was at risk, Judith prematurely lost this old, secure, unchangeable affection. She lost her deep and only source of strength. She was ill with grief.

'I had a very nice letter from Judith Catulle Mendès,' Flaubert wrote to Princess Mathilde. 'She seems to me so sad. I'm told that her mother is in abject poverty, which I think is true.'[32] Ernesta lived well into the century. Towards the end, she lingered on *en pension* at Auteuil, spending every Sunday with Judith; but sometimes she would call on Mme Sabatier, la Présidente, whose fortunes had improved since her liaison with the wealthy philanthropist Richard Wallace. Ernesta, then an elderly woman, her face all raddled by years of theatrical greasepaint, used to hint 'that her daughters did not always satisfy all her needs, since times had changed and her poor old carcass was no longer good for anything. But Ernesta exaggerated, as old people generally do when they have come to depend on their children. She wanted to touch her kind-hearted hostess and to keep her favour.'[33]

Gautier was to be commemorated by *Le Tombeau de Théophile Gautier*: a tribute in seven languages by more than eighty poets. Soon after Gautier had died, Catulle Mendès invited Victor Hugo to contribute 'some stanzas of farewell to our great and excellent father'.[34] Gautier had died without knowing of Judith's marital problems, but Hugo understood what this 'excellent father' thought of this son-in-law. It was largely for Judith that, on 2 November, he wrote his heroic valediction.

Judith herself understood this, and it was she who thanked him, and asked him for the manuscript of his poem. Hugo sent her a copy.

> Maître, thank you [she replied]. It is the first pleasure that I have known since he died. I breathed for a moment, I admired, and I was proud. How delighted he would have been if he had seen this homage from the god to the disciple! But the lines are not in your dear hand. Won't you send me the manuscript?
>
> I do not hope to be consoled. I feel a spiritual collapse, an irremediable ruin [within me]. I was very ill at first. Now I am physically better, and I regret it. The physical suffering drowned the other. Is Mme Drouet well? Give her a thousand kisses from me.
>
> When are you coming back? It is a very long time since you went.
>
> I embrace you, and thank you with all my soul.[35]

'Here, Madame, is the manuscript you were kind enough to want [this from Hugo on 23 November]. I lay it at your feet. The dear great poet who was your father lives again in you. He gazed so long on the ideal that he created you: you who, as woman and as soul, are perfect beauty. I kiss your wings.'[36]

On Christmas Day he wrote again:

> You should have come to this great solitude to spend the grievous months of your mourning. I think of you very often, I think of our good, dear and charming Gautier. I sent you the manuscript you wanted. Do you still remember me, Madame?
>
> I kneel before your great soul, the daughter of that great spirit.
>
> V.H.[37]
>
> I trembled as I read your letter, Maître [answered Judith], I felt so guilty, but I was counting on your kindness.
>
> I have it now, this dear manuscript, this Titan's manuscript! And there is not a day when I do not give myself the delight of reading it again (I even read under the crossings-out).
>
> Someone had told me that you were expected in Paris – and I hoped for you every moment, but in vain. Of course I guessed, when you went, that you didn't mean to come back this winter. What a joy it would be for me to go and see you down there! I may try to escape for two or three days at the end of January. Until then, I shall be a prey to the thousand vexations which add still further complications to great griefs; they are like pinpricks in a wound.

You are not one of those whom one forgets, as you know full well. You alone help to make life bearable and make one believe in God. But you make me too proud.

Remember me to Mme Drouet, and do not forget me too much, you who are in everybody's thoughts.[38]

Hugo's drama *Marion Delorme* was to be revived on 10 February 1873. Early in January, still on mourning paper, Judith wrote to him: 'Maître, I cannot resign myself to missing the première of *Marion Delorme*, and, if I can have a pit-box, I shall go in spite of my mourning. I trust in God rather than his saints, and that is why I address him directly, although he is so far away. But is he not omnipresent and omnipotent?'[39] Hugo reminded Paul Meurice to reserve a pit-box for Judith. She did not get it, and she seems to have suspected Juliette's intervention. However often she sent her kind regards to Mme Drouet, Juliette was naturally mistrustful. Escholier maintains that she kept a watch on Judith's correspondence; so much so that, in the spring, when Judith wanted to recommend an actor for the part of Saint-Vallier in *Le Roi s'amuse*, she was afraid that she would not be heard.

I don't know [this to Hugo] if a recommendation of mine means anything to you. Perhaps it is because I did not write to you after *Marion Delorme*. I couldn't get the box and I didn't want to inform against anyone to you.

I have not entirely lost the hope of seeing you. I shall come and ensure that I am forgiven.

Your faithful disciple,
Judith Mendès

My new address is 50, rue des Martyrs.[40]

Her recommendation was not ignored. Hugo told Meurice: 'Mme Judith Mendès recommends M. Marc for the part of St Vallier. What do you think?'[41] But Judith remained enamoured of Hugo, and she was anxious.

She wanted to see him all the more since her marriage was increasingly unhappy. When the impoverished poet Albert Glatigny died on 16 April, at the tragically early age of thirty-four, Catulle was in Bordeaux, and it was Judith who wrote a note of condolence to Glatigny's widow.[42] Judith was preoccupied, and her correspondence suffered. She did not send the expected greetings to Wagner on his birthday. On 25 May, from Bayreuth, Cosima wrote anxiously: 'You haven't answered my last note, . . . and as I know you are very susceptible, I imagine that I have committed or omitted something which has vexed you; I'd rather think that you are ill, and, as I know that you still love me despite your injustices, I want to tell you that we were sad not to have had a sign of life from you on 22 May.'[43]

If Judith was Victor Hugo's mistress, her infidelity was understandable. That year, so she later told Suzanne Meyer-Zundel, she and Mendès had gone to do 'a series of readings and some reporting in Vienna'.[44] They had arrived, so it appears, during a cholera epidemic. Judith caught the cholera, and the doctors decided that she must return to Paris at once. It was not Mendès who took her home. Louis Benedictus, a Dutch composer, was already much in love with her. He was revolted by her husband's unconcern, and he undertook, she recalled, 'to bring me back, half dying, to Paris. I shall never forget this service, which was rendered with such devotion. In the apartment next to the one we occupied in Vienna – but a more luxurious apartment – Mendès had in fact installed his friend and mistress, Augusta Holmès.'[45]

Sometime in the summer of 1873, Judith had gone for relaxation – perhaps for convalescence – to Normandy. She had always been responsive to masculine beauty. She had been enthralled by Catulle, who had seemed Apollo in person; now that her marriage to him was ending, she was all the more aware of beauty in other men. At Fécamp, this summer, as she was swimming, she saw a young man bathing. 'It seemed to me,' so she remembered, thirty years later, 'that I was in the presence of the Archangel Michael. He was beautiful, and in him grace was allied with strength. He was the ideal hermaphrodite, my type of beauty.'[46] Judith – an intrepid swimmer – swam after him, and she made her admiration plain; she felt that he was much intrigued, but was escaping her. Their emotions remained unspoken, except by their eyes. Judith later learned that her Adonis came from a strait-laced bourgeois family. She assumed that she must have frightened him; but he continued to haunt her dreams. Among the papers of Charles Clermont-Ganneau is a prose-poem by Judith, dated 25-27 July 1873. It ends: 'Hélas! j'aime d'amour l'archange Saint-Michel!'[47] It was, again, for her archangel that she wrote the poem *Châtiment* that December.[48] For René Gérin, a painter of almost celestial beauty, she felt a similar attraction. She delighted in the mere sight of him; their relationship, too, remained unexpressed, though it inspired her with the poem *Tigre et Gazelle*.[49]

Meanwhile, on 29 August 1873, Léon Dierx reported to Mallarmé: 'Catulle has come back. His wife is at Fécamp, and is due to return, so he tells us, in five or six days. It all leads one to think that things are not as final as rumour had suggested. A thousand times the better for both of them.'[50]

On 31 July, after nearly a year's absence, Victor Hugo had returned to Paris. He had come to see his son, François-Victor, who was slowly dying of tuberculosis of the kidneys; he had also come to continue a new liaison.

The previous year, Juliette had taken a young maid, Blanche, into her service, and Hugo had found himself afire for the girl, who was half a century younger. According to Louis Barthou, she had become his mistress on 1 April. She remained an inspiration for six years. Hugo was seventy-one; yet his liaison with Blanche did not prevent his continued relationship with Judith. 'Master, you are in Paris!' she wrote to him. 'I have come back from far away [from Normandy], from a part of the world where I was very bored. I learned of your return and I hurried back with a great delight on my horizon. Which days and times can one see you without disturbing you?'[51] They saw one another secretly, but, on his first visit to the rue des Martyrs, Hugo looked in vain for his Dea, on the wrong side of the street. Judith was desolate at this mischance:

> What evil spirit is so vexed with me that it suggested such a strange address to you? It's 50, rue des Martyrs, not *neuve* [des Martyrs] at all. You were opposite this house and I didn't guess. How can you believe in magnetism after that? Yet I was waiting for you. I'm still waiting for you, and I didn't go out for a single moment that day. It's enough to drive one mad. I am in despair, and all the more furious since we are having some people to dinner this evening, and Tuesday is the day we receive our friends. (How I detest them, my friends!) After Tuesday, I escaped into hiding so as to go and see you, but twice in succession my absence might be noticed. So I shan't even have the consolation of seeing *Marie Tudor* again. But at least don't imagine that I'm going to give you back the seats.
>
> I shall come and see you on Thursday evening, if that suits you. You will try to console me, won't you? It will be difficult. I should like to kill someone: the occupants of nos. 47 and 49, for example. Why don't I have the power of Marie Tudor?
>
> I kiss your hands, divine Master. I shall see you soon.
>
> Judith M, <u>50</u>, rue des Martyrs.[52]

Catulle continued his love affair with Augusta Holmès; Judith and Hugo continued to see each other secretly, and in public. Throughout the autumn, both the Mendès were invited to the Master's table, and the poet of *L'Art d'être grand-père* took his granddaughter to 50, rue des Martyrs. Jeanne, he recorded, 'saw the dog which played the piano and stood up on its hind legs at the name of Hugo. Mme Judith gave Jeanne a Chinese doll, and she gave me a French doll.'[53]

Juliette Drouet was forced to suffer from Hugo's enduring love for Blanche, and to be reminded of Judith's presence. On the night of 27 November, as she lay uneasily awake, she re-read Hugo's sonnet, *Ave, Dea*. Next day she wrote: '*Ave, Deo*, your very humble worshipper blesses you even in your infidelities.'[54]

Chapter Ten

The goddess still continued to visit Victor Hugo. Sometimes she went alone, and sometimes Mendès went with her. Once they arrived with a curious companion.

> Maître [she explained], We are having some people to dinner this evening, and it is difficult, isn't it, to let them dine alone? But we shall have the pleasure of coming to see you at nine o'clock with the sorcerer.
> My respects to Madame Drouet.
> > I kiss your hands.
> > Judith M[1]

On 4 December 1873, Hugo recorded: 'Mme Mendès brought me her *sorcerer*, who is none other than the abbé Constant, once the husband of the beautiful Claude V., today occupied with the Kabbala under the pseudonym of Éliphas Lévi.'[2]

There was to remain an element of mystery and magic about Judith. On 28 December, after the funeral of François-Victor Hugo, Goncourt reported:

> We are accosted, Flaubert and I, as we leave Père-Lachaise, by Judith . . . Théo's daughter is beautiful, with a strange and almost frightening beauty. Her complexion is of a whiteness hardly tinged with pink. Her mouth is shaped like a Primitive's mouth over her big ivory teeth. Her pure and somehow somnolent features, her great eyes, where animals' lashes, stiff lashes like little black pins, do not soften the glance with a shadow: all give the lethargic creature the indefinable majesty of a sphinx, of flesh and matter in which there are no human nerves.
> And the young woman sets off her dazzling youth. On one side of her she has the Chinese Tsing [sic] with the flat face and turned-up eyes, and, on the other, her mother, the aged Grisi, so shrivelled and shrunk that she looks like an old tubercular monkey.

And then, so that everything about the meeting is bizarre, eccentric and fantastic, Judith apologizes to Flaubert for having missed him yesterday: she had gone out to have her *magic* lesson – yes, her magic lesson![3]

The war had suspended the collective effort of the Parnassians, and life was finally to disperse them; but the Mendès remained devoted to Leconte de Lisle. Appointed librarian to the Senate, where François Coppée had nobly resigned his place to him, Leconte de Lisle moved in 1873 to an apartment in the École des Mines, off the boulevard Saint-Michel.[4] It was a classic salon, furnished with rosewood and grey rep, with austere armchairs upholstered in green velvet. There were few ornaments except the poet's bust on the mantelpiece, an enormous sculpted head – a copy of Michaelangelo's Moses – and a Japanese lantern with fringes. Among the old habitués were Heredia, Henry Houssaye and Anatole France; among the newcomers were Maurice Barrès, Edmond Rostand, Swinburne and Pierre Louÿs. In 1873 Mallarmé introduced John Payne, the English poet and translator. Payne described Leconte de Lisle as 'a marble colossus.'[5] Little love was lost between Leconte de Lisle and the ageing Victor Hugo. Leconte de Lisle would make sharp observations about the Master, which duly found their way back to him.

At the very beginning [said Calmettes], Hugo had not denied himself the pleasure of returning the impertinences, which he sent back indirectly, as he received them. A year or two after Leconte de Lisle had published the translation of the complete works of Aeschylus, Hugo had some Parnassians to dinner: Léon Dierx, Jean Marras, Judith Gautier. Taking advantage of a silence at table, after the soup, he said: 'I spend every morning reading the great Greek poets. I spent this morning reading Aeschylus, who has never been translated into French.' Then he emphasized his insinuation by looks which the Parnassians naturally refrained from meeting.[6]

In 1873, not without occasional demonstrations from the audience, French orchestras began to play Wagner again. On 12 December Wagner himself sent a fulsome note to the Mendès, whom he had not seen since the Siege.

Dear, dear friends!
. . . All I want, as far as you are concerned, is to have you with us. We were hoping to see you this summer – but you have been silent . . .
But you will come and visit us – I hope – next summer. It can't go on like this – believe me. In the spring, you will find us settled at last in our new house, which is still giving us a great deal of trouble. It will be very convenient, you'll see . . .

Goodbye, dear friends! Give us your news, and please God it may be good![7]

His own news was good. In 1870, after the performance of *Die Walküre*, it had been decided to build a Wagner Festival Theatre. Wagner's patron, Ludwig II of Bavaria, had offered to build it near Munich. Wagner had opposed the idea. In 1871 he had decided to build his own theatre at Bayreuth. He had secured a site for it, and another site on which to build a house for himself, the villa Wahnfried. In 1872 he had finally settled in Bayreuth. On his fifty-ninth birthday, 22 May, the foundation stone of the new theatre had been laid. Now, in 1873, the building was rising grandly on its hill, a lasting monument to Wagner's dream.[8]

Judith admired the god of Bayreuth. She felt intense admiration and physical passion for Victor Hugo. This passion was mutual. On 4 April 1874, he wrote the poem 'À Madame J***':

Âme, statue, esprit, Vénus,
    Belle des belles,
Celui qui verrait vos pieds nus
    Verrait des ailes.

À travers vos traits radieux
    Luit l'espérance;
Déesse, vous avez des dieux
    La transparence.

Comme eux, vous avez le front pur,
    La blancheur fière,
Et dans le fond de votre azur
    Une lumière.

Pas un de nous, fils de la nuit,
    Qui ne vous sente
Dans l'ombre où tout s'évanouit,
    Éblouissante!

Vous rayonnez sous la beauté;
    C'est votre voile.
Vous êtes un marbre, habité
    Par une étoile.[9]

Victor Hugo cruelly showed the poem to Juliette Drouet. He seems to have told her that he had also written a second.

Thank you, my great beloved [she answered], for your loyalty in telling me this morning that you had written another poem for Mme M . . . Thank you too for your kindness in offering to read the lines to me and not to send them to her until later.

I had at first accepted this postponement, but, on reflection, I understood that what was deferred was not lost, that I should gain nothing by opposition to your conjunction with this statue inhabited by a star, and that I should quite simply make myself as ridiculous as the ostrich which thinks it is avoiding danger by burying its head in the sand.

That is why, my great beloved, I ask you to act with absolute freedom, and to send the lines you have dedicated to your beautiful inspiration. Since this poetry was tapped, it is quite natural that you should both become intoxicated with it, and so much the worse for my thirst . . .

My dear, great friend, I beg you not to stint yourself, and to behave as if I were already no longer there. That will give me time to rest from life before I take flight for eternity. Try to be happy if you can.[10]

It is not clear when 'Nivea non frigida' was written, but it was dated 5 April. It leaves little doubt of the relations between 'Madame J***' and her 'divine Master.'

> Elle prouve que la blancheur
>   N'ôte à la femme
> Aucune ivresse, aucun bonheur,
>   Aucune flamme;
>
> Qu'en avril les coeurs sont enclins
>   Aux tendres choses,
> Et que les bois profonds sont pleins
>   D'apothéoses;
>
> Qu'une belle fait en tout lieu
>   Son doux manège,
> Et que l'on peut être de feu,
>   Étant de neige.[11]

Victor Hugo had not been single-minded in his love of Judith. All-embracing in his love of women, he remained faithful, at heart, to Juliette Drouet, who for forty years had sacrificed herself in his service. Juliette was to remain the rock in his existence. But his affair with Judith, which caused Juliette such grief, such helpless jealousy, was perhaps a factor in ending Judith's marriage to Mendès. In May 1874, eight years after their wedding, they separated.

Théophile Gautier had been justified in opposing his daughter's marriage; Cazalis and des Essarts had been right to doubt if it would last. Mendès was a man who preferred conquest to responsibility, who needed constantly to prove his masculine attraction. He was fundamentally unsure of his own importance, he was always conscious of his wife's superiority. Mendès had a great esteem for intellectual women. As Fernand Calmettes observed, in *Leconte de Lisle et ses amis*,

> . . . he particularly admired Judith, and it is not in their incompatibility of mind, it is in the secret of their psychologies that one must seek the reason for their famous separation, of which the Press were the clamorous confidants.
>
> And that is what stops me. Mendès, impulsive by nature, is easy to define; but Judith had a reflective disposition, spoke little and stirred little, she was the heir of a great intellectual, and all of the mind; she cannot be judged by appearances. For that very reason one would have to penetrate the innermost recesses of her deep thoughts, and draw a detailed portrait of the greatest interest . . . But one cannot analyse the [intellectual or the] emotional life of a woman without the risk of being indiscreet, and one's duty is to say nothing if one does not feel entitled to say everything, for rare subjects cannot be partially treated.
>
> There is no doubt that this psychological study would wonderfully complete the great figure of Théophile Gautier, for Judith is his daughter three times over: by descent, and beauty, and intelligence; but, once again, it could only be written if it were presented whole, complete and unrestricted, just as it is. I do not feel authorized to do this, and I renounce the task with the utmost regret.[12]

Calmettes is tantalizing in his omissions and in his implications; but he is surely right to emphasize that Mendès was impulsive and superficial, and that Judith was reflective and profound. She had an innate sense of justice, a contempt for compromise, she was open and she was generous. She knew that she was beautiful, but she was not vain about it, and she had no time for coquetry. She was a private person and, since her childhood, she had always been reserved. She preferred to hide her inner self. In love, as in friendship, she was, by nature, faithful.

Mendès was quite otherwise. Early in their married life he had been unfaithful to her, and he had long ago returned to Augusta Holmès. His relationship with Augusta was now virtually a marriage. He gave her five children: Raphaël, Huguette, Claudine, Hélyonne, and a son who died in infancy. Of these, it seems, at least the first two were born before his separation from his wife. Augusta had been essential to Mendès before he had known Judith; she was to remain essential years after he and Judith had separated. He was clearly more drawn to her than he ever was to the daughter of Théophile Gautier.

Many years later, Judith talked to Suzanne Meyer-Zundel about·the relationship between Mendès and Augusta:

> As always in these cases, I was the last to know the truth . . . For everybody except me, this scandalous behaviour was an open secret. But when a friend, and then several friends – being charitable souls – finally opened my eyes, and

added that, if I insisted on staying with him, . . . I should just be considered his
accomplice, I turned him out . . .

Mendès packed his things that evening, and left without a protest the next
day, taking under his arm a picture which he had unhooked from the
dining-room wall. 'So long, goodbye, good luck,' he said as he left the house.

'My good luck begins today,' I replied. And, as a final word of advice: 'You
should try to work yourself instead of making people work for you.' 'Oh,' he
said, 'what a nuisance it is to have that reputation!'[13]

Mendès, too, had given some explanation of the irretrievable breakdown
of his marriage. In the Bibliothèque Nationale there is an unpublished
letter to Jean Marras, which is dated simply 'Wednesday morning'. It may
be placed more precisely in April or early in May 1874.

My dear friend,
    . . . I shall see you again before 12 May. But if, by chance, we don't
encounter each other before then, do please come and see me that day. You will
meet two of our friends, Dierx and Mallarmé, whom I shall be informing soon.
I will talk to you at length, at great length. Many things which are obscure will
be illuminated for you. You will learn, among other details, why, though my
resolution was made a fortnight ago, I am still waiting until 12 May to carry it
out. In the life of a man who earns his living from hand to mouth, there are
some cruel necessities, and I may not have what I need in order to act until 12
May. Perhaps you will ask why I haven't at least allowed my friends to
understand that the present situation was about to end? Because of the
embarrassment I should impose on them: an embarrassment from which I
should suffer much more that they did. I should perhaps have explained that I
have only borne [this situation] because I am certain that it is nearing its end. If
I have still said nothing, even to you, whom I love and esteem, it is because you
would have been obliged to reply, and I did not want to impose the
responsibility of such terrible advice on anyone. On 12 May the whole of my life
for the past eight years will be revealed to you; at that moment there will be no
going back: it will all be over, and you will be my adviser and my judge.
Whatever you decree, I shall obey it. You will understand many things, my
friend . . .[14]

Judith had ample grounds for her separation from Mendès. In the past
eight years he had degraded her, abused her, changed her from a
passionate, idealistic girl into a wounded, disillusioned and embittered
woman. Judith had embarked on her marriage innocent and intensely
romantic. Perhaps she and Mendès had found themselves physically
incompatible, perhaps she had been unresponsive, even frigid. Perhaps
she had been unable or unwilling to have children, or disgusted by his
sexual demands. Whatever the truth, on 15 May 1874 John Payne wrote to
Mallarmé about the breakdown of the Mendès marriage. On 18 May, the
innocent and perhaps uncritical Mallarmé wrote to his old friend:

My dear Catulle,

. . . You are acting wisely, bravely, with your head held high; beside the thousand wrongs which you will probably have in the eyes of strangers because of your discretion towards them, I think I do not need in the least to add that you have my entire sympathy . . . I see you as one of the most loyal and most right-minded men one can meet, and as someone endowed with great goodness . . .

In my moments of leisure, since last Tuesday, I have looked for you, wanting to be alone for a minute so that I could listen to you. I wanted in fact to speak first yesterday and to see Mademoiselle Holmès again. But it is decreed that we shall always write to one another, and that the best of our friendship, at least of mine for you, will be what I feel from a distance . . . You know that you are, with Villiers, the only man whom I really seriously love, and from an old habit which one must not allow to fall into disuse, I will see you tomorrow evening, if you are still receiving at home: after dinner, probably . . .[15]

On the evening of 19 May, he duly called on Mendès, and no doubt heard his version of events. Next day he wrote: 'I grasp your hand – and I shake hands warmly with Augusta.'[16]

Mendès – who was living, now, at 16, rue de Bruxelles – was clearly disturbed by the thought of the effect which his separation might have on his career. He was, above all, anxious not to lose favour with the great. Hugo was devoted to Judith. Mendès wrote to him with a nicely calculated sadness; he took the occasion to present himself not only as an admirer of Hugo, but (with a certain condescension) as the loyal son of Tibulle and Sara. He needed to restore his tarnished image.

My beloved Master,

Are you settled in your new house [in the rue de Clichy]? . . . I, too, have moved house in the last few days, very sadly, and I am sending you my new address.

A supplication, my dear Master: my father and mother have come to join me in Paris. They are worthy and excellent people who taught me, as a small child, to read you and love you. They would like to see you once, just once. Would you let me bring them to you, one day, whenever you choose? . . .[17]

There remained the forbidding thought of Flaubert. Mendès had always been anxious to keep Flaubert's friendship.[18] Now, it seems, he was writing a libretto for an opera based on *Salammbô*;[19] he was all the more anxious to keep his connection with the author. It was, presumably, this May that he wrote to him. It was a disagreeable letter; and its shifty and ingratiating tone did not, one assumes, impress the recipient. Mendès' protestations of his blameless behaviour to Judith were too insistent to be credible.

Mon cher Maître,

   You already know that there has been a momentous change in Judith's life
and in mine. I am sure that I have nothing with which to reproach myself, but I
am making no reproaches to Judith. The present misfortune originates from a
long and painful misunderstanding, about which I shall also be silent, unless I
am obliged to defend myself, should I be accused – which I cannot foresee. I
should not even have written this to you. Loving you as I do, I should have
been very careful to do nothing which looked like giving you the unacceptable
role of judge and arbiter. But there is *Salammbô*, and you are an old friend of
Judith's. I had become accustomed to the idea of this work in which my poetry
would have done as little damage as possible to your wonderful prose. But you
understand that, without taking sides – which in no case, I am quite sure, you
would or could do – it might be possible that your very old and almost paternal
affection for Judith inspired you, in the present case, not with antipathy for me
– since I am sure, as I say, that I have no reproach to make myself – but with a
certain dislike of the idea of seeing your work abandoned to my discretion, and
of being in constant touch, which would be the necessary result of this
quasi-collaboration . . . All this is very difficult to write, and I beg you to
understand me through this scribble and through the confusion of my ideas.

   It goes without saying that if, before you make a decision, you want to be
enlightened about everything, I should be entirely at your disposal; and,
without making an accusation, I should have the wherewithal to defend myself.

   As for the importance I attach to your reply, you can imagine it. From you to
me, that is to say from the admired master to the disciple, the slightest word
assumes an extraordinary value – and then I love you as much as I admire you.

Your
Catulle Mendès[20]

Mendès was eventually discarded as a librettist. His letter could only have
strengthened Flaubert's affection and sympathy for Gautier's daughter.

   Henry Stuart, an American author, declared that the reverberations of
Mendès' famous separation 'filled the air in Paris for several years'.[21] The
marriage had been a catastrophe in Judith's life; yet Suzanne Meyer-
Zundel, who was to know her well, believed that, even in her final years,
Judith did not cease to love Catulle:

   Despite the cutting words which were exchanged, the humiliations which were
   suffered, the wounding insinuations, my fundamentally indulgent friend would
   certainly have been ready to forget and to forgive, at the slightest attempt to
   return. At least, that was my deepest conviction. And then, since first love is
   always the most passionate and the most tenacious, too, the memory of it must
   have persisted for years. It certainly left ineffaceable regrets in her heart.[22]

III

Madame Judith Gautier

Chapter Eleven

When the wax of the candle is burnt out, it is replaced. Is it not so with a thousand things?

So he behaves, my faithless husband.

He loves another than myself, another beautiful as jade! . . .

The magnolias have not forgotten the time at which to close their corollas.

The pairs of teals still remain tenderly united, and never does the female go away, to sleep alone.

But he, beside his new beloved, who is laughing,

Does not even want to hear the once-beloved who weeps.[1]

So Tu-Fu had written, long ago; so Judith had recorded in *Le Livre de Jade*. Now, in 1874, she remained, alone, in the rue des Martyrs, and she withdrew into silence. On 2 June, Cosima reminded her:

I am still waiting for you to send me a word about your new life, which implies a new establishment; as you are silent, I am afraid that you might think we were indifferent. In any case, this is to say that we are thinking of you . . .

I cannot from a distance pass judgement on the situation, or give you advice . . . When we see each other again you can talk to me without reserve, and I will tell you quite frankly what I feel. In the meanwhile we are anxious about you and about your future . . .

Goodbye, my dear Judith. Send us your news soon, because, as I say, we are concerned about you. Can you write, and what are you writing? Rest assured of the fate of your letters; I burn them *all*, so you can speak freely. I embrace you with all my heart.[2]

Judith promptly sent her explanation of events to Bayreuth. On 26 June, from Wahnfried, Cosima replied:

My dear,

Never, since the institution of marriage, has a woman separated from her husband for such good reasons, or in such a sensible way; I think it is quite

right that you should have stayed in the apartment and that Mr M should have
had to leave, not you; it is much more suitable like that, and, since the wretched
question of money was involved, I can quite see that one couldn't be patient
. . . You're going to laugh, but I am a little afraid of the friend.[3]

The friend was Louis Benedictus. He had for years been much in love
with Judith. He now devoted his life to her, and his one idea was
eventually to marry her. Benedictus was the son of a Dutch diamond
merchant. He was French by naturalization, but he spoke French with
such a heavy accent that he was sometimes taken for a German. As
Ludwig Benedictus he had contributed, in German, to *Le Tombeau de
Théophile Gautier*. He was later described, with transparent jealousy, by
Judith's confidante, Suzanne Meyer-Zundel:

> Tall, powerfully built and handsome, Judith's friend was oriental in appear-
> ance, with Assyrian features, matt white skin, dark hair (although he was nearly
> bald when I knew him), dark bright eyes, and a high forehead. His moustache
> and goatee were the only masculine things about his face. Fiery, jealous,
> egocentric, like most composers, he was ill-tempered, irascible, grumbling and
> difficult. He would grow angry and exasperated about nothing. He was
> ultra-sensitive. A false note, a dissonant chord, a different way of judging or
> understanding, became an immediate reason for disagreement, even for a
> quarrel; then he would vanish for a few days, sometimes for several weeks.[4]

He seems to have made little mark as a composer, possibly through lack
of talent, possibly because he did not seek publicity and appreciation; but
he composed some settings for poems by Gautier and Leconte de Lisle,
and incidental music for some of Judith's plays. He also collaborated with
her in transcriptions of oriental music. Perhaps he asked no more.

> Apart from his fidelity and devotion, which never failed, he had [continued
> Suzanne] a real cult for Judith. It was more than a cult, it was a fetish . . .
>   His erudition was extraordinary. It was literary – one could leaf through him
> like a dictionary – as much as musical. He interpreted Wagner's music, and
> Beethoven's symphonies, from memory, and to perfection . . . And, besides,
> what would he not have done for Judith?[5]

Benedictus spent the rest of his long life in her service. He suffered from
her bitterness and her unhappiness, and no doubt from the presence of her
other admirers, many of whom were handsomer and more distinguished
than himself. At moments of frustration he left, but he could not bring
himself to leave her for ever. In time, as Suzanne recorded, he always
returned to do Judith's errands, compose for her, pour out her medicines,
and to find his peace in her presence. He finally outlived her, and he was

buried near her. He had been the most loyal of the men in her life, and he had been the most sorely tried.

On 15 July 1874, from Saint-Jean, Carlotta Grisi wrote to Estelle Bergerat: 'I was grieved to learn of Judith's separation from her husband, though it was something which had been foreseen since her marriage, and all the rights appear to be on her side . . . You should rejoice, my dear, that you met a good man. Love him well, because honest men are rare nowadays, and thank God for the good fortune He has given you.'[6]

Estelle remained solidly married to Émile Bergerat. Now that her marriage to Catulle had foundered, Judith lost herself in writing. She needed, more than ever, to escape reality, to live in her imagination. She sought relief in distant and exotic worlds. She recalled the Japanese of noble demeanour whom she had glimpsed in London, long ago, the Japanese who had expressed such melancholy grace, such sweetness and disdain. He served, now, as a model for the Prince of Nagato in *L'Usurpateur*, her novel about feudal Japan. In 1875 *L'Usurpateur* was published by the Librairie Internationale, and crowned by the Académie-Française. As Anatole France recalled:

> At the moment of publication it was lost in a great publishing bankruptcy. The public hardly knew it. And yet it is a pure marvel, Mme Judith Gautier's masterpiece, and a masterpiece of our language. It re-appeared, later, under a title which is better suited to the enchanting splendour of the book; it was called *La Sœur du soleil*. I know of nothing to compare with these pages steeped in light and happiness, in which all the forms are rare and beautiful, all the feelings proud or tender, in which the cruelty of the yellow race is half effaced in the glory of that heroic age . . .
>
> With this (and *Le Dragon impérial*) one must set *Iskender*, which is the legendary history of Alexander according to the traditions of Persia. These three books are the three finest jewels of this queen of the imagination.[7]

'How can one answer such sweet flattery?' Judith was to ask Anatole France. 'With heartfelt gratitude and smiling doubt.'[8] She sent him a photograph of herself, taken by Nadar. Riotor declared that *L'Usurpateur* 'revealed the iridescent glory of the woman of letters'.[9] Leconte de Lisle would have liked to put certain passages from the book into verse; he considered it a masterpiece.[10]

Judith needed more than acclaim from eminent contemporaries. Now that she found herself alone, she desperately needed money. André Billy, in his life of Mme Sabatier, recorded that since literature does not always give a living to beginners, 'the author of *Le Dragon impérial* had had the idea of trying to fill her empty purse in other ways. She had tried to slim by taking a drug which she thought a marvel, so she assured her friends and acquaintances who – like la Présidente – had put on weight. Judith exploited this find, and sold it for a while at a certain profit, under the name of Élixir égyptien.'[11]

She had a more conventional way of earning her living. Throughout 1875 and 1876, an irregular series of articles appeared in *Le Journal officiel*, under the signature of F. Chaulnes (listed in the index as Ferdinand Chaulnes). Mathilde Camacho identifies this as a pseudonym of Judith Gautier;[12] her statement is substantiated by the fact that many of the pieces were reprinted, at least in part, in Judith's book, *Les Peuples étranges*, in 1879.

In this disparate series of articles on exotic subjects, Judith discussed the Cro-Magnon skull and the grottoes which M. de Baye had recently discovered in Champagne.[13] She paid a generous tribute to her friend Charles Clermont-Ganneau, who had rediscovered Gezer, one of the most ancient cities in Palestine.[14] Eagerly she watched the uncovering of the buried past; she was anxious that oral traditions should be recorded before they had irretrievably vanished. 'We must make haste, for civilization is penetrating everywhere.'[15] As André Beaunier observed, Judith had a horror of progress.[16] She was fascinated by General Palma di Cesnola's archaeological expedition to Cyprus. He had undertaken it in 1873, and he had unearthed amazing treasure. On its way back to New York, where it had been acquired by a museum, 'the treasure had been brought back to Europe, and, as M. di Cesnola passed through Paris, we were able to see the gold and silver artefacts which had come from the precious find.'[17]

Whatever her other interests, most of the articles in *Le Journal officiel* were Judith's 'Notes sur la Chine'. She discussed Chinese music and poetry. She dwelt at length on Li-Tai-pei, one of the greatest of Chinese poets, to whom the Emperor himself had served as secretary; for in China, as she wrote, 'poetry is the magic key which opens every door, the sign of nobility before which the loftiest heads bow down'.[18] She described the Chinese theatre, and painted a lyrical picture of itinerant actors, travelling by junk down the rivers through pen-and-wash landscapes. She gave an affectionate account of ancient Chinese cures and simples, and discussed the Chinese fear of medicine. She wrote of the Chinese gods and poussahs, and her article on Miou-chen, the goddess of mercy, reflected her own simplicity, her love of poetry and heroism, her continuing fascination with violence. She wrote a delectable account of a marriage in Peking, a poignant description of a funeral.

Her interest in Eastern themes was not confined to China. She discussed Persian poets. She described a day in the kingdom of Siam. It began with a picture of daybreak, a multicoloured account of Bangkok, where the crowds were watching the torture and execution of criminals. Prah-Klang, the mandarin-minister, passed by, on his way to report to his master on governmental affairs. After his audience, he gave the people permission to see the royal elephants in their stables. 'Once upon a time these white elephants were free . . . Now, amid the gold and marble, they force themselves to forget the beautiful fields and the mighty forests . . .'[19] Here, perhaps, was the inspiration of the children's book which Judith was one day to write: *Mémoires d'un Éléphant blanc*. Then night fell on Siam:

> Bangkok was enveloped in darkness and tranquillity, and great stars blossomed in the heavens; it was the time when sorcerers were going to do their magic, cast their spells. Things were distorted and assumed terrifying shapes; the domes of the pagodas looked like great bald skulls; the palm trees seemed to fill with dark birds . . . The sounds of humankind gave place to the murmurs of the night . . .[20]

Judith's account of Siam was rivalled only by her description of Cochin China. In September 1875, *Le Journal officiel* published two articles, 'Douze heures dans la baie de Tourane en Cochinchine'.

> Is there a more agreeable awakening than the one which surprises you, after a long sea-voyage, in the tiny cabin of a ship as it reaches port? . . . It was in the bay of Hane, in Cochin China, that I woke up like this one morning, after a fortnight's voyage; we had come from Singapore . . .[21]

Judith recalled the coast of Cochin China as they approached it, the festival in progress ashore. She painted a panorama of a wedding procession and a wedding ceremony. She described the marble grotto dedicated to the god of the sky, earth and sea. None of these things, which she recalled down to the smallest detail, had she seen.

Like her father, she was intensely aware of the visible world. Théophile Gautier had been renowned as a travel writer; but, thirty-five years earlier, as he had crossed the Spanish frontier, he had remembered the challenge of Heine: 'How will you talk about Spain once you have been there?'[22] Judith had the power of poetic evocation; she travelled in her well-informed imagination. She would not risk destroying her own authentic dream by comparing it with reality.

Her literary manner – her ironic humour, her visual style, her romanticism – often recalled that of her father; and, like Gautier, she became a critic of art. On 2 May 1876, in *Le Rappel*, she published her first, somewhat chauvinistic, impression of the Salon. 'As always, in the presence of this enormous flowering of works of art, one's first emotion is national pride . . . This creative power, this vital ardour which nothing can abate, is found in France alone.'[23]

During the next two months her articles continued to appear in *Le Rappel*. On 6 May she turned to Gustave Moreau, whose exotic fantasies had always been much in sympathy with her own:

> These vanished cities, these gracious figures of which the ancient poets have given us the memory: it is in oneself that one must see them; it is from one's mind alone that they must spring. Gustave Moreau draws everything from within himself . . . To see this *Salome*, he has closed his eyes and concentrated his thoughts. Inspiration has led this young girl before him, this girl who is so perilously beautiful in her wondrous raiment. He has painted her according to his dream.[24]

Since one could not copy a god, one had to invent him. For Judith, Moreau's invention transcended his technique. 'You are hardly concerned with the medium . . . You forget that you are looking at a painting.'[25] In time she met Moreau himself, and found him 'absolutely delightful'.[26]

On 7 May, Judith discussed *Mahomet II*, by Benjamin Constant: an exotic, violent, brilliant canvas which seemed like a scene from one of her own novels. On 23 May she deplored the everyday subjects of modern artists. 'Certainly, the real Quai aux Fleurs is better than M. Firmin Giraud's picture. There, at least, the flowers smell sweet and the people are alive.'[27] On 15 June she discussed the Orientalists in painting, and turned to Fromentin and Gérôme with something of the nostalgia which her father had once felt for Spain:

> How often has one not perceived, through a gilded frame, the long file of a caravan unroll, snake-like, across the desert sands? And yet one is always happy to see, yet again, the bizarre silhouettes of the camels against the sky; one contentedly follows their rolling gait, and envies those who lead them. One is overcome by a vague nostalgia for the countries that one will not see . . .[28]

One country she longed to see again. For all the anguish of the war and the Siege of Paris, Germany remained the land of Wagner. The first two parts of *Der Ring* had been produced several years earlier; now the final part, *Götterdämmerung*, was to be added to them. On 13 August 1876, the first complete performance of *Der Ring* was due to begin at Bayreuth.

——————Chapter Twelve——————

Wagner's new theatre stood on a hill some distance from Bayreuth. A wide road, lined with trees, led up to it, and, from its doors, one could see the old town and the countryside far beyond.[1]

Mendès duly reviewed *Der Ring*. 'Think what you like of the work itself,' he told *La République des Lettres*. 'I do not intend to impose my admiration on other people; but you must announce loud and clear that the success was colossal. After *Das Rheingold*, they applauded, stamped and shouted with enthusiasm for twenty-four minutes. The next two evenings only increased the emotion and enthusiasm, and *Götterdämmerung* ended in incomparable triumph.'[2] On 29 August, Édouard Dujardin continued: 'One came out of *Die Walküre* (the third series) broken with emotion . . . On every side one heard the stifled sobs of women, and one saw men wipe away their tears.'[3]

After the first performance of *Der Ring* at Bayreuth, the idolatry shown towards Wagner knew no bounds. 'This state of mad and unconsidered passion for the art and especially the spirit of Wagner lasted,' considered Vincent d'Indy, 'for a good ten years. Then it calmed down, and became balanced. In about 1888 everyone could estimate the giant's works at their true value.'[4]

The mad and unconsidered passion had not, perhaps, subsided. As Camille Mauclair was to write in 1922: 'When I was an adolescent (in about 1892), men knew the enchantment of Wagner: fascinating, peremptory, total. And no similar enchanter, not even Debussy, has since appeared to offer a comparison, to those who are twenty years old, with what we knew when we ourselves were twenty – that religion, that ecstatic state of grace.'[5]

Judith, too, had been to Bayreuth in 1876 to hear *Der Ring*.

The theatre . . . is a very simple building in appearance; it is like a smaller version of the Palais du Trocadéro.

When, for the first time, I saw it standing majestically on its hill, illuminated by the rays of the setting sun, when I saw that crowd of worshippers slowly ascending, from every side, towards the temple of art, I could not restrain my tears of joy. The lifelong dream of that man of genius had been realized at last! This world which had so persecuted him was hastening to acclaim him with a fanaticism until then unknown . . .

Those who attended those wonderful performances in 1876, when everything had been prepared and directed by Wagner, will never forget them. Such a solemnity had not been known since the great theatrical festivals of ancient Greece, and it will remain, in the future, a capital event in the history of art.[6]

The solemnity also remained a capital event in the history of Judith's relationship with Wagner. She had, she said, been a Wagnerian since the days of her childhood at Neuilly, when she had found a Wagner score, by chance, on her piano, and his particular magic had enthralled her. It was eight years since she had written of Richard Wagner in La Presse: 'He assumed his glory as a sovereign assumes his rightful throne.' It was seven years since she had first visited the Master at Tribschen, and she had 'seen God face to face'.

Judith's feeling for Wagner was, above all, a feeling of romantic admiration. She had found felicity in watching him at work, at being accepted by Cosima, loved by the children. The daughter of Théophile Gautier, she had found her satisfaction in fighting Wagner's fight, as her father had fought for Hugo and Hernani. She had been elated by the warmth of Wagner's welcome. In 1869 there had been no question of a love affair. She was only recently married. Wagner was the lover of Cosima, 'the woman who, alone,' he told Judith, 'makes life bearable for me.'[7] He was the father of Isolde and Eva, and of the infant Siegfried. Within the year, he and Cosima were married. Judith was godmother to Siegfried. There could hardly have been a clearer indication that she was a close family friend.

Now, in 1876, Wagner met Judith again, for the first time since her marriage had ended. The girl of twenty-three who had come to Tribschen with her husband was now a disillusioned woman of thirty-one, separated from Mendès, and grateful for the devotion of Louis Benedictus. Possibly she gave Benedictus physical favours; if so, she gave them out of gratitude. She did not return his passion. If any man stood, now, between herself and Wagner, it was more probably Victor Hugo; and, if Escholier is correct, his love affair with her still continued.

Long afterwards, recalling her visits to Wagner, Judith told Suzanne Meyer-Zundel:

The year 1876 was the most brilliant, the most astonishing year. It was that year that he said to me one day in his house – and he also wrote it to me –'you are my deliverance,' and he passed his hands over my cheeks, . . . 'you are of my race . . . I should have found you! I have missed my destiny, but we must be sensible.' And, again in 1876, the day of my arrival in Bayreuth, it was in the afternoon. I had changed my dress and put on a particular pink dress with blue bows to go and visit Wagner. It might have been half-past six or seven. I went quite unannounced into a big drawing-room where Wagner and Cosima were alone, in evening dress. They were ready to receive, and they were awaiting their guests. There was a big reception that day. We exchanged eager greetings, and joyfully, hand in hand, we circled round the big drawing-room for quite a while. Cosima adjusted her lorgnette and declared that I had become much more beautiful since the last time; they made me turn round and round again, and they examined me in every detail . . .

Every day I had *déjeuner* at Wagner's, and nearly every day I went back to dinner there. He was very keen on elegance, and one day he wanted everyone to dress up, and beautify themselves just for him, as if it were a grand evening reception. I had put on an old-gold dress which, I knew, was very becoming to me . . . When I made my entrance: 'There's the goddess!' Wagner exclaimed, and he offered an arm to each of us.[8]

A few days later came another evening reception. As the guests were leaving, Judith could not find her coat, and Wagner promptly lent her his own. As she remembered:

When I got back to the little apartment which one rented for the duration of the performances, I called out to Benedictus, who had just arrived with Saint-Saëns: 'I've got Wagner's overcoat!' Immediately, like wild animals leaping on their prey, the two passionate disciples of the Master both threw themselves on to the 'sacrosanct' coat, delved into the pockets, and pulled out a white scarf. They snatched it from each other, but it remained in the hands of the stronger one – Benedictus – who purely and simply took possession of it . . . Next morning, at about half-past eleven, there was a visit from Wagner. Himself, in person, all alone, superb under his broad-brimmed buff felt hat. He was followed by two magnificent Newfoundland dogs. As always, I received him alone, and did not spare my enthusiasm for him . . . And, all at once, I caught sight of a sudden change of expression. He was very moved, and curiously troubled. 'I wasn't listening to you . . . I was looking at your mouth . . .' Then an inexpressible sadness came over him, and he added: 'I hadn't seen you as you are.' That day, it was as if a veil had suddenly been torn.

From that moment a new Wagner revealed himself in a very violent form. I tried to hold him back, and I introduced Benedictus to him . . . They stood there for a long while, looking one another in the face, unable to say a word to one another. Benedictus was dumbfounded. Wagner was charmed. And they threw themselves into each other's arms, and embraced each other. 'Since he is your friend,' Wagner said to me, 'he is worthy of you.'[9]

Judith had been invited to the second series of performances, which had ended on 23 August; but Wagner insisted that she remained for the next.

He had arranged [she told Suzanne] to keep a place for himself between Benedictus and me. He wanted to be on my left. As soon as the lights went out, he came back to his seat, and grasped my hand, my arm, so violently, that it was a long while before I could move them again. From time to time he completed some passage in his work with explanations or commentaries. He whispered, in a very low voice: 'I never want to hear my music again, except like this.' And he added: 'I should like to hear all my works in your arms . . .' For me it was as if Christ had suddenly begun to pay court to Mary Magdalen . . .

  He often used to say to me: 'You are my reward,' or again, 'my intoxicating luxury,' 'the abundance of my life,' and he recognized that I had inspired certain passages in his work. When he could catch me alone in some or other doorway, he used to kiss me. 'Not so loudly,' I said to him. 'Of course it must be loudly,' he would answer.[10]

Judith remained at Bayreuth until 2 September. That day, in his inadequate French, Wagner scribbled to her: 'Did I embrace you for the last time this morning? No! I shall embrace you again – I must – because I love you. Goodbye – be good to me!'[11]

For the first time, Wagner had seen Judith as an intensely desirable woman. It was not surprising. One day, at Wahnfried, as she was lying on a chaise longue, he had caught her looking at him. 'You were looking at me with such eyes,' he recalled. 'Like eyes which had gazed upon God Almighty.'[12] Judith had responded to his embraces; but it is almost certain that she did not surrender. She was elated, but she did not want to be Wagner's mistress. She did not love him, or desire him; and Wagner, who desired her, did not love her as he loved Cosima. As Pourtalès wrote in *Wagner: Histoire d'un artiste*,

  Judith certainly did not touch Wagner to his depths; none the less she stirred a poetic current in him . . .
  What he enjoyed in her was the proof that his power remained active. All he sought in the eyes of this beautiful Frenchwoman was a mirror which reflected back to him the image of the Parsifal that he wanted to be, the Parsifal without an age, without origins, as fabulous as himself. The words that he addressed to her were those of a ghost who was speaking to a ghost.[13]

Wagner had hoped that Judith would visit him again before she left Bayreuth. She did not do so. 'It would have revived me,' he confessed, 'to see you again . . . The good Benedictus has written some fine things to me. Could he have forgiven me for loving you? And I do love you! That is true! Oh, dear soul, sweet friend!'[14]

Judith returned to France, but Wagner continued to romanticize: 'I have come back from the first walk I have taken since – when? Instinct drew me towards Moritzhöfen . . . I spied the window. I delighted in your embraces. You do well not to write to me. But write to Cosima, to let me know how you are.'[15] Late that month he sent another letter: 'Dear soul, sweet friend! I love you still! . . . For me you were full of gentle fire, soothing, intoxicating! Oh, how I should love to embrace you again, dear sweet one! . . . I pity you your life. But everything is to be pitied. And I above all should be pitied if I followed your advice to forget you.'[16]

She had clearly indicated that she did not want a love affair with Wagner; but she did not wish to be forgotten. She was proud that she inspired him, eager to have her influence on his work. She answered him by sending some of her books to Bayreuth; but Wagner and Cosima were now resting from their festival exertions at the Hotel Vittoria at Sorrento, and it was from here, early in October, that Cosima wrote to her:

> The postmark of this letter will explain its delay, my dear Judith, . . . and now your beautiful books have arrived at Bayreuth, which I have left for God knows how long . . . *The Usurper:* isn't that the pretty Japanese novella I like so much? I shall send it to my father [Liszt], who is spending the winter at Pest. Did you go and see Victor Hugo in the end?[17]

Judith remained devoted to Hugo; she remained in correspondence with Wagner's wife. The new year opened, and Cosima continued to write. She entrusted Judith with buying clothes for her in Paris. Wagner was to conduct some concerts in London in May, and she needed her trousseau urgently. Cosima's demands for clothes were repeated and insistent, and Judith's kindness was severely tested. On 2 May, Cosima and Wagner arrived at 12, Orme Square – the Bayswater house where they were to spend their month-long London season. Wagner had invited Judith to London; whether or not Cosima knew of the invitation, Judith refused it. She preferred Paris and Brittany.

It was through the publisher Albert Lacroix that she had acquired the villa which she was to call Le Pré des Oiseaux, in honour of Walther von der Vogelweide – Walter du Pré des Oiseaux – in *Die Meistersinger*. Lacroix had wanted to establish Saint-Enogat as a resort, and he had had a series of châlets built there, round the Hôtel de la Mer. It was then, wrote Guichard, that, having lost the manuscript of one of Judith's stories, he suggested to her, by way of amends, that he would put one of his châlets at her disposal the following summer.[18] Judith went to Saint-Enogat, and fell in love with it. She and her friends used to spend the evenings at Mme

Lacroix's, and there, one day, they were asked to sign a list if they wanted to buy a plot of ground for building. Judith signed – so legend goes – without reflection. She had forgotten all about it when she was told that the foundations of her house were laid. She was dumbfounded, because she could hardly afford such a luxury. However, she had signed. She became a householder in spite of herself, and she had to borrow money to fulfil her obligations.

Le Pré des Oiseaux was to be a much-loved and much-used retreat. Among her guests was to be the aristocrat and aesthete Robert de Montesquiou (said to have been the original of Huysmans' des Esseintes and Proust's Charlus). In the mid-1870s he had begun to establish himself in literary salons and coteries; he had also met Judith, who was to have a strong influence on his developing tastes.

> I was very fond of Judith Gautier [he recalled in *Notes et Réflexions inédites*]. I often proved it to her in my writings. I went to see her at Saint-Enogat, where I spent a night at the bottom of her garden, in a little house she had put at my disposal. I called this retreat a *hat-box* or *cigar-box*, it was so diminutive . . .
> I have never been a real coward; all the same, this shelter, which was scarcely bigger than a beehive, seemed to me a trifle precarious. So we visited it, stopped up the holes, casemated it, and, when everything was finally done, we noticed that it was equipped with a service lift which gave on to the open country.[19]

Yamamoto, the Japanese artist, also came to Le Pré des Oiseaux, and decorated the wooden panelling.[20] Other visitors arrived to escape their creditors, as Sâr Péladan did on several occasions. Judith's old admirer Mohsin Khan, now first secretary of the Shah, used to stay at the villa; so did Charles Clermont-Ganneau, professor at the Collège de France. In the 'cigar-box', Pierre Louÿs wrote *Aphrodite*: the book which helped to determine the renaissance of the historical novel in France. Among Judith's other guests was the politician Paul Deschanel, one day to be the President of the Republic.

Suzanne Meyer-Zundel was notoriously inaccurate about dates; she said that Judith had first been to Saint-Enogat in 1867, and that Le Pré des Oiseaux had been built in 1868.[21] Whatever the truth of these statements, the letters from the Wagners suggest that Judith was newly installed there in 1877.[22] Alas, the world soon discovered the charm of the little seaside town. By 1892 *A Handbook for Travellers in France* described Saint-Enogat as 'a favourite watering-place, with good bathing,' and found the Hôtel de la Mer 'unpretending, but tolerable'.[23] By 1905, Saint-Enogat had merged into Dinard, and Dinard was a smart resort, and drew the fashionable world who wintered in Nice and Arcachon and Biarritz. Saint-Enogat – 'a resort of quieter character frequented by families' – now boasted half a dozen hotels; and visitors admired 'the picturesque *plage*, formed by a crescent bay,' overlooked by cliffs.[24] Le Pré des Oiseaux remained a small oasis of civilization among the hotels and the tennis courts, the constant ebb and flow of visitors. Two miles away, at another small resort, Saint-Lunaire, Émile Bergerat built the Villa Caliban, and there he and his family spent several months each summer.[25]

Meanwhile, in 1877, Wagner, like his wife, entrusted Judith with various errands. He wanted 'a very pretty ornamental sachet, in silk, etc.' for his stepdaughter Daniella's birthday. 'You must choose a fragrance for it which you like yourself, but really like, and perhaps you would add half a dozen paper sachets of powder, so that I can put them among my own linen in the morning. It will help me to be properly in touch with you when I sit down at the piano, to compose the music for *Parsifal* . . . And when shall I see you again? You were wicked enough to refuse my invitation for London. And why? Of course I know! Oh, how wicked you are! . . .'[26]

During the days of apotheosis in 1876, Judith had asked Wagner if he was still thinking about the Hindu drama for which she had sent him the *Bhagavad Gita*, the *Bhagavad Purana* and the *Mahabharata*. Wagner had preferred to write *Parsifal*. Now, at last, he had turned to his new opera, and Judith at once decided to translate it. Since she knew no German, Cosima offered to make a rough translation into French; Judith, 'with all possible devotion and care,' was to produce the final version.[27]

> Dear soul [this from Wagner on 9 November]!
> How fortunate they are, the waves of the sea and the caves of Fafner [in *Siegfried*], which have charmed you for so long! – But what about the perfumes of correspondence? . . .
> As for our perfume of correspondence, think about it seriously. Perhaps Rimmel's *Exquisité*, if that suits you. I should also like the pure Rose, but it must be strong . . .
> Goodbye, dear soul, sweet friend! –
> Love me for ever! –
>
> R W[28]

Judith remained content to be the friend and the translator, the faithful and devoted partisan. Her letters to Wagner have been destroyed, but she was patently embarrassed by the thought of her flirtation in Bayreuth. She had refused to visit Wagner in London; she did not intend the passionate encounters to recur. She began to feel disquiet at his tone. 'Dear soul!' he pleaded. 'Protest no more! I only remember your embraces as the most intoxicating, the most elating event of my life; it was a last gift from the gods . . . I do not protest, but – in my better moments – I keep a sweet, beneficent desire – the desire to kiss you again, and never to lose your heavenly love. – You are mine! Aren't you?'[29]

In a certain intellectual sense, she belonged to him. She had been his admirer since her youth, one of his foremost partisans in France. She had been his champion since the days of *Tannhäuser* in Paris; she had travelled to Munich and Baden, Brussels and Bayreuth, to hear his work. She had proclaimed his genius boldly and consistently, and she was to do so all her life. She was to be not only the translator but the inspiration of *Parsifal*.[30] She was to give him the bout of fever which he needed to create his Kundry. 'Was she Kundry?' asked Pourtalès. 'Was she Klingsor? Or a flower-maiden in his secret garden? . . . We do not know. But Wagner's erotic sense certainly found its final inspiration in her.'[31]

Judith was naturally flattered by this *amitié amoureuse:* and, in the heady atmosphere of Bayreuth, she had allowed herself to respond. But a kiss, even when it is passionate, does not always prove that a woman abandons herself completely. Henri de Régnier, who knew her in her later years, wrote that 'Judith Gautier denied that she had given in to Wagner's entreaties, which had gone as far as suggesting an elopement. She gave reasons for her refusal, which it would seem to me indiscreet to reveal . . .'[32] Possibly she was the mistress of Louis Benedictus; possibly she was still drawn to Hugo. Perhaps the recollection of Mendès still made her deeply contemptuous of men. Perhaps she found Richard Wagner unattractive. Whatever reason she chose to give for her refusal, she was clearly not in love with him. She was, however, feminine enough to make a mystery of the episode. Long after Wagner's death, towards the end of her own life, she made conflicting statements about it. She allowed a shadow of doubt to linger over the nature of the relationship.

In 1877, Wagner continued to send her ardent letters. Yet – curiously for a would-be lover – he made it plain where his devotion lay.

Dear soul [he wrote, on 20 November]!
    . . . I should have liked to have a word from you. Because I always see you, here – from my writing desk – on my right, on the chaise longue, looking at me (God, with what eyes!) when I am writing notes for my poor singers! – Oh! the most extraordinary thing is that you are the abundance of my poor life, so calm and sheltered since I have Cosima. –
You are my wealth – my intoxicating luxury![33]

It was a strangely cerebral courtship. Two days later, he wrote yet again:

. . . I want to have the rarest and most beautiful covering for my chaise longue – a covering which I shall call Judith! Listen! Find me one of those silk materials which they call lampas, or something like that. A yellow satin background – as pale as possible – sprinkled with networks of flowers – roses; not too big a pattern, because it isn't for curtains; it's generally used for small pieces of furniture. If there isn't any yellow, then very bright *blue*. I should need six yards.

All of this for the good mornings of *Parsifal!*

Goodbye, my dearest, my *dolcissima anima*.

Your

R W[34]

Wagner was insensitive, incorrigible, persistent. Judith wanted to forget what had happened at Bayreuth. He continued to refer to it, and to send her passionate letters. On 28 November he enquired: 'How are you? Dear, dear Judith! That *is* your name, isn't it? Oh, I know! And I often pass that house . . . down there – But everything has vanished, and the *Niebelung* with you. I don't think about it any more, and I only keep the memory of what happened down there, [what happened] down there! – Oh, sweet friend! Dear soul! Be good to me!'[35] On 4 December: 'Dear beloved! You will have the proofs of the German *Parsifal* within a few days; the only manuscript I have is the one which helps me to compose the music . . . Love me! Forget the linguistic problems! I love you.'[36]

Wagner was romanticizing about the unattainable. He thought, now, about his early struggles in Paris, and he imagined how it might have been had he discovered Judith in those desperate days:

. . . And now! Dear friend! Good angel! I dream of being once again in the muddy streets of Paris, a refugee abandoned by all the world! Suddenly – I meet you, Judith! You take me by the arm; you lead me home; you cover me with kisses! – Oh, it's very touching, very touching! – Oh, time and space! Those enemies! – I should have found you – then – a long time ago!

I embrace you.[37]

Judith reproved him for his fantasies.

Dear soul,

Do not think ill of me [he answered]. I am old enough to indulge in childishness. – I have three years of *Parsifal* ahead of me, and nothing must tear me away from the gentle peace of fruitful retirement . . .

Oh, dear soul, beloved soul! Everything is so tragic, everything which is *real!* But you will always love me – and as for me I could not fail to love you, even with the strongest will.

A thousand kisses.[38]

Christmas approached, and Judith sent boxes of presents to Bayreuth.

They were opened at once. On 24 December Wagner wrote again:

> Oh! My Judith! You are beautiful, and you are quite excessively kind! – I wept
> when I took the work of your grace out of that box. It contained more for me
> than I can tell you: the perfume of your soul!
>   Oh, how good and kind you are! May you be happy!
>   These boxes, this multitude of things must have caused you unheard-of
> trouble, looking for them – And yet, there was something which had been
> forgotten: – one of your kisses, which intoxicated me when I was utterly weary.
> – But come, let us be content.[39]

There was enough in Judith's boxes to content them all. Next day, Cosima
continued: 'The Japanese dressing-gown is an inspiration, the Henri II
bottle is a masterpiece, and the rest is incomparably delightful and
charming.'[40] Wagner had no doubt remained silent about his passion for
Judith; but he had naturally told Cosima that they were discussing the
translation of *Parsifal*.

> My husband [added Cosima] has told me all about your correspondence, and I
> laughed a good deal at the idea that I might be ruffled by your remarks on my
> translation! I had sent it to you in order to have them, and if you knew me you
> would know that I am *unruffleable* . . .
>   And so I deny that there can be an exact translation, but I certainly think that
> there can be an elegant and poetic translation, and I am doing the spadework,
> and allowing myself the most bizarre constructions, the most impossible
> expressions, to give you a *rough* glimpse of the original. It is for you to be
> elegant and poetic.[41]

Judith was about to translate *Parsifal;* she was also contributing an
occasional series, 'Les Muses de l'Orient,' to the *Journal officiel*. She
found it difficult to work. Late in December she was ill. 'It's your
bronchitis which distresses me,' wrote Wagner. 'As for the rest of your
worries, I'm not anxious . . . Oh, beautiful sweet one, whom I should
have found long ago! . . . Keep well, and always be sure of me, I shall
always love you.'[42] On 4 January he wrote again: 'And your bronchitis? I
want to know how it is getting on, and you say nothing about your health
. . . I embrace you, beautiful beloved, dear and adored soul!'[43]

Judith was silent. On 13 January he sent another letter: 'You will soon
have two acts of *Parsifal* in translation . . . But I'm talking about all this
simply to fill up the paper: it should only tell you that I am deeply and
seriously anxious about your silence. Could you be ill? Bronchitis? You
must reassure me, dear cruel one!'[44] Their letters crossed. She wrote to say
that she was still unwell. She still blamed much of her ill-health on her
privations during the Siege. Anxious to keep Wagner at a distance, she
also made much, so it seems, of her affection for Benedictus.

Your note today confirms my anxiety about your health [Wagner wrote on 14 January]. Happily I see you're still a little kind to me. But what bitterness is mingled with your kindness! You remember your sufferings in the Siege? It's horrible! We must always avoid any quarrels about things which are not worth the gunpowder they cost . . .

Oh, keep well and look after yourself! Believe that all I suffer from is knowing you so worthy of a love which makes you entirely happy. – Do you still love me?[45]

Cosima, too, was anxious about Judith's health; but she sent her the rough translation of *Parsifal*. 'Be kind enough to welcome it warmly and overlook all its faults, small and great, or, rather, do not overlook them, but correct them so that it is metamorphosed by your magic wand . . . We are still waiting for your news; none has come. Please don't go on frowning at us. Do tell us how you are . . .'[46]

Judith wrote more than once to Bayreuth. 'My beautiful abundance!' answered Wagner. 'Thank you for your dear letters. I should love you less because you are still unwell, which proves to me that my love does not have enough power over you. Try to get completely well, to give me confidence in myself . . . Oh, sweet soul! How inspired I felt in your arms! Must I forget it?'[47] He continued to remember, though Judith herself felt increasingly anxious to forget the interlude. On 27 January he wrote again:

My Judith! I say *meine Judith!*
Geliebtes Weib!
(see the dictionary! Ah!!) . . .
I absolutely insist that you are well, because – I often pass that poor house in Bayreuth, from which you drove me . . .
My soul! My dear! – In a day or two I shall have finished composing the first act. And then you will have samples of it.
Love me! Beautiful, ailing abundance![48]

I had hardly posted my last note [added Cosima], when my husband showed me your letter. It explained your silence, in the way that must sadden us most. Count on Le Pré aux Oiseaux [*sic*] to restore you completely and make you forget that miserable Siege! In the meantime you should have received the *Sonate d'Album*, and we shall soon send you the *Idyll*, which will give you even more pleasure . . .
Goodbye, my dear proprietress – why didn't you buy your land at Bayreuth? We should certainly have taken the place of the sea for you.[49]

Judith's ill-health continued into February.

Liebe Judith [this from Wagner, early in the month],
Your dear letter was not made to reassure me. – When you were here for the

Festspiele, you seemed to me so radiant, so strong in your constitution, that it increased my joy in seeing you again. Do try, I beg you, to avoid these bouts of illness: that is all you have to do to please me . . .

Dear beloved! I have finished the first act; you will have a sample of it as soon as I have attended to a multitude of affairs which I had neglected recently . . .

But – I love to see my address written in your hand! Oh – if! – if? – but that is the way of the world! Why – in the name of heaven – did I not find you in those days after the failure of *Tannhäuser* in Paris? Were you too young at the time? Silence, silence! – but let us love, let us love![50]

Then, suddenly, the months of passion were over. Possibly Cosima had suspected the warmth of Wagner's feeling, and decided to remove the pretext for correspondence. More probably Wagner himself had recognized, at last, that his love would remain in the mind: a necessary passion of the imagination which would not become a passion of the flesh. On 15 February he sent a final letter:

Dear soul,

I have asked Cosima to take charge of these·commissions now, or rather of the final arrangements about these commissions with which I have troubled you for so long . . . At the moment I am so worried by my affairs – which are not pleasant in the least – that I no longer find the freedom to continue writing *Parsifal*. Take pity on me! It will all end soon, and I shall again have these good moments of leisure, in which I like to talk to you about myself.

But don't torment yourself about me: my vexations will soon be over . . .

Be good to Cosima: write to her fully and properly. I shall hear everything. Love me for ever . . . We shall see each other again one day, at last.[51]

Chapter Thirteen

The passionate letters ceased to arrive from Wagner himself, but Cosima continued to show concern. She had never felt that Judith was a threat to her marriage, especially since Judith had extolled Benedictus, and dwelt at length on his devotion to her. Cosima could be light-hearted.

> My dear [she wrote on 26 February 1878], . . . now you must relax in Brittany, and spare yourself any further vexations . . .
>
> Time has hardly changed for us, for Wahnfried is like Tribschen, and here we are quite as much out of the world, the children have grown up but they haven't altered . . . Instead of *Siegfried*, it is *Parsifal* which is being composed . . . It is all on a slightly grander scale, but life is still the same. For you, my dear, it seems to me that life has improved. You [had] struck me [before] by your beauty, but also by your pallor and your unhealthy look; while, whatever you say, at Bayreuth you were dazzling: beauty has remained, and health, let us say Satisfaction, has come. You have found a friend who is worthy of you, 'what you dream of and do not find,' as you told me when you were here, and *estates* in the picture, too! The only objection to your *ownership* is the distance from Bayreuth – you really should, like Shakespeare, have set the sea [coast] in Bohemia! In short, if the Exhibition [of 1878] does not draw us to Paris, Le Pré aux Oiseaux [*sic*] will draw us to Brittany. Your godson is learning French with me, and he will understand you.[1]

Judith was silent. She was immersed in work: not only in her writing, but in the decoration of Le Pré des Oiseaux. Besides, she was not a natural correspondent. 'You could not imagine,' said Suzanne Meyer-Zundel, 'the anguish that came over her at the idea of writing a letter.'[2] On 2 March, Cosima wrote again:

> My dear, please don't ever apologize; I am better able than anyone to understand silence, for if the life of Paris and the great cities eats up time, solitary life absorbs it; I go through days and weeks and months without

knowing how, and without having done a quarter of what I wanted . . .

I am sure that your little house will be charming, original and graceful all at once . . .

The idyll is wonderful, a great little masterpiece, says our friend [Hans] Richter, and Mr Benedictus will say the same to you.[3]

On 13 July 1878, when they had lived apart for four years, Judith was granted a judicial separation from Mendès. He did not appear in court, and he was not even represented. It was Judith who had asked for the case to be heard, and it was decided in her favour, on the grounds of his adultery (a few months later, Augusta Holmès was once again pregnant by him).[4] The separation was, it seems, discussed in the Press. On 24 July, Flaubert told his publisher Georges Charpentier: 'I've read about Judith's assignation, and her husband's letter. It's *monstrous*' (he used the word *gigantesque*).[5] And there matters rested for many years; divorce was not yet legal in France.

Louis Benedictus was still determined to marry Judith; yet perhaps she was privately grateful that she could not commit herself. She was touched by his devotion; but when, at last, divorce became possible, it was, she wrote, 'too late. I had thought things over . . . One disappointing experience had been enough for me. I was no longer resolved to try again.'[6]

More than ever [so she told Suzanne Meyer-Zundel] I feel that the union is worthless. One is not made for that, because there is a mystery which the man does not understand . . . When by chance you meet your true complement, this state cannot in any case last more than two years with the same person. All the strings on the lyre have been played. And then other feelings have to be considered: love of the children, habit, comradeship, attachment, the bother of undoing something which has been done, and of changing what has been established, but none of that has anything more to do with love, properly speaking.[7]

In the meanwhile, Benedictus was established as Judith's worshipper. He was an old friend of Mallarmé and Villiers de l'Isle-Adam, and he was among the habitués of the Nouvelle-Athènes, in the place Pigalle. Villiers introduced Mendès to the little café. The novelist Paul Alexis reported to Zola that he had played chess there 'two or three times with a German [*sic*] who was very good at it, whom Duranty introduced to me: Benedictus – Mme Mendès' Benedictus.'[8] The Nouvelle-Athènes brought some unlikely characters together.

The separation from Catulle had not kept Judith from her writing. On 8 August 1878 Huysmans announced to Zola: 'The printer is so ill-equipped that he cannot undertake two books at the same time. The place is occupied at the moment by a book of Mme Judith Gautier's .·. . When this *chinoiserie* is set up, then the two little girls [*Les Sœurs Vatard*] will go to press.'[9] The *chinoiserie* in question was no doubt *Les Peuples étranges*, which Charpentier was to publish in 1879. Judith was also writing a series of articles for the *Journal officiel* on the latest International Exhibition. In February she had toured the sites and the unfinished buildings at the Champ-de-Mars and the Trocadéro; in May, June and July she had discussed the Chinese sculpture, costumes, jade and ivory, the Japanese exhibits, the fairy-tale Persian pavilion, the French furniture. Until late November she was to continue her impressions of English, Russian, Dutch and Portuguese furniture, furnishing fabrics and glass, and the jewels of imperial India. She still remained an art critic; and Flaubert, anxious to see his niece successful at the Salon, told her that he knew 'Judith Gautier on *Le Rappel*'.[10]

On 6 January 1879, Cosima wrote once again:

> We are afraid that we can't accept your kind invitation this year, my dear Judith; all of us, including Parsifal, are so well for our year of complete seclusion, that we have promised ourselves to live in 1879 as we did last year; but we have great plans for next winter: we should like to spend some time in Naples, and go from there to Spain, and make our way home through Saint-Enogat. Would that suit you? There will be nine of us descending on you, just as you urge us to do, and we shall leave when you dismiss us. So be patient!
>
> Thank you for your good wishes; one of my hopes is already fulfilled, because we know that you are free of drudgery. What a nice country, France! Whether or not there is an Emperor, it is enough to be gifted there to be given a competence and esteem. And so we greet you as head of a department, and congratulate you.[11]

Judith's appointment as head of a department remains a mystery: Guichard suggests that she might have had a post at the *Journal officiel*.[12] Suzanne Meyer-Zundel was to recall how, as a functionary appointed by decree, Judith had written for the paper under the pseudonym F. Chaulnes.[13] 'Why haven't you sent us your book on the Exhibition?' added Cosima.[14] Judith had presumably hoped to publish her collected articles, but it seems that the book did not appear.

Judith sent a sonnet to Wagner in honour of his birthday, and Cosima read it aloud to his birthday guests. Sending their thanks to Judith, she added: 'Do you remember telling me at Tribschen that you had no women friends? Now you have them in plenty . . . It would be enough to prevent me from coming to see you, but I have a passion for generosity, and there

– you have already been forgiven.'[15] Judith already inspired the jealous devotion of other women – as she was one day to do with Mme Lepelletier and, above all, with Suzanne Meyer-Zundel. Whatever her self-sufficiency during her marriage, she now had a number of women friends. She dedicated *Isoline* to the Comtesse Alphonsine Bowes; she was later to dedicate *Tristiane*, a play for marionnettes, 'to the memory of my dear friend Antoinette, baronne de Poilly, *née* du Hallay-Coëtquen'. Cosima continued to chide her: 'I clasp you tightly to my heart, and as if you had no woman friend but me.'[16]

In the autumn of 1879, Cosima and Wagner were planning a visit to Saint-Enogat; but Wagner's movements still remained uncertain. 'As for Naples [this from Cosima on 5 September], I daren't say anything, because either I am much mistaken or the affair is decided, but I still don't see us there . . . And now here's a proposition: if we settle in Naples, why shouldn't you come and see us there? . . . And then we can make our way back by easy stages to Saint-Enogat, from which we can descend on Bayreuth. Doesn't that itinerary appeal to you?'[17]

Judith waited hopefully for a visit from the Wagners. She continued to show her devotion to Victor Hugo; and Hugo gracefully acknowledged his copy of *Les Peuples étranges*: 'Madame, I should be stranger than your people if I did not finally read you and write to you. Let me tell you that I am with you, that I am enchanted, and that I very humbly kiss your feet.'[18]

Judith did not only enchant him, she continued to be his guest. On 26 December he invited her to dinner, and demanded that Mendès was kept away. Juliette Drouet, relegated to the role of steward, was obliged to bow before his will:

> I am going to busy myself to have Catulle Mendès warned that he mustn't come this evening because his wife will be here. Yet it is very much against my feelings that I resign myself to receiving her. I hope that you will not make me repent it and that you will spare me everything which might remind me of a past which I detest. For my part I promise to be perfectly polite to her, nothing more, nothing less.[19]

Juliette, wrote Escholier, tried in vain to intercept the love letters which were sent to the avenue d'Eylau. Judith was not troubled or deterred. Having written to Hugo in Chinese, she sent him – in translation – an eloquent poem by Sádi: 'I am with you and I cannot reach you . . . As, in the desert, the camel pants with thirst, and it is burdened only with water.'[20] On 24 July 1880, sorting Hugo's correspondence, Juliette chanced to read a letter from the publishers, Charavay:

They ask you for the famous sonnet [she wrote bitterly] . . . The sublime wretch who wrote [*Ave, Dea*] and the woman to whom it was addressed are wonderfully well, for nothing fattens and maintains body and soul like betrayal.

Suffering is only for the stupid in love, the lovers who trust. Which explains why I suffer so in body, heart and spirit this morning.[21]

————Chapter Fourteen————

On 20 February 1880, *L'Événement* announced that Mme Judith Gautier had organized a series of six Wagnerian evenings. Through the generosity of Nadar, they were to be held in the hall of his photographic studio in the rue d'Anjou-Saint-Honoré. It was indeed a generous gesture, for Nadar detested Wagner, especially since he himself had been a character in *Une Capitulation*; but he was prepared to lend his hall from time to time for artistic gatherings (in 1874 he had lent it for the first Impressionist Salon).[1] On 28 February, in *Le Figaro*, 'Un Monsieur de l'Orchestre' indulged in journalistic fantasy: he waxed indignant at the noise produced by four pianos in concert in a crowded street, and he proposed to banish the performers to the esplanade des Invalides. 'For the past two days, all Nadar's neighbours who are not compelled to stay in Paris for business are making preparations to travel. They have resigned themselves to leaving for the country three months earlier than usual . . .'

These performances, recorded Servières,

> were attended only by Wagnerians, and the Press were not invited. They consisted of a reading by M. Émile Marras of a text by Mme Judith Gautier, the analysis of the works given in the programme, and the performance of excerpts from Wagner's lyrical dramas.
>
> The singers were MM. Herman Devriès, Pagans and the tenor Provost; the women's roles were taken by Mme Irma Marié, Mlles Abella and Zélo-Duran; the usual accompanists were M.G. Fauré, M. André Messager, M.H. Ghys, MM. Chevrillard, Esposito and Luzzato.
>
> For the performance of the extracts from the symphonies, four pianists represented the orchestra. They were conducted by M. Benedictus. Thus prepared to appreciate the finest pages in Wagner's work, the audience went home with an impression which was no doubt incomplete, but favourable.[2]

On 4 March, at the first Wagnerian evening, there were extracts from

Rienzi and *Der fliegende Holländer*. On 11 March there were excerpts from *Tannhäuser* and *Lohengrin*. On 18 March came *Parsifal*, the *Faust* overture and *Huldigungsmarsch*. On 25 March came *Tristan* and *Die Meistersinger*. On 1 April there followed *Das Rheingold* and *Die Walküre*. On the final evening, 8 April, there were excerpts from *Siegfried* and *Götterdämmerung*. The Wagners were delighted by Judith's enterprise.

> We are enchanted for you [wrote Cosima] that it has been such a success, and we congratulate your friend [Benedictus] on all the courage he has shown. We were sure that it was you who had been the soul of the campaign, and we admire the order of the programme . . .
> As things stand at present, Brittany seems to have come to nothing, but when the warm weather arrives we may perhaps think differently . . .
> Goodbye, my dear Judith. I am sad to know that you are sad, and I should like to know the passing reason for your grief.[3]

Posterity would also like to know the reason for her grief. Possibly it was the thought that she was thirty-four, disillusioned by marriage, embittered by separation, and hardly compensated, now, by the presence of Benedictus. She had demanded much of life: a passion as intense and as single-minded as her own. She had found devotion only in admirers whom she could not love.

Lesser mortals continued to love and admire her. On 3 June, in the handsome hôtel de Poilly, in the rue du Colisée, Mme de Poilly staged Judith's Chinese play, *Le Ramier blanc*. Invitations had been sent to 'the élite of aristocratic and artistic society'.[4] The invitations and programmes were printed in French and in Chinese. A member of the Chinese Embassy had instructed the performers in the etiquette of Peking. The Chinese entertainment, said Vento, in his study of the salon, 'became the most refined of Parisian pleasures'.[5]

The Wagners returned from their travels to Wahnfried. Their visit to Le Pré des Oiseaux seemed as far away as ever. 'There were too many obstacles cast on our path,' Cosima confessed, 'for me to pronounce the word St Enogat.'[6]

It was Judith who made the journey. On 29 September 1881, she herself returned to Bayreuth. It was, she wrote in her diary, with a beating heart that she entered Wahnfried,

> this house which, despite the warm welcome we always find there, still remains a sacred place for us . . .
> All the family were gathered in the salon, which was lit up by a ray of sunlight. Liszt had come to spend a few weeks with his grandchildren; he was

superb, with his long white hair, his bushy eyebrows, under which his lion's eyes were shining. My godson was already quite tall; he had a massive forehead, and blue eyes of exquisite sweetness.

The Master came in from the garden. Still the same! Or, rather, younger! Really, the immortals defy time.

He welcomed us with the affectionate warmth he feels for faithful friends – the friends by whom he knows he is truly loved.[7]

The next day, she arrived early at Wahnfried, to take a solitary walk in the garden.

In front of the salon, round the fountain, lies the pleasure garden: pretty lawns, baskets of Bengal roses, flowers of every kind, though many of them are already shrivelled by the frost. A dense wood, like a wall, encloses this open space. One must plunge into its shadows to approach the tomb of which so much has already been said: the tomb which, in a rather lugubrious fantasy, the Master had built at the same time as his house. It is completely enveloped by the thick copse, from which there is no outlet. Only when autumn strips the trees does one perceive a big slab of grey marble through the confusion of branches . . .

The bell rings, and summons us back to the house.[8]

Years later, in conversation with Suzanne Meyer-Zundel, Judith recalled the overwhelming sadness of the visit. This time, perhaps, she had found herself more attached to Wagner; he had wisely kept a distance between them.

In 1881 it was, alas, the heartrending time of regrets. Unfortunately Wagner was already touched by illness. The whole of the drama lies in the displacement of those two dates. It was for him in 1881 what it had been for me in 1876. This time he chose to keep something distant, far-away between us, the logical reaction to my exuberance . . .

It was on a fine September afternoon, at about two o'clock. 'The sun is out for you,' he said to me . . .

I still remember that I picked a small bunch of flowers from the garden. Next day everything was touched by the frost. The cold had suddenly come. . . .

And the withered flowers that Judith sometimes took out of the casket with its touching mementoes went back [recalled Suzanne] with the other relics: locks of hair, crumbs of bread gleaned from the Master's plate, . . . and a little white paper collar from a lamb cutlet which had been served to him . . .

When we had occasion to be alone for a moment [Judith continued], Wagner spoke of his great sadness at growing old in every way . . .[9]

Judith had no financial sense, and she was apt to spend money without counting. Victor Hugo, who was himself a multi-millionaire, had once obtained a pension for her father from the Government of National Defence. Now, in his imperial tone, he asked the Republic for an annual

Théophile Gautier. From a photograph by Nadar, *c.* 1856

Ernesta Grisi in 1850. From the pastel by Léon Riesener

Ernesta Grisi in old age. From a photograph

Carlotta Grisi. From a photograph by Nadar, *c.* 1865

Théophile Gautier with Ernesta Grisi and their daughters, probably at Neuilly, 1857. From a photograph by Richebourg

Estelle and Judith Gautier. This photograph of the poet's daughters was taken by Nadar in about 1862

Catulle Mendès in 1863, at about the time he met Judith Gautier. From an engraving by Fernand Desmoulin

Mme Judith Mendès. From a photograph by Nadar, *c.* 1870

Mme Judith Gautier. This photograph by Nadar was taken in about 1875, after her separation from Catulle Mendès

Augusta Holmès, composer. This portrait of Augusta in her later years was one of a series of pictures of celebrities issued by Chocolat Guérin-Boutron

CHOCOLAT GUÉRIN-BOUTRON

428 Augusta Holmès, Compositeur de musique

Victor Hugo in later life. From a
photograph by Nadar

Richard Wagner. From a photograph
taken in London, 1877

M. and Mme Théophile Gautier *fils*.
These drawings by Princess
Mathilde were done at Saint-Gratien
in October 1874

Le Pré aux Oiseaux. This villa at Saint-Enogat was Judith Gautier's retreat for the last forty years of her life

Judith Gautier. From a pen-and-wash drawing by John Singer Sargent, now in the Royal Collection at Windsor *(copyright reserved. Reproduced by gracious permission of Her Majesty the Queen)*

M. and Mme Émile Bergerat. These photographs of Judith Gautier's brother-in-law and sister were taken in later life (*Phot. Bibl. nat. Paris*)

Catulle Mendès in middle age *(Nadar)*

30, rue Washington. A fancy-dress party at Judith Gautier's, at the turn of the century
(*Phot. Bibl. nat. Paris*)

Judith Gautier in her garden at Saint-Enogat. Two photographs first published in 1910

Suzanne Meyer-Zundel and Judith Gautier. From a photograph taken at Le Pré aux Oiseaux, 1 June 1917 (*Phot. Bibl. nat. Paris*)

grant to the daughter. 'My dear Minister, my dear friend,' he announced to Jules Ferry, the Minister of Public Instruction, ' . . . Théophile Gautier's daughter, Madame Gautier, needs a pension. It is enough that this is so, and that I tell you, for the pension to be given.'[10] It was given.

The pension eased immediate problems, but it could not be a livelihood. Judith continued her prolific writing. In 1882 Charavay published *Isoline*, a sentimental novella, romantic almost to the point of innocence. It was set in Brittany, near Saint-Malo; and one is tempted to see a reflection of her own intense melancholy in that of the young naval officer, Gilbert Hamon:

> The sea and its oppressive solitude, that was all he found in his heart. The earth seemed foreign to him. He never felt far away or near, no one loved him and he loved nobody; and so it was that death, which had just brushed against him, had drawn from him no sigh of regret.
>
> 'All sailors are like that,' he told himself. But he was only outwardly resigned, and very often, on the calm sea, though his cold face bore no trace of them, there were tempests raging inside him.
>
> Now, as he tried to feel a little joyful impatience at coming home, he was more than ever aware of the destitution of his soul.
>
> 'Spleen!'
>
> The word rose to his lips, and he felt himself enveloped in grey clouds, like the sky.[11]

Gilbert Hamon is, of course, on the eve of romance. He falls in love almost at once with a mysterious girl who lives in a local château – entirely alone except for her servants. She is imprisoned there by her father, who cannot forgive her for the fact that his wife had died in giving birth to her. Isoline is rescued from thoughts of suicide, and from taking the veil, by the ardent, chivalrous young man. She disguises herself as a ship's boy, and sails away with him, proving the omnipotence of love.

A second edition of *Isoline* was published, again in 1882. On this occasion it appeared with a collection of other tales. *La Fleur-Serpent* is a macabre fantasy, in the manner of Edgar Allan Poe. In *Trop tard*, Judith, like her father, writes of the romantic love of the impossible. The narrator falls in love – as Guy de Malivert had done, in *Spirite* – with a dream woman. Unlike Malivert, he finds that she is real. He had recalled her from his childhood; when he finds her again, she is old and grey. 'We were destined for one another,' he writes, 'but our lives have not coincided.'[12] This story – down to the detail of the big Venetian mirror, the mirror which had hung, once, at Neuilly – is strangely reminiscent of Gautier's novel.

Yet, as Anatole France was to observe, Judith lost her charm and poetry when she wrote on European themes; and, whatever the merit or interest of *Isoline* or *Trop tard*, it is her Japanese tale which enchants the reader.

L'Auberge des roseaux en fleur is the story of two young samurai in love. Early one morning they set out in the hope of meeting two sisters whom they had seen at an inn a year ago. 'The air was deliciously fresh, the sun, still overcast, seemed like a ruby lost in muslin, and pink clouds rolled from the horizon, like silk cushions cast aside by a man awakening from sleep.'[13] The story is infused with poetry, lit up by a delighted visual sense. The girls return to the inn, 'their creamy complexions slightly flushed by their transparent pink parasols'.[14] The samurai spend the day with their family. Alas, both have fallen in love with the same girl. She marries the one who proposes to her, but she herself loves his rival. He is obliged to marry her sister. For love of one another, they both accept a marriage which is not an affair of the heart.

A copy of *Isoline* was inscribed: 'To the amazing and delightful poet and friend Robert de Montesquiou, this book which is much too simple for him'.[15] Another copy of *Isoline* was sent to the Wagners, who were once again on holiday. 'It is making the rounds of Palermo,' Cosima announced on 2 March, 'after giving us the greatest pleasure.'[16]

It was this year that Judith published *Richard Wagner et son oeuvre poétique*, the latest of her tributes to the god of Bayreuth. The first pages of the book were, she explained, 'a fragment of the memoirs which I may perhaps publish some day, not because my life is worth the trouble of being told, but because it has often touched the lives of very illustrious artists'.[17] The recollections of Wagner were in fact to reappear in the volume of memoirs which she was one day to devote to him.

Yet, in 1882, Judith published her study of Wagner with an unexpected sense of disappointment and resignation. After more than twenty years of devotion to his cause, she was now lost in despondency.

> I have recently abandoned all idea of proselytism; having fought for a long while, I am giving up the struggle, at the moment when for many people victory appears to be probable. I have reasons for doing this which I shall merely indicate, and they seem to me to be decisive.
>
> What I have long considered to be ordinary and inevitable resistance, the instinctive hatred which any public feels at first for the innovators of genius, is, I am much afraid, more than this in France . . . For us, art is above all an amusement, seriousness frankly bores us, and if, by chance, we happen to accept a masterpiece in one of our theatres, it is simply as a curiosity . . .
>
> *Lohengrin* will probably be a success in Paris, but we shan't go further than that. The great Scandinavian epic, the metaphysical loves of Tristan and Isolde, the mysticism of Parsifal, will not reach us. That is why I have recognized the generous error in which I have persisted for so long, and I am giving up the fruitless struggle . . .

This book is addressed, then, only to the few initiates who have entered the veiled inner sanctuary of the new art.[18]

Ernest Reyer was, like Mendès and many others, so angered by *Une Capitulation* that, in spite of Judith's pleading, he could not now consider Wagner the man.[19] Here, if nowhere else, Judith remained above questions of nationality. Wagner had always been, to her, an international figure. 'My one ambition,' she confessed, 'is to be as useful as I can to that intelligent minority which, for me, alone fills this world, and, I earnestly hope, will alone fill the other, if it exists; for I am quite convinced, as Charles Baudelaire maintains, "that it is the small number of the elect which makes Paradise".'[20]

It was that July that the theatre in Bayreuth summoned the patrons of the Wagnervereine, that is to say the members of the Wagnerian societies, to hear the master's new work, *Parsifal*. The first performances, restricted to the patrons, were given on 26 and 28 July. The profane were not allowed to hear the opera until 30 July. This time, many French enthusiasts had made the journey to Bayreuth. Among them were Saint-Saëns, Delibes, Vincent d'Indy, Mendès, and Édouard Dujardin, one day to found and edit the *Revue Wagnérienne*.

Judith also went to Bayreuth. It is said that, at the première of *Parsifal*, she sat with Wagner in his box. He wept unceasingly, and told her: 'All is well, but I should need to be twenty to enjoy it.' He was already stricken by illness. One day he fainted during a performance; when he regained consciousness, he said: 'I have escaped again.'[21] It was probably this visit that Judith had in mind when, years later, she told Suzanne Meyer-Zundel:

The last visit, the farewell visit [to Wagner], was terribly poignant, but moving and beautiful. [He was] very pale, grave and sad, and his fear and anguish were visible. 'Are you leaving?' . . . He wept, and kissed me on the eyes. And, as if all his strength abandoned him, he murmured: 'Life is a tragedy.' Then he went over to the piano and improvised some phrases of unheard-of beauty, but of inexpressible sadness. These phrases were the echoes of his grief.[22]

Some months later, on 13 February 1883, just before his seventieth birthday, at the height of his international glory, Wagner died in Venice.

My poor beloved friend [Judith wrote to Cosima],
    Have the heroism to live for your children, for Siegfried who is his flesh and soul – Siegfried, whom you must see grow up to manhood. Draw this strength from the inexhaustible and grievous treasure of memories, from the sublime

existence that was yours. Regain possession of it day by day, and try to live on
memory, poor dear Friend!

What is our grief, the grief of us who were so far from his heart, beside your
despair? And yet we feel great sorrow!

I kiss your hands with much affection.

Judith Gautier[23]

Now that Wagner was safely dead, and buried, as he had wished, at
Bayreuth, the Parisian public could admire him. On 11 April 1884 he
entered the programme of the Société des concerts du Conservatoire, with
the overture to *Tannhäuser*. It was official consecration. On 8 February
1885 there appeared the first issue of the *Revue Wagnérienne*.

Chapter Fifteen

On 11 May 1883, half a century after she had become Victor Hugo's mistress, Juliette Drouet died of cancer. She had given him a lifetime of love and of abnegation. Hugo was in his eighty-second year, and, as Paul Meurice told Maurice Barrès: 'From the day she died, he was finished . . . He wanted the end.'[1] On 12 August he arrived at Villeneuve, on Lake Geneva, 'all white and wrinkled,' remembered Romain Rolland, 'with pursed brows and sunken eyes. He seemed to me to have emerged from the distant ages.'[2]

If Charles Mount, the critic, is to be believed, Judith embarked this summer on another love affair. Mabel de Courcy Duncan, who knew her well at the end of the century, thought that John Singer Sargent 'visited Judith quite often when she first bought her villa at Saint-Enogat'.[3] Whether or not that was true, in the summer of 1883 Sargent spent much of his time in Brittany. He stayed at Les Chênes, at Paramé, the château of Pierre Gautreau, the Parisian banker, while he was painting a portrait of his wife in the sporadic sittings she allowed him.[4] According to Mount, he seems to have spent much of his enforced leisure at Le Pré des Oiseaux.

Judith Gautier [writes Mount] had refused Lembach when that artist, then at the height of his fashionable reputation, asked her to sit, and this she did for no better reason than a distaste for keeping still. Sargent, however, declared himself an ardent admirer of her beauty, and because of this and an apparent desire to humour him, she felt greater need to let him have his way . . . What their relationship might have been early that summer, when his visits began, cannot be said. Wagner figured in his mind as a titanic genius, . . . and to know someone who had been intimate with him doubtless flattered this young painter of twenty-seven. As the summer wore on, and he continued to visit, painting her again and again, some gentle trace of a faint incense comes out of his pictures, and the revelations they supply of both artist and model. More and more one becomes conscious of trampling over the stale remains of a romance.[5]

There appears no evidence in Judith's correspondence that she was enamoured of Sargent: indeed she does not even mention him. Charles Mount himself offers no facts to support the suggestion of a romance, or his statement that three oils, a watercolour, a wash drawing, and a pencil drawing, all date from that summer.[6] A love affair appears improbable. The date remains a matter of speculation, and Richard Ormond, in his book on Sargent, his great-uncle, observes that 'stylistically a date of 1883 or soon afterwards is acceptable', but that there is no proof that Sargent and Judith met that summer, or that all his portraits were executed at the same time.[7] However, the Ormond family own a pencil and watercolour sketch of Judith which was done in about 1883. All the likenesses show a woman of similar age; and their number and inspiration suggest that Sargent, like many others, was haunted by Judith's beauty.

In 1883 she was thirty-eight, buxom and seductive as an oriental princess. He was the only painter to reflect her magic. He himself, recorded Mount, said that the one likeness which satisfied him was the pencil drawing of her head. Yet neither Judith nor her admirers could have wished for a more amorous series of portraits: a series which caught the atmosphere of the early 1880s, the prevailing oriental influence, and her own unique, enthralling presence. In the oil study called *A Gust of Wind*, Sargent records her standing on the dunes at Saint-Enogat, wearing a long white robe with flowing sleeves. One hand holds her broad-brimmed hat in place, the other holds her skirt against the wind. She is seen from below, against a gentian summer sky.

One weekend [continued Mount], interrupted again in his work on the portrait of Mme Gautreau, . . . he appears to have travelled with Judith Gautier, for the wooded landscape and the stream which figure in the picture called *In the Country* are totally unrelated to her Brittany home . . .

Filled with enthusiasm, . . . he decided to do a large picture of her, evoking visions of a full-length portrait. Mlle Gautier later said he drew her many times for this portrait, and then, because he did not have a suitable canvas of the right proportions with him, went out and broke up a kitchen table to provide a wood panel over which he could paint in the white heat of inspiration.[8]

The painting was indeed inspired. The largest and most ambitious of his portraits of Judith, it shows her standing beside a grand piano in a dark interior lit by candlelight; she is wearing a kimono, and a flower in her hair. It is a serene and intimate evening scene. Mabel Duncan declared that it was 'the best portrait of Judith Gautier by Sargent, in my opinion, and almost by the common consent of her friends.'[9] Judith herself later said that, having finished his sketches for her portrait, Sargent had thrown down his brushes in despair, 'saying that he would never succeed in rendering her mouth and smile in oils'. It was after this that he made the crayon sketch which he signed.[10]

There are other pictures of Judith at Saint-Enogat, reflected in her undated letters to Robert de Montesquiou.

> Dear friend [goes one of them],
>   It is under your lovely parasol, set up in the peaceful shade of a rose laurel, that I thank you for the charming gift which has been my delight for the past week. I have already wanted, twice, to write to you, because I have an indiscretion to confess and some news to tell you. When I left you, on the way back from Montrouge, I showed some of your sonnets to Leconte de Lisle, who, as you know, is to me the ultimate judge. As I expected, he was very interested and charmed by certain stanzas, especially by the one which begins 'dans le pré nébuleux des anémones pâles.' He saw you as a true poet, and he advised me to make violent efforts to tear you away from *Mallarmisme* once and for all . . .
>   The parasol really enchants me; thank you again, write to me soon, and don't let me lack sonnets.[11]

The sonnets were apparently lacking. Annette de Poilly admonished Montesquiou: 'I have had a letter from Judith; she spends her life under her Japanese parasol, and she is worried not to have heard from you.'[12]

Under her Japanese parasol, or in her salon, which recalled the Second Empire and the Empire of the Green Dragon, Judith meditated on literature. In October 1883, Hugo sent her a copy of his latest book, *L'Archipel de la Manche*.

> Beloved Master [she answered]!
>   How happy I am to have to thank you!
>   How could it be that you were concerned with me and that I did not divine this providence in my dark sky? Yet I think about you very often on my rock, where I am more afraid of the blows of fate than the buffets of the sea, although I am extremely cowardly in the face of a tempest.
>   Your study of Guernsey and Jersey is exquisite, and it has a charm the more when one reads it a few knots from the islands . . .[13]

Judith thought not only of Hugo but of her father, his disciple. In 1884, with loving admiration, she introduced a new edition of one of his most famous works of fiction:

> How many novels, already imagined and sketched out, might have taken their places beside *Le Capitaine Fracasse!* . . . One, among the rest, the most

regretted of them all, was called *Le Vieux de la montagne*. It was an oriental story, full of fairy-tales and wonders, which my father was particularly fond of, and he very much hoped to write it. But the terrible toils of journalism did not allow him to; he could never break this chain which weighed so heavily upon him.[14]

Nine years later, she herself was to publish a historical romance set in the Holy Land, and called *Le Vieux de la montagne*. One wonders how much it owed to the fairy-tales and the wonders of her father's story.

Meanwhile, in 1884, she brought out *La Femme de Putiphar*. It was her first contribution to a series, *Les Grandes Amoureuses*, which was published by Albert Lacroix. It was a notable gallery of historical vignettes: Mendès offered Messalina, Daudet was to write on Mme Roland, Houssaye on Mme de Montespan, and Leconte de Lisle on Chimène. Judith created a lyrical picture of ancient Egypt, a primitive impression of Potiphar's wife, burning with unrequited love for Joseph, her husband's slave. Lacroix had grand ambitions for his pantheon of love. He announced that Judith would contribute a further fifteen essays on the great loves of the past, from Venus and the Queen of Sheba to St Theresa. A book on Iseult duly appeared in 1885; Lacroix then announced that Judith would also write on Mary Queen of Scots and Cleopatra. It is not known if any of these books was written.[15]

On 22 May 1885 – on what would have been Wagner's birthday – Victor Hugo died. He was eighty-three. Judith left no record of her feelings; but, while his lying-in-state and his national funeral were planned, she scribbled to Montesquiou:

> My dear,
>   The papers say under the Arc de Triomphe; do you want to see him on his deathbed? I may perhaps learn something today. Until now the house has been very much shut. If one can get near I will let you know . . .[16]

She herself went to see Hugo on his deathbed in the avenue Victor-Hugo: the street – once the boulevard Haussmann – had for years borne his name. She modelled his head in wax: the head of a Jupiter who had dominated French literature in his century.[17]

Leconte de Lisle was now, said Fouquier, in *Profils et Portraits*, 'the grandest, at least the most grandiose, of our poets'.[18] He kept his hatred for utilitarian civilization. Yet he did not scorn the admiration of the younger generation, or of his latterday Egeria, Mme Guillaume Beer. Mme Beer, who wrote under the pseudonym Jean Dornis, was one day to publish *Leconte de Lisle intime*. She had a *salon* 'much esteemed by the élite of Paris', and Leconte de Lisle often used to visit her at her lodge at Louveciennes, an eighteenth-century folly in which she settled late every spring. She used to give the most enchanting dinners.[19]

There were other compensations for living in the vulgar nineteenth century. Leconte de Lisle had not hated conventional life enough to disdain his appointment as librarian to the Senate; nor had he finally rejected the prospect of the Académie-Française. 'As for the Académie,' he had explained to Heredia on 9 August 1883, 'I renounce it absolutely, unless Hugo should die before me. It would be a fine speech to make and a tribute which it would be my duty to pay him . . .'[20] Now Hugo had died; his chair remained vacant, and the election was to be held on 11 February 1886. 'Leconte de Lisle counted his votes, and he knew that Immortality was imminent . . . His friends Paul Hervieu, Judith Gautier, Psichari, Henry Houssaye, Verlaine, vied with each other to assure him so.'[21] Leconte de Lisle won Hugo's seat on the first ballot. On 31 March 1887, he was finally received among the Forty.

He spent his last, Immortal years in physical decline.

My dear friend [this to Judith],

Forgive me for not having answered your affectionate letter before. It is true, I have no reason to offer you for my silence except the sad state of my brain, where nothing stirs any more. Add to that a perpetual malaise, and constant neuralgia and fits of choking, in short a foretaste of absolute decrepitude. Flaubert said that he seemed to be crossing an endless solitude to go he knew not where, and that he himself was at once the desert, the traveller and the camel. Personally I am, above all, the camel, to judge by the tedium which weighs upon my shoulders . . .

Your old rheumaticky, pituitous, ailing and ragged

Leconte de Lisle[22]

Chapter Sixteen

In that little house in the rue de Longchamp where, as they say of the princesses in the fairy-tales, she grew in wisdom and beauty every day, Judith learned from her childhood to understand and appreciate the rarest, the most exquisite, the most curious forms of art . . . That little house, bathed in winter in the mists of the Seine and the vapours of the Bois, was filled, by the master's voice, with all the poetry of the Orient of which he dreamed . . .

It was there, as a child, that Judith Gautier fed on poetry and learned to love exotic beauty. Nothing was lacking to complete her education as an artist, except perhaps the commonplace and the ordinary.[1]

Anatole France spoke truly; but the inspiration of her father, the lessons from Tin-Tun-Ling, the vision of the Japanese in the London arcade, had not been alone in fostering Judith's passion for the East. Hugo had written of Egypt, Turkey and Persia in *La Légende des siècles*, Baudelaire had dreamed of Mauritius. Leconte de Lisle had sung of Persia and of India, Heredia had written a Chinese sonnet. Another of Gautier's friends, the art critic Philippe Burty, had become the most fervent of the apostles who proclaimed the beauty of Japanese art to the Western world.

The taste for the Japanese had been encouraged by historical events. In 1868, Japan had undergone a political transformation. The Mikado had grown tired of being set apart on the pretext of preserving his sanctity. He himself had seized power.[2] The revolution which he had started had brought the ruin of the great feudal families and their dependants. People had begun to sell their treasures, and an admiring Europe had found itself in the presence of an unsuspected, captivating art.

Edmond de Goncourt, who possessed a virtual museum of *japonaiseries*, had been among the first in France to create the fashion. He and Heredia scoured the Left Bank for Japanese works of art. 'The Japanese is triumphant,' *La République des Lettres* had declared in 1876.[3] It triumphed even in the theatre, with plays by Ernest d'Hervilly and William Busnach.

La Vie moderne diagnosed that the Japanese illness was acute, and that 'it might be considered a kind of artistic *jaundice*'.[4] The Paris Exhibition of 1878 had fostered the general infatuation. A retrospective exhibition of Japanese art was organized in the rue de Sèze, in April 1883, by Louis Gonse, the editor of the *Gazette des Beaux-Arts*. The exhibition was based entirely on private collections. Among those who lent exhibits were Philippe Burty, Sarah Bernhardt and Heredia – who lent no fewer than thirty-nine pieces from his collection.

Judith had lent nothing, but her passion for Japan remained intense. In 1885 there appeared *Poèmes de la Libellule*. In Burty's charming phrase, she had collected Japanese poems just as the Japanese themselves collected fireflies in miniature cages. She had translated them after the literal version by her friend the Marquis Saionzi, the Japanese Minister to France, and they were illustrated by Yamamoto, a Japanese artist living in Paris. The de luxe edition was a bibliophile's delight; on 22 May, Burty reviewed it in *La République Française*. He kept the book in his library; he also kept *Les Trois Baisers du serpent* and *Le Livre de Jade*, *Le Dragon impérial*, an inscribed copy of *L'Usurpateur* and two copies of *Les Peuples étranges*.[5]

Judith's love of the oriental embraced a number of civilizations. In 1886 the *Petit Bottin des Lettres et des Arts* described her as 'a Chinese princess, brought up by subtle mandarins.'[6] She was not only enamoured of Japan and China. The same year, Frinzine published *Iskender* in book form. It was, wrote Paul Ginisty in *L'Année littéraire*, 'a Persian story told with every sort of magic in style'.[7] It was introduced by a sonnet, *L'Orient*, by Leconte de Lisle. 'It is a sort of fairy-tale,' so he explained, 'a story from the Arabian Nights, but it is all brilliant in its style and imagination.'[8]

Judith deserved the tribute – as an orientalist and as his loyal friend and admirer. She had been among the most assiduous visitors to his *salon*; she had entertained him at Le Pré des Oiseaux. When the critic Jules Lemaître attacked him, she called it treachery.[9] After the death of Leconte de Lisle in 1894, she was to dedicate a series of poems to his memory. *Les Rites divins* recorded the gods drunk with love and power and pride; they were unmistakably in his manner.

Since her childhood days at the rue de la Grange-Batelière, when she had helped her father to write *Le Roman de la momie*, Judith had also been enthralled by ancient Egypt. In the winter of 1887-8, at a fancy-dress party given by Mme Juliette Adam, she created a sensation as Cleopatra. Her headdress, recorded the critic Maurice Guillemot,

consisted of a stuffed guinea-fowl, which Lecomte de Noüy asked her to give him as a model (a stuffed bird might easily lead one to define the artist's talent);

the dress was absolutely original, copied from a papyrus in the Bibliothèque Nationale; on one of her fingers shone the ring once brought to her by Maxime du Camp: the ring which he had actually taken from the finger of a royal mummy, from a very ancient Sesostris.[10]

Who, enquired Claude Vento, 'has forgotten her "desperately pure" medallic profile, her sculptural form, her hieratic poses, if he saw her dressed as Cleopatra? . . . She was dazzling, this reborn Cleopatra! Rather buxom, tall, and very fat, like oriental women: the evocation seemed to be complete.'[11]

It was at Mme Adam's ball, so Henri de Régnier remembered, 'that Judith Gautier, as Cleopatra, and Pierre Loti, as Pharaoh, had felt drawn to each other by one of those deep and sudden affinities which go back beyond ourselves, to those "secret affinities" of which Théophile Gautier had sung.'[12] Judith and Loti had greeted one another with the intimate form of address, and

she had complimented her companion on the rare proportion – only to be found in Greek statues – of the second toe in relation to the big one: according to the canon, it should be noticeably longer.

By wearing sandals on his bare feet, Loti had succeeded in emphasizing this detail, of which he was, in fact, very proud. He was flattered by his friend's judicious observation. There followed an original correspondence, written entirely in Egyptian hieroglyphs . . .[13]

The American writer, Stuart Henry, later alleged that Judith married Loti in 1913.[14] 'I was amazed to learn of my marriage to Pierre Loti,' Judith confessed to her friend Mme Monod. 'It was the first news I had of it, and it came to me from America! You must never believe such things, and you must rest assured that I am in my right mind. Is Loti a widower, or divorced? I don't know anything about it. He is quite capable of such a deed, but I am not.'[15]

The allegation was ridiculous; but the deep affection between Judith and Loti remained.

In 1888, in a letter dated only 'Monday', Jean Lorrain announced to Edmond Magnier, the editor of L'Événement: 'My piece on Japonism in the theatre and Mme Gautier's play . . . will reach you tomorrow evening at seven o'clock. I was at Mme Gautier's on Saturday before I left, and I have some amusing information.'[16]

The letter was presumably written some time in April. On 21 April, La Marchande de sourires, a Japanese drama in five acts by Judith Gautier, with a prologue by the faithful Armand Silvestre, and music by

Benedictus, was to be performed at the Théâtre de l'Odéon. Judith was nervous, and instructed Loti: 'Burn a few joss-sticks before the most influential of the gods which you have brought back from afar.'[17]

La Marchande de sourires, which had already been performed by her marionnettes, was in fact a Chinese play which Judith had transferred to a Japanese setting. The seller of smiles of the title is a ruthless courtesan, Coeur-de-rubis, bent on the destruction of her lover Yamato's marriage. She does not care for him; he is simply a step on her path towards her own marriage to Simabara. Yamato's wife, Omaya, dies of grief, and Simabara casts Yamato into a river to drown. Coeur-de-rubis sets fire to his house and steals a coffer from it, as the basis of her prosperity. Yamato's infant son, Ivashita, is given by his nurse to a prince, who vows to bring the child up as his own, but finally tells him the story of his life. The young man goes to find the courtesan and take his revenge, but he goes reluctantly, for he is much in love with Fleur-de-roseau, a girl whose reflection he has seen in the lake (this is a curious echo of Gautier's Chinese novella, *Le Pavillon sur l'eau*). Ivashita finds his nurse, and his long-lost father, now reduced to beggary; he also finds that his future wife is the daughter of the courtesan. Virtue is rewarded, and wickedness is punished; the courtesan commits suicide, and, as in all fairy-tales, the young couple live happily ever after. *La Marchande de sourires* is something of a fairy-tale. It might, more properly, be called a morality.

Gustave Kahn dismissed the play in *La Revue indépendante*, and spoke of 'sombre boredom', but he seems to have been the only adverse critic. Jules Lemaître recorded:

> Mme Judith Gautier is an honest artist, and she is worthy of bearing a great name. For her, 'the visible world exists' almost as much as it did for her father. In *La Marchande de sourires* (which is, in fact, a play of Chinese origin) she has kept much of the Japanese theatre: the simplicity, the violence, the ferocity of feelings and passions, the innocent romance of the adventures and the picturesque poetry of the details; being of good Latin stock, she has added clarity, nobility, a sense of proportion and the art of composition.[18]

Twenty years later, in *L'Évolution du Théâtre contemporain*, Léon Séché and Jules Bertaut still remembered 'that delightful *Marchande de sourires* which Porel staged with such sumptuousness and taste . . . Mme Gautier's precious and subtle mind had,' they said, 'made these crude and childishly violent scenes into an artistic trinket, rare and wonderful. All Paris raved about it for some weeks.'[19] 'This victory,' wrote Émile Bergerat, 'is inscribed in the golden book of hundredth performances.'[20]

It was also immortalized by the camera of Nadar.

Dear friend [wrote Judith],
  Everyone will be enchanted if you do the *Marchande de sourires*. I am at your
disposal when you want.
  The success is growing all the time, they're turning people away from the
Odéon!
  I shall see you soon, dear friend. Let me know the day, and I will come with
the greatest pleasure to watch you at work.
All good wishes,
Judith Gautier[21]

La Marchande de sourires – dedicated to the Marquis Saionzi – was not
her only collaboration with Benedictus in the theatre. He had already
composed the music for *Le Ramier blanc*. In 1894 he was to write the
music for *La Sonate du clair de lune*, a one-act opera based on her poem
about Beethoven's unhappy love for Juliette Guicciardi. This sentimental
work was performed at a Rosicrucian evening. Benedictus was – with Erik
Satie – the accredited composer of the Rosicrucian Order.

It was late one night, in the foyer of the Odéon, after the dress rehearsal of
La Marchande de sourires, that Judith met a man after her own heart:
Prince Bojidar Karageorgevitch, a member of the dispossessed royal
family of Serbia. Bojidar was not only a prince in exile, but a lover of the
arts and of the East. He was almost as unworldly as herself. He was in
desperate need of money; he turned to journalism and translation, played
the guitar, gave singing lessons, and tried his hand at decorative art.
Somehow he found the funds to go to India, and to write his *Notes sur
l'Inde*. In 1903 the Karageorgevitch dynasty was to be restored, and Peter
I became King of Serbia; but Bojidar continued his extraordinary double
life in Paris. He remained a working man, so poor that he invariably dined
off a tin of tuna fish and a cup of tea – unless, that is, he dined in high
society. To Judith, Bojidar remained 'a beautiful hot-house flower, which
had happened to grow in a quite unsheltered spot, assailed by the tempest,
and resisted it with the strength of the oak – the heraldic oak, the emblem
of his race.'[22]

After their chance meeting at the Odéon, Prince Bojidar became a
frequent visitor to 30, rue Washington. Since 1885, when she had given
her address as 108, avenue des Champs-Élysées, Judith had moved to this
fifth-floor apartment, near the Étoile, where she had established her *salon*.
On 21 April 1888, discussing her drama in *Le Figaro*, Maurice Guillemot
recorded her in her setting.

This glory-hole is peopled with memories: perhaps one ought to call it a temple rather than a glory-hole, a temple in which Wagner is the god. His bust, in gilded bronze, presides over the mantelpiece. One of his last photographs, framed and inscribed, hangs over the piano. A curious picture glows red in a corner; the subject is taken from German legend – a knight in armour is lying beside a fiery sea. And, finally, Mme Judith Gautier treasures an autograph from the composer of *Lohengrin;* it is written on a song from *Tristan und Isolde:*

> *A wretched story set to music to please Mme Judith Gautier*
> *Richard Wagner*

There are a portrait of Liszt with an inscription, a medallion executed by the enameller-poet, Claudius Popelin; a Puvis de Chavannes; a Baudry; several paintings by John Sargent . . . There are curiously coloured chests; statuettes in tinted wax . . .

Under a pretty silken cover there is a box stuffed with autographs, and they are worth leafing through. First of all there is a superb manuscript of Victor Hugo's, the manuscript of the poem he wrote for *Le Tombeau de Théophile Gautier,* and then innumerable letters: 'Daughter of a poet, wife of a poet, you are yourself a queen. More than a queen, a Muse!' '. . . I kiss your wings . . .'. 'I am an imbecile, and I am waiting for you . . .'. Verses from Richepin and Silvestre (whole volumes from Silvestre) . . .[23]

Poor Armand Silvestre, now forty-nine, plain, bearded and balding, had long since lost his hopes and his verve; he had, he confessed, no pretentions left 'except as a poet, a fencer and a cook'.[24] Judith kept relics of other, more distinguished, admirers, sonnets from Hugo and Leconte de Lisle.

'Singular charm . . . oriental languor . . .' The Goncourts saw these qualities in the young girl, and they are [continued Guillemot] still possessed by the woman of today.

. . . It was said of Mme Judith Gautier that she had 'the desperately pure profile of a Syracusan medal'; the description is fair, witness a particular unfinished pencil sketch by John Sargent who, with the sobriety of a master, recorded the marvellous line of this cameo with a single stroke. The eyes are very gentle, sometimes bright with energy, sometimes with sensual pleasure . . .

The body is powerfully built; the broad brow and the robust hands suggest strength and vitality, and they are signs of easy creation. Mme Judith Gautier is a creator; she paints in her leisure hours; she is an accomplished sculptor, and the daughter's chisel is as good as the father's pencil: witness the candelabra on the mantelpiece in Auguste Vacquerie's big salon, and also a wax head done a few days after the fatal date, a Victor Hugo on his deathbed, a striking likeness, with the corner of the mouth ominously open. Mme Judith Gautier is a worker; she spends little time in Paris, and most of the year she prefers her little house by the sea. There, playing round her while she sits at her piano or writes, is her little Chinese dog, Mousmé, a curious creature with no fur and a bristling moustache, a creature who only feeds, poor little thing! on lilac blossom or Parma violets.[25]

Mousmé showed such intelligence that Judith was convinced that she was the reincarnation of an oriental princess. When Mousmé died, Judith sent her friends a printed *faire-part*. The dog was embalmed and sealed in a lead-lined coffin; it was buried in an enclave in the garden at Saint-Enogat. Here, on a cement scroll, in Chinese characters, Judith engraved the names of her favourite cats and dogs, the companions of her solitude.[26]

Now, in her mid-forties, she became an increasingly romantic, mysterious figure. In 1889, in *La Littérature de tout à l'heure*, Charles Morice wrote: 'Madame Judith Gautier is, perhaps, in this generation, the most uniquely poetic soul, the proudest, and, beyond all passions, in her land of dreams, the most serene . . . In this Poet's soul, there is only room for the Dream of Beauty. And, in this Dream, this soul finds both its happiness and its creed.'[27] Anatole France agreed; and he knew that Judith dreamed most happily of the Eastern world. In 1890, when he read *La Conquête du Paradis*, he almost wished

that the splendid thoughts of Madame Judith Gautier, like Baudelaire's Malabaraise, never came to our grey and humid climes, which are not in the least made for her rare beauty . . . When the poet of *Le Dragon impérial* and *Iskender* leaves the fairy-tale East which she has dreamed, leaves her own East, in which she has set her soul, when she enters the realities of contemporary life, she loses her heavenly grace in our fog-bound world.[28]

Edmond Haraucourt went further:

Her Orient [he wrote] was a total splendour from which she had systematically removed the stains and blemishes; she kept it irreproachable, because she needed to imagine that an essential paradise existed on earth. Indeed, her Orient resided in herself much more than on the maps of the world, because for her it was the symbol of what we lack here below: it was the article of faith essential in a life which was only an act of faith.[29]

In the early summer of 1889, after an interval of eleven years, Paris enjoyed yet another International Exhibition. 'Rome is no longer Rome,' wrote a critic, 'Cairo is no longer in Egypt, or the island of Java in the East Indies. It has all come to the Champ de Mars, the Esplanade des Invalides and the Trocadéro.'[30] It was enough to captivate Judith Gautier. All Paris, she recalled,

was enamoured of the Javanese dancers, those hieratic bayadères who had escaped from the harem, since the Sultan of Jakarta had been good enough to leave the door half-open . . .

Le Tout-Paris, in particular, never tired of the spectacle. They met each other almost daily at the Japanese Kampong, they greeted one another with smiles of complicity, they drew up closer to each other to make more room round the little tables, where the froth dissolved on the glasses of beer, the sorbets melted under the distracted spoons. And, unendingly, they listened to the indiscernible music, they gazed at the strange young girls, . . . at the mystic, enthralling dance, which finally made them drowsy like hypnotism. It lulled the spirit in veils of dream, which seemed at times to be shot through with confused recollections of an earlier life. These recollections were so transient that they were poignant, almost painful. And so, of all the masterpieces, all the wonders that adorned the last Exhibition, what memory has most faithfully kept, with the illogicality of passion, is the bizarre, seductive vision of these exquisite dancers. Everyone recalls them with a little of that languor which is caused by a regret in love. It is the intoxicating flower, with the clinging scent, preserved between the pages of the memory, the fragile petal which, alone, survives from the splendid summer.[31]

In 1890, in their Bibliothèque de Romans Historiques, Armand Colin re-published *Le Lion de la victoire* and *La Reine de Bangalore*. The original works had been abridged, and they now appeared as a single novel, *La Conquête du Paradis*. The Paradise of the title was India, and the novel was concerned with the French conquests in India in the eighteenth century. The Marquis Charles de Bussy rescues Ourvaci, the Queen of Bangalore, from a tiger. He falls incurably in love with her, and, finally, a fakir's prediction comes true, and he realizes his dream. He rescues Ourvaci once again – this time from the funeral pyre where she intends to die for love of him. Ourvaci abdicates, and makes him not only her husband, but her king. Judith had, she said, studied Bussy's history for ten years. The background is multicoloured, poetic, and wholly original. The story is as naïve, as impossible as that of *Le Dragon impérial*, but it remained one of Judith's favourites among her works.

When it was published, Anatole France took the occasion to discuss its author in *Le Temps:*

In *La Conquête du Paradis* one rediscovers that pure, heroic imagination, that indefinable, noble, divinely childlike quality which is the charm of Judith Gautier's novels . . .

It is no doubt an historical novel. Deep down, Madame Judith Gautier understands history in the manner of Alexandre Dumas, and I think it no bad manner for a novelist. She likes messages brought mysteriously in the middle of festivities, messages which suddenly turn joyful nights into armed vigils. She likes great sword-cuts, and lovers' trysts, when they are very dangerous. Her Bussy is delightfully brave. It's surprising that he hasn't been killed a thousand times over . . .

I should have liked to put more order and clarity into these simple notes on one of the most original talents in contemporary literature. I should at least have liked to show you the somewhat rare sight, which is worthy of consideration, of a woman of perfect beauty, made to delight, indifferent to her beauty, escaping the world and caring only for work and solitude.

This indefinable quality of disdain and fierceness which one senses in everything she writes, Madame Judith Gautier carries in the depths of her soul. She is glad to live entirely among her attendant dreams, and it is true that no court could give her such a splendid retinue. She has a love of all the arts, she is profoundly musical, . . . she has a taste and a feeling for painting. The walls of her salon are covered with bizarre animals which she has painted, in the style of the Japanese kakemonos, animals which reveal both her childlike taste for pictures and her mystic understanding of nature.

As for her natural talent as a sculptor, it amazed her friends, long before she and M. H. Bouillon signed the bust of Théophile Gautier which has recently been unveiled at Tarbes.[32]

Robert de Bonnières confirmed: 'Madame Judith was then modelling clay and making pretty figurines. In particular she created an ingenious model of a clock: a sphere on which the twelve Hours of day and the twelve Hours of night, personified by women, were each devoted to a characteristic occupation. Some were drinking or sleeping; and some were kissing one another [sic]. This composition had all the imaginative richness which we have since admired in the vases and goblets of Gustave Doré.'[33] Such praise was more of a condemnation than the writer knew.

On 5 March 1892, Hachette published the first of a series of illustrated monographs, Les Capitales du Monde. Sir Charles Dilke wrote on London, François Coppée on Paris, Carmen Silva, the poet and Queen of Roumania, on Bucharest. Judith contributed the monograph on Tokyo.

A railway now connects Yokohama with Tokyo, and it is by the railway that most visitors from Europe now arrive.

A railway in Japan! Is not that an extraordinary thing? When one hears of it, one immediately jumps to the conclusion that this artistic people . . . would surely turn bronze locomotives into bronze dragons vomiting forth fire and smoke, and dragging behind them chariots of gold and lacquer-work . Not a bit of it! This railway is exactly like any other . . .

The first view of Tokyo from the station is anything but pleasant . . . Fortunately, however, we soon get away from it, and we quickly find ourselves in little streets lined with little wooden houses, their wide roofs forming penthouses, with glazed paper windows in movable frames . . .[34]

These narrow streets were crowded with traffic: private and public palanquins had all but vanished, but tramways and carts were beginning to appear. At the fish market, the visitor marvelled at 'a great variety of grotesque-looking monsters of the deep . . . The stalls, tastily arranged, form scales of colour and marvellous richness, ruby-like purples, metallic blues, tender, gleaming mother-of-pearl-like shades, shining amongst the pale emerald green of the edible algae, of which the Japanese are very fond.'[35]

It was a remarkable essay, written by a woman who hăd never set foot in Japan. But she had been there in imagination. All that she had read in books, seen in pictures, heard from her friends, had been used in this authentic fantasy. In her mind's eye she saw the Palace of the Mikado. In her waking dream she visited the gardens of Asakusa, where she admired

> the fruit-trees – whose marvellous spring blossoms are the delight of poets . . .
> But suddenly the gaze is arrested, fascinated by the mighty mountain: . . . the surprising, the marvellous, the unique Fujiyama! It rises up in the south-west, a gigantic, solitary cone, very lofty, of a pale rose colour, with blue shadows looking like furrows on its sides. The base is wrapped in mist, and it looks as if it hung suspended in the air, upheld by clouds alone.[36]

It is like a painting by Hokusai.

Judith's name was often before the public. In 1893 appeared a book which, one suspects, had been in her mind for nearly twenty years, ever since she had described a day in the Kingdom of Siam in the pages of the *Journal officiel*. *Mémoires d'un Éléphant blanc* are the engaging reminiscences of Iravata, a white elephant given, as a dowry, to the Princess Sapphire-of-Heaven when she marries the Prince of Golconda. The elephant saves its master's life in battle, and rescues his little daughter from drowning; it is appointed the child's chief attendant, and, after a series of adventures and misunderstandings it is finally reunited with her. *Mémoires d'un Éléphant blanc* is a classic children's story; it was reprinted by Armand Colin in 1900 in the Bibliothèque du Petit Français, with illustrations by Alphonse Mucha.[37]

In 1893 the same publishers re-issued *Le Dragon impérial* in their Bibliothèque de Romans Historiques. This new edition was dedicated to the memory of Théophile Gautier.

> I should not swear that it was a perfect novel [confessed Théodore de Wyzewa in the *Revue bleue*]. Perhaps the novel needs more analysis and less painting, more complex characters and a simpler setting.
> And I shall not swear that this is a very accurate picture of Chinese customs and Chinese nature. I shall not swear it, since I have never been to China, although deep down I am almost convinced. But I do swear that *Le Dragon impérial* is a beautiful, indeed a marvellous poem, one of the masterpieces of our poetic literature . . .
> Mme Judith Gautier does not know the East like those travellers who spend their travels in regretting Paris. No doubt she lived in those adorable lands, during one or other of those previous existences of which every one of us finds the images deep inside himself. Whether she bears her dream to China or to Japan, or to Egypt or to Palestine, or to the forests of India, in which her

Éléphant blanc was born, she is at once at ease there, and at once the eternal voices of things tell her the secrets which they reveal there alone . . .

Even in Paris, it is the East which presents itself to her . . . Like the poets of the East, Mme Judith Gautier prefers pictures to thoughts, and dreams to realities: all her books are not only poems but fairy-tales as well . . . In one way alone she is French: in her deep feeling for our language, its dignity and beauty. And this, to be honest, is where she touches me most.[38]

The year which saw the re-appearance of *Le Dragon impérial* also saw the publication of *Le Vieux de la montagne*. It was dedicated to Clermont-Ganneau – who had re-discovered Gezer – 'as a token of sisterly affection'. It was another extravagant historical romance, this time set in the Holy Land; and, once again, it showed two strangely different sides of Judith's character. The historical detail was complete, authentic and intense, the work of a dedicated intellectual. The story was, as usual, curiously unsophisticated, full of heroic deeds, inaccessible castles on mountain peaks, intense love, primitive violence and saintly abnegation. *Le Vieux de la montagne* was the work of an idealist, of a youthful mind which had not much changed in thirty years. For all her scholarly pursuits, and for all her worldly experience, Judith remained an innocent at heart.

Her innocence was apparent, too, in *Fleurs d'Orient*, a collection of historical short stories which Armand Colin published in this same fecund year. *Zuleika* is simply *La Femme de Putiphar* reprinted under another title. *Le Tapis des mille et une nuits* and *Les Danseuses du Sultan de Djog Yakarta* are reminiscences of the 1889 Exhibition. The themes of the collection range from Arabia to China, and *L'Étoile aux cheveux d'or* recalls the Three Kings on their journey to Bethlehem. The most felicitous story is *Le Livre de Thot*. This fairy-tale about ancient Egypt is told with a strong visual sense and childlike fantasy. It is characteristic of Judith at her best.

On 15 August 1894, *La Revue de Paris* published *Le Resplendissement d'Atenn:* an Egyptian novella said to be based on fragments of a papyrus. It was the history of a priestess enamoured of a king; she refused to give herself to him, although 'two desires of equal ardour, mingling their fires, are the most divine thing which life can offer.'[39] Instead she died, and she was found 'lying in her blood as on a bed of purple lotuses. In her heart she had a dagger, standing erect, its golden hilt represented Amon with the ram's head.'

Time and again, in Judith's work, one is aware of this central paradox. Judith, the outwardly impassible, who impressed so many by her nonchalance, concealed a violent, impassioned nature. Perhaps it was enough for her to record such passion to be free of it, and no longer to be troubled by it.[40]

Chapter Seventeen

Judith, like her father, remained an ardent, unrepentant idealist. She deplored the mediocrity of the French theatre. She would have liked to see only masterpieces performed. 'For us [the French], art is first and foremost an amusement. The serious frankly bores us, and if by chance we allow a masterpiece on one of our stages, it is simply as a curiosity. Is there a theatre in Paris, the capital of the world, where the masterpieces of all the world are performed? Calderon, Schiller, Flaubert, Shakespeare: who cares about them?'[1] Like many of her compatriots in literature, she felt herself to be a dramatist. She would have liked to create a theatre. 'My one wish . . . would have been to have had a theatre of my own, like Sarah Bernhardt, a stage of my own, to produce my plays and sometimes to perform in them myself.'[2]

She had been emboldened by the success of *La Marchande de sourires*. In 1893 she had published a ballet-pantomime, *La Camargo*, written in collaboration with Armand Tonnery. In 1894, she returned to the Odéon with a Russian drama, *La Barynia*, adapted from one of her own novellas with the help of Joseph Gayda. She also published her one-act opera, *La Sonate du clair de lune*.

For the moment, however, her dream of her own theatre remained unfulfilled. For want of means, she realized her dream in miniature, with her Petit Théâtre. It was, perhaps, a dream she had known since her childhood days, when she had played with her dolls at Montrouge. Her marionnettes, as she observed, were more obedient than live actors. Émile Bergerat was to recall how '*La Larme du diable* was performed in a marionnette theatre, at Judith Gautier's, . . . by wooden and cardboard actors, and the privileged audience who watched it have kept the ineffaceable memory of her art.'[3] Mme Alphonse Daudet remembered 'a really delightful marionnette show, mingled with music, with dreamlike

settings, and Shakespearean costumes.'[4] In 1894 Pierre Louÿs recorded a
more significant occasion:

> Two new companies of marionnettes have made their first appearance in Paris.
> The débuts of these little people only last an evening. When they have once
> sung, they all die, suddenly, together; but these ephemeral appearances are
> great events . . . The shorter a life, the more exquisite and the more perfect it
> should be.
>   Such was the life of Mme Judith Gautier's marionnettes.
>   They were modelled by skilful hands from a fine grey clay. Mme Gautier,
> who is a poet, is also a sculptor and a painter. When the little Tanagra figures
> were created from friable clay, she herself gave them life and coloured the folds
> of their costumes green and blue. The marionnettes had to perform *Die
> Walküre*, but, as they were made of clay, their attitudes remained unchange-
> able. So there had to be several for each character: Siegmund sitting, standing,
> lying, bearing Sieglinde away or holding her asleep during the Announcement
> of Death. It was all as it should have been, and those who saw it will not forget
> Sieglinde's movement of passionate attention, while she was listening to the
> Narrative at Hunding's table. M. Lecomte de Noüy had lent the old warrior his
> deep bass voice for the occasion. Mme Paul Hillemacher [the wife of Gounod's
> biographer] sang the lamentations of Sieglinde in a delicate and tender voice.
> Mme Simone Labatut as Brünnhilde, M. Bagès as Siegmund, M. Vals as
> Wotan and Mme Fath as Fricka, were irreproachable. M. Benedictus, that
> skilful composer, was at the piano, and, thanks to him, the score was played in
> excellent tempo. Finally the décors were done by M. Gérin, who is an exquisite
> painter, and the mechanism was regulated by M. Dorado . . . A very select
> company watched these miniature marvels: M. and Mlles de Heredia, M. and
> Mme Thadée Natanson, MM. Robert de Bonnières, Clermont-Ganneau, Jean
> Marras, Haraucourt, Henri de Régnier, R. de Montesquiou and his whip,
> Ferdinand Hérold, another director of marionnettes, and André Fontainas
> . . .[5]

Fontainas recalled the occasion and the hostess. Judith Gautier, he wrote,
'was welcoming in her Japanese-style apartment in the rue Washington,
where she was sometimes pleased to give Wagnerian festivals with
marionnettes . . . Her rather heavy body had thickened, but her beauty
was still evident; the features in her perfect oval face were noble and
regular; her eyes, a deep velvet, caressing and sometimes dreaming, shot
brilliant shafts of intelligence and kindness. A placid idol, indulgent and
inspired, she exuded a benevolent charm, and her friends adored her.'[6]

Fontainas was not alone in recording Judith's physical decline. It was, it
seems, in the summer of 1895 that another visitor observed her.
Saint-Georges de Bouhélier Lepelletier was the son of Edmond Lepelletier
(the friend and future biographer of Verlaine). Mme Lepelletier had

rented a house at Saint-Enogat for the season, and here the young man arrived from Paris for his holiday.

I had not [he remembered] been at my mother's for twenty-four hours before she told me how she had met Judith Gautier. In fact this very famous woman had a villa at Saint-Enogat, where she spent the summer seasons in company with a rather singular composer called Benedictus. This personage had the face of an Abyssinian and the voice of a eunuch. Judith Gautier put up with him, but showed him no affection. My mother, who looked for superiority, had a violent infatuation for this woman. Judith Gautier enthralled her, and repaid her for her idolatry with indifference. She was forty-five or fifty [Judith was fifty], but she looked imposing and splendid . . . She did me the honour of receiving me.

Her life as a woman had begun early. Legends lingered on in the folds of her dress . . .[7]

Legend was sometimes stronger than fact.

Dierx maintained [continued Bouhélier] that, while she was living with her father, who received all the youth of the day, she thought of nothing but creating trouble. She appeared naked in the sight of the most fervent, though nothing went any further. Catulle Mendès was twenty-two or twenty-three and she was eighteen or nineteen when he endeared himself to her, and, since Théophile Gautier refused her to him, he had carried her off [sic]. They had not been made to please one another for long. They had broken up. She seemed, now, to have forgotten that old folly. Beauty was not absent from her royal features. Her extraordinary dark eyes enlivened her face – which, otherwise, would only have shown extreme slackness. Accepted in her house, I thought of her as the object of a cult, not as a living person.

She professed a passionate interest in the oriental sages, and that did not fail to keep me at a distance. In Paris, she saw many men of letters of Chinese origin, and she took pleasure in their company, for she considered them as men of a superior race . . . At Saint-Enogat, she lived in solitude. Her body had grown heavy with fat, and it only seemed to be comfortable among silk cushions and in deep armchairs. Sometimes she spent hours with us, but one hardly heard a word from her. My timidity aggravated the situation. My mother was not very expansive either, and did not break the silence any more than I did. Each of us followed their own thoughts, oblivious to the others.

August was drawing to an end, and I had to think of going back to Paris. Around Saint-Enogat, the country was brilliant with gorse in bloom. Saint-Malo began to grow empty . . . So I went to Judith Gautier, and paid her a final visit. Did she want to be amiable to a young man who was, like her, imprudently engaged in the world of letters, of which she and her father had known the cares? Judith Gautier grew animated. She asked me about my impressions of Saint-Enogat, and she made me talk. The poetry of the countryside had overwhelmed me, and I could not hide the fact in the least . . .

'If you have a day to spare,' said my hostess, 'stop at Dol, which is on the way.'

She explained to me that there was a very old menhir there, and that sacrifices had been performed on it in ancient times . . . I felt little interest in this kind of thing, but, so as not to disappoint Judith Gautier, I promised to make the excursion as she asked.[8]

In July 1894, Leconte de Lisle had died at Louveciennes. Judith had been among the first to send a telegram of condolence.[9] The Parnassians had been generous in their enthusiasm for each other; and, even now, in 1895, a strong sense of fraternity remained. On 8 August, Coppée recorded:

> The other evening, at the Grand Hotel, we celebrated the red ribbon with which – after so many years of inexplicable forgetfulness – a brave young Minister, M. Poincaré, has finally adorned the buttonhole of Catulle Mendès. And there, with a lively pleasure, I saw once again a few grey beards of old Parnassians . . . I am not talking about Catulle, who is not in the least bi-metallic, for his golden hair still has no silver threads. But – we must come to terms with it – the Pleiad of 1862 is turning grey.[10]

Coppée was not alone in observing a certain youthfulness in Mendès. Frantz Jourdain, the architect of La Samaritaine, remarked that 'his youthful verve is seen above all in his love of movement, which drives him never to attach himself to a school, never to set up his tent without a thought of departure . . . His vast intelligence has constantly been enamoured of beauty, however it has made itself manifest.'[11]

Yet, in his *Figures contemporaines*, published this year, Bernard Lazare relegated Mendès to the past.

> He was famous, once, and only a few years ago one could still see him on the terraces of certain cafés, surrounded by young men whom he took to be his disciples. He governed the Parnassians, a long time ago, and it is said he taught prosody to Coppée . . .
> M. Mendès represents the last of the elegiacs, the final shepherd boy; he is . . . as languorous as the Roman flautist, and as empty as a leather bottle which once held aromatic wine. But he is above all the last magician in French literature.[12]

Over the years, despite the birth of their five children, Mendès and Augusta Holmès had grown apart. When she was twenty-two, Cazalis had admired 'the male and female Monster' in her; in her thirties, the masculine element had become more pronounced. She had come to have rather brusque and mannish ways. Perhaps the inconstant Mendès found these hard to accept. The relationship turned sour. There had been a first rupture in November 1885, and this had soon been followed by a final separation.[13]

Augusta – who was thirty-eight – was bitterly hurt when Mendès left her. In two years, it is said, she aged by fifteen years. Mendès had run through her fortune, and she was reduced to giving piano lessons for a living. Her financial difficulties increased when Mendès finally remarried and stopped the small allowance which he had made her since their separation. Her reputation as a composer began to decline. Occasionally, she was recalled to the public mind: in 1889 her *Ode Triomphale*, a glorification of France and the Republic, was first performed at the Palais de l'Industrie during the International Exhibition. It was reported to have been a superb success; but Augusta, it was said, could not be decorated since at the time she found herself in debt.[14] That year her photograph appeared in the *Album Mariani*. It was hard to see the youthful goddess in the middle-aged woman with the short hair and severely tailored suit, the woman whom Péladan addressed as 'Mademoiselle & Androgyne'.[15] When she died of a heart condition on 20 January 1903, she was poor and almost forgotten. Until the end, she was determined to appear an untouchable goddess. It is said that she never admitted the existence of her four surviving children. She saw them only in secret, and she forbade them to call her 'mother'.[16]

Mendès himself, in the 1880s, was hardly a desirable man. Early in his Parisian life, P.–B. Gheusi had a letter of introduction to him.

Mendès [he reported] received me at 18, rue Berlioz, between the Bois and the avenue de la Grande Armée . . . When he came to meet me in his salon, he was wrapped in an ample gandoura striped in mauve and green, and had just, it seemed, emerged from a battery of shower-baths and massages. He was wan, and spotted with freckles, his eyes protruding, his grey and tawny mane was dishevelled . . .[17]

Gheusi was asked to stay for *déjeuner*.

There were our host's sister, Mme Debar, self-effacing as an English governess, and Mendès' three daughters, with clouds of hair the colour of ripe corn; the eldest, Hélyonne – later married, I believe, to Barbusse – was fifteen, with the profile of an immaterial fairy and eyes of intense blue, of an innocence which was mischievous and sweet, worshipping the paternal genius. The other two were adorable, delectably badly brought up . . .

As for Mendès, groomed, and recently shaved, luxuriously slovenly in a kind of Eastern woman's kimono, he displayed without innocence the disorder of his dress, the audacity of his anecdotes, the wear and tear of the network of fibrils on his wan, moon-shaped face, the 'imitation youth' of his enervated character . . . His daughters listened to his ragged voice as if it were some music of their mother's . . . They understood nothing – happily – of the tales of the bard in his artificial delirium. But I was choking with distress and provincial shame . . .

'Mésange,' Catulle confided to me as a final shock, 'is my new mistress. She is sixteen . . .'[18]

Gheusi was understandably shocked. Albert Samain, who met Mendès – apparently with Mésange – was only enthralled by his conversation.

The other day [this on 6 December 1893], I spent three delightful hours with Mendès . . . I went to the Harcourt concert . . . Mendès came in with his current mistress, M***, a pale, pale, pale little woman, thin, thin, thin . . . And at the end of the evening we all went down together chez Pousset. It was a quarter to twelve. We came out at three o'clock in the morning. From the beginning, I manoeuvred so as to bring Mendès round to his recollections . . . And I felt a childlike joy to hear him say to me: 'One evening, at the piano, Wagner was playing me the prelude to *Les Vaincus*, an opera on Buddha which he had just planned . . . "They accuse me of being an apostle of musical anarchy," he said, "of destroying all harmony, of lording it in dissonance deliberately sought. Nothing is less true. All my chords, without exception, are found in Bach . . ." And he shook with violent exasperation in his yellow satin dressing-gown.'[19]

Mendès remained the friend of the great. He often entertained them. His table, said Léo Larguier, was that of a farmer-general of revenues. The old Parnassian was a past master of the art of cooking, and he could turn his hand to *carpe au bleu*, *suprême de bécasses*, or *lièvre à la royale*. He expressed contempt for the gastronomic ignorance of Sarah Bernhardt. 'Sarah,' he said, 'can regale herself with a steak cooked over a spirit lamp, and tinned beans.'[20]

Many of his contemporaries felt respect for him. Edmond Rostand agreed to be his executor. Chabrier wrote the music for his opera *Briseïs*. Massenet collaborated with Mendès on his opera *Ariane: 'Ariane! Ariane! The work which made me live in such lofty spheres! Could it be otherwise with the proud collaboration of Catulle Mendès, the poet of ethereal hopes and dreams?'[21] Mendès delighted in the society of composers: not only Massenet and Chabrier, but Messager, d'Indy and Saint-Saëns. He remained both a creative writer and a dramatic critic:

At performances, he was one of the 'figures' in the audience . . . As soon as the curtain rose, he appeared punctually at the front of his box. He listened attentively, stroked his ash-coloured beard, or fidgeted with the floating ends of his white silk necktie, which was spread out on his evening shirt. In the intervals one came across him in the corridors, perorating in his raucous voice, or distributing handshakes with an air which was both insolent and distracted, surrounded or accompanied by numerous listeners or clients.[22]

Mendès' success was undoubted; but his personality was flawed, as it had been from the beginning. He remained – as he himself was aware – a failed human being. 'Why should I be a better judge than I was in earlier days? A young mind, full of sparkle, lucidity and loyalty, is worth as much as a regretful, diminished, degraded mind. Indeed, it is worth far more.'[23] Mendès was certainly degraded. In 1887, in his novel *Le Désespéré*, under the transparent disguise of Properce Beauvivier, Léon Bloy had drawn him with hatred: 'He married, this conqueror, and he married the most beautiful woman he could find, in the hope (which was not disappointed) of conquering others more easily . . . From the point of view of baseness of soul pure and simple, . . . Beauvivier's originality seems impossible for any human being to surpass.'[24] Antoine Albalat, who met Mendès in about 1894, never forgot the sight of him 'walking up and down, and talking, and breaking off from time to time to toss down great glasses of beer and then calmly spit in front of him on the carpet in his own study.'[25]

Mendès remained a desperate decadent; yet if Stuart Henry, the American francophile, is to be believed, he also remained a curiously sad figure. Talking of Wagner, he recalled how 'my wife and I went to Lucerne and passed three months with him [*sic*]. Villiers de l'Isle-Adam went with us. Those three months were the happiest I have ever known.'[26]

In 1896, after eighteen years of judicial separation, Mendès asked Judith for a divorce. 'Since I obtained a letter from my husband in which he recognized all his wrongs, there was,' added Judith, 'no pleading in court. In this letter he explained everything, and he went one better, and said much more than he was asked to do.'[27] It is even possible that he explained how, under cover of darkness, using Machiavellian stratagems, he had tried to have himself replaced in bed by one of his friends, who was passionately in love with his wife.[28] The lawyers, recorded Judith, 'were speechless at such confessions, and the divorce was granted in my favour. Mendès thus avoided the scandal which would certainly have roused the derision of all Paris.'[29] The divorce was granted on 28 December, and Catulle was ordered to pay all the costs, since he had been in the wrong at the time of the separation.

Léo Larguier, who was one day to write a life of Gautier, remembered:

Catulle Mendès never talked to me about Judith, except on one summer day when a big fly was buzzing between the curtain and the window-panes.

'Judith was very clever at swatting flies,' he murmured, 'they used to say that that was connected with Satanism. The demoniacs called Beelzebub *Lord of the Flies!* . . .'

The old man who had been as beautiful as a Greek poet, and still kept the prestige of that beauty, was silent, no doubt lost in his memories . . .

After all these years, did he feel regret or remorse? . . . He finished his glass of absinthe, and lit another cigar.[30]

Catulle was anxious to remarry. Jane Boussac, the mother of the famous
industrialist, had ended her first marriage, and left the prosaic life of the
provinces for Paris, where she had been instinctively drawn to intellectual
circles. She was beautiful, passionate, and a gifted writer. Mendès fell in
love with her; and, surprisingly, she accepted him. Jane Catulle-Mendès
established herself as a biographer and poet, a lecturer, and dramatic critic
of *La Presse*.[31] She gave Mendès a son, Primice, who was killed in action
in 1917.[32] Mendès also had a son by the actress Marguerite Moreno.[33]

Suzanne Meyer-Zundel was to notice Judith's absolute and sometimes
cruel contempt for men. Her infinite sadness came from her bitterness,
disappointment and regrets. She was to show a distant coldness, an
exquisite indifference; but 'through her, though she was unaware of it,
there really showed a temperament quite different from the one she
wanted people to attribute to her . . . To those who did not know her, it
seemed that nothing, and no one, could leave the slightest mark on her
heart. One would easily have called her unfeeling and inhuman, but all her
worshippers . . . very soon became aware that she was not like this at all,
that there was a volcano burning underneath this snow.'[34] Judith was
incurably passionate; and nothing, so Suzanne maintained,

> could vex and humiliate her more than such a discovery. She would have liked
> to conquer men by her mind alone, and she scorned the untimely part which
> physical attraction always played for her male admirers.
>   Idleness, boredom, dreadful boredom filled her with terror; and so she tried
> to occupy her leisure by distracting her mind . . . Gounod was one of those who
> did not mistake the true state of her soul. 'Madame,' he said to her one day,
> 'what you regret is that you are intellectually alone, . . . alone of your kind.'[35]

She was alone, and she remained profoundly distressed. Suzanne was
one day to find among her papers a prose-poem of biblical intensity; it
was, perhaps, the answer to the riddle of her nature.

> I have vowed you a cult to make them blush with shame, all the gods whom
> men adored, and I have built you a temple more splendid than that of Solomon.
>   In this temple I am both the priest and the victim, my spirit is the lamp
> which burns unceasingly, my heart the smoking censer.
>   The robust pillars of my faith are lost in the mist of my dreams and of my
> fervent desires, and the hymn of my glory rises up towards your glory, day and
> night.
>   But if you were only a deceiving idol, if your soul were not as I have imagined
> it to be, if you proved unworthy of my ecstasy, if you made my faith a vain
> idolatry!

By the grandeur of my hopes! By my untiring love! By my soul, which has made itself a pedestal for your beauty! O you whom I adore without reserve, tremble with fear to the very marrow of your bones!

For I shall trust neither God nor Satan to accomplish my revenge.

I shall tear you from the altar which you have usurped, I shall tear your body asunder, and I shall drag you out of this life.

And, through the infinite abysses, through the whole eternity of time, I shall pursue you with my cries of rage, and I shall drive you mad with the ever-increasing cruelty of my hatred, the hatred which nothing will ever assuage.[36]

Everyone, Judith told Suzanne, 'has their emotional core round which their whole existence revolves, and besides which nothing else exists.'[37] Her emotional core had been her disappointed love for Catulle.

Chapter Eighteen

Love had long since disappointed Judith's aspirations, failed her romantic imagination. Even established friendship sometimes failed her. On 23 May 1898 the first performance of *Parsifal* ever to be given in Paris was to be staged on her Théâtre des Marionnettes.

The audience? Invited guests. The actors? Wax dolls. The play? *Parsifal*. Two performances, maybe three. For this [wrote Edmond Haraucourt], Mme Judith Gautier has written a new translation. For the past year, with patient art, she has modelled her thirty or forty figurines, invented springs and articulations to move them. Illustrious artists have painted the anonymous décors; the costumes have been discussed at solemn sessions by the [Almanach de] Gotha of contemporary art; the glories of literature have sought the honour of being stage-carpenters; the electrician is a Member of the Institut [de France]; some prince or other sings in the chorus and some or other noble lady, who would not dare to tread the boards of a real theatre, comes in a brougham to lend her talent to a wax doll, which walks but doesn't speak. The rehearsals take place in great secrecy. The performers' names can be guessed from their voices . . . Happy are those who live on dreams![1]

This Lilliputian Bayreuth, as Henri de Régnier described it, was Judith's affectionate and original tribute to Wagner, whose fame she had fostered in France for some thirty years. Yet if her devotion to his music remained as strong as ever, her relationship with Cosima had long ceased to be close and confiding. Since Wagner's death, Cosima had devoted her life to the furtherance of his work; she was concerned not only with the theatre at Bayreuth, but with foreign performances and foreign royalties. She seems to have understood, now, from the Press, that there was to be a performance of *Parsifal* at the Galerie Barbazanges in Paris; she thought that Judith had planned to give a public performance without permission, and therefore to infringe the composer's rights. Cosima considered legal action. She treated Judith as if she had been an unscrupulous theatre director, and sent her an unforgivably harsh letter.

Judith was wounded:

My dear Cosima,

You are right to think that you are ill-informed. So rest quite assured: it's only a question of a private evening, absolutely barred to the public. If the papers talk about it (and they always talk), it cannot be in any other way.

It is true that I was approached, six months ago, and asked if I would give a public evening in aid of charity. It was then that I asked for information from the Société des Auteurs. They assured me that what I was asked to do was permissible, and that with their permission I should be perfectly in order, provided that I paid the royalties. It was no doubt out of deference, and completely without my knowledge, that the society wrote to Mr Gross. I learned at one and the same time of the request and the answer, which in fact no longer answered anything, since I had already turned down the charity plan. Besides, the society added that its own authorization was all that was needed, and that I could proceed, which I took good care not to do.

When I received your letter, I asked for a copy of the letter sent to Mr Gross, the contents of which I did not know. The idea of representing me as director of a theatre explains your inexplicable feelings to me. So let me tell you, my dear Cosima, that in fact the little theatre does not exist. The four posts which it consists of are brought out of a cupboard once a year, for two or three private evenings, then it goes back into the cupboard and it's forgotten. Indeed, last year, when my old apparatus had fallen to bits, I declared that I would throw the débris into the fire, and give up a folly which costs me endless trouble and a great deal of time and money. My wiser friends approved. The rest protested, and when they tried to establish a small [financial] basis for the crumbling theatre, they obliged me to restore it.

Only once have I opened my door to the public: for a mystery of my father's, in which his grandson [Théo Bergerat], my nephew, an actor, wanted to perform. Then I closed it again, and I closed it more [firmly] than ever this year.

I am sorry that you will not be at my soirée tomorrow. It might perhaps remind you of the time when you were rehearsing the *Rheingold* for Eva's birthday. But those days are distant, now, and the present is different. I try not to know about it, so that I can remember better; for rest assured that through all the changes I have remained unchangeably loyal and ever yours.

Judith Gautier[2]

The heartfelt friendship which had begun in 1869 had ended over a question of business interests. This letter seems to have been the last in the correspondence.

Other friends proved to be more affectionate and more understanding than Cosima. On 28 May, in *Le Gaulois*, Edmond Haraucourt, who was a frequent visitor to Judith's salon, paid tribute to her and to her idealism:

Mme Judith Gautier lives on a desert island, indifferent to all glory, and innocent because of her solitude. Literature, for her, is not a career in the least, but the pleasure of an anchorite; and quietly, in retreat, she cultivates her genius as a solitary cultivates his oasis, in the depths of the desert.

Had she been richer, I imagine she would have kept the fruits of her garden, and no one would have known her poetry. With an egotism which is tinged with modesty and jealousy, she would have kept it for herself alone, and no doubt she would have taken care to burn it before she died. She has published it, however, because one needs to live, but she keeps a grudge against the book which rushes off to the publisher and prostitutes itself in shop windows . . .

In her childhood, she was lapped in dreams . . . The Orient called her. By what atavism did she bear within her the memory and the regret of an oriental world, brilliant, fairylike: a world which she had seen herself before anyone had told her about it? She had already travelled through it when books described it to her; she knew it as a native land, and she recognized it. As a child, when she opened a book which revealed the East to her, she rediscovered the memories of another childhood; immediately, she wanted to know, to know more, to know all: in learning, it seemed to her that she was refreshing her memory . . . In accounts of travels, she saw again the visions of her dreams, a whole Eden which was already familiar . . . She wanted to study the languages of these familiar people, to re-learn their forgotten existence; and her soul, full of palaces with marble floors, with golden roofs, and gardens, became a sunlit paradise.

Then she peopled it with heroes and princesses, lovers and their ladies with hearts as pure as her own, with noble, unreal souls: in the setting of *The Thousand and One Nights* there shone the deeds of Roland. Warriors who clove armies asunder were there as chaste as virgins, and man, proud and gentle, had something of the lion and of the lamb . . . Sadness was sweet and friendship deep, and vows were kept. Love blessed human beings; life was good; the world was beautiful!

She lived in such a world, while she created it.

Of our own world, she knew nothing. She chooses to know nothing of it. Paris is for her a distant capital which she does not even wish to visit. The shapes in Paris lack splendour and mystery, the houses there are grey; the multitudes of people are lustreless, the sky too pale . . .

She has beautiful eyes which see nothing at all. She passes through existence, but without perceiving . . . Her whole vision is an inner vision, so is her whole life. Things flow about her without echoing in her. She is jealously enclosed in a sort of cloister which she has fortified with indifference and distaste, perhaps with fear. A nun of art, she is in ecstasy in a retreat which sometimes seems like prayer, and she only recalls the outside world when she looks to the bolts on her gates.[3]

The bolts were sometimes drawn. On 29 January 1899, Pierre Louÿs announced to Claude Debussy: 'I'm dining this evening with Mme Judith Gautier, 30, rue Washington.'[4] It was one of his last visits as a bachelor. On 15 May he explained to Judith:

Madame,

    I haven't been able to come to the rue Washington for several weeks, because a great event was imminent. I am delighted to tell you that I am engaged to Louise de Heredia. You can be sure that, apart from all the reasons I had for wanting this marriage, I am delighted to marry a young girl who is a friend of yours . . .

    Always rest assured, Madame, of my affectionate and profound respect.

Pierre Louÿs[5]

It was this same year, 1899, that Judith came to know two English sisters, the Misses Mabel and Ethel Duncan. Ethel was later to translate the memoirs of Judith's cousin, the daughter of Giulia Grisi; Mabel was to write her own memoirs, which, alas, remained in manuscript. The Duncans became close friends of Judith's; and, recorded the francophile Sisley Huddleston: 'It was always a pleasure, in their spacious apartment by the quiet place Saint-Sulpice, to listen to their stories of the vivacious old lady [sic].'[6]

Mabel Duncan recalled, years later:

Judith once told me that all records of her birth had been destroyed, that nobody could determine her age, and I strongly suspect that she made herself out younger than she was. She was a stout, heavy woman when I knew her, and affected loose, flowing robes, but she had remained wonderfully young in character, and liked to be surrounded with young people. We knew all her friends, and when she had accepted to review the Saturday and Sunday concerts for the paper Excelsior, though she often sent someone to replace her on Sundays, for she received that day from 2 p.m. to midnight, there were often concerts given by celebrities that she had to go to. She would send us a note asking us to come to her house and receive her friends and keep them till she got back at five o'clock.[7]

The first number of Excelsior, an illustrated daily, was to appear on 16 November 1910. It contained an article by Judith: 'Le Conflit des compositeurs'; and, for the next year and more, she remained the accredited music critic: writing under her own name and, perhaps, under the pseudonym Fortunio.

Some time towards the end of the century, the American author Stuart Henry called on 'the talented daughter of Théophile Gautier, the celebrated poet, and of Carlotta Grisi'.[8] This somewhat unreliable visitor, who accorded Judith the wrong mother, and underestimated her age by five years,

was struck at once by her resemblance to her father – by her powerful physique, and by the dead white color of her face, and by a certain plastic grandeur that would tempt the chisel . . .

She spoke of many things. First, of *Japanism*, since she was one of its earliest devotees in France. The Goncourts had started the fashion . . . But Judith Gautier was the first to translate Yellow romances for French readers, and to prepare a Saffron drama for the Paris stage. This drama, *The Merchant of Smiles*, was given at the Odéon in 1888, and was played in Daly's in New York under some other title. Her Japanese novel *The Usurper* was awarded a prize by the French Academy in 1875, when the author was twenty-five years old [she was in fact thirty] . . .

'My Japanese books have not met with success in England and America,' she said in her echoless voice. 'I am told that the English and Americans are interested in the Japanese for their grotesque drollery, whereas I have tried to treat the sad side of their nature.' . . .

The subject changed to Wagner. Judith Gautier was one of his most intimate friends. 'I was born a Wagnerite,' she said. 'As far back as I can remember, his music was magic to me . . . Ah, if he could have lived a few years more! He had got things yet in store. He told me of the new opera he was meditating. Hindustan was the scene and Buddha was to be introduced. But he had to go – he was very weary – he had suffered so much.' . . .

She showed me (with the excuse that they were fabulously idealized) some photographs of herself as a Valkyria [*sic*] in magnificent attitudes and with small white Valkyrian wings on her black hair. There was an aspect of grandiose humility, of valiant strength, of unconscious appeal, in these goddess pictures – a helpless triumph gleaming at me with probing eyes. Amazing eyes, indeed, were the eyes of my hostess! – those two deep torrid lights of lustrous jet shining forth from a soul that lived, not in France, but in distant tropics where restless coralline understreams rise and find solace at tranquil ocean surfaces . . .

As I came away through the low ante-chamber, and down the five flights of stairs, I was thinking, not of Wagner and his Valkyrias, but of austral seas and white, immobile statues – of a yearning soul from the East locked within the placid contours of some pearl and ivory Buddha.[9]

Judith yearned, still, for the East. On 15 December 1897, *La Revue de Paris* had published *Le Prince à la tête sanglante*. It was a short story which, again, revealed all the violence and colour of her Orient.

A young Chinese shepherd is bewildered by a loud, continuous murmur:

What is it? It sounds like the distant rumble of chariots of war, the rhythmical trampling of horses on the march and the muffled clash of arms.

No, it is not that.

On the other side of the pool, a jasmine tree is in wondrous bloom: on the bare branches, nothing but flowers, little white and yellow flowers of enchanting fragrance; and, in the troubled water, the bush is reflected, there it is nothing more than a cloud; but a whole world of bees, insects and butterflies whirl round among these blossoming branches, and with what commotion, what delight! They gorge themselves, grow drunk, grow mad; their wings tremble and quiver; drops of gold, emeralds and flames, rush passionately down on the scented petals, kiss them, bite them, suck the honeyed saliva, knead the tender pulp which is swollen with a bitter milk. At moments, the tree seems to shake itself, reject these insatiable lovers; but they rush upon it again: avid, still, with a tremor yet more sonorous.

The shepherd smiles and half closes his eyes.

The amorous bees, assaulting this tree, seemed to him to imitate the sounds of the chariots of war, reverberating in the mountain gorges! . . . And why does he think of war? . . . The bees are not thinking of it.[10]

It is a prose-poem, sexually charged: a measure of Judith's lyric imagination and, perhaps, of her own frustrated physical and emotional desires.

Her longing for the East was recalled once again when, on 1 April 1900, *La Revue Blanche* published another felicitous prose-poem. *L'Oiseau-fleur lisse ses plumes* describes the *lever* of a Japanese courtesan. Intensely Japanese though it is, her beauty recalls the beauty celebrated in *The Song of Solomon:* 'The pure and elongated oval of her face is shaped exactly like a half of a water-melon; her hair is as black as the lacquer of Kyoto, and the curve of its locks draws on her brow the snowy summit of Mount Fujiyama . . .'[11] L'Oiseau-fleur is bathed, and dressed 'in a satin robe the colour of weak tea, all covered with poems embroidered in black upon squares of gold'.[12] Then, in her garden, she sings of her grief at the passing of her love.

L'Oiseau–fleur lisse ses plumes, so delicate and so intense, was followed, on 15 April, by *L'Oiseau-fleur conte une histoire*, the tale of the same courtesan overcome by maternal love. Whatever Judith's cool behaviour, her Parnassian impassibility, these two brief tales again reflect her passionate nature.

The year 1900 saw a new International Exhibition in Paris. Its exotic splendours delighted her. At the last Exhibition, in 1889, Benedictus had transcribed the curious music he had heard, and published a collection of *Musiques bizarres*. Now 'he accomplished a tour de force, and caught in flight the indiscernible music which is never written down. He has,' wrote Judith, 'fixed it and wonderfully caught its enveloping charm.'[13] He transcribed the music of six oriental countries; she herself provided a commentary. Ollendorff published the results in half a dozen pamphlets which were later collected in book form.

The Javanese dancers had returned to Paris, and they did not disappoint their admirers. The Egyptian section at the Exhibition earned Judith's eager praise. She listened to 'the two delectable sisters, Ouan-Ta-Pa and Ouan-Eul-Pa, singing at the Théâtre Chinois at the Trocadéro, accompanying themselves on the pi-pa and the two-stringed violin'.[14] At the Japanese section, she watched 'the great artist who is at once comedienne, dancer and tragic actress: Sada-Yacco, who is all the rage in Paris. She brings us, as it were, a brief and final vision of that feudal Japan which we have not known, that feudal Japan which is no more. Only the great courtesans and actors of Japan piously keep its traditions, which will be submerged under the tide of the new civilization.'[15]

Judith was later to discuss the differences of character between the Japanese and the Chinese. To her the Japanese were like the Germans. They exploited other people's inventions, and in general they were aggressive. There remained a permanent barrier between the Japanese and the French. She herself had only two Japanese friends: Komiosi, and the Marquis Saionzi. With them, alone, this barrier had been broken. As for the Chinese, they were like the French. They were fundamentally peaceful and artistic, and they were content to seek, discover and invent.[16]

Among her Chinese friends was Yu-Keng, the new Minister to Paris. In April 1901 he improvised some stanzas in her honour:

> Upon a sovereign order, entrusting me with an embassy, I have had to leave my country, and travel across the oceans to the distant West, to the illustrious city of Paris . . .
> Between the leaping waves I gaze, hoping that I shall see a vision of the beautiful goddess Siang-Ling, holding the golden lyre in her white arms . . .
> But it is not Siang-Ling who appears to me; she whom I meet is a poetess of the West, who, to my delighted surprise, clasps to her heart the poems of my native land! . . .
> And so I write these few lines for her, and, as I hand them to her, I rejoice to think that we can talk together of poets and of poetry.[17]

On 15 June, *Vers l'Occident* was published in *La Revue de Paris*. It was followed by a number of Chinese poems translated by Judith Gautier. She had long lived in a West to which she did not belong. One of the most poignant works in her *Poésies* was to be the poem she had written to Yu-Keng to thank him, in turn, for the poem he had sent her.

> Comme une graine, au vent jetée,
> Par une rafale emportée
> J'ai fleuri, loin du ciel natal,
> Sous le brouillard occidental.
>
> Mais, dans mon ennui nostalgique,
> Toujours l'Orient magique

Mon rêve, au tournesol pareil,
Se tourne vers le vrai soleil.

Loin de la glorieuse aïeule,
Je me sens orpheline et seule,
Et dans mon coeur jamais lassé
Veille le culte du passé.

O Yu-Keng! illustre poète,
Par vous la Chine me fait fête,
Et, comblant mon plus cher souhait,
Pour son enfant me reconnaît.[18]

Judith longed, insatiably, to learn about her adopted country. Albert de Pouvourville, the author of *La Chine des mandarins*, remembered with affection:

On my return from the Far East, Judith Gautier monopolized my days, . . . for the countless recollections I had stored up in my memory and for all the exotic fragrance with which twelve years of Asia had impregnated my words, my ideas, and even my actions . . .

I shall never forget the calm and friendly atmosphere of that house, . . . and the conversations which degenerated into monologues, and the long silences full of savour, between the mistress of the house, always smiling but already struck by illness, Satan the cat, which listened to us, motionless, and no doubt understood us, and Juliette the snake, which had become a friend of mine and which, one cold and humid day, when I was already in the street on my way home, I found in my overcoat pocket, curled up snugly round my fur-lined gloves.[19]

All that was oriental enthralled Judith Gautier. The vision of the East remained before her and within her: a vision which owed much to books and pictures and conversations, but more to her intense and loving imagination. Through her imagination she had seen reality: not merely photographic reality, but enduring spiritual truth. She had found what Victor Hugo, in the preface to *La Légende des siècles*, had called 'la réalité historique condensée ou . . . la réalité historique devinée'. Her work was sometimes fiction, but it was never falsified. When Bojidar Karageorgevitch sailed for India, to write his *Notes sur l'Inde*, he had slipped two books into his trunk: *La Conquête du Paradis* by Judith Gautier, and *L'Histoire de la littérature hindoue*, by Jean Lahor. 'They both recalled a legendary past,' he wrote. 'One of them, an admirable novel, showed an India which had changed so little over the ages that it was the one I recognized.'[20]

Judith escaped not only to the distant East, but to her own past. As Pouvourville recorded, she was struck now by illness – perhaps already by a heart condition. In September 1902 she wrote to Loti: 'I have wanted to send you my *Livre de Jade* for a long time, but I am in a curious state in which any action is an unbelievable labour for me. I feel I'm living in a mist, on yielding ground, with a boneless body. So much so that I've let the summer pass and I haven't looked at the countryside . . .'[21] Her condition persisted. On 14 January 1903, she confessed to an unnamed correspondent: 'I have recently been very unwell. It was impossible for me to answer you. I am just recovering . . .'[22] It was now, in her late fifties, when she felt alone, and ill, and wretchedly uncertain of her future, that she embarked upon the work that was to remain one of her best titles to fame and to the affection of posterity. She returned to her own past, and began to write *Le Collier des jours*, her iridescent autobiography.

The first volume appeared in 1902; the second followed in 1903, after it had been serialized in the *Revue de Paris*. In February, in the *Mercure de France*, Rémy de Gourmont reviewed the book. It was, he said, written by someone

> who seems to find with each new year still more vivacity, more freshness, and more grace. Between *Le Dragon impérial* and *Le Collier des jours* there is so little distance that one would think the two books contemporary and born of the same youthfulness. Judith Gautier knows every language, living or dead, she knows every literature, philosophy and religion, and, when she writes, it is with the smiling innocence of a surprised and enchanted young girl. Innocence is perhaps the real form of feminine genius: innocence, which means in this context something like perpetual youth of spirit . . . A real woman is always young, . . . always a little childlike, even when the intellectual part of her being is enriched by several sciences and numerous talents. That is why *Le Collier des jours* is a delightful book.[23]

Rémy de Gourmont did not merely review Judith's latest work. In 1904 he also assessed her in the series *Les Célébrités d'aujourd'hui*.

> Judith Gautier seems, with Pierre Loti, to represent the taste for the exotic in contemporary French literature. To judge by her novels, her poetry, her plays, she would rather be Chinese than French; and not only Chinese but Japanese, too, or Persian, or Egyptian . . . She does not only read Chinese, she speaks it and she writes it . . .
>
> Here, then, is a woman whose imaginative life has been entirely spent in Asia . . . Even her social relationships have been affected by this pronounced taste for the exotic. It is difficult to go to Judith Gautier's without meeting some Japanese ill-disguised by European clothes, or two or three brilliant mandarins in national dress with their pigtails swinging on their backs as they make their bows with exquisite politeness. Her salon is an Asiatic academy.

But look at the power of race and heredity. This woman, completely nurtured on the exotic, is among the best purely French writers of today.[24]

One day, recalled Judith, Sarah Bernhardt wrote to Pierre Loti: 'I should like to act in a Chinese play in which I took the part of an Empress.' Loti replied: 'I haven't got such a play myself, but let me collaborate with Judith Gautier.'[25] 'Dear friend,' came Sarah's telegram, '. . . the collaboration you mention will give me great delight because I adore that exquisite woman. It will be heavenly to work under the inspiration of two people who are dear to me. I embrace you in fraternity of heart.'[26]

Judith was enthusiastic. In May 1903 she happily told Loti:

I will do all you want; and of course I shall be delighted. The only thing which causes me a little anxiety is my wretched health; but I am gradually getting better and I am hurrying my work so that I can be completely free.

I am very impatient to begin the great enterprise – there won't be too much time.

In the meanwhile, I'm translating a history from the Chinese annals: the history of a beautiful, bloodthirsty and glorious Empress. It may be useful to us . . .

But I shall see you soon, dear Loti; it will be a double festival for me, as you can imagine, to see you a little consistently at last.[27]

During the next few months, there was a lively correspondence between them. Loti, a naval officer, was either on the *Vautour* at Constantinople, or else continually on the move, in Paris or Rochefort. 'I am meditating about the play according to the indications you give me, which is rather terrifying,' Judith wrote. 'But we'll talk about it soon.'[28] On 30 May, 1903, she sent an express letter to him at the Hôtel Meurice, rue de Rivoli: 'Welcome, dear Loti! Iouen-Poa-Ki will be delighted to see you. I hope that you will devote a few hours to *La Fille du ciel*. Whatever hours you like. If you'd care to have *déjeuner* or dinner with me – you decide. I shall always be free.'[29] On 4 June she sent another letter, again by express: 'My dear, I'll send all I've managed to do at four o'clock.'[30] And again: 'What a rush! I'm worn out, and I haven't time to re-read. Do explain that the last act, in particular, is hardly sketched out. It would be very kind of you if you'd return the manuscript so that I can copy it; I'll send it back if you're in a hurry, or give it to you next time you're passing.'[31] 'Sarah very nice and very pleased,' came Loti's telegram. 'And so am I (very nice and very pleased). Returning the manuscript by registered post.'[32]

The summer passed in intensive work. It was presumably about now that Judith explained to Robert de Montesquiou:

Very dear friend,
    . . . Tomorrow I am even more tied up than usual. Georgette Leblanc is
coming to rehearse some of the *Poèmes de Jade* which she is going to sing in
London (my débuts in musical composition!!! You may die of laughter . . . But
literature is so deceptive!)
    And, besides, Loti is in Paris and he's going to come and talk to me about *La
Fille du ciel* . . . As you see, I can't go out, no need to say I'm sorry, but also
why choose that particular day? . . .[33]

In July, once again, she wrote to Loti:

I have kept these two months' holiday free from chores so that I can work at the
play consistently and in peace. I will send you what I've done as I do it. Always
tell me where you will be. Even Constantinople is not on the moon, and one can
correspond . . .
    Jot down the ideas that occur to you and send them to me, without any link
or order.
    We'll need quite a bit of music. I have already set my collaborator in the
Musiques bizarres to work; he is used to it. Give us what information you have
for the orchestra. I haven't forgotten the flutes in unison . . .[34]

And again:

Dear Loti,
    I am very happy that you are pleased. But I beg you to correct and amplify
and only to take what I send you as a very incomplete first draft . . .
    I'm very glad that you haven't said anything to Sarah. Don't let the delays
come from us. There will be quite enough as it is. If we told her [that the play
was unfinished], she would arrange her season without us.[35]

Loti was no doubt diplomatic, but he put gentle pressure on Sarah.

Madame amie [he reported to Judith],
    Yesterday evening Sarah answered my letter asking if she was really going to
act it by a telegram from Belle Isle: 'Yes, of course, dearest friend, yes, a
hundred times yes.'
    We mustn't yet cry victory, but at least we can hope . . .[36]

Alas, there was still trouble with Sarah. She had thought the drama was
written, and she understandably refused to take the unfinished play for
that season. Judith was desolate. 'The news you gave me in your last letter
was a catastrophe for me [this to Loti]. It was terrible to see the play put
off for years to come, when one had dropped everything for its sake – but,
when you are not stunned by the blow, you get up and move on.'[37]
    A gleam of hope appeared, for Lucien Guitry seemed to want to stage
La Fille du ciel. Then he decided against it. 'I thought for a moment that

we might have a quick solution,' wrote Judith, 'but when he knew the truth – no doubt he feels some affectionate obligation to his great colleague, and he had qualms about it . . . When our play is finished, Sarah either performs it or not. If she doesn't, she is in the wrong and we are free. The sooner that is, the better. Let's share the work, and finish first; we can polish it up later.'[38]

Judith and Loti had perpetual problems with Sarah Bernhardt; and, as the months went by, they grew increasingly impatient. Judith considered Jules Claretie, administrator-general of the Comédie-Française. She thought of Porel, sometime husband of Réjane, and director of the Vaudeville. She wondered about Coquelin aîné, director of the Théâtre de la Porte-Saint-Martin. Sarah Bernhardt herself explained by telegram to Loti: 'Dear friend, La Fille du ciel has a remarkable first act. An unactable second, where the Empress has four monologues. A fine last act but three times too long. I embrace you in fraternal affection. S.B.'[39]

Judith was angry and frustrated. In March 1904, she scribbled again to Loti: 'If Sarah says that she detests the monologue, she is lying. That's all there is in every play she acts in, and she hardly lets her partners say a word.'[40]

La Sorcière had recently opened at the Théâtre Sarah-Bernhardt. Judith went to see the drama by Sardou which Sarah had preferred to her own. It was, she told Loti, 'an inept play where they bawl and yell like market porters. You can hardly hear what they say. It's a frenetic pantomime.'[41] Yet, for all her vexation with Sarah, Judith was prudent: that year, when Eugène Fasquelle published her new collection of short stories, Le Paravent de soie et d'or, she sent her a copy, suitably inscribed.[42]

Meanwhile, in the spring of 1904, Judith accepted all Loti's ideas and all his advice.[43] La Fille du ciel remains romantic, but her own concern for history and realism and his concern for moderation and balance make it a powerful and solid work. Unlike her other plays, which are engaging fantasies and entertainments, La Fille du ciel reflects the ideal so frequently discovered in her novels: the ideal of grandeur, purity and sacrifice. The novelist Claude Farrère, who was among the first to read the play, found himself 'moved a thousand times more than I could say'.[44] La Fille du ciel did not see the footlights of a French theatre. It was, however, published in 1911. A seventh edition appeared in 1912.

'Someone to cajole and someone to murder are,' wrote the critic William Archer, 'the two necessities of artistic existence for Mme Sarah Bernhardt; and the illustrious Academician [Victorien Sardou] is her most active purveyor of victims.'[45] La Fille du ciel owes something to the Sardou model; the widowed Empress shows her impassioned love for the Tartar Emperor, her enemy, and she finally takes poison in his arms, upon her throne. *La Fille du ciel* has the grandiose melodrama of Sardou, the visual magnificence of the Yellow Empire. Trumpets are sounded, courtiers prostrate themselves, eunuchs keep the common herd from gazing on the sacred imperial person. Before the Empress walk attendants bearing the yellow parasol with three flounces; behind her, other servants bear tall feather screens, emblems of sovereignty. *La Fille du ciel* was written as a vehicle for Sarah Bernhardt, who moved strong men to tears when she died on stage; but – at least in France – only Sarah could perform it.

Ironically, she accepted a play by Catulle Mendès. On 10 November 1906, after an absence of eighteen months, she returned to the Paris stage in *La Vierge d'Avila*, in which she played St Theresa. All Paris flocked to see Sarah as a nun. She added one more to an imposing series of death scenes.

Perhaps she had been mistaken in refusing *La Fille du ciel*. Six years later, in October 1912, it was performed in New York. A critic observed that

> this sensational event had gathered in the auditorium of the Century Theater all the high society of New York and a few celebrated Parisians who had come over for the event [*sic*]. The French Ambassador and Mme Jusserand attended the performance in a centre box, adorned with the French and American colours. On their arrival, they received a veritable ovation.
>
> The evening ended in the midst of endless applause, and, to escape the enthusiasm of the crowd, M. Pierre Loti had to leave the theatre by a back door before the end of the performance.
>
> *La Fille du ciel* will certainly run for several months; it already exercises an indirect influence on the social life of New York. Five great Chinese balls are announced for next month, and elegant American women are going to dress their hair like the Filles du ciel. That is a triumph which M. Loti certainly did not expect.[46]

IV

Maya

Chapter Nineteen

Suzanne Meyer-Zundel was born in 1882, the daughter of wealthy parents in Alsace.[1] They lived in the rue Thiers, in Mulhouse, in a massive mansion with extensive stables and outbuildings. Robert de Montesquiou, the aristocrat and aesthete, to whom Suzanne once sent a photograph, no doubt had his private thoughts about such bourgeois opulence.[2] The Meyer-Zundels did not figure in *Le Livre d'or de la Ville de Mulhouse*, when this record of distinguished local families was re-issued in 1883; but a certain Jules Meyer-Zundel, of Wesserling, was listed among the subscribers. The family was not mentioned in the two volumes of local archives published in 1895 and 1897; but Jules Meyer-Zundel was among those who guaranteed the publication. The Meyer-Zundels, one suspects, were barons of industry with a longing for social acceptance.

Suzanne herself had two brothers, one of whom was married, the other a confirmed bachelor; her sisters made conventional marriages. Nothing is known of her father, whom she does not even mention in her memoirs, but her mother was unsophisticated and recklessly indulgent. Suzanne had scant respect for her; she seems to have learned in childhood that, if she persisted long enough in her demands, her mother would always finally grant them.

'I never in my life,' she wrote, 'had to suffer any constraint.'[3] She hardly suffered the constraint of education. Since the Franco-Prussian War, Alsace had been part of the German Empire, and all lessons were given in German. Some families, like the Meyer-Zundels, who kept their old allegiance to France, and could afford private tuition for their children, engaged French tutors from Belfort or Nancy three or four times a week. Suzanne gained little from this sporadic education. She was intellectually lazy, she had small interest in books, and she could not write acceptable French. Her only gift appears to have been the unusual gift of modelling flowers out of breadcrumbs, an occupation in which she showed an unchallenged skill. She refused not only the discipline of learning, but an education in manners. She was irremediably spoilt, stubborn with her family, arrogant to servants, and effusive to her social superiors. Mademoiselle Mie-de-Pain, as she was dubbed by Ferdinand Bac,[4] had no notion of behaviour. In her early twenties, she remained provincial and immature. There is no record that she was ever attracted to men, no record (despite her wealth) of prospective suitors; but she needed some grand passion. She was kind, intensely sentimental, and increasingly frustrated.

One summer, in Switzerland, where she was staying with her married brother, she happened to meet Prince Bojidar Karageorgevitch. He much admired her skill at modelling, and he watched with fascination as violets, fuchsias and forget-me-nots appeared under her dexterous fingers. By the time she was obliged to rejoin her mother in Alsace, Prince Bojidar had become a steadfast friend.[5]

She herself was all the more unhappy in her everyday routine. Life in Mulhouse, so she wrote, was as monotonous as that of molluscs clinging to their rock. One day she found her means of escape. The paper *Femina* announced an exhibition which was soon to open in Paris. Le Grand Concours de la Jeune Fille was designed to bring to light some undiscovered feminine talent. Mme Meyer-Zundel refused to let her daughter go alone to Paris. Suzanne replied that either her mother went to Paris with her, or she would go to Paris by herself.

A few days later, bearing a glass case of model flowers, mother and daughter settled in a hotel in the rue Carnot. The unknown talent was revealed; Suzanne shared first prize for her modelling. Financial arrangements were no problem for the Meyer-Zundels. Soon afterwards she was installed in a little villa, Florilège, near the Bois de Boulogne, to establish herself in her career. When her mother returned to Mulhouse, Suzanne's unmarried brother moved into Florilège to live with her.

Prince Bojidar, who was now a neighbour, often called on her. A year or so later, in the spring of 1904, he decided to introduce her to 'a great friend whom I love and admire'.[6] The following Sunday he presented Suzanne and her brother at the rue Washington.

> Was it an intuition [she wondered, long years afterwards]? For me this visit had the significance of an event . . . I still see myself, in the intoxicating light of that fine April day, in the rather overwhelming sun, during those few minutes' walk, . . . then climbing a broad staircase up to the fifth floor.
>
> There was a small seat on the landing. Above it were some Japanese engravings. Beside the door hung a strip of Chinese embroidery which served as a bell-pull. These simple details already revealed tastes like those of the young

mandarin – they had given me this affectionate nickname as a child, because of my liking for everything exotic. What eager delight I felt when the door opened, and a Chinaman stood before me! A real one, clad in a sumptuous robe of royal blue silk. A superb black pigtail hung right down his back. Very slim and slender, with a gentle, welcoming face, this original guest, with his undulating walk, led us to the salon. This was separated from the hall by a simple curtain of rustling pearls. An open French window led on to a broad terrace which ran the length of the apartment. A Pleyel grand piano stood in front of a window adorned with stained glass with Turkish arabesques. This window, a memento of Gautier's visit to Constantinople, had been given to him by the Sultan.

There were large divans in the two corners of this very low-ceilinged salon. On the wall was a huge painting by René Gérin: a scene inspired by *Tannhäuser* . . . There were portraits of Judith by different artists, friends of the woman of letters. You saw her at home, wearing an ample white *peignoir*, standing in her *salon;* Judith on the dunes at Saint-Enogat, wearing a robe with wide sleeves and protecting her big straw hat from the fury of the wind. Judith in the country, sitting at the edge of a wood in the middle of a green field, . . . bare-headed, wearing a pure white dress. Judith on a summer day, walking in her garden.

Laughter and bursts of gaiety announced the end of a happy dinner . . . The sudden pushing back of chairs marked the end of the meal, a door creaked on its hinges, and, from the far end of the hall, leading her guests, a woman came forward, slowly, dressed all in white, that slightly creamy white, in a straight, loose, silk gandoura. It was like a Chinese goddess come down from her kakemono. This woman made an immediate and deep impression on me . . . When the first banal formalities had been exchanged, my hostess made me a sign to sit beside her . . .

I seized the first occasion to move away from her, so that I could take in her expression and features, and fix them in my mind. Her eyes had struck me; they were an extraordinary colour like that quartz, with reflections of greenish gold, which is known as 'cat's-eye' . . .

Her gaze was suffused with a deep melancholy . . . Her expression let one divine a disillusioned soul, ennobled, made more generous, by the bitterness of life . . . There was a very unusual contrast: the glossy black of her hair set off the marmoreal whiteness of her skin. And then her attitudes and her pure features, wonderful in their regularity, gave her the appearance of a Greek statue.

That day I made my irrevocable decision. Whatever the cost, I would win the friendship of this woman whom I felt to be so perfect and so accomplished. This wish, to gain her friendship, became the one object of my life.[7]

As they walked back to Florilège, Suzanne repeatedly asked Bojidar for his impressions of this first meeting. Judith had expressed no wish to see her again; but 'she never asks people to come back,' Bojidar explained. 'When they come back of their own accord, and show that they aren't counting the visits, then they are accepted as friends.'[8]

Several Sundays passed, and he made no further allusion to the visit. At last the longed-for occasion occurred.

Suzanne Meyer-Zundel is notoriously inaccurate in her account of events. In *Quinze Ans auprès de Judith Gautier*, she records, repeatedly, that she entered Judith's life in 1904. If this is true – and one accepts it – then her book should be called *Treize Ans auprès de Judith Gautier*, for Judith died in 1917. Suzanne Meyer-Zundel also refers to President Fallières, but from 1899 to 1906 Émile Loubet was President of the Republic. Biographies of Loubet, and contemporary papers, make no reference to a visit from King Sisowath of Cambodia, either in 1902 or 1904; they record that, on 12 July 1904, the President entertained the Bey of Tunis to a dinner and a soirée, but there is no mention of a garden party. What follows is Suzanne's account of an occasion which is doubtless true in spirit, if not in fact.

In the first half of June 1904, so she records, King Sisowath of Cambodia was on a visit to Paris, and the President gave a garden party for him at the Élysée. The royal Cambodian dancers were to perform on the palace lawn. Suzanne and her brother had procured themselves an invitation. A flood of guests invaded the Presidential gardens. Suddenly Suzanne cried: 'There she is! She's here!'[9]

There was no time for protocol or even for decorum. Abandoning her brother, she ran off 'in pursuit of the woman who had become the hope of my life, the secret wish of my affection'.[10] She found her, and, recollecting that Judith had no memory for faces, she introduced herself. 'But of course I remember you,' Judith said.[11] Suzanne remained immovably, inexorably, beside her, and, during the course of the conversation, she mentioned that she would soon be leaving for Saint-Lunaire, where her mother had rented a villa for the summer. 'But I spend every summer in that part of the world,' said Judith. 'I am a stone's throw from Saint-Lunaire. I have a little house at Saint-Enogat. I hope that you will come and see me there.'[12]

The numerous Meyer-Zundels duly assembled at Bon-Abri. One day in mid-July, in a heatwave, Suzanne and her brother called at Le Pré des Oiseaux. They were ushered into the salon. The walls were painted reddish-brown, and almost entirely covered with kakemonos and with elaborate pictures on gold backgrounds: portraits of Chinese poets and poetesses. A Japanese parasol – Robert de Montesquiou's parasol? – hung, open, from the ceiling, and quivered in every tremor of the breeze. A window looked across the steps and the terrace towards the sea. There were so many windows that one seemed to be inside a lantern. 'At last the door opened. It was Her! She was astonished by the sight of the two audacious people who had braved such heat. There was a certain anxiety in her face . . . She gave us a very warm welcome.'[13]

Two days later, brother and sister returned to Saint-Enogat. Suzanne paid a third visit, alone. Mme Meyer-Zundel invited Judith to Saint-Lunaire. Suzanne – who now considered herself the daughter of the house – returned to Le Pré des Oiseaux with the invitation. Judith promised to come with two Chinese friends.

> As for me [recalled Suzanne], I already felt a certain web of hostility woven by my family round this new friendship. It was not without a secret apprehension that I saw the arrival of the day when my friend, accompanied by 'her Chinamen', would be taken to pieces by all of them: these strait-laced bourgeois with tastes and ideas so diametrically opposed to her own – these bourgeois, stiff with prejudice, who had certainly never in their lives had any contact with people of a foreign race, whom they dismissed as dagoes and expatriates, let alone with real Chinese!
>   Then Judith herself gave an oriental note to her very personal style of dress. She did not lack originality, and she might appear eccentric to them.[14]

The *déjeuner* went well, but, the moment that the guests had gone, the family divided into two opposing camps: those who were in favour of Judith, those who were not. Mme Meyer-Zundel was resolutely neutral; the sons-in-law were hostile, and their hostility affected their wives. Suzanne understood that she would have to fight every inch to keep the friendship. A few days later, the Meyer-Zundels decided to go home a fortnight early.

Suzanne predictably insisted that she stayed in Brittany. As usual, for the sake of peace, her mother gave in. She agreed that the girl might stay, on condition that a maid remained with her. There was no need for such arrangements. Judith promptly offered to give Suzanne the 'cigar-box' in her garden.

The next fortnight, recalled Suzanne, passed 'in the sweetest beatitude'.[15] When at last she felt obliged to mention her departure for Paris: 'Oh, Suzanne,' said Judith, 'you aren't going to leave me all alone? I've arranged to go back on 28 September. If you really want to please me, and prove your friendship, stay till then. We'll go back together.'[16]

Judith was fifty-nine, and Suzanne was twenty-two; because of this disparity in age, Suzanne found a name for her which was both intimate and respectful. 'Call me Marraine,' said Judith. 'Anyway, am I not your spiritual godmother already?' Suzanne later called her Maya – the goddess Illusion. The name was used by some of Judith's friends.[17]

On 28 September, with Judith and her *ménagerie intime*, Suzanne returned to Paris, leaving behind us [so she wrote] a thousand regrets: the desertion of such a happy home, of the Bengal rose which so touched my friend. It was as old as the house, and it would continue to flower far away from us . . . With the final preparations for departure – taking down the kakemonos, putting the precious trinkets in order – we finally gave the Pré its uninhabited 'winter' look; while dogs, cats and birds, in their baskets and cages, waited anxiously for the moment of departure . . .

When Judith travelled, she liked to do so in comfort; and so she used to reserve one, two, or sometimes three extra seats [on the train]. She had soon made the compartment look like a lived-in-room. Papers, books and reviews were spread over the seats; then she let her animals out of their prison, and, so as not to disorientate them too much, she explained, when *déjeuner* came, she laid a cloth and places as for a picnic. It was a tradition to serve, among other things, a particular 'Balzac' concoction, a nicely calculated mixture of sardines and butter without which, it appears, the great writer never set out on a journey. The mixture was easy to carry, and it did not displease the cats, who licked their chops at the very thought of it. The banquet ended with the traditional cigarette. [In Paris], getting out of the omnibus was always a particular amusement for the local shopkeepers and the passers-by. This menagerie on the pavement, waiting to return to its winter quarters, was really very comical: there was an entertaining cacophony of barks, miaows and whistles. Finally, the whole little world, let loose in the apartment, sniffed out, examined, and gradually resumed possession of their favourite pieces of furniture, impregnated with the familiar smell, which Judith tried to mask with various essences . . .

Since she had always lived among them, Judith – like her parents – quite certainly preferred animals to human beings.[18]

That September day, when Suzanne was about to leave for Florilège, Judith said abruptly·: 'I expect you for dinner this evening.' It was the first time that she had used the intimate form of address. 'It took me quite a long while,' remembered Suzanne, 'to become accustomed to this sudden *tutoiement* . . . Of course this state of things was delightful, but I also felt a vague anxiety when I thought about my family . . . And, besides, what would Judith's friends say when, only a few months earlier, I had been an outsider?'[19]

Suzanne was to speak of friendship, maternal and filial affection. Ferdinand Bac, who visited Saint-Enogat in 1910, managed to record his impressions in a non-committal but suggestive way:

At table, there was another guest whose relation to the poetess remained ill-defined for newcomers. But in this romantic kingdom are not all relations placed beyond the notions established by an astute and secretive society? It was her adopted daughter, her secretary, her friend, her only friend, without a doubt, in the fullest sense of the word. She was called Mlle Meyer, like the

Egeria of the artist Prud'hon. She was absolutely straightforward, shrewd on
several subjects, solidly built and industrious . . .

The life of these two inseparable women was the successful bonding of two
solitudes which requited them for all their sorrows.[20]

The relationship remained ill-defined, and the speculation continued.
After Judith's death, Émile Bergerat felt constrained to write: 'She
remained all her life an old-fashioned Frenchwoman of her own sex. She
did not belong to the Thermodon of the Amazons.'[21] It was an official
denial, by her family, that Judith had had a Lesbian 'marriage'.

Suzanne Meyer-Zundel's inclinations are perhaps more open to question.
If her statements are to be accepted, it was she who had fallen in love with
Judith at their first encounter; and she was to recall that moment, many
years afterwards, recall every detail of Judith's appearance, as a man might
remember his first meeting with the transcendent love of his life. It was
Suzanne who had pursued Judith at the Élysée, she who had called at Le
Pré des Oiseaux again and again. In *Quinze Ans auprès de Judith Gautier*,
she recorded a devotion which – for all her protestations – was quite unlike
the devotion of a close friend or a daughter. It was exclusive, jealous, and
burningly intense. It was the devotion of a worshipper for a goddess; it
was also a devotion which was patently frustrated. 'I had finally,' she
wrote, 'come to feel absolute idolatry for my friend, so much so that my
youthful ardour, which sometimes clashed with her attitude of deliberate
indifference, often made me very unhappy. Whatever she might say to the
contrary, Judith did nothing without passion. One felt that she was
exclusive, even jealous, and quite capable of affection.'[22] There is much
insistence in these memoirs – too much, perhaps – on friendship; there is
also much regret that Judith failed to be demonstrative.

Thanks to a life together which was based on this deep friendship, there were
[wrote Suzanne] such exchanges of thought that in the end we answered one
another's ideas without needing to express them. So it was that, after one of
these long but eloquent silences, Judith tried to convince me: 'Look, darling,
do you still find me so cold and indifferent?' And, enveloping me in a gaze of
unforgettable tenderness: 'It's very deep . . . It's better when it's private, it's
more genuine. There's no need to express feelings like that.'[23]

Suzanne was unconvinced, and she remained disappointed; but,
whatever disappointment she felt, she loved Judith with perception. She
recognized that,

however paradoxical it might seem, Judith combined the wisdom and philosophy of an old Buddhist priest and the delightful candour, innocence and freshness of a child. She agreed as much herself. It was touchingly childlike. When we happened to walk down the Champs-Élysées, Judith forgot her age and her personality. Instinctively, as in the days of her nurse, she held on to a fold of my coat, and allowed herself to be guided . . .

And then the roles would be reversed . . . And I had the clear impression that Judith was putting herself under my protection.

In these circumstances, how I should have liked to be very old, and to have the envied role of the humble nurse for whom, from her first steps, Judith had always shown the greatest feeling, a feeling which had lasted until the poor woman's death . . .

Too late! I used to think, and I was often in despair. Yes, I had come into her life too late! She would never be able to mind more about me. She couldn't believe in anything, now, least of all in real human affections, which for her were just Utopia. She believed only in the love of animals, which, she said, disillusioned as she was, 'does not fail, does not disappoint you and never betrays you. No man is capable of such a love.' And so it was only with animals that she became 'human' and affectionately demonstrative. When I pointed this out to her: 'This is our only means,' she said, 'of proving our love to them in exchange for theirs; that and never failing in our duty, and in the engagements which we have undertaken towards them.'

'What an incomparable mother you would have been,' I ventured.

'There is certainly no sacrifice that I would not have made,' she said, 'in order to assure a child the happiest life. [I should have had] to make amends to it for the misfortune of its existence.' Then she added: 'I am sure that I can make my animals happy, but I couldn't have ensured the happiness of a child; that is why I didn't want to have one.' And she quoted Chateaubriand's profound reflection, with which she completely agreed: 'After the misfortune of being born, I don't know a greater one that that of giving birth to a man.'[24]

It was a nihilistic creed which Judith had professed for some years. Tolstoy had maintained 'that absolute chastity was the ideal aim of man, that it was absurd that novels insisted on ending with a marriage'.[25] In 1902, two journalists, Dan Léon and Edgar Jéhut, had asked a number of celebrities for their opinions. 'I have no definite opinion,' Judith had said, 'except on one of the questions you ask: the question of birth. To prevent and end the misfortune of life seems to me to be the only wisdom.'[26] Perhaps the words had merely been intended to deter her questioners, to indicate her need for privacy; but one suspects that they had reflected her desperate melancholy. To Robert de Montesquiou she wrote: 'The little Breton phalanstery is happy. I alone brood on an invincible sadness which is beginning to worry me very much. It seems to me that I've outlived myself, and I look in vain for the shock which might restore me to life.'[27]

Judith had been deeply hurt; she was wary, now, of emotion. Life was, for her, an eternal conflict, in which her hopes had often been disappointed. 'I suffered very much,' wrote Suzanne, 'to think that my friend, so often disappointed or deceived, doubted or appeared to doubt – was that perhaps to test it? – the sincerity of my affection. And yet, as every new year came to strengthen this friendship, it could only confirm my valiant hopes. Slowly, but surely, I was winning my secret victory. I was removing Judith's apprehensions and fears about the fragility of human things.'[28]

On their return to Paris, in September 1904, Judith settled once again in the rue Washington. Suzanne returned to her villa,

> but with this difference: that, every day, after the hours I spent on my work – I was in fact preparing for my second *Salon* – between four-thirty and five o'clock, I went to Judith's, dined there, and on the stroke of eleven – which suited him very well – my brother, an inveterate noctambulist, came to fetch me . . .
>
> He generally found me in the agreeable company of those intimates who were not only admitted on Sundays: Dr Albert Prieur was one of them, Liao, Benedictus, Clermont-Ganneau, who was always sparkling with wit, and of course dear Bojidar, and sometimes, too, Georges Soulié de Moran, a remarkable young man. With a sure instinct, Judith had soon discovered his brilliant aptitude for oriental languages. She had directed him towards China. He recognized that it was his path. He has since acquired an international reputation. On his first journey he wrote an enthusiastic letter from Peking: 'One sees *Le Dragon impérial* everywhere one goes.' It was still quite rare for the two of us to be alone together. Those evenings were of course the ones I very much preferred.
>
> When we sat by the fire, with the curtains drawn, completely cut off from the noise of people and the street, and isolated from the outside world, my Friend set out to confide in me about Wagner, Victor Hugo, Armand Silvestre and Paul Baudry. It was a delight quite unparalleled![29]

On such occasions, Judith sometimes seemed to regret the burden of her beauty. 'She would have liked to conquer men by her mind alone, and she scorned the untimely part which physical attraction had always played for her male admirers.'[30] She had found her power calamitous. Sometimes, too, she regretted her failure to marry Mohsin-Khan. Until his death, she told Suzanne,

> Mohsin-Khan kept this love for me, this feeling which finally turned into inalterable friendship. He used to say to me: 'You have let your destiny pass you by.'
>
> During his last stay in France, he fell ill in a hotel in the Champs-Élysées. . . . I was at Le Pré des Oiseaux, where he had been a guest. When I learned what had happened, I didn't hesitate. I made the journey at once, to be with this peerless friend until the end.

I had asked Mohsin to give his Master the Shah of Persia a copy of *Iskender* from me; the Sovereign was touched and delighted by my book. One fine day, from far away, from Persia, by the ordinary post, there came a tiny box: a ring – a splendid ring, one single and magnificent diamond: a diamond from Golconda, which . . . cast dazzling fires. I discovered later that it was part of the [Imperial] treasure. I called it Iskender.[31]

Even before she came of age, Judith had known the power of her extraordinary beauty. Soon after their first meeting, her half-brother, Toto, had addressed some poetry to her. It had revealed an emotion 'against which he had had to struggle quite hard'.[32]

An explorer, Wiener [Charles Wiener, who published books on South America], had also conceived a very violent passion for Judith, but as this passion was not reciprocated in the slightest, he had set out again on the most perilous and distant explorations. 'I'm going,' he said, 'you will never see me or hear of me again.' He kept his word; never, in fact, did Judith see him again. It was the same with Paul Baudry, whom she did not love either. He contented himself with reproducing the likeness or the features of the young woman of his dreams in nearly all his frescoes at the Opéra. Armand Silvestre, too, sent her a sonnet or a piece of poetry every day for more than a year . . . Jean Richepin sent her a rondeau; Jean Lorrain had written her several series of sonnets and other poems which would have made a small collection in themselves. Then there was old Count Barni, who was equally taken with his beautiful cousin. Judith was not unaware of the empire which she had over him, and she had sometimes liked to put his love to the test. He had submitted to all her fantasies, however baroque they were.
     'Even my godfather, Maxime du Camp, felt more than affection for me [Judith confided to Suzanne]. It was he who brought me that famous ring one day.' And Judith made me examine the seal of Thutmose III, king of the most ancient Egyptian dynasty, which people date back 8,000 years . . .
     And, finally, Judith spoke of Hugo. 'He, too, was seriously in love with me. He paid court to me like a schoolboy . . .'[33]

Suzanne insidiously brought the conversation round to Wagner. 'Oh,' sighed Judith, 'that love was as heavy as a paving-stone; it was always weighed down by the sad reflection: "Too late" – by that atrocious thing, Regret. For he really felt that it was I who should have been his wife, his true other half, 'his female', as he said . . .'[34] On such evenings, under Judith's gaze, Suzanne would open the coffer of relics, and take out Wagner's letters, impregnated, even now, with essence of roses. It was the perfume which he had chosen for their correspondence. One day, Judith remembered, Wagner had asked if she would like a son by him. 'You have Siegfried,' she had answered. But she told Suzanne: 'I admit that, now, I should like to have had a son by Wagner – I should have given him to you as a husband.'[35]

Now, in her sixties, Judith longed for a tranquil life. 'Friendship is so superior to love,' she used to say. 'Love is generally based on lies.' Love, to her, was only a malady, 'a crisis of the instinct to which the poets have given wings'.[36]

The tradition with Théophile Gautier, and with his daughter, had always been to receive one day a week: Thursday with Gautier, Sunday with Judith. The habitués remained to dinner. Suzanne and her brother became the pillars of these Sunday dinners, and, once a week, on Thursdays, Judith, Benedictus and Clermont-Ganneau used to gather at Florilège, where Suzanne had an early phonograph, and they made their amateur recordings. Benedictus played classical music on the piano; Clermont-Ganneau forgot his academic dignity, and he and Judith improvised hilarious dialogues. Then they played the records back to themselves, and collapsed with laughter.

The Meyer-Zundels planned to have a family Christmas in Alsace. As December approached, Suzanne

> counted, in anguish, the days which were implacably passing and would separate us again . . .
>
> As for Judith, she spent all her evenings devising mementoes and presents for her friends: statuettes, medallions, cards she had illustrated herself . . .
>
> Judith disliked saints' days and birthdays, because they added another year to her own age; but she was very touched by the faithful remembrance of her friends, who never failed to send her baskets of flowers, or sweets in pretty wrappings. Green, mauve and pink fondants were always in favour . . .
>
> Judith had adorably childlike enthusiasms . . . She always felt a double pleasure just from receiving a parcel and having the surprise. On her birthdays, she sometimes sent herself trinkets, . . . and so she had the illusion of receiving a great many presents that day.[37]

Christmas dragged on in Alsace.

> Though every day the beloved letter came from my Friend [Suzanne continued], . . . I only counted the days that lay between me and my return . . . This dear letter helped me, more than all my mother's spoiling, to be patient about my homesickness. It was my spiritual daily bread. I read it and re-read it: 'I have your two letters, darling, happy to have them. And sad to have to have them! Patience and courage, your return will cure everything . . . My darling, it is really true, a few days more and then the celebration of your return!'[38]

Ton amitié m'a fait comme un nid duveté,
Où ne m'atteignent plus ni le vent ni l'orage;
L'oiseau de mon esprit a de nouveau chanté
Et remonte gaîment le noir courant de l'âge.

L'arme, qui se rouillait inerte dans ma main,
Est de nouveau fourbie et prête à la bataille;
Et puisque tu le crois, c'est hier, non demain:
La Walküre a son casque et redresse sa taille.

En avant! . . . J'ai plongé dans le Styx de ta foi,
Et nous vaincrons le temps et ses ruses moroses.
Fondons sur l'adversaire, en reniant sa loi,
Allons reconquérir des lauriers et des roses![39]

The poem *À Suzanne* was to appear in Judith's *Poésies* in 1911; it suggests the despair of her middle age, and the consolation and comfort, the spiritual rebirth, that the girl had brought her.

Mme Meyer-Zundel might have been disturbed by her daughter's overwhelming relationship. Yet, far from discouraging Suzanne, she appears to have shared in the 'daily delight' of Judith's letters; and, when Suzanne went to live with Judith, Mme Meyer-Zundel seems to have shown only relief.

> I was infinitely grateful to my mother [wrote Suzanne] for her complete understanding of this friendship: this intensely strong friendship at which she took no umbrage at all. At most, when she had no doubt been inspired by some item of news in the papers, a sudden anxiety would enter her letters: an anxiety, made more acute by absence, at the idea that her daughter was often all alone in that villa, and could be exposed to burglars or marauders.
>
> I put an end to these anxieties. Enchanted to seize the pretext, I announced to my mother one fine day that Judith had prepared a room in her own apartment, and was delighted to offer it to me . . . It was more than enough to reassure her . . .
>
> Finally, after several pressing invitations, Judith wanted to know the setting in which to place me; and, when she left Saint-Enogat, she decided to end a splendid autumn at our country house in Alsace. Benedictus came to fetch her – and he, too, spent a few days at my mother's.[40]

It is difficult not to feel sympathy for Benedictus, who had devoted himself to Judith for more than forty years.

> He spent hours at the Bibliothèque Nationale, doing research for her.
>
> He accepted every errand, and went in search of the most diverse things: hair for her marionnettes, materials, anything which her whims or tastes or ideas suggested to her . . . He had chosen to appoint himself her protector in life – more than that, her convict-warden. If, on doctor's orders, she had to take drops, pills or medicines, he was there to remind her.
>
> It was I [Suzanne recorded] who later assumed all these responsibilities. Benedictus must certainly have suffered from this interference in his life; but he finally accepted it.[41]

Benedictus' sight was failing; by 1917 he had become completely blind. After Judith's death, Suzanne gave him shelter at Le Pré des Oiseaux. He died in hospital, in Dinard, in 1921.

Suzanne had been more, from the first, than an adopted daughter. The relationship was now so close that Judith granted her 'the signal favour of being allowed to copy every letter she sent her friends . . . She ended,' wrote Suzanne, 'by not sending any letter until I had seen it. If I were not there, she kept a duplicate for me.'[42]

Judith tried to make amends for Suzanne's neglected education; she introduced her to the works of Gautier, Balzac and Shakespeare. She also talked to her about her own attitude to writing. She had once thought, like her father, that writing should be purely instinctive. Now she always corrected it, scribbled notes on scraps of paper, warned Céleste, her maid, not to touch her manuscripts, polished and re-polished her work. She always remained in control of it. 'My only concern is to keep a good balance. When I write, a kind of tap opens inside me, and it turns off again when I want. I am in no way the slave of my inspiration, I don't allow myself to overflow with it, or to be possessed by it. Some writers are cerebral, their brains occasionally make baroque demands in exchange for the effort which is asked of them. It was like that with Pierre Louÿs, with his owl-like ways: he rested all day, and only worked at night, with orgies of black coffee. As for Mendès, he absorbed quantities of ether . . .'[43]

Judith also taught Suzanne her philosophy of life. 'Never stop furnishing your mind, acquiring new knowledge, and walking, ceaselessly, towards perfection.' Judith had been initiated in magic by Éliphas Lévi, to whom she had regularly gone for lessons. He had shown her the secret principles of psychic force and magnetism.[44]

> Another time [recalled Suzanne] she said to me: 'It's only a question of seeking the reasons for the existence of everything . . . Eurythmia – which means harmony in order and proportion – should be the law of the artist . . . Rhythm is perhaps the great master of movement and of life: without even knowing it, we submit to rhythm all the time. Doesn't your heart beat to a rhythm? Doesn't our earth turn to a very strict time? How terrifying if it were distracted, if it missed its rhythm by a quarter of a sigh! The most terrible things would undoubtedly happen . . .'[45]

There were other, more mundane, subjects of conversation, for Suzanne patently needed an education in manners:

> 'Don't ever forget,' insisted Judith, when I was late, 'that punctuality is the politeness of princes . . .'

I was always profoundly vexed [continued Suzanne] when, at some gathering, the conversation turned to subjects which were rather free, and I was asked to leave the room or cover my ears. I considered that a personal offence which humiliated me to the marrow.

'But, darling,' Judith used to say, 'it's just the contrary; we women should always inspire such feelings, and be proud of them.'[46]

Judith, wrote Ferdinand Bac, 'still had an unused mother's heart. She had adopted a girl who was not like her in the least, but who could love her and serve her memory in proportion.'[47] Judith showed a truly maternal solicitude; she tried to make this pedestrian, unformed girl into an accomplished young woman. It was an impossible task; but, as time went by, Judith herself became dependent on her to a quite unusual degree. For the first time in her life, since her infancy with Damon, she was given constant, entire, uncritical devotion. It was what she had always needed, and she had responded. She had come, at last, again, to love a human being. The letters which she sent Suzanne reveal an intensity of feeling more common between lovers than between mother and daughter. The extracts which Suzanne was to publish were, it is true, quoted out of context, and they were chosen to prove Judith's devotion to her. They prove that she had come to feel a desperate need for her companion, an inability to live without her:

Darling, in spite of my work I am struggling against a great indifference to everything; when you aren't there, I find it very difficult to react . . .
A Sunday without you is hard, dull and charmless, and to think that there's a whole week more, a Sahara to be crossed!
The slightest word is something, but nothing – that makes me sad all day! It's wonderful weather, but I don't want to go out . . . without you . . .
Darling, it is very long, and I feel very much alone in spite of the crowd. I miss you enormously, but one must be patient and calm. I hardly have time to think, but I always look for you beside me, and, really, you are lovingly there.[48]

Henri de Régnier was to praise Judith. She bore, he said, a noble name, and round her floated, like a halo,

Attestant que les Dieux vous ont fait divine,
L'hommage de Wagner et de Victor Hugo.[49]

The woman who had once loved Catulle Mendès with passion, who had been the mistress of Hugo, the inspiration of Wagner, the love of Mohsin-Khan, the admiration of Baudelaire, Leconte de Lisle and Sargent, the woman who had enslaved Benedictus, Baudry, Armand Silvestre and innumerable other men, had now become, in her sixties, dependent on a dull, uneducated, infatuated girl.

Chapter Twenty

By 1904, women writers had earned such literary status that Mme de Broutelles, the editor of the women's magazine *Vie heureuse*, decided that the time had come to create a women's academy similar to the Académie-Goncourt. This institution was also to award an annual prize of 5,000 francs, the funds for which were to be supplied by the publishers Hachette.[1] The idea was ingenious, and excellently timed. There is no longer a *Vie heureuse*, but there still remains a Vie heureuse prize, now the Prix Femina.

In 1904 the Académie des Dames, or jury, was soon established. The Comtesse de Noailles presided. 'I remember how moved I was,' she said, 'when I first saw Mme Judith Gautier: the face of a tranquil goddess, the daughter of an illustrious poet . . . She dazzled my heart.'[2] There were twenty members of the jury, including Judith, Mme Juliette Adam and Rachilde (who, with her husband, and Jules Renard, had founded the *Mercure de France*). There was Jane Dieulafoy, wife of Marcel Dieulafoy, the engineer and archaeologist; she had gone with him to Persia, published a book about her visit, written novels, and lectured on the Greek and French classics. With her, now, on the jury were the Duchesse de Rohan, Mme Edmond Rostand and Mme Alphonse Daudet. Some of the Académie des Dames still sheltered behind masculine pseudonyms. Mme le Barillier was better known as Jean Bertheroy; Mme Guillaume was more familiar as the Jean Dornis who published *Leconte de Lisle intime* and studies of modern Italian literature. The Baronne de Pierrebourg had established herself as Claude Ferval; Mme Lapauze as Daniel Lesueur. Mme Logerot (Gabriel Reval) left some recollections about the origins of this prize. The first discussions were held in the editorial offices of *Vie heureuse*. Some of the later meetings took place at Mme Alphonse Daudet's. Her cooking was reported to be excellent.

Suzanne recorded sadly that, between Judith 'and the only people who could really have interested her, fate set up obstacles which were insurmountable from her point of view, playing on the difference of age, sometimes in one direction, sometimes in another. Besides, her loyalty made her incapable of creating trouble in a household, or of being the cause of its destruction.'[3] However, thanks to her sister's warning – or perhaps her jealousy – Julie Daudet had waited almost thirty years to make Judith's acquaintance.

> I was friends first with Estelle [she explained], who was married to Émile Bergerat, a friend of Alphonse Daudet's, and I secretly hoped that I should meet Judith Gautier there – she very soon resumed her maiden name, because the Mendès marriage did not work; but Estelle said to me:
> 'Don't make friends with my sister, don't invite her home, she would make love to your husband.'
> And it was true. Judith was aware of her beauty, and wanted it always to triumph and overcome.
> 'Now listen,' the witty Mme de Banville said to her, 'listen to me, Judith dear, you must leave my husband in peace: he's too old for you! . . . '
> And I was frightened, myself [continued Mme Daudet], and mistrustful of women who stole other people's property; and this warning had been enough for me. I did not know Judith until very late, [seven years after my husband's death], and then it was among my acquaintances on the *Vie heureuse*.[4]

On 28 January 1905, the first Vie heureuse prize was awarded to Myriam Harry for *La Petite Fille de Jérusalem*. Huysmans wrote to congratulate 'the glorious elect of the Blue Amazons'. 'The remarkable thing,' he added, 'and it will take a very clever man to explain it, is that today the women have more talent than the men. Judith Gautier, Rachilde, Myriam Harry: there are three women with great talent.' He admired Judith 'as much for the purity of her style, which she had inherited from her father, as for the dignity of her isolated life.'[5]

She did not need to be alone in order to write. 'If I were condemned to the solitude of a study, I should go to sleep,' she confessed, 'and I shouldn't do anything worthwhile . . . . There, again, I am like my father, I need life around me. Even if my friends are talking, they don't worry me at all, provided that they don't speak to me. If I have a subject in my head, and I want to write it, it has the right proportions . . . . And when the book is finished, it no longer concerns me.'[6]

> Madame Judith Gautier has an almost hostile indifference not only towards her works of art, but even towards her finest works of literature [so decided Anatole

France] . . . . She would willingly set down her noblest thoughts on rose petals, in the corollas of lilies, which the wind would bear far from the eyes of men. She writes as Bertha spun, because it is the occupation most natural to her . . . . Never, I think, did a woman show such natural contempt for success, never was a woman so far from being a woman of letters.[7]

Judith remained indifferent to the public and the critics, and she asked no favours of them. Literature, for her, was a priesthood. She wrote to enchant, and that is why she did not obtain the favour of a large public, but she delighted the more thoughtful readers. In her poems, novels and plays, she sought to describe the beauty of landscapes, the beauty of characters, their thoughts and deeds. She has sometimes been reproached for being superficial. 'Oh, she was not a reasoner!' Paul Souday was to write. 'No sort of metaphysics or intellectual effort of any kind pleased this beautiful, superbly nonchalant sovereign, whose Olympus tended to dissolve in Buddhic nirvana. She was marvellously gifted. But terrestrial activity added nothing to the divinity that was in her.'[8]

Yet perhaps Souday was mistaken. In 1900 she had published an anonymous pamphlet, *Le Livre de la foi nouvelle*. It expressed her creed with the brevity of a Chinese poem. Judith had sought the truth in vain and, suddenly, like a stream undammed, the truth had flooded into her soul. 'My soul was, for the Truth, an instrument of thought, my voice an instrument of expression . . . .'[9] God Himself had assured her:

> My deliverance is the aim and end of the struggle: *To free, in death, through every creature, a pure particle of Myself.*
> Just as the coal becomes the diamond.
> And if you want a symbol, or a sign, take this: *The diamond, the perfection of coal.*
> Until now, death has been *sterile!* It is the fruit which falls without having ripened; the flame extinguished; strength exhausted to no purpose; *and every death has been in vain.*
> Today, man is the finest result of the struggle, and, *since he knows, he can help deliverance.*
> All his efforts should tend towards the creation of his diamond – which you may call the Soul –*by creating fruitful death.*[10]

One evening, wrote Suzanne,

in one of those moments of silent reflection and almost divine serenity when her face assumed incomparable sweetness, Judith revealed her Great Secret to me: *Le Livre de la foi nouvelle,* into which she had initiated only a few of the elect. She had had taken fourteen years to work the book out [sic]. She had had it printed at her own expense, when she was suffering from a serious illness; and, abandoned by the doctors, harassed by this idea, she had decided on this last financial sacrifice before she died.

Her face was pale, and seemed to be veiled with a slight cloud, and, as if she were speaking in a dream, Judith said to me:

'The few phrases in this book are too hard for most of humankind. One would need commentaries . . . . But I shall no longer be the one to make them . . . . The seed is sown, that is the essential. When minds agree with one another, hearts soon understand. Who knows? Perhaps one day you yourself will be my disciple . . . . I want the book to remain anonymous.'

It was then [Suzanne continued] that she promised me that, after her death, if there was another life, she would struggle in every way to express, through me, what she would have to reveal.

Then her expression was veiled by a deeper sadness, and she went on:

'We spend life trying not to die . . . We resist death. Don't we discover skeletons and teeth and nails intact, centuries later? That really proves that we die too soon.

When the time comes, the Divine element should be able to free itself from the matter which engulfs it . . . . All of us should therefore work to perfect ourselves so that, when we die, body and soul can be more easily separated . . . We should be able to foretell our death so that, when the moment comes, we let ourselves be deliberately gathered in by it – like a ripe fruit which is naturally picked from the tree.'[11]

Her creed was simple; it is hard to understand why she had taken fourteen years to set it down, why she had been so anxious to publish it, why she had also called it her Great Secret, and wished it to remain anonymous. *Le Livre de la foi nouvelle* does not seem unorthodox, nor does it seem to be strikingly profound. It did, however, find favour with Yu-Keng, the former Chinese Minister to Paris. 'Sublime as the Dragon,' so he wrote, 'Judith Gautier has understood the secret of birth and death, and reconciled Good and Evil. One listens to her voice, which is like the voice of the wind in the pine trees. It will extend into the future and it will be eternally heard.'[12]

Judith remained enthralled by her study of the supernatural. More than once her maid would turn a visitor away: 'Madame is out. Madame is having her magic lesson.'[13] Judith considered these studies dangerous for all but the strong-minded, and she advised her friends not to follow them, and, above all, not to attempt to practise magic. She herself did not practise it, and all she kept from her lessons were the metaphysical ideas. She was a friend, too, of Joséphin Péladan, author of mystical dramas and of *Le Théâtre de Wagner*. Péladan was now involved in a revival of the eighteenth-century philosophy, half occult and half religious, known as Rosicrucianism; he called himself Sâr – or High Priest – Péladan. He had founded the Théâtre de la Rose-Croix, in opposition to the naturalism of the Théâtre Libre; and in *L'Art Idéaliste et Mystique* he set out his theory of beauty: 'There is no Reality but God. There is no Truth but God. There is no Beauty but God.'[14] Judith had followed his ideas closely, and she had also been concerned with Rosicrucian mysticism. She belonged to a Rosicrucian order, and often wore the robes. Her maid Céleste spent hours embroidering them.[15]

Judith led an intense inner life, and she lived retired within herself. 'She had a horror of the outside world,' recorded the Tharauds, 'of everything that was foreign to her or simply indifferent. She felt ill at ease everywhere, except at Saint-Enogat or in her little apartment in the rue Washington. She used to stay there for months on end, writing, talking, listening to music, dreaming of Persia, India, China and Japan . . .'[16] She revealed herself only rarely, and that is why she had few intimate friends; but her intimates were devoted to her.

Life had not been kind to her, but, as Suzanne Meyer-Zundel was to write: 'Judith always kept a radiant altruism which went materially beyond her means, doing a thousand kindnesses to her friends and acquaintances, lavishing her counsels; despite herself she encouraged confidences.'[17] No one ever appealed for her help in vain. She was always ready to help a colleague, to write something favourable in a paper. There was no shadow of jealousy in her, and she rejoiced in other people's triumphs. You could not say a word against her friends, or else 'this languorous creature became a lioness and her drowsy eyes blazed with anger.'[18]

Her *salon* was not a worldly *salon*, but a place which brought together those who loved her, those who admired her, the intellectual élite of her time. Sunday afternoon was reserved for her friends. They arrived early and stayed for dinner. The first to come were the Chinese and Japanese passing through Paris: Ministers, embassy secretaries and other mandarins. Laurent Tailhade recalled that the Emperor of Annam

> was the object, in her house, of a ceremonial which barred her door even to most of her intimates, when he visited her in the rue Washington. 'You know that the Emperor's there!' she used to say. And indeed one soon discerned a little gentleman in a corner. He was very yellow, very short, and very ugly. He wore a three-piece suit, while the mistress of the house appeared in robes of scarlet or buttercup yellow silk bedecked with irises and dragonflies.[19]

The Emperor Hâm Nghi had reigned, briefly, in 1885. Defeated and dethroned by the French, he had been deported to Algeria. His fate had inspired Judith to write a play, and she had already finished it when the Emperor came, one summer, to stay near Saint-Enogat. 'I made his acquaintance,' she told *Le Temps*. 'I was brave enough to read the poor man the drama in which I related the wretchedness of his Court, the sadness of his fall, and we became friends . . . . Today he is a king in exile, intelligent and good, and, in spite of his long resistance, imbued with our culture. He has married a Frenchwoman, and his son is my godson. His history is in my play. Who will perform it?'[20]

The Annamite play remained unperformed, but the friendship flourished. She had, it seems, felt more than friendship for this exiled sovereign. Suzanne recorded that he was 'absolutely delightful, a man of great moral and intellectual superiority'.[21] Certainly, she added,

> Judith had an ardent feeling, a hopeless feeling, sealed up in her heart, for this oriental Prince who inspired her with a very fine play, *Les Portes rouges*, based on historical facts, which she had wanted Antoine to stage. He had also inspired her with acrostics and other poems which likewise appeared in her *Poésies*. It was in 1900, through Pierre Louÿs, that Judith had made her hero's acquaintance. Perhaps this unpublished piece of verse casts some light on the nature of the feelings which were, in time, transformed into unchangeable friendship.

> Parler de désespoir à vous, quelle ironie!
> Rien ne peut attendrir un coeur si bien fermé.
> Il n'aura pas pitié de la longue agonie,
> N'écoutant que le mal dont il est consumé.
> Cependant, des douleurs, longue est la litanie
> Et la pire c'est bien de n'être pas aimé.

> De votre exil, l'absence est une soeur jumelle,
> Aussi bien que gardé par un geôlier jaloux,
> N'est-on pas prisonnier d'un rêve trop fidèle?
> N'écoutez pas une ennemie à vos genoux,
> Au moins, laissez-la vivre et vengez-vous sur elle,
> Meurtrissez-la, tout sera bon venant de vous![22]

During the last years of her life, Judith's habitués included Pierre Louÿs and Émile Vedel – a frigate captain, a friend of Loti, and a translator of *King Lear* and *Faust*.

> Who [asked Vedel] could ever express the delights of a close friendship with her? Who could suggest the charm of her welcome, the healing sense of serenity you feel as soon as you enter her apartment, in which dogs, cats and birds live in peace together for love of her? How, without spoiling the magic, could one describe the enchanted hours at Saint-Enogat, where, every evening, sitting on the beach in front of the chalet, beside the sea, one watches, in silent reflection, the symphony of the setting sun, which she sometimes likes to record in colour? For Mme Gautier possesses all the gifts which Jupiter distributed among his daughters, the Nine Muses, and I have seen her do everything, paint watercolours, compose waltzes, model busts of astonishing resemblance, talk

Chinese with mandarins, debate with oriental scholars, and even sew, everything except one thing: put pen to paper – if, by that, one means to isolate oneself and to think and write out, more or less painfully, a certain number of pages . . . .[23]

Maurice-Verne, a journalist, was also fascinated by Judith's setting:

The walls [in the rue Washington] were covered in brilliant vermilion lacquer . . . . Painted swallows flew aslant across the low ceilings . . . .
    In these little rooms, cluttered with flowers and plants, there darted, miaowed and wheeled, with a sense of freedom and security and space, a blackbird, afflicted with a limp, which whistled a bar of Wagner, canaries dizzying with their songs a number of cats whose collars set off a bunch of shrill bells . . . . Obviously the salon smelt, all at once, of sandalwood, amber, green plants, and the sharp smell of the animals – which enjoyed their freedom. There was a prolongation of this gimcrack palace, but here a touch of magic brushed against you: this was the terrace. This terrace, overlooking the rue Washington, consisted of a wide balcony among a confusion of chimneys, grey roofs and dismal attics. Judith Gautier had adorned it with currant bushes in boxes, crocuses and chrysanthemums according to the season, and they appeared to flourish in the long wooden coffins which served as flower-beds . . . . Judith Gautier was above all proud of her cherry tree. I think that it produced occasional fruit. In the spring it burst into blossom, striping the chaos of zinc and slates with the blossom of a Japanese print.[24]

The flow of visitors continued. Lucien Descaves arrived, with Charles-Marie Widor, composer, critic, organist at Saint-Sulpice, and César Franck's successor as Professor of Organ at the Conservatoire. Widor, a lover of art and literature, was an original companion. 'Do you believe in metempsychosis?' he once enquired. 'Personally, I remember having been a duck!'[25]

Émile Bergerat, too, would appear at the rue Washington. His jet black beard and curly hair were now turning white, and seemed 'a real anachronism round his bright and kindly face, as shining and rosy as a red apple'.[26] His glance was less keen, nowadays, behind his monocle, but Caliban – as he signed himself – remained an accomplished journalist with an extraordinary understanding of Parisian life. Bergerat was always conscious of his distinguished marriage. He wrote some engaging memoirs of Gautier, and in 1896 he produced a five-act drama based on Le Capitaine Fracasse (Mendès had long ago turned the novel into a comic opera). It was to Bergerat's credit that he remained both a friend of Mendès and a friend to Judith all her life.

The attic in the rue Washington – where the name of Zola had been banned since the days of the Affair – was thronged, now, with celebrities and friends. Mme Juliette Adam sometimes made an appearance; and so, it seems, did the converted Mme Daudet. Judith, she wrote, 'pleased and interested me, and her décor was picturesque and charming: a fifth-floor apartment in the rue Washington, a very small apartment with a big terrace, a salon with exotic decorations, from which you could hear a blackbird whistling Wagner in the next room, which was purposely darkened. Judith spoke little; she seemed to be following an inner dream.'[27]

Julie Daudet found Judith 'very beautiful, orientally beautiful, with a placidity which suited her extremely well – a placidity which she kept throughout her life.'[28] Henri de Régnier, too, remembered her placidity:

> The windows [at the rue Washington] gave on to a wide balcony on which there were rows of flowerpots and boxes with climbing plants springing from them. It was there that Judith had her hanging garden, under the sky of the 'modern Babylon': the Carthaginian terrace of which, her arms encircled by her familiar snakes, she was the nonchalant Salammbô . . . .
>
> Her work was not in the least a replica of her father's work. It was certainly to Judith Gautier herself that we went to pay homage, and it was this feeling which gathered her regular visitors round her on Sundays . . . . Assiduous and respectful, they listened with fascination when, caressing the irascible Mousmé or the diabolical Satan, playing with her slippery snakes, or toying with some or other amulet, she summoned up her recollections . . . .
>
> If Judith Gautier had her father's voice, she did not have his truculent and paradoxical verve . . . . She had inherited from him a sort of placid nonchalance, a somewhat indolent kindness which sometimes appeared like indifference. Indifferent she certainly was to all that concerned the realities of everyday existence. Apart from reading and writing, she scarcely had any occupations but playing with her domestic animals, cutting out materials, modelling and painting puppets. These occupations were enough for her. She rarely went out. She lived at home among her memories . . . .
>
> At the rue Washington you saw passing guests who had come from afar, some from Persia, others from China, others still from Japan. For a time we used to meet a young Peruvian there who claimed to be descended from one of the ancient Inca kings.[29]

Judith liked to entertain. She did so liberally, and, as she was far from rich, especially in her later years, she used to tell Céleste to economize during the week so that she could kill the fatted calf on Sundays. Sometimes Mme Meyer-Zundel, Suzanne's ever-generous mother, allowed them to enjoy a taste of luxury.

> Very dear friend [wrote Judith, one Christmas Eve],
>
> You should be represented like certain images of the Virgin whose hands shed a rain of golden rays, and they are so abundant from your hands that one always has arrears of gratitude. Before the splendid surprise of today, we had already had the delicious pâté. We shall begin our assault on it tomorrow,

Christmas Day, continue it on Tuesday and complete its defeat on 1 January, when, as usual, we shall drink your health – and then there are the foot-muff and the beautiful coverlet which we took to the Opéra the other evening. The car is so agreeable at the moment and we are so comfortable in it, but we shan't be entirely happy until you have tried it. And so it is a whole sheaf of affectionate thanks which I send you . . . .

Now I am going back to my extravagant work, which consists of making dolls. But first I embrace you with much affection and send you the most fervent wishes from the very depths of my heart.[30]

Her heart remained young. She still loved dressing up, as she had done since her childhood. She still loved giving fancy-dress parties. Mme Marguerite Jules-Martin – one day to found the Société de Poésie – was invited to the rue Washington, and asked to recite one of her poems on the god of war; she herself arrived as a goddess of war, 'with a splendid Japanese costume, a diadem and authentic make-up, . . . and that a year before 1914! I never think of it,' she confessed, 'without a certain fear.'[31]

Judith's Sunday evenings inescapably recalled her father's distant Thursdays at Neuilly. They had the same Bohemian brio, the same international, artistic distinction.

Every Sunday [recorded the notorious Willy, sometime husband of Colette], every Sunday, round the copiously laden table (mortadella, loucoum, black olives, pineapple, pickles, anchovies, various sweetmeats), there crowded dinner-guests who were invited at random, I think, or had asked themselves: Hungarian artists, nameless boulevardiers, members of the Chinese Embassy, some of them quite decorative, others notable for decorations rather than decorum . . . . Sometimes Judith needed information:

'Tell me, Willy, that fat little man who is sitting between Paul Hillemacher and Comte François de Chevilly: who is he?'

'It's the first time I've seen his phiz. Why don't you ask Benedictus?'

'But he's the one who told me to send the maid to invite him! Otherwise I wouldn't mention it. It doesn't matter to me in the least.'

In fact, nothing mattered to this Islamic woman with the fine expressionless dark eyes, indifferent, indolent, drowned in melted fat . . . .

The Ancients had spoken only with ecstasy about her beauty. It had never much concerned her . . . .

Even about her talent – which was very real – she was no more concerned than she was about anything else. She wrote effortless, well-mannered prose: prose which owed nothing to paternal lessons, for Théophile Gautier, she often told me, had given her only one single piece of literary advice: 'Don't begin two consecutive paragraphs with the same word: it looks ugly.'

Frantz Jourdain accused her of not having the slightest personality, and, perhaps, this was ultimately true.

At table, somnolent, her cat on her lap, she neglected her guests, absorbed in her three favourite animals: a melancholy tortoise, a lizard with a whimsical

digestion, and M. Clermont-Ganneau, a member of the Institut de
France . . .[32]

Willy, it must be said, recorded his conversations with Judith long after
she had died; and Willy frequently preferred invention to fact. None the
less, there is still a certain truth – as well as innuendo and scandalous
invention – in his memoirs:

> Judith Gautier often, very often, gave me details [about Liszt] which she alone
> knew, details so extraordinary that I dare not publish them all – out of modesty.
>   Dear Judith, how many secrets she poured out in her little apartment in the
> rue Washington, too cluttered up with knick-knacks for the maid to dare to
> sweep it properly!
>   She lived there . . . in company with an amorphous Dutchman who had a
> falsetto voice and a beard dyed mahogany colour – the fat composer
> Benedictus.[33]

The *Tout-Paris* of 1912 recorded that Benedictus lived at 157, faubourg
Saint-Honoré.

At one time Judith could afford the luxury of a manservant, Chrétien, the
husband of her faithful maid, Céleste. Chrétien summoned the guests to
table by playing the theme of *The Ride of the Valkyrie* on his cornet. Later
on, when her means were more restricted, Judith was obliged to part from
Chrétien and Céleste, and all she had was a girl of fifteen who used to come
and help pass the plates. None the less, she would still ask one of her
Sunday visitors: 'My dear, would you tell the staff to serve?' It amused her
and entertained her guests.[34]
    They crowded in as best they could among the Chinese, Japanese and
Turkish bric-à-brac, in the shadow of a gilt Buddha lost in eternal
meditation. Albert de Pouvourville remembered:

> 'Be careful of Satan, and don't crush Juliette when you sit down in that
> chair.'
>   So Judith Gautier greeted the cautious friends who came to see her . . .
>   Satan was the black cat with green eyes, enormous haunches, and
> night-coloured fur, who sometimes sat, an indifferent sphinx, on the grand
> piano, and sometimes merged, through his sombre immobility, with the
> sombre hangings of the studio.
>   As for Juliette, she was the friendly and familiar snake who rolled herself
> round the brimming glasses of saké, or, more simply, round our cups of coffee.
> Her saucer of milk had its place at table . . .
>   All the domestic life and all the aesthetic talent of Judith Gautier were
> decided in her adolescence, when she talked to Théophile Gautier's Chinaman

. . . And it was the Far East, invisible and secret, but all-powerful, which presided over those extraordinary evenings, those enclosed and precious conversations, when, beside the mantelpiece covered with 'Chinese Aubussons', Heredia recited still unpublished sonnets, and, from the mysterious, dim depths of the salon there rose the harmonies, then wonderfully new, of Widor and Benedictus.[35]

In this *entre-ciel*, as Pierre Louÿs called it, where Paul Nadar could hardly stand erect, they also played charades. 'What a pity,' lamented the Tharauds, 'that one of the familiars of this salon, Henri de Régnier, Heredia, Pierre de Bonnières, has not described one of Judith's Sundays for us. He would have described the Parisian *salon* which was the most sincere, the most idealistic, and at the same time the simplest and the kindest.'[36]

Henri de Régnier may not have left his impressions of Judith's Sundays, but he described the apartment and the châtelaine.

No. 30, rue Washington. A broad staircase with echoing, well-polished steps. The fifth floor. Beside the door hangs a bell-pull. Tug it, and there is a peal answered by furious yapping. Heavy footsteps. The door opens. A massive, corpulent figure stands before us. Judith Gautier herself holds out her hand in greeting. She is wearing an ample Chinese robe. Despite the thickening of age, the face is still beautiful, the features noble. A mouth with rather full lips, splendid dark eyes with a kindly smile. The hair, which is still black, is curled and piled up in opulent tresses. The thick neck is encircled by a necklace of sparkling stones. The voice is warm, rather dull and drawling. It is exactly like Théophile Gautier's voice, say those who have heard it. He has passed on the tone and inflexions to his daughter. Followed by her Japanese dog, Mousmé, with its smooth-skinned body, which looks as if it is truffled, Judith Gautier leads us into the little salon where she receives her guests . . . You would hardly believe that you were in the heart of Paris. There is something of the Oriental and indeed of the Far-Eastern woman in the author of *Le Dragon impérial* . . . Is it from Egypt or from Persia that her nostalgic, distant and vagabond soul came once upon a time to be incarnated in her young and impetuous beauty?[37]

It was tempting to believe that her soul came from a distant past, for Judith had a horror of progress. Despite the presence of Suzanne, the throngs of visitors, she lived in a world which was peopled by the dead. It was in this spirit that she had written, continued to write, *Le Collier des jours.*

In the first two volumes of this autobiography, all the figures of her past had appeared once again, as they made their appearance in her own life. *Le Collier des jours* is, as Bergerat observed, 'the account of the only journey she made in the realm of the realities . . . Under the folds of the veil, there appears the enchantment of a radiant youth.'[38]

Paul Souday complained that she did not analyse the famous people whom she had known. 'Did she make a great distinction between human beings and those marionnettes which she carved and dressed with her magician's fingers? . . . . Her artistic loves and hates are ardently affirmed, but they do not go beyond affirmation.'[39] Souday's comments were unfair. *Le Collier des jours* is written with the verve, delight and sadness of spontaneous recollection. Théophile Gautier presides over Judith's life: the god of her youth and, perhaps, of her later years. Flaubert, Baudelaire, *père* Gautier, with his silver-knobbed cane, the two eccentric maiden aunts are living individuals whom one would recognize in the street. The impasse d'Antin, Notre-Dame de la Miséricorde, the original, brilliant life at the rue de la Grange-Batelière and the rue de Longchamp are faithfully remembered. *Le Collier des jours* is more than a self-portrait of its author, or an engaging period piece. It is a considerable contribution to literary history. The only valid criticism that one could make of it is perhaps its vagueness about dates. Chronology has no place in Judith's memoirs. For her, a true oriental, time does not exist. 'Your son must already be delightful,' she wrote to Pierre Loti. 'Is he walking? I can't remember how old he is. I share your horror of depressing things, things that one doesn't talk about. I deny time. Dates and figures go through my memory as if it were a sieve. But you will understand me, and you won't laugh at my ostrich nature.'[40]

It was in fact a sad time for Judith. On 23 May 1908 came the death of François Coppée, the breaking of another link with her Parnassian past. She was, one suspects, more moved by the death of Bojidar Karageorge-vitch. On 1 June she paid tribute to him in *La Revue de Paris*.

On 1 February 1909 the same periodical began to serialize the third volume of *Le Collier des jours*: the volume entirely devoted to her memories of Wagner. The first episode began with the day, early in her marriage, when she and Mendès and Villiers had arrived to visit Wagner at Lucerne. Before the second instalment appeared, that episode was set still more firmly in past history.

─────Chapter Twenty-One─────

'To me Catulle Mendès' life is very tragic. It is the eternal tragedy of the talent that would fain be genius.'[1] So an acute American observer had written in 1900. Despite his unremitting work, his endless publication of poetry and dramas, novels and criticism, despite his involvement in Wagnerian politics, his well-earned place in literary history, Mendès himself felt a sense of failure; and, desperately seeking an explanation, he assured Léon Dierx: 'If I hadn't been a Jew, I'd have been a genius!'[2]

At the turn of the century, his life was pitiful. At Mallarmé's funeral, in 1898, he was 'hiccoughing from a combination of alcohol and tears, and looked terrifyingly pale.'[3] Mendès, wrote Henri de Régnier, the son-in-law of Heredia, 'had nothing, now, of that fair Apollonian beauty which in his youth had justified the name of the Latin elegiac and had led him to be compared with an adolescent god. The fatigues of his nocturnal life and of his laborious existence had marked him cruelly.'[4]

'I only knew him when he was faded,' said J.-H. Rosny, 'his eyes protruding, bloodshot and discoloured, his gait unmannerly rather than ponderous, his torso heavy and ill-set on rather short legs, his hair thin, his beard indifferent.'[5] Nowadays he had a paunch, and his straggling beard and hair were turning grey, but he continued, as Fouquier said, 'to paint the vices with the accuracy of a mediaeval artist illuminating a missal'.[6] Jules Lemaître, the critic, declared: 'If I were a legislator, I should have him conducted across the frontiers of the Republic, wreathed with the faded roses of his last nocturnal banquet.'[7] But the nocturnal banquets continued; and, even now, Mendès had a curious, slightly sinister attraction:

> When I made the acquaintance of Catulle Mendès [remembered Eugène Montfort], he was already on the wrong side of forty, but he still cut quite a

figure, he was in all the brilliance of his renown, and he enjoyed considerable literary standing. He was then living in an apartment in the rue Lafayette, . . . in which there was a series of little scented rooms, adorned with divans, which looked like boudoirs. He had just married a beautiful young poetess, who, having spent some years in the provinces, leading the grey and monotonous life of a notary's wife, had felt herself attracted by the hazardous existence of artists in Paris, and had come and thrown herself into the arms of her great man. Yet another adventure which, to our childish eyes, enhanced the figure of Catulle Mendès, embellished as it was by duels, love affairs and poetry . . .[8]

Mendès had invited Montfort to *déjeuner* at their first meeting: a curious meal, for 'the double window-curtains were drawn, and the lamps were lit . . . In the somewhat artificial atmosphere of a lamplit supper at the daylight hour of *déjeuner*, one began to grow torpid.' On the stroke of two o'clock, Mendès roused himself, and left for work.[9] Later that day, he set out from *Le Journal* for the Café Napolitain, near the Vaudeville, 'wearing his yellow overcoat, his head thrown back, superb, walking slowly down the boulevard . . . Once at the Napolitain, he settled down at the table with Courteline, sometimes with Bergerat, his former brother-in-law.'[10]

Jacques Porel, the son of Réjane, was sitting with his father at the Napolitain when,

suddenly, one saw him enter, like a brig in harbour: Catulle Mendès, with . . . the head of a Bohemian Gambetta, and that white silk kerchief which looked like a seagull caught at his neck. Behind him, a head taller than himself, was his wife. She was very beautiful, but pallid and dreamy, and she looked like her own effigy for the Musée Grévin. My God, how pale she was, how dark and distant was her gaze! She was the mother of Primice, who was about my age . . .
  Years later, during the 1914 War, I heard someone say:
  'You know, young Mendès is dead. He was killed at the Front. Oh, his mother will never be consoled! . . .'
  How pale she was! How dark her gaze, . . . and how distant, at the Napolitain! That gaze already seemed as if it knew.[11]

It knew already her husband's depravity and violence. At a wedding breakfast, Gheusi saw Catulle Mendès, 'drunk as a demi-god at the grape-gathering, raise a dessert-knife over his wife, whose face was always thickly and carefully painted. He threatened to scrape her pallid cheek down to the skin, and said: "I'm tired of being called *the keeper of the rouge.*"'[12] In his *Portraits-Souvenir*, Jean Cocteau recorded Mendès and his wife in the early years of the twentieth century:

Catulle Mendès in the corridors in an interval! I hardly dare to venture on a description . . .
  Catulle Mendès was corpulent and he walked buoyantly. He undulated with

his hips and shoulders. A sort of billowing, like a balloon, pushed him blindly on. The astonished multitudes drew aside to make way for him. He had something of the lion and of the turbot. His face, with its cheeks and eyes and little fish's half-moon mouth, seemed to be imprisoned by a sort of frost which kept him at a distance and set a mysterious, transparent, quivering barrier between him and the rest of the world. He had the lion's arrangement of little locks and curls, and a reddish moustache, the proud mane and tail in the form of a long-tailed dinner-jacket which went beyond the putty-coloured bum-freezer which was thrown on anyhow. The bum-freezer displayed the red splash of the Légion-d'honneur, the starched shirt-front was stained with coffee . . .

He was accompanied by Mme Mendès, tall and painted like an idol, who, behind the aquarium of her veils, and followed by the foaming frills of pagoda sleeves and trains, was like a wonderful Japanese fish.[13]

Her appearance had its poignant reason. A friend once asked her why she chose to paint her face so much. 'Because Catulle is used to actresses' greasepaint, and it doesn't shock him. Behind this mask, he never sees that I am growing old.'[14]

For the last three years, explained Georges Grison, the journalist, in 1909, Mendès had rented a little house at Saint-Germain for the summer. This year, for personal reasons, he decided to spend the winter there.[15]

There was, it seems, one decisive reason: he wanted a divorce. Despite her desperate (and, to some, strange) desire to keep him, he had separated from his second wife. In the summer of 1908 he had left 160, boulevard Malesherbes. Jane Catulle-Mendès and Primice, now a pupil at the Lycée Carnot, continued to live in their handsome apartment. Mendès settled at the villa Mackenzie, on the corner of the rue de Sully and the rue de Médicis, at Saint-Germain. The villa stood in a little garden, among centennial trees. He lived there alone except for a housekeeper, Mme Julie Ruelland.[16]

His work and his social life demanded frequent visits to Paris. The young Jean Cocteau used to have *déjeuner* with him every Saturday. 'At four o'clock, Mendès rigged himself out, injected remedies into his eyes [*sic*], and into his thighs, through his trousers . . . As soon as he was ready, he caught the train, and he did not stop again until he had reached the terrace of a café on the boulevards.'[17]

He was now, in his sixty-eighth year, an increasingly unhealthy figure. In the last few months he had repeatedly complained of headaches. Dr Guimard, the doctor at Saint-Germain, had diagnosed an abscess behind his ear, but Mendès had dreaded trepanning and had constantly refused it. As a result, he was sometimes deaf for several days in succession. On 6 and

7 February he suffered from this temporary deafness; perhaps it was one of the causes of the catastrophe.[18]

On the morning of Sunday, 7 February,

> he had an apéritif with a few friends, including Mme Liane de Pougy who was collaborating with him on a new work. Then he went home for *déjeuner* and settled down at his desk. He had several works in hand . . .
>
> At five o'clock he got dressed to go – as he did nearly every Sunday – and dine and spend the evening with Baron Félix Oppenheim, in the rue de Villejust. He was to come back at one o'clock, and he had asked his maid, Mme Ruelland, to have some cold soup ready for him.[19]

'He was melancholy, even a little drowsy,' the Baroness remembered. 'Several times he complained of feeling tired. He . . . only emerged from the sort of torpor he was in when he talked about a journey which he had made in his youth with Villiers de l'Isle-Adam.'[20] No doubt it was the journey which Judith had just described in *La Revue de Paris*, the journey which he had made to Tribschen, with Judith and Villiers, in the early years of his first marriage. Mendès left the rue de Villejust at about half-past eleven, and went to the Gare Saint-Lazare with the novelist and critic Charles-Henry Hirsch. He chatted with him until he got into the train which was to take him back to Saint-Germain. Normally he got into the *wagon-bar* on the 12.15 train; this evening, a Sunday, the train left at 12.13, and, as there was no *wagon-bar*, he got into a first-class carriage. He fell asleep almost at once, and woke up in the short tunnel just outside the arrival platform at Saint-Germain. Still drowsy, he got out of the train, and fell on to the rails.

At six o'clock that morning, an official of the Compagnie de l'Ouest informed M. Carrette, the local superintendent of police, that there was a body in the tunnel. M. Carrette went at once to the scene of the accident, and identified the body as that of Mendès. The face was recognizable, but the back of the skull was crushed, and the right arm and foot had been severed. In Mendès' pockets there were 750 francs in notes, a Crédit Lyonnais chequebook, and Mme Ruelland's watch. He had borrowed this, since his own was being mended.

His mutilated body was taken back to the rue de Sully. Dr Guimard sent a telegram to Jane Catulle-Mendès, who arrived that morning, in anguish, with the engraver Fernand Desmoulins. Guimard and Desmoulins laid out the corpse, and Jane kept watch by it, with Léon Dierx. Cocteau remembered:

Mendès' death struck me with consternation. The news was telephoned to me by his maid. He had dined with his friends the Oppenheims, where he had drunk nothing because of some or other wound to his self-esteem. He had come home in an abnormal state and thought that the tunnel and its lamps were the shadows of the station platform . . .

At Saint-Germain, a crowd had invaded the garden and the hall . . . Léon Dierx was weeping. The mutilated body was covered by a sheet, and the candles illuminated a face of wonderful beauty. The face of a dead man rediscovers the contours of adolescence. The mask of Napoleon at St Helena shows us the cheekbones and profile of Bonaparte. Mendès, after death, looked like Heinrich Heine.[21]

Maurice Talmeyr, the journalist, was less sympathetic: 'We know how the wretched Catulle died. He had become an etheromaniac, and everywhere he went, in editorial offices, theatres and cafés, he exuded an intolerable smell. He had no doubt stretched the dose that evening.'[22] Maurice de Waleffe, the Belgian man of letters, also suspected ether. Mendès not only took ether, and injected himself – presumably with drugs; he drank absinthe, and he had long been known for his heavy drinking.

It was a grim end to a life which had often been peculiarly squalid. It was an end which he himself had predicted, ten years earlier, to Waleffe: 'I had an abominable dream last night. I had fallen from a train . . . I was dying slowly, interminably, far from all human help. It was atrocious. I shall die like that.'[23]

Now, in February 1909, Le Goffic shuddered at this 'appalling, sinister death.'[24] Gheusi considered that, by his fearful death, Mendès had expiated all his sins.[25]

His sins had been many; yet the news of his death caused genuine grief, as well as a sense of a flawed talent, a destiny unfulfilled.

> What a death! Good God, what a terrible death [wrote Émile Bergerat in *Le Figaro*]!
> He had braved it, almost challenged it, in one of his ballads: '*Tu peux venir, camarade!*' he had cried. But if he had known it would come to him like this, poor Catulle, he would have asked it to spare him, all the same . . .
> Catulle was, first and foremost, a great man of letters . . .
> As for me, my voice fails me, and I cannot find the words . . . to express my grief at losing such a friend. Forgive me.[26]

Coming, as it did, from his former brother-in-law, it was a tribute that should be remembered.

The death of Mendès brought a surprising show of admiration and affection. André Beaunier wrote in his *Éloges:* 'He died in the twofold darkness of night and a tunnel, the man who had sung of life and of light

. . . What a savage revenge of brutal power on the delicacy of mind, on its subtle and ingenious refinements!'[27] Jules Claretie, in *La Vie à Paris*, gave him generous praise: 'The talker was equal to the poet in him, and like Barbey d'Aurevilly, like his master, Banville, he like to scatter truths and witticisms broadcast . . . It is a marvellous craftsman with words, a very gallant colleague, who today completes his destiny.'[28]

Mendès' body was taken home from Saint-Germain to 160, boulevard Malesherbes. On 10 February he was buried at the Cimetière Montparnasse. Jules Renard observed that there was a street full of people at his funeral. 'Someone pointed out Verlaine's son, a big strapping fellow, the stationmaster at some or other Métro station.'[29]

In *Le Théâtre des Poètes*, Ernest-Charles wrote a devastating epitaph:

> Mendès' death was only a cause for national grief in a few literary cafés. Yet he deserves to be judged by literary history. But history must make haste, because there soon won't be anything left of him . . .
>
> The work of Mendès is already decomposed. But variegated lights still sparkle and shine on these pernicious ruins. The work of Mendès is a building-yard of demolitions decked with flags, a cemetery illuminated *a giorno*.[30]

'No doubt he had talent,' added Dubeux, 'but talent is not enough, alas, to cross the abyss to posterity.'[31]

Judith's emotions on the death of her former husband have not been recorded; no doubt her pain and bitterness were tinged, at least for a moment, with regret. And yet, a year later, if we are to believe Ferdinand Bac, she talked about the visit to Wagner in 1869, and 'about her life with the no less divine Catulle'.[32] It is difficult to know whether Judith was embroidering events, or if Bac himself was writing with a certain licence; but,

> . . . with a sweet tenderness, Judith recalled . . . those four people 'struggling with the demon', and she revealed the shadows to us. There was also a certain resentment against her husband, who, even on the morrow of their wedding, had explained the poet's duties to her in a light which was far from her own conceptions . . .
>
> Fortune favours the bold. The future depends on the favours of the great. Even genius could not flourish without them . . . One must take care not to offend their self-esteem, and to understand their passion, like that of the gods, whom nothing resists for long. That was the theme of his conversation, in those glorious days.
>
> Her own position was less complicated. She loved Catulle and she admired Wagner, the Titan. For her Mendès was Cupid, and the friend of Ludwig II was Jupiter. But women do not like to pursue mythology any further.[33]

Chapter Twenty-Two

The Duchesse de Rohan was one of the *grandes dames* of republican France, and her social grandeur was to be only marginally increased when one of her daughters married the Duc de Caraman and the other married Prince Lucien Murat. The Duchess herself was a talented poet. She was also, wrote Maurice Rostand, 'one of the great literary hostesses of the age. All the poets gathered eagerly in her *hôtel* in the boulevard des Invalides, which has now become some or other geographical institute, and one heard them all in turn stammer out their poems . . . . It was easy to make a joke of this very mixed society: the Duc de Rohan himself, when he made a brief appearance there, called it the Gare de Lyon.'[1]

Suzanne Meyer-Zundel saw it through eager provincial eyes. 'Judith and I rarely missed the poetry teas on Thursdays . . . . Or again, one of those sparkling Tuesday evenings, where the guests, like itinerant reliquaries, made their appearance streaming with diamonds and pearls.'[2] In his *Trente Ans de dîners en ville*, Gabriel-Louis Pringué, the socialite, recalled the procession of 'all literature, all music, all art in general, not to mention ambassadors, crowned heads, ministers, great explorers, great scholars: everyone who occupied the stage boxes of life'.[3] At Mme de Rohan's Tuesdays in the boulevard des Invalides,

I used [continued Pringué] to meet Mme Alphonse Daudet and her beloved daughter Edmée, the Abbé Mugnier, Pierre Loti, Hélène Vacaresco, Paul Bourget, M. and Mme Henri Lavedan, and a prestigious prelate clad in mauve moiré silk with long trains and surplices of precious lace, who seemed to belong to the household of Louis XIV. This was Monseigneur Veye de Veya, the Hungarian Apostolic protonotary, whose clothes vied in beauty with those of the pretty women . . . I often sat in a corner with Judith Gautier . . . Judith had the head of a cameo, she possessed a subtle, enveloping charm, her voice, both clear and gentle, was a crystalline murmur. There was much unreality about her; the body had grown heavy, but the head remained superb. She vibrated with a great passion for the East . . . . She used to say to me: 'The colonization of Asia will remain the great task of the twentieth century.'[4]

In the early years of the century, Mme de Rohan's Tuesdays were among the pleasures of civilized Paris. A rare but exquisite pleasure remained le Petit Théâtre: the marionnette theatre which, for years, had delighted Judith's friends. The cramped conditions in the attic in the rue Washington had naturally limited the audience. In 1897 she had established her own puppet theatre in the old Salle Kriegelstein, in the rue Charras. She had adapted her father's mystery play, *Une Larme du Diable*, for the first night. The venture in the rue Charras seems to have been short-lived; but in 1910 – inspired, perhaps, by Gautier's imminent centenary – Judith decided to give another performance of his mystery. Her puppets would again perform it. Benedictus would provide the music. It was, no doubt, in the spring or early summer of that year that she scribbled a postcard to Montesquiou:

My dear, it's very kind of you to trouble yourself about me, and it's very useful because I'm contracting terrible expenses: choruses and orchestra!

It's not at Devandy's [?] any more, that's too small; it's at the Galerie Barbazanges, near Poiret, the couturier's—he's lending us his illuminated garden as the carriage entrance. The date is a little delayed by this change, and it hasn't yet been fixed. It will certainly be before 15 June . . .

Affectionate thanks from us both, and we shall see you soon.

Judith G.[5]

The performance was given on the evening of 13 June. Montesquiou was dissatisfied with Benedictus' music; at times it seemed to him 'somewhat luxuriant, and the mystery veered towards an opera'.[6] But the production itself enthralled him:

Yes, I saw Adonai, Jehovah, the Eternal Father under His mountainous shock of hair and His fleecy beard, both of them mingled with spun sugar, tinsel and sprigs of silver; I saw Christus with the emaciated features, crowned with the golden disc of his halo . . .

But this is not all: I saw rabbits scratching their noses and philosophizing, and others dancing like the Nijinskys of the grass; I heard crickets talking, butterflies singing, snails in argument . . .

I saw all this on the evening of the 13th, at the Galerie Barbazanges, by magic, and also through the piety of Mme Judith Gautier, a filial piety which had taken it into its head to perform, with home-made puppets, *Une Larme du Diable*, a Mystery by Théophile Gautier . . .

One of our friends once compared Madame Gautier to a prisoner of genius who, in the intervals of writing her fine books, used her leisure in her terrestrial prison to toy with dreams, to cut them out and model them; never was this appreciation more accurate than it was when the prisoner of genius, on the heights of her terrace, created, dressed and animated all the creatures of heaven and earth, with a view to this unique performance . . . .[7]

The article remains among Montesquiou's papers;[8] it was duly published, and republished in his *Majeurs et mineurs* in 1917.

My dear friend [this from Judith],
   It's nice, this recollection of my little puppets, and the whole article was very pretty!
   You are a rare friend, from every point of view!
   My very affectionate thanks and faithful remembrance.
                                                    Judith Gautier[9]

Montesquiou continued to endear himself. That year he also published *Les Paroles diaprées:* a hundred poems, each of them dedicated to a different friend. Two copies of the book were presumably sent to Le Pré des Oiseaux: one addressed to Suzanne, who had a poem to herself, and one addressed to Judith:

Chère et grande Judith, admirée entre toutes,
Amie (et qui mieux vaut), déesse, enfant d'un dieu . . . .[10]

Judith was again enchanted.

                                                    Le Pré des Oiseaux
                                                    3 August

Very dear friend,
   A fortnight ago last Sunday, in the rue Washington, Henri Monod was reading your dedications aloud to some select listeners. Now, in the peace of Le Pré des Oiseaux, we are reading the whole book again, and with what pleasure! And now the fine article on the theatre has been sent on to us, and brings us a delight the more with its friendly and delicious smell of incense.
   The article is delectable in itself, and what it says delights and deeply touches me.
   My delight is, however, slightly mixed with terror, because you have the terrible claws of the tiger, while all I have is a few fitful reflections in the eyes! . . .
   Thank you, my dear, you have been wonderful in this diabolical adventure, and I shall always be moved when I remember it.
                                        Ever yours,
                                                    Judith Gautier[11]

Judith had recognized the terrible claws of the tiger. Yet even she would have been surprised by Montesquiou's concealed ferocity. He wrote a series of satirical portraits, in verse, and the most successful, to his mind, were the ones 'inspired by people *for whom I felt no animosity*'.[12] He refused to publish them during his lifetime; but he died in 1921, and four years later they appeared in a limited edition. The originals of these portraits were not identified here, in print; but Edith is identified, in Montesquiou's papers, as Judith Gautier. The portrait is a revelation of his duplicity, and it is savage in the extreme:

Un gros éléphant blanc, sacré, vaincu par l'âge,
La dèche, les ennuis, l'orgueil, le maquillage,
C'est EDITH. Elle étonne encor les jobards
En faisant manoeuvrer un guignol de poupards
Assez ingénieux, en écrivant des livres,
Et surtout en pesant cinq cent quatorze livres.
– Avoir été déesse, en descendant d'un dieu,
Avoir connu l'amour des mains d'un prince bleu;
Du poète inspiré des Chants du Crépuscule
Avoir été la Muse, Omphale d'un Hercule,
Avoir aimé Wagner dans son beau, dans son neuf . . .
Et ne plus rappeler que le Baron de Boeuf![13]

Mme de Rohan did not only entertain her friends in the boulevard des Invalides; she also entertained them at the château de Josselin, in Morbihan, and in September 1910 she invited Ferdinand Bac to stay. Bac was said to have a touch of Bonaparte blood: he was thought to be an illegitimate descendant of King Jerome of Westphalia. He was also musician, artist, creator of gardens, and historian; and, in his *Intimités de la Troisième République,* he recorded how the Duchess had invited him 'on a little journey round Brittany' with her neighbour, 'the gentle Judith Gautier'.[14] The Duchess was devoted to Judith: 'She was marvellously gifted; her mind was masculine and her grace was that of a daughter of Eve . . . I think that the jewel in that woman's character was kindness.'[15]

Judith Gautier [remembered Bac] was still the handsome dark-haired woman with the matt complexion, indolent and improvident like her father, an excellent writer, poetic and colonial [*sic*]. She had kept the traces of that grave beauty which so enchanted the last of the Romantics . . . She was light-hearted in misfortune, laughing at her worst disasters, shedding tears of compassion at the sight of a stray cat which asked her for hospitality. She was constantly in ecstasy, and she had the voice and the ample manner of George Sand . . . Impetuous, omnivorous, she opened her arms to Mother Nature and she blew kisses to ruins . . . She would have loved, whatever the cost, to camp for the night in haunted castles, to sleep among the menhirs, to become the bride of the Druids and the Muse of Prehistory . . .

As soon as we got back to Josselin, it was agreed, with Mme de Rohan, that we should go and visit her at her house at Saint-Enogat. As we arrived, we were reminded, before we even crossed her threshold, of the generosity of her heart. All the spikes on the surrounding wall, intended to stop people climbing over, she had adorned with champagne corks. She could not bear to think that one night some poor burglar risked tearing his trousers and even his buttocks . . .

And so she had drunk champagne until there were as many corks as there were spikes. Now that the number was right, she could sleep in peace.[16]

It had been an appropriate solution for the writer of a prize-winning *Ode au Champagne*.[17]

On the left of the entrance [continued Bac], in the delightfully neglected garden, there was a little summer house where she could work, like those of her friends who needed their independence . . .

The interior of the villa was decorated with a thousand Japanese curiosities. Panelling, doors and ceilings, cushions, carpets, chairs and sideboards, all [*sic*] had been painted by her hand and bore the traces of her noble Asiatic frenzy. Everything seemed to me to be abandoned to the mice and the saltpetre, divinities of the Styx which gnawed away at these illusions and made nonsense of them . . .

Judith had a great love for the Far East. Had her father not shown her the way, with his mandarin air, his narghile and his embroidered skull-cap, seated on *sublime* Persian cushions? . . .

All this glorious Past one found in the villa at Saint-Enogat. Everything was in disorder. But what august disorder! Nothing recalled the hideous rules of the bourgeois for whom the broom is a sceptre and a speck of dust a domestic disgrace.

On the mantelpiece, supreme, reigned the bust of Judith, when she was very young, her contours already marked at fifteen. It was the marble bust by Étex. In it one could see a Judith who was fatal in the Romantic manner, with her bandeaux and her pensive air, a Judith already lost to the world . . .

Since her childhood, she had sat in the front row of Romanticism. She had known those giants! . . . They had held her, as a child, on their knees, they had stuffed her with marshmallows, with oriental sweetmeats, loaded her with toys, and then with flowers, . . . and then with confessions and madrigals.[18]

It was a memorable visit. Judith was often said to be inert, lost in her melancholy or her dreams. Now, in this sympathetic company, she recalled her marriage to Mendès, her relationship with Wagner – which she (or Bac) appears to have embroidered.

During the meal [continued Bac], she told us about her honeymoon journey to Switzerland [*sic*] with the charming, handsome Catulle. They had been invited by Richard Wagner, who was living in semi-exile with Cosima. The daughter of Liszt and Mme d'Agoult had stayed behind in the chalet to superintend the

preparations and give a proper welcome to the young couple. But Wagner –
impatient, as Titans are – had gone to meet them with his cabriolet. As he
helped Judith down from the carriage, he had taken her into his arms 'to give
her the burning kiss of Immortality' . . .

Judith did not confide in us all the details of this visit, but it was right that
she let us guess the most flattering in her memory, without equivocation or
vanity. What was noble about her was this frankness. She only veiled herself at
the limits of the confessions which one confides in oneself alone . . .

The good Judith described these rather disconcerting things – with less
periphrasis than I am using – in her innocent autumn. It had borne so much
fruit, and, yet, it had left her in the state – which is a kind of innocence – of
those good, simple souls who have walked along the edge of a precipice . . . She
was rather frightened, too, at her fate, which had left her so disarmed in the
presence of the laws of men. And yet, *she had no regrets at all*. Everything had
come to pass as had been decreed . . .

On the evening of that memorable day, we set off home, leaving the good
Judith and her fair-haired companion outside the hedge of the little wild
garden. A bit of gilt paper still shone on the corks which softened the cruelty of
the spikes. That was my last meeting with that excellent poetess. She died a few
years later, mourned by Mlle Meyer, whose piety perpetuated the memory of
the last Romantic, a soul outside everyday life.[19]

She was indeed outside everyday life. Suzanne recalled her two tame
lizards, one of which was so docile that it never stirred from the position it
was given; Judith used it as a headdress at first nights at the theatre. And
then, one evening, Suzanne continued,

we were dining out of doors, in a grove, and the soup was on the table.
Suddenly there was un untimely splash . . . A young blackbird had fallen into
the soup tureen . . . As soon as he'd been fished out, he escaped. There was a
wild rush across the garden to save him from pursuit by the cats. Finally he was
caught again, and henceforward nothing mattered to Judith until the bird had
recovered from its emotions, had been installed in a fine cane cage, and seemed
to accept its new setting.

Every morning and every evening, with extraordinary patience, Judith
undertook to educate the young blackbird with a little flute.

One fine day – what a surprise! – the bird began to whistle the few notes of
the great composer's three famous themes: *Der fliegende Holländer; Walter von
der Vogelweide* – from *Die Meistersinger* – and *The Woodbird*, from *Siegfried*,
which my friend had so often, and so patiently, taught him.[20]

When Edmond de Goncourt died, in 1896, he left his considerable fortune
for the establishment of the Académie-Goncourt. It was to consist of ten
members. No poet, and no member of the Académie-Française, was to
belong to it. The members were to meet monthly, at a *déjeuner* in some
Paris restaurant, and their first duty was to choose the best imaginative

prose work in the French language which had been published in the previous year. This was to be awarded the Prix Goncourt. At the beginning of 1903, seven years after Goncourt's death, the Académie was finally founded. It was, wrote E. A. Vizetelly, 'certainly subjected to a good deal of ridicule during its early years. It was derided for presumption and pretentiousness. But, all considered, it has been a very harmless institution.'[21]

On 22 May 1910 Jules Renard, the diarist, and author of *Poil de Carotte*, died at the early age of forty-six. His death left a vacancy at the Académie-Goncourt. There were at least eight candidates, including the diplomat and dramatist Paul Claudel, and the vituperative but arresting novelist Léon Bloy, author of *Le Désespéré*. On 28 October, the Academicians met for their forty-seventh *déjeuner*, this time at the Café de Paris. There were long and impassioned arguments.

> It was clear [remembered the novelist J.-H. Rosny] that they didn't want Claudel. He wouldn't get more than three supporters, even if they discussed it for years . . .
> 'What do you think about Bloy?' asked someone slyly.
> There was an outcry. Bloy had insulted Goncourt deplorably. He would be an intolerable guest . . .
> Descaves waited for a moment, and then, with a smile, he asked:
> 'Why don't we elect Judith Gautier?'
> He had hardly spoken before we were won over . . . Judith Gautier had a crushing majority.[22]

Léon Deffoux, in his *Chroniques de l'Académie-Goncourt*, recorded that, in the first round, she obtained seven votes, against two for Paul Claudel. And then, it seems, her supporters made their way immediately to 30, rue Washington. 'When the news of the election was taken to her, . . . Judith Gautier declared that she did not know any of the people who had chosen her, except for Descaves, whom she had seen twice, and Octave Mirbeau, whom she had sometimes glimpsed.'[23]

Rosny, too, recalled the visit which they had paid to the rue Washington. 'A crystal chime announced our arrival. A monkey started up, and cats observed us with mistrust, and the châtelaine appeared, fat and rolling, with a face in which there still remained the traces of great beauty, and something indefinable in her manner which belonged to another age, something which recalled the heroic era of Romanticism.'[24] Georges Ravon, in his book on the Académie-Goncourt, remembered that

> they had found her in her apartment, in the midst of her Chinese trinkets, followed by her cats and her marmoset, with a tortoise making its way across a pouf, a lizard dozing by the window, snakes rolling up their coils in a basket, a

parrot tracing threatening circles round the visitors. The new Academician
threw her arms round Lucien Descaves:
  'I'm sure this is the chief conspirator!' she cried.
  And it was true.[25]

No doubt her election owed much to the fact that she was the daughter
and literary heir of Théophile Gautier. In doing her this honour, French
literature had, in a sense, belatedly repaid the debt it owed her father. He
had failed, repeatedly, for all his distinction, to enter the Académie-
Française. But Gautier had been the first to recognize his daughter's
achievements, and, whatever name she bore, she would not have been
elected instantly, and by a large majority, had her own distinction not
been evident. She had inherited one of the best-loved names in
nineteenth-century French literature; and, at a time when women writers
had acquired a new, undeniable importance, when the status of women
was rapidly changing, it might have been thought appropriate for a woman
to be elected. Yet learned institutions do not always do justice; academies
are not always renowned for their enlightened views; and this election was
without precedent. Judith Gautier was the first woman to be an
Academician in France. Her election was a signal honour.

It was warmly welcomed. Gaston Deschamps declared in *Le Temps* that
'it was more than a proof of the good feminist feelings which move this
literary company. It was also the just reward for a life completely devoted
to the pure cult of literature and the arts.'[26] Had women been allowed to
enter the Académie-Française, there was no doubt, said Bergerat, that
Judith Gautier would have been elected; but, 'since they could not do
better, the Immortals had crowned her complete works in 1892, and so got
round the regulations'.[27]

On 25 November 1910, Raoul Aubry announced in *Le Temps*:

> Mme Judith Gautier, newly elected, will take her place this evening [*sic*] in her
> chair at the Académie-Goncourt, that is to say on the restaurant chair accorded
> her by the suffrage of the nine. It will be very simple and cordial, and there will
> be no speech. And so Mme Gautier will not feel any of the emotions which must
> assail an Academician who enters beneath the Cupola for the first time. Here
> there is an annual income of 4,000 francs, but there is no ceremony, or green
> uniform, indeed there is no uniform at all. It is a distinct advantage.[28]

For Judith, the annual income was an advantage in itself. As Vizetelly was
to write, some of the Academicians had been 'well able to forgo the
allowance of £120 a year, but this may have been of help to others – it

certainly was to Mme Judith Gautier, the Academy's first lady member.'[29]
All her adult life, Judith had known the meaning of financial problems,
even of hardship. On one occasion the bailiffs had arrived while she was
entertaining some friends; she had persuaded them to leave, and none of
her guests has suspected the drama. 'You cannot imagine,' she confessed,
'what it is sometimes not to be able to pay your coal merchant or your
cleaning woman.'[30]

Now, in November 1910, Raoul Aubry asked her what emotions she felt
at being the first woman in the Académie-Goncourt:

> 'No emotions!' she said to me. 'I know all my colleagues, and they are as kind as
> they are civilized. I am grateful to them, and I am really delighted at the honour
> which these good and brilliant writers have done me in admitting me, a woman,
> to join in their work and meetings.
>
> 'At the moment, my dignity has earned me, first and foremost, an absolute
> avalanche of books and letters . . . I am, in fact, a very important lady, because
> I dispose – at least in part – of 10,000 francs to be distributed this December:
> 5,000 francs for the Vie heureuse prize and 5,000 francs for the Prix Goncourt.
> So I am beset. I receive books by the parcel. And I read, I read incessantly, I
> read nearly everything! At our dinner this evening, we may discuss the
> candidates; and then, next week, we'll meet again, this time without a dinner,
> for the official vote.'
>
> 'Have you a candidate?'
>
> 'I am Chinese. I have no literary *salon* [sic] and I live apart. So I have an open
> mind, and my vote will simply go to the book which I've thought best. I've
> lived independent, and I'm growing old independent, and I shall die
> independent. I shall be, all my life, a sort of Far-Eastern woman detached from
> her time and her setting. That has been so for forty years, and I hardly feel it's
> time to change . . .'[31]

'I am Chinese,' she repeated. 'I am the reincarnation of a Chinese
princess.' It was hard to see the princess in the photographs of the
ungainly woman in her kimono at Saint-Enogat, which adorned the recent
translation of her memoirs, *Wagner at Home;* but, thinking of the Far East,
Judith turned, once again, to her childhood at Neuilly and to the distant
figure of Tin-Tun-Ling. He had, she told Aubry, filled her youthful mind

> 'with all the treasures of his distant Empire; and we read the poets of his
> country, and he described its customs and landscapes to me, and he recalled the
> sacred legends with such magical art that my imagination was completely filled
> with the lights and dreams of the East . . . And years have passed! And, as I
> told you, I am still Chinese . . .'
>
> 'And you have only visited in spirit those wonderful lands which you've
> described in such detail in your novels?' . . .
>
> 'I haven't visited the Far East . . . I know it precisely and delectably through
> its poets, its history, its men of letters. What could I hope for that would be

superior to the idea I had formed of it? I couldn't possibly risk being disenchanted!' . . .

The work of the Académie-Goncourt [Aubry continued] is very undemanding. You meet for dinner [*sic*] ten times a year, you read the books that are published by young writers, and that's all. It isn't much. Was Mme Judith Gautier going to take advantage of the happy re-awakening of public interest that has come from her election? Was she about to give us a new work?

'My drawers,' she cried, 'are cluttered with manuscripts, and you want me to produce something else! Yes, there is something which tempts me and has always tempted me: the theatre. But I have known such disappointments in the theatre that I have abandoned the struggle for dramatic glory.

'My last two plays, *Princesses d'amour* at the Vaudeville, and *L'Avare chinois*, at the Odéon, were taken off for some reason which I never understood, in spite of their obvious success. And my troubles began for my next play, *La Fille du ciel*, even before we came to cast it . . .

'And so I am simply going to publish my dramatic works . . . It's the best way of being performed when I choose, and forgetting the directors!'[32]

One important work she did not mention: the fourth volume of *Le Collier des jours*. She was just completing it, and she meant to call it *Dans l'intimité des dieux*. It was, said another journalist, 'a book of recollections of Victor Hugo, Wagner and Leconte de Lisle'.[33] Émile Vedel was also to record this book.[34] We do not know if it was finished, and it does not seem to have been published. The remaining volume of *Le Collier des jours* was to be called *Pendant les jours sanglants*, and very little of it was done.

Meanwhile, she delighted in her election to the Académie-Goncourt. 'L'Académicienne est heureuse.' So went the headline in a paper which had asked her for her comments.

With tarot cards [so she explained], I always draw a number nine, which means solitude, and people have often said that I live in an ivory tower – a nice euphemism for my fifth-floor apartment, my *entre-ciel*, as my friend Pierre Louÿs calls it; they say that I rarely come down from it, and that's true. So people hardly know me, and personally I only have the vaguest notion of what is happening outside . . .

[I am not] aware of anything that is going on, and I am very little involved in life. That's not because I don't open my eyes to people and things, but it seems to me that my eyes can't keep the pictures; everything becomes confused, faces are obliterated, and this causes me great embarrassment on the rare occasions when I venture into the world.

I have so little contact with the public that I always feel surprise shot through with anxiety when it is suddenly concerned with me; most of the time I am not aware of it, and the rumour has to be loud for me to hear it.

In the last few days, it has been quite terrible: they've been laying siege to my tower . . .

But it was a great honour and pleasure which came to me, quite unexpectedly . . . I was touched and amazed, and I gratefully accepted them; and after the delight they've shown, my known and unknown friends, after all those affectionate handshakes, perhaps I am going to change, come down from my *entre-ciel*; perhaps, with tarot cards, I shall no longer draw number nine, which means solitude.[35]

'I am not a feminist', she told another journalist, 'at least in the exaggerated sense of the word. All the same, I am glad to have breached the prejudice which says that a woman of letters cannot belong to a literary or learned society.'[36]

Rosny remained among Judith's warmest supporters at the Académie-Goncourt.

Her presence among us had great charm . . . How often, when I was next to her, I extracted some anecdotes about her father, Banville, Wagner . . . She described Hugo among his family, a mixture of M. Prudhomme and the pontiff.

'Did he really love his grandchildren as much as he professed?'

'He certainly loved them to play with, . . . like some people love kittens . . . And he needed them . . . But if they were ill, he didn't bother about them, and he hardly went to see them, especially if he was afraid of catching something, because he was enormously concerned about his health.'

'An egoist?'

'Not exactly . . . Self-centred, with great self-esteem, . . . a bit of a cult, . . . which of course was right.'

'Wasn't he a miser?'

'He was economical . . . Obviously, he didn't throw his money away, and he didn't readily give it . . . But he had his budget, his tiny little budget for charity . . .'

Married to Catulle, she had separated from him, because she did not share his ideas and did not like his behaviour, but she never showed the slightest trace of rancour. He had, she said, a terrible impulsiveness, he was always being carried away by a sudden impulse, and leaving his ménage in the lurch. And so he made domestic life difficult, and he forced Judith into work which was too regular for her, . . . because she could hardly count on him. So as to put some order into her life, she withdrew, and lived literally like the bird on the branch, letting the money flow through her hands and trusting for the rest to obscure providence. In Wagner she excused everything . . .

'But what do you think about his morality?' . . .

'I admit that he had very liberal ideas, . . . but there was no corruption. He started from the sense of his own greatness, which was almost divine . . . Did not a man of his stature honour the man whose wife he took? If I'd been M. X——, I don't think I'd have been offended by the love he felt for my wife.'[37]

There are numerous impressions of Judith at this time. André Billy, the engaging man of letters, had his memories:

> When she was elected [to the Académie-Goncourt], I also went to visit Judith Gautier . . . . She looked like an old Chinese or Byzantine empress, hieratic and taciturn, immobile and, it seemed, congealed in her stoutness, which was ill concealed by silk draperies with multicoloured floral patterns. In spite of everything, in spite of her fortune-teller's appearance, one was aware that she had been very beautiful. Her still-perfect profile, her still-smooth complexion and her dark eyes made a powerful impression, even now. Those who knew her speak of her grave and velvet voice, which was, it seems, exactly like her father's, but she spoke so little that her remarkable voice left no impression on me.[38]

Robert Harborough Sherard, the English journalist, also recalled

> the first woman who had enjoyed the proud title of *académicienne* . . . .
> I saw her shortly after her election, and it was pleasant to see how delighted she was with the honour done to a woman writer. She took the election less as a tribute to herself and her years of arduous labour than as a recognition of the equal rights of women to the rewards and honours of artistic merit.
> Woman-like, she was already discussing the dress she would wear at the meetings of the Academy . . . . The Ten meet at different restaurants, where they dine together and discuss literature. Madame Judith Gautier had designed for her toilette for these dinners a green dress embroidered with flowers; and, to show her predilection for things oriental, she proposed to wear a small Chinese sword [*sic*] . . . . She declared that she meant to play her part as an Academician very seriously.[39]

Her visiting cards were duly engraved 'Judith Gautier de l'Académie-Goncourt'; but her membership of the Académie was not to be entirely happy. Deffoux observed that 'she soon exercised a firm but friendly dictatorship over her colleagues, which one Academician appeared to deplore when he confessed "that it would be wise, in future, not to elect a woman".'[40] Ravon confirmed that, for a long time afterwards, the Academicians restricted themselves 'to this one feminist experience. They liked to feel at home'.[41]

Descaves observed that Judith stopped attending their dinners 'after we politely refused to accept the presence of her lady companion'.[42] Since none of Judith's colleagues thought of bringing their wives, the presence of Suzanne would have been all the more extraordinary. Descaves remained convinced that Judith was bored by her fellow Academicians; but, recalling her journey to Tribschen with Mendès and Villiers, he could understand her boredom 'with men as devoid of fantasy as ourselves'.[43]

No one could say that she herself lacked fantasy. Léon Daudet, the son of Alphonse, was fascinated by her:

In her languid way, she told wonderful stories . . . . She told me how she had bought a splendid carp for a dinner party for twelve people. She hadn't had the courage to see it killed and plunged into the stock. She had rescued it, brought it up, and tamed it, so much so that the carp used to recognize her and show its joy when she approached by making leaps and somersaults in the fish-pond. So Judith Gautier . . . led a life which was both melancholy and fairy-tale, like that in a German story of the early nineteenth century. I used to imagine her in a small German court, among her talking animals, and attended by dwarves in golden helmets. She only passed among us.[44]

─────Chapter Twenty-Three─────

Judith had always loved the theatre, revelled in disguise.[1] Not long before the Great War, she was asked for a short play for a charity performance at the Théâtre Femina. She chose *La Tunique merveilleuse*. The one-act play had been performed at the Odéon in 1899. Now it was revived. Two days before the performance, the leading actor developed erysipelas. The organizers of the fête called on her in despair. She decided to play the old Chinaman herself. The takings were magnificent, and Pierre Louÿs paid an engaging tribute to the distinguished débutante:

> Chère Madame,
>   I know everything. You have been acting for twenty years under an assumed and certainly illustrious name . . . You will never convince me that that marvellous talent, that understanding of the stage and that fine indifference to the ovation which greeted your entrance, came to you quite naturally on your first performance.
>   You were extraordinary. I had my friend Claude Farrère with me. He is actually publishing a novel on the Far East today, and he knows the Chinese well, since he saw them in their setting. He wanted to be introduced to you, to express his admiration, but we waited a long while behind the door of Box No. 5, which was impassable and jealously guarded . . . All the same, I am passing this letter through the keyhole.
>   Your respectful friend,
>   P. L.[2]

The Comtesse Greffulhe asked hopefully if there would be a second performance. 'There is no other matinée,' answered Judith, 'and, even if there were, last Wednesday's comic adventure would not be repeated . . . One doesn't repeat such lunacies.'[3] 'If you had only seen me the other day!' she wrote to Émile Vedel. '. . .I was a ridiculous Chinaman, bearded, with a curious phiz and spectacles. I was abominable, but I must say that I was a huge success.'[4]

Ungainly though she had become in the early years of the century, Judith still delighted in theatrical transformations. One day Suzanne gave a tea party in her studio. It was youthful party, except for a number of more or less eligible bachelors. Judith justified her presence by appearing as an attaché from the Chinese Embassy. It was an audacious hoax, for the guests included Clermont-Ganneau and a talented poet, Alfred Drouin, who had often been to China. Judith maintained her imperturbable gravity to the end, even when Drouin talked to her about Judith Gautier, and questioned her at length on Chinese politics. Never, for a moment, by her gestures, or by her accent – the unmistakable accent of a Chinaman speaking French – did she fail to give him a complete illusion.[5]

Another day, recalled Suzanne, Paul Deschanel arrived with his wife to spend the evening at Le Pré des Oiseaux. Judith dumbfounded them. She sat in her armchair, under Auguste de Châtillon's portrait of Théophile Gautier as a young dandy. She had dressed up as her father, to whom – despite her age and stoutness – she bore an extraordinary likeness. The impression was unforgettable.[6] Like Sarah Bernhardt, Judith was fond of male disguise. She had once dressed as Ruy Blas to visit Victor Hugo, and she had gone as Romeo to an evening party. Once, in the rue Washington, sheathed in gold, she appeared as Buddha, and sat on her grand piano, cross-legged, in the traditional pose. She remained immobile until the last of her guests had arrived. One or two bewildered visitors admired the work of art, and congratulated Suzanne on this splendid acquisition.[7]

With or without such fantasies, Judith's social life continued. Even at Saint-Enogat, so she reported, 'the serenity of Nature is very disturbed . . . The Sarah Bernhardt of the North, the illustrious Modjeska [Helena Modjeska, the Polish actress], has passed through Le Pré des Oiseaux, declaiming excerpts from Schakhespeare [sic] in delectable English . . .'[8] Mme Guillaume Beer invited Judith to dine at Louveciennes, where she met Gabriele d'Annunzio, 'an adventurer in glory, a condottiere and a clown.'[9]

Siegfried Wagner came to dine at 30, rue Washington, and Judith was moved when she discovered that his hands were just like his father's.[10] He had come to Paris to conduct a concert of works by Liszt, by Wagner and by himself; and, at the Concert Lamoureux, Judith heard him conduct the *Siegfried Idyll*.[11] In Paris, too, she and Suzanne were invited to Robert de Montesquiou's receptions at his Pavillon des Muses, in the boulevard Maillot at Neuilly; they often met him at private views, and, after these meetings, wrote Suzanne, 'he generally sent us a remembrance, in the form of a rare plant – rare because it was out of season, or rare because of

its colour and species.'[12] He sent them a may tree in memory of his friend
Gabriel de Yturri.

> My dear [wrote Judith], we are charmed and touched by the arrival of the may
> tree. In memory of Le Chancelier des Fleurs and as a reminder of yourself, we
> are going to look after it, and when it has shed its blossoms we shall take it
> down to Brittany so that it becomes a tree, a robust symbol of friendship.[13]

The may tree remained in Paris. A year later, writing to thank him for an
article on her marionnettes, Judith added: 'The may tree which you gave
me last year . . . is on my terrace, full of blossoms and buds. Suzanne and
I are delighted to see it in flower.'[14]

Robert de Montesquiou was indeed, as Judith told him, 'a rare friend,
from every point of view'.[15] He sent her enchanting presents: 'A triple
thank you,' so she wrote, 'for the Magic, phosphoric and Moreautique
necklace! I am giving you a present with less lustre, but perhaps it will be
precious to you: a lock of the Abbé de Montesquiou's hair, which was part
of my inheritance.'[16] Perhaps the Moreautique necklace explains the
presence of a photograph of Judith among Montesquiou's papers. It shows
her in profile, wearing a necklace, with draperies round her shoulders.

This social life was enchanting to the girl from Alsace. Suzanne
delightedly recalled the distinguished circles in which she and Judith
moved:

> There was Mme de Pomairols, who lived in a splendid *hôtel* in the rue
> Saint-Dominique where, on Sundays, all Paris gathered at her famous poetry
> teas, and we used to meet old friends and new ones. Among the latter was
> Comte Paul Biver. The sonnets and poems he wrote for Judith would double
> the size of his collected poems. And there was a certain Zoltan de Havas de
> Guehmeure, a very handsome young Hungarian . . .
> He came to see us at Le Pré des Oiseaux, and he stayed there on several
> occasions. Judith did a very fine life-size medallion of him, and a bust.
> Did I not also have occasion to know that famous Prince of Annam, who had
> always so intrigued me, and his wife? They became our best and most devoted
> friends.[17]

Indeed, they spent three consecutive summers in Brittany so as to be near
Saint-Enogat.

Judith was an innocent in the world of literature, unable to intrigue or to
make demands, averse to cultivating people of influence. When she was
elected to the Académie-Goncourt, *Le Figaro* observed that the Académie
had 'honoured itself by sparing her even the expression of a wish'. She had

not seen fit to ask to be decorated. 'No Minister,' the paper continued, 'has ever had the charming idea of climbing her five flights of stairs to take her the cross. She would have had to ask for it . . . Mme Judith Gautier was not capable of that.'[18]

She did not need to ask for it, now, or to wait for long. In January 1911, at the age of sixty-five, she was appointed Chevalier de la Légion d'honneur. Her name shone brightly, now, in the firmament of letters.

> Everyone is talking about her [recorded Émile Poiteau, with a mixture of bewilderment and envy]. People who know her slightly talk about her as an old acquaintance, and people who don't know her at all pretend that they have always known her.
>
> Important dailies, reviews and magazines are vying for her photographs and her work . . . Judith Gautier is in fashion! And, since fashion is an essentially French epidemic, everyone wants to read Judith Gautier – which is the strangest thing in the world. The most obvious results are . . . big sales for the publishers, . . . and a few more *chinoiseries* in French literature.[19]

Poiteau was waspish. Judith's fame was now becoming international. Her memoirs of Wagner were translated into English and published, in 1910, by Mills & Boon. *Les Princesses d'amour* was done into Spanish, and her name and works were known in countries as distant as Poland, Russia and Brazil.

Her star was indeed in the ascendant. In January 1911, as the music critic of *Excelsior*, she went to Dresden for the premiere of *Rosenkavalier*. It was the first time she had seen the city, which she found under snow. It was also, she recorded,

> the first time I had come to Germany not impelled by the wish to hear a work by Wagner, and I was tormented by remorse, because it was still a question of hearing music. Who knows, perhaps the veteran scents an ambush, and marches instinctively towards the gunfire to defend his flag yet again? Are there not some extreme modernists who oppose Strauss to Wagner?[20]

She filled nearly three columns with her analysis of this 'intricate, singular and powerful work'.[21] She was clearly drawn to Strauss, though, back in Paris, at the Concerts-Colonne, she found Mussorgsky 'rather strange and disconcerting'.[22]

For a moment, Judith's life must have seemed rewarding. In February her one-act Japanese play, *Embûche fleurie*, was given at the Théâtre-Michel.[23]

Early in May the Grand Season opened at the Théâtre du Châtelet. The

Beethoven Festival began. Judith considered Beethoven 'the greatest composer of all time'.[24] Discussing the second concert, on 7 May, she asked:

> Can one imagine the void that there would be in the soul if the work of Beethoven no longer existed? It is, for those who know it, a familiar palace, a garden of dreams, in which the spirit delights to wander; one knows every turn in its paths, and one makes discoveries there, as in nature, with the changing effects of light.
>
> Mme Pauline Viardot used to say, apparently, that she loved Beethoven more than her mother and father. Isn't the great family of art in fact the closest, and does it not overwhelm us with incomparable largesse?[25]

Whatever her admiration for Beethoven, her deepest personal loyalty remained. In June 1911, Wagner's work was once again performed at the Opéra; and, on 11 June, introducing *Rheingold*, she recalled how, long ago, Charles Garnier had taken her and her father round his new Opéra,

> round the grandiose building that he had just erected . . . I duly admired it; then, leaning over a balustrade on the sumptuous staircase, between my father and the architect, I said: 'Dear Monsieur Garnier, you have no idea for whom you have brought this temple to perfection . . . It is for a man whose name alone causes tumult today, a man who will soon fill this place with his sovereign glory: it is for Richard Wagner.'
>
> Garnier abruptly brushed the stray curls away from his bright eyes, and he looked at me in terror . . . But he forgave me because of my youth.
>
> Yet I was a good prophet. Such a work was destined to impose itself, and the hour of triumph has come.[26]

Now, fifty years after the uproar over *Tannhäuser* in Paris, Judith announced that 'the triumph of the Wagnerian cycle at the Opéra is confirmed with each new work. There are endless recalls, flowers, shouting, stamping of feet . . . The public is conquered.'[27] Late in June, the second cycle of *Der Ring* began, and she confessed: 'I have always had a special predilection for *Siegfried*; that is no doubt because Wagner himself revealed the work to me. He was finishing the music when I saw him for the first time . . .'[28] On 30 June, discussing *Der Ring des Niebelungen*, she recalled her own puppet Niebelung – 'the pocket Bayreuth', Wagner had called it – which she had sent in a huge box to Wahnfried.

> I had the honour [she remembered] of a fine performance at Wahnfried, for Eva's birthday, in the presence of Wagner and Liszt . . . There were five scene-shifters involved in the proceedings, not to mention the pianist and singers, and it was a great success.
>
> Alas, the 'pocket Bayreuth' no longer performs, and now it is over, too, at the Opéra.[29]

The year 1911 was an eventful year. That summer Fasquelle published
Judith's *Poésies*. When she had first thought of publication, she had asked
advice from Léon Dierx.

> My dear great friend [he had replied],
>   You tell me that you hesitate to publish your poetry, which is superior in its
> art. But why should you, the perfect and delightful writer, feel alarmed at this
> début as a poet, when the poet equals the writer of prose? Adding a wreath to
> your illustrious name will double the paternal glory in you, and will that not be
> the most pious and praiseworthy way to celebrate the centenary of Théophile
> Gautier?
>
> > Your old and devoted admirer,
> > Léon Dierx[30]

Reading her poems, said Ernest-Charles, in *Excelsior*, it was difficult not
to be constantly aware of her father's poetry. Judith Gautier revelled in the
countless spectacles of the world, but her intelligence was moved rather
than her sensibility. Théophile Gautier was continued and renewed in his
daughter's verse.[31]

The observation was largely true. Judith's collection of poems recalled
her Parnassian days and the magisterial influence of Leconte de Lisle. A
birthday sonnet reflected her devotion to Wagner; a fragment of a lyrical
monologue recalled her thoughts of musical collaboration with Gounod.
'Billet à Robert de Montesquiou' recorded the aesthete's visit to Le Pré
des Oiseaux.[32] There were poems dedicated to Suzanne's mother, and to
the Duchesse de Rohan. There was a three-act opera based on Gautier's
novella *La Morte amoureuse*. Two poems remain in the memory, and they
were the two that sprang, not from the intellect, but from the heart. One
was the poem of gratitude to Suzanne; the other was the sonnet 'Soir de
Chine':

> Sur le ciel fin, d'or et d'orange,
> S'étage, en la gloire de soir,
> La haute tour qu'entoure et frange,
> Aux toits, l'aile du dragon noir.
>
> Le lac, qui se ride en losange,
> La renverse dans son miroir
> Et vers ce reflet, très étrange,
> La saule penche pour mieux voir.
>
> Accroupi dans sa barque frêle,
> Un homme frôle, d'un doigt grêle,
> Le vibrant pi-pa de santal
>
> Et sur un ton très aigu chante . . .

Brisant l'air clair, sa voix touchante
Jette au ciel des cris de cristal.[33]

On 31 August 1911 it would be a hundred years since the birth of
Théophile Gautier. Late in June, a committee, including Judith and the
Bergerats, was formed, somewhat belatedly, to decide how to celebrate the
occasion.[34] Émile Bergerat marked the centenary with the first volume of
his *Souvenirs d'un Enfant de Paris*, in which he recalled life at Neuilly.
That year Charpentier also published the fourth edition of Bergerat's
Théophile Gautier, in which he recorded some of his conversations with the
poet and published some of Gautier's correspondence.

Judith had long ago sculpted a bust of her father as part of the official
memorial, designed by herself and Henri Bouillon, erected in Tarbes, near
the Pyrenees, where Gautier had been born. On 2 July 1911 there was a
civic celebration. 'Hundreds of young girls wreathed with flowers the
brow of the author of *Émaux et Camées*, . . . whose bust will henceforward
remain in the Jardin Massey, in the wonderful setting where it was
unveiled in 1890.' There was a lecture by Laurent Tailhade, and there was
a speech by the Mayor of Tarbes. 'Our happiness would,' he said, 'have
been complete if Mme Judith Gautier had been able to join us in the
commemoration of her illustrious father, whom she holds in pious
memory.'[35]

That year, when the young poet and journalist Léo Larguier published
his life of Théophile Gautier, he dedicated it to Gautier's elder daughter.
Judith invited him to call.

If my heart was beating [he confessed] as I reached her door, it was certainly not
because I had run up the stairs four steps at a time.

I pulled a broad ribbon of pale blue silk which served as a bell-pull, a Chinese
silk embroidered with flowers and butterflies, and, behind the door, a silvery,
crystal chime announced me. The maid took my card and asked me to wait in
the salon.

I was all eyes.

The garnet rep of a Voltaire chair stood next to the branch-patterned
brocatelle of a low-seated Louis XIII chair.

This furniture had belonged to Théophile Gautier, and I was very moved . . .

That mirror had reflected his noble Olympian head. He had sat in this
armchair, while Judith tied his cravat for him, and Estelle parted his hair.

While I was waiting for Mme Judith Gautier, I thought of the wonderful
young girl she had been in the rue de Longchamp, at Neuilly . . .

She had seen all the Romantics; she had slept at Tribschen, in Richard
Wagner's oratory, which was all blossoming with white roses . . .

A door-curtain was lifted. Mme Judith Gautier stood before me. I bowed . . .

She was a corpulent woman in a cream silk dressing-gown, and I seemed to
see, beardless, the heavy face of her father . . .

Massive, and apparently somnolent, Judith Gautier seemed to me older than she really was. She did not thank me for the dedication of my book, but she said to me:

'You know my father very well . . . I had forgotten many things which I have remembered, thanks to you.'

She showed me the poet's bed, an oak bed, with twisted pillars.

Two kittens were playing on the eiderdown, a shaggy log was burning in the bedroom fireplace. On a small round table, among the Chinese trinkets, were some lace, a discarded piece of work, a needleful of thread, a thimble.

So Judith Gautier could sew, like other women? . . .

She offered me a chair; and, in a distant voice, so muffled that it seemed to be lifeless, she talked to me mostly about her brother-in-law, Émile Bergerat, whom she did not seem to approve of very much. I was so disappointed I could have wept.

I thought of ancient legends in mythology, I thought of those slim nymphs whom the irate gods imprisoned in the trunks of mighty trees, and it seemed to me that this corpulent woman was a prison for the beautiful young girl of Neuilly . . .

I had come to this 'porcelain tower' with pictures which dated from too long ago . . .

Too late! All I had before me was an old woman who did not trouble to shine, and said something-or-other, thingummy-jig, when the proper word escaped her.

Yet I had one moving moment at the end of my visit.

The evening dusk was filling the room, and no lamp was lit.

Just as she was saying: 'My father', someone rang the bell.

I turned my head towards the door, and, for a few moments, it seemed to me that Gautier was going to arrive with Alexandre Dumas or Baudelaire, coming back from the *Le Moniteur* with his heavy ratine coat, and his hair, the hair of a Merovingian king, about his shoulders.[36]

Late in 1911, with a preface by Jean Aicard, there appeared *En Chine*. The book was one of a series designed for schoolchildren and for the general reader. It allowed Judith to discuss the antiquity of China, Chinese language and Chinese teaching, music, poetry and dramatic art. She wrote of Chinese houses, Chinese furniture and dress, of China tea and the method of making it set down by the Emperor Kieng-Long. Some of the passages on poetry and music bore a close resemblance to the text of *Les Peuples étranges*, published thirty-two years earlier: indeed at times they followed it verbatim. *En Chine* is the book of a weary author. Now, it seems, Judith was tired of writing, vexed by the demands of publication, more anxious than ever to escape the twentieth century. As Tailhade said: 'She had a long nostalgia for China, for Annam, Cambodia, for the saffron-coloured lands where the plum trees in blossom sow the young girls' cymars with white stars, where the warriors compose songs to the marguerite, where the sages drink pure wine from cloisonné enamel goblets and recall the glory and the virtue of their ancestors. She dreamed of imperial processions, of mousmés, of samurais, of peonies, chrysanthemums, and pavilions on the water's edge.'[37]

Early in 1912, again with a preface by Jean Aicard, there appeared *Le Japon*. It, too, is an uneven book, and more than once it suggests the author's boredom. The first half, a guide to Tokyo, bears a remarkable likeness to Judith's earlier essay. The second half of the book, *Contes et Légendes*, is almost unrelated to the first. It is, perhaps, most interesting for the glimpse it gives us of Judith and her Japanese friends: Mitsouda Komiozi, a former attaché at the Legation, and M. and Mme Motono, the Japanese Minister and his wife. There is an impression of Judith attending a tea ceremony which would have delighted Gautier's heart.

It was to the Motonos that Judith owed her friendship with Maurice de Waleffe. In 1911 the Belgian man of letters had launched *Paris-Midi*. The publication had its offices at 9, rue de Beaujolais, the address which was one day to be made famous by Colette. In his memoirs, *Quand Paris était un paradis*, Waleffe recorded:

> I owe the pleasure of having known and loved Judith Gautier to the Japanese Ambassador [*sic*], Motono . . .
> One evening, at the Embassy, before we went in to dinner, the Motonos were teaching me the difficult art of carrying several grains of rice, balanced on two ivory chopsticks, to my mouth without spilling them on the table, and I was beginning to manage it when they announced Mme Judith Gautier. There entered a woman who had grown heavy with age, a woman whose impressive face kept its wonderful dark eyes, shining with intelligence and kindness. Japan brought us together, Egypt cemented our friendship. I had come back from the Nile, infatuated with the Pharaohs and *Le Roman de la momie*, to which I had written an answer, *Le Péplôs vert*. Judith had read it, liked it, and told me that she had just voted for me on the jury for the Prix Goncourt. My Egyptian novel was as un-Goncourt as could be, and it only ever obtained that single vote. But it brought me her friendship, which was of a far greater worth.[38]

In 1912, the year which saw the publication of *Le Japon*, there also appeared *Le Roman d'un grand chanteur*, the life of Mario de Candia, the lover of Giulia Grisi. It was based on the memoirs of his daughter, now Mrs Pearse, and on the French version of Ethel Duncan. 'It has,' wrote Judith in her introduction, 'given me pleasure to transcribe and present to the French public the *Souvenirs* which my dear cousin mistress Cecilia Pearse has just published in England with such success, and to add to them the memories which I have kept of my most illustrious and affectionate relations.'[39] The result was a romanticized biography,

supported by her own recollections, largely taken from *Le Collier des jours*.
It had none of the charm, conviction and brio of her autobiography; it was
a work of piety which, perhaps, brought her a little money.

'Judith,' said Théophile Gautier, 'has much more talent than Madame
Sand, and so, as you will see, she will never be successful.'[40] Like her
father before her, she could not subsist on literature alone. She was often
obliged to write for money, and sometimes an unexpected friend made use
of her gifts. Early in 1913, Mme Rouzaud, director of La Marquise de
Sévigné, the famous *chocolatier* in the boulevard de la Madeleine,
published the *Lettres inédites de Madame de Sévigné*. It was purely a work
of publicity. There were twelve hundred numbered copies for private
distribution to favoured customers. The letters, said to have been
collected by Judith Gautier, had in fact been written by her. Dated from
Paris, in 1912, they give an engaging account of Mme de Sévigné on her
brief return to modern France.

Still in her seventeenth-century dress, the Marquise finds herself in the
early twentieth century, bewildered and bemused in a Paris street. She
summons a cab, which predictably takes her to 11, boulevard de la
Madeleine. The shop bears her name in letters of gold; her picture is
displayed above the door. Mme Rouzaud receives her, and Mme de
Sévigné promptly begins a letter to her daughter. As she writes, she eats
delectable sweets: 'It is my hostess who invented them. She has recently
set up big factories, where they make such quantities of them that they
could satisfy all the universe.'[41]

Terrified at the sight of a Paris omnibus ('a public carriage, which goes
by fire'), and astounded by the telephone, Mme de Sévigné feels more at
home at a performance of *Andromaque*, but she is vexed to see the lasting
glory of Racine, whom she has always set below Corneille. She is,
however, delighted to attend a Tuesday *soirée* at the Duchesse de Rohan's,
and she finds the Duchess 'the most affable, the most vivacious, and the
wittiest person in the world'. Rapidly, it seems, she becomes acclimatized
to the twentieth century. She goes by car to see Versailles; she goes by
train to Vitré, to see a statue of herself unveiled in the square. Finally, by
aeroplane, she returns to her immortality. It is an engaging fantasy which
endears her to the reader, and it shows Judith in a rare, light-hearted
mood.

'Judith Gautier seems to us very original and interesting,' wrote Émile
Poiteau this year in *Quelques Écrivains de ce temps*.[42] Poiteau ventured,
none the less, to criticize her writing on the East, for 'she had only peopled
China and Japan with her dreams'.[43] While Poiteau criticized her for her
invention, others recognized it as, perhaps, her real distinction. Vance
Thompson, the American francophile, wrote: 'She has made the East her

own. The streets of Pekin, the blue hills of Japan are as familiar to her as the tresses of her shining hair. Read her books, and then you will know her – those marvellous Eastern books, haunted with strangely magnificent figures, Chinese and Japanese, full of heroic candors, of pure and ancient passion, chivalrous, tender – there you shall see the white soul, the proud heart, the chaste word.'[44] 'Never did an opium-smoker or a hashish-eater, never did a creator of artificial paradises make his dream so rich and so coherent, his vision so powerful. Madame Judith Gautier,' wrote Robert de Bonnières, '*saw* China and Japan.'[45]

In some ways she remained enchanting; in others she continued to disappoint her would-be admirers. Bonnières observed her with wonderment, and with regret:

> This excellent writer [he continued] expresses herself rather badly, it must be said, in ordinary conversation . . . Her indifference to good speech, her habitual silence, her air of boredom, make her look more like a sultana than a bluestocking. I have never in my life seen a woman of letters who looked less like one, and had such charming unconcern for everything she wrote.
>
> She is hardly a Parisian, either, in her walk or manner, and she behaves like a Greek. Other women show little approval of her dress. But she isn't ruffled, and instead of thimble, needle and thread, she takes up paintbrush, gum and brass and spends her leisure making wonderful little masterpieces: a magic lantern for the grandchildren of Victor Hugo, with the whole of the poet's work painted on the slides [*sic*], and a marionnette theatre, with all the décors and all the characters of Wagner's dramas, which she sent to her godson, one of the master's children.
>
> Those are her amusements. That is how she rests from her writing, happy if by doing so she has for a moment warded off her unique and terrible enemy: boredom.
>
> She has made no demands of life: a little place by the sea; a room under a Paris roof, that is all she possesses in the world. She passes across this earth like a beautiful stranger. She knows nothing but her thoughts, she sees nothing there but her dream.
>
> She remains alone in her tower of porcelain.[46]

This tower had now become a place of literary pilgrimage. 'I often used to visit Judith Gautier, daughter of *le bon Théo*,' recorded André de Fouquières in 1951. '. . . She had lived on intimate terms with the giants of 1830 . . . To me she was the incarnation of the last century.'[47]

Another frequent visitor, now, was Maurice de Waleffe:

> I dined . . . at Judith Gautier's, at 30, rue Washington, every Sunday for years. She lived in a little glory-hole in the attic, low-ceilinged, cluttered with hangings and dusty carpets thrown over priceless manuscripts of Wagner and Victor Hugo, and inhabited by cats and dogs, which were the household gods.

But not a mirror! Only a noble portrait of her, by Sargent, recalled the sculptural beauty of this George Sand of the exotic for whom the friends of her youth, who were now old men, still sighed:

'Oh, if you'd seen her on the beach! It was the most beautiful sight at Étretat [*sic*]!'

These friends remained faithful to her in the evening of her life. I recall them at these Sunday evenings: Robert de Montesquiou-Fezensac, the poet of *Les Hortensias bleus*, tyrannical, imperious, capricious, erect as a fighting-cock, perpetually strutting about . . . The composer Benedictus, a Dutch Jew descended from Benedictus de Spinoza, a specialist in Asiatic music, chatting with a young French consul from Yunnan, Georges Soulié, who was a specialist in Chinese writing . . .

Some of her familiars met her again in the summer at her villa, Le Pré des Oiseaux, near Dinard . . . But those who came to see her by car could not expect to park their noisy machines there. The sedentary mistress of Le Pré des Oiseaux felt an intellectual's aversion for them. To those who were fanatical about the new way of travelling, and rushed past her door like a whirlwind, she used to cry, mockingly: '*Go on! You'll be as stupid when you arrrive as you were when you left!*'

I was finally allowed to give her the baptism of the road: a ten-minute trial run, in an inoffensive closed car which, going at full speed, if the road was straight, touched forty miles an hour. There was one condition: you had to put some water into the radiator at once, for after this exploit it used to steam like a racehorse which had just won the Grand Prix. My tyres burst. Judith was triumphant. She had christened my chauffeur the Death-cheater, and she never forgot to ask, when she wrote to me: 'Is the Death-cheater still alive?'[48]

In *Quelques Fantômes de jadis*, Laurent Tailhade noted the same qualities: the residual beauty, the apparent indolence, the kindness, the intense dislike of the modern world:

At first sight the woman had nothing sympathetic or attractive about her.

With the profile of a Syracusan medal, the countenance of Juno, a body whose obesity drowned, in a shapeless mass, the contours which had once been harmonious, with her torpid movements and her air of boredom, Judith Gautier gave the impression of someone conceited, overweening and affected . . . She spoke monotonously, and as if she disdained to lift the weight of her sentences. A sovereign indifference emanated from her movements, and from her conversation, as if, dragged out of the beatific torpor of opium, she had cast upon the objects of human curiosity the unsleeping gaze of the theriaki . . . One admired the beautiful idol, enthroned on high and seated as it were in dream on the lotus of Çakya-Mouni, without feeling the desire to continue the conversation further . . .

From her father, in fact, she had inherited a hatred of movement 'which displaces the lines': an Olympian attitude, Mahometan impassibility. Everything discordant, useless, deceptive and frivolous about the Western races inspired Judith Gautier, like her father, with an insurmountable repugnance. One would have thought her born to live in the vague and sumptuous setting of the fairy-tales, in the cool halls of a Japanese palace, or in the Alhambra, so that she might, to the plashing of the fountains, sing of the willow leaf, and make necklaces of jasmine petals . . .

And then, when the first steps had been taken, the first ice had been broken, the woman had disengaged herself from the Idol, Judith Gautier appeared in her true nature, childlike and timorous. This Princess Far-away with the classical and majestic face, . . . this beautiful, indifferent woman hid beneath her icy exterior a genuine kindness, a very noble tendency to see men and life through rose-coloured spectacles. Through the malevolent world of literature, where all is perfidy and treachery, where everybody strives to hurt his neighbour, she passed, benevolent and serene, never allowing herself or those around her the slightest jibe about the most discredited. She was timid, afraid of the public and of new faces, which was enough to explain the apparent haughtiness of her greeting. And yet, when the occasion arose, she could defend her friends, and even hold her own with the famous.[49]

In 1912 she was to have good cause to do so.

It was in about 1892 that Mme Alphonsine Lafitte, who had been a friend of her father's, had called on Judith in the rue Washington. Alexandre Lafitte, the organist at Saint-Nicolas-des-Champs, had left her a widow 'with five or six children'.[50] He had also adopted one of his favourite pupils, Ernest Fanelli. The son of a Bolognese bank clerk, Fanelli had been born in Paris on 29 June 1860. He had begun to study music at the age of ten, and had later entered the Conservatoire. Mme Lafitte was full of Fanelli's musical promise. Judith introduced 'a composer of merit who was somewhat strict [in his criticism]': presumably it was Louis Benedictus. He was enthralled by the compositions which Alphonsine showed him. Fanelli himself was invited to the rue Washington, and 'played the first three pieces of the *Tableaux symphoniques* based,' as Judith remembered, 'on *Le Roman de la momie* by my father. It was dazzling, like the appearance of a splendid fresco, which one seemed to see as much as hear. The impression was profound, and it was unforgettable.'[51]

For a while, Fanelli continued to visit the rue Washington; then, suddenly, he disappeared. Had he not left two compositions with Judith, she would have thought that she had been dreaming. The years passed by. Then, as the *Musical Times* reported:

Towards the end of February [1912], a surprising piece of news spread through Paris like wildfire: M. Gabriel Pierné [the conductor of the Concerts-Colonne], had discovered, by sheer accident, a totally unknown composer of genius . . . He was now living in the utmost poverty; and, having applied to M. Pierné for work as a copyist of music, had submitted as a specimen one of his own scores, which had greatly interested not only M. Pierné, but all the members of the Colonne Orchestra.[52]

It was the set of tone-poems inspired by *Le Roman de la momie*.
Early in March, remembered Suzanne Meyer-Zundel,

> my Friend was reading the papers in bed, as she always did the moment she woke up. Suddenly, on the front page of *Le Matin*, printed in bold type, she saw the headline: '*Discovery of a musician of genius*' . . . She seemed almost electrified, and rushed into my room: 'Suzanne! Suzanne! It must be Fanelli, it must be him, it can't be anyone else . . . Read this article.' In fact the composer's name was not mentioned; but soon afterwards, when the post arrived, Judith's presentiment was justified. Among the pile of letters was one in a large and beautiful hand: it came from Fanelli.
>
> In it, the composer of genius humbly begged forgiveness for remaining so many years without giving a sign of life. 'O Fanelli,' she wrote to him, 'I have been thinking of you and waiting for you for more than twenty years! . . . So come when you like – tomorrow, any day before four o'clock. Faithfully, J. G.'
>
> 'Madame,' he answered, on 10 March 1912, 'I received your letter, and its enclosure, this morning. Thank you a thousand times. Life has often been so difficult for me that I must become accustomed to happiness. I will come on Tuesday, if that suits you, with my daughter Estelle.'
>
> And so he came, with his small daughter, as he had promised, and told us that, on 17 March, at Le Châtelet, Pierné would perform his *Tableaux symphoniques* based on *Le Roman de la momie*, which had for so long been dedicated to Judith. This concert, needless to say, was an unprecedented triumph.[53]

Fanelli was triumphant, but he still remained destitute. Since 1894, recorded the *Musical Times*, 'he has not composed a single note. From that time to the day when he was introduced to M. Pierné, his tale has been one of resignation and poverty . . . Certainly, he is a man of whom much may be expected; and, despite his misfortunes, he has never lacked confidence in himself. It is to be hoped that now, the burden of poverty being removed from him, he will find fresh inspiration.'[54]

Judith and Suzanne determined to lift the burden from his shoulders: to give him a small income until he found a publisher. They approached possible patrons, and Edmond de Rothschild showed his generosity. As soon as his means of livelihood were more or less assured, Fanelli began to compose again. Judith wrote untiringly to her influential acquaintances to bring his case to their attention, or to engage those who – like Antoine, now director of the Odéon – had a theatre or an orchestra at their disposal.[55]

Among her influential friends was the politician Raymond Poincaré, who in 1913 became the President of the Republic. With Henriette, his wife, she maintained an affectionate, understanding correspondence.

> Très chère Madame [goes a card from the rue Washington],
>   . . . There are many writers who would be absolutely delighted if Péladan were given the post of assistant keeper at the [Bibliothèque] Mazarine. They are all persuaded that if M. Poincaré said a word in favour to the Minister of Public Instruction, the affair would be in the bag. I put [Péladan] under your protection, intercede for him . . .[56]

Another undated note from Judith suggests a remarkably close relationship with the First Lady of the Republic:

> Très chère Madame,
>   We readily give up the Jeu de Paume but not the pleasure of making the journey with you.
>   Do you want to go straight to the Embassy? Send us the car – and we will come and pick you up – that would save time . . .[57]

Among the Poincaré papers there is also a card of explanation from Judith, dated only 'Wednesday'. She had mislaid a presidential invitation for Suzanne. 'I tell you this,' writes Judith, gaily, 'so that you don't think Suzanne is getting into the Élysée on false pretences.'[58]

In the intervals of her social life, Judith continued, laboriously, to write. In 1913, under the imprint of a London publisher, there appeared a children's book, *Dupleix:* her fervent, chauvinistic account of the eighteenth-century French administrator who had tried to undermine English power in India. That year also saw the appearance of *The Daughter of Heaven*, an English translation of *La Fille du ciel*. Some time after March 1912 she had also embarked, with Fanelli, on a dramatization of her father's most celebrated novel.

The idea of her doing so had already occurred to Émile Bergerat. On 22 December 1911, in a letter to Robert de Montesquiou, he had discussed a stage version of *Mademoiselle de Maupin*.

> . . . From a literary point of view, there is only one woman who can treat the subject. And for want of [George Sand], the author of *Lilia* [*sic*], Gautier's own daughter seems to me the only person able to undertake the work and to be absolved in advance . . .
>   Since you want the thing to happen, it must, and absolutely must, be her, . . . and it is now for you, son of the d'Artagnans, to capture the redoubt and the hills. Your little quarrel is quite trivial, and I am sure it is only based on a misunderstanding. That doesn't count in families, and you belong to the family of Fracasse, and all you have to do is forgive the Rohans.[59]

The quarrel with the Rohans was, it seems, inspired by a question of literary jealousy. In his *Notes et Réflexions inédites*, Montesquiou explained that he was devoted to Judith.

> I was also very fond of the Duchesse de Rohan; I am still fond of her. Judith had also grown fond of her very much later, but very much less. This had almost led me to a break with [Judith]: she actually dared to reproach me for having run down the great Lady who, not content to be a charming hostess, also claimed to be a poet . . . I myself had the courage to sacrifice the friendship of the delightful châtelaine of Josselin to my cult for Orpheus, since I could only find her verse detestable. And here I am, reconciled with Judith. But when with Herminie?[60]

Montesquiou continued to brood. After Judith's death, he told Suzanne that Judith had been unkind to him.

> My dear Count [replied Suzanne], this conclusion is quite mistaken. Not only did she appreciate you at your true worth, she was actually fond of you . . . The fact is that when you involved her in your quarrels with her friend the Duchesse de Rohan, she was very hurt, and she was obliged to appear reserved towards you. Besides, as we only saw you when we had the good fortune to meet you, here and there, . . . on occasions which were all too rare, Maya could not show you this admiration as often as she would have liked.[61]

In the meanwhile, to the satisfaction of Montesquiou and Bergerat, Judith dramatized *Mademoiselle de Maupin*. Alas, like *L'Apsara*, her Hindu play, and *Les Portes rouges*, her Annamite drama, her version of *Mademoiselle de Maupin* remained unperformed.

In 1914, Judith was to be sixty-nine. Her health was still delicate, but in May she accepted an invitation from the Emperor and Empress of Annam. She and Suzanne would stay with them at El-Biar. It was a last-minute decision. Suzanne had been determined to see Algeria. Judith could not bear to part from her, and finally she decided to go, too. 'At least, that way,' she told Suzanne, 'if you're drowned, I shall drown with you.'

'And God knows,' added Suzanne, 'what it cost her to leave her setting, and her cats and birds!'[62]

Her visit lasted for seventeen days. It was the first time that she had left the confines of Europe, and it was, alas, to be the last.

————Chapter Twenty-Four————

In the final and unfinished volume of *Le Collier des jours*, Judith recalled the day when France and Germany found themselves, once again, at war.

> On the peaceful afternoon of 1 August [*sic*], under the scorching sun, the tocsin suddenly began to sound from the belfry at Saint-Enogat. War! War! One hesitated to believe the rumours. From all sides we ran to the little town square. Workmen left the work which they were not to resume. Housewives were pale and already in tears.
>
> Monsieur le Curé crossed the square.
>
> 'I was ordered to sound the tocsin,' he said.
>
> He was crying, too.
>
> Parisian women came out of the villas, left their tennis matches, climbed up from the beach. A few cars stopped.
>
> And there was the town crier rushing up on his bicycle. He stopped and blew his bugle. He usually announced lost property; what he proclaimed today was terrible, out of all proportion to his usual functions. The devastating news chilled the blood, contracted the heart. That was the end of the freedom to live . . .
>
> And the Herald set off again, to spread consternation in the neighbouring communes . . .
>
> It seems to me that I am the victim of an injustice. At the other end of my life, I suffered the war of 1870, and here is war again, the disasters, Sedan, the Siege, the hardship and the cold! The Commune! That was enough. Like an evocation of ghosts, those distant days arise once more and file past, through my mind, with cruel reality. Must one live them again?[1]

In recollection she did so. In these poignant pages she moved backwards and forwards in time, from the war of 1870 to the war of 1914. All too little of her book remains, but there is still enough to show that it would have been another coruscating rope of pearls.

At Dinard, at the Hôtel Royal, the few visitors who still remained were asked to

leave, because the hotel had been requisitioned. It was going to become a
military hospital for the wounded. The wounded! What a grievous, cruel
certainty! . . . Has humanity come to this? It is the same as the Stone Age, with
the weapons perfected. What men have most perfected since their origin is the
means of destroying one another . . .

There's a crowd round the Hôtel Royal today, and one can't get past. They
are expecting some casualties. The big grille over the entrance is decorated with
flags and flowers . . . The first car goes through the gate, an open car, and in it
a single soldier. His face is pale beneath his tan, he is tired, and yet he is hardly
leaning back on the cushions; he is trying to hold himself erect, hiding his
wound. A major is sitting next to the driver. Other cars follow. One sees the
white linen, arms in slings, bandaged heads padded out with cotton wool,
swaddled feet propped up on the seats . . . Out of respect, one does not weep,
and suddenly everyone claps, they applaud the wounded men as if they were
actors!

There they are, then, in the beds which have been prepared for them, . . .
and their presence is for us the first material contact with the war. Until now it
has been, so to speak, a fiction . . . Now the proof is there.[2]

Suzanne, too, recalled the continuing procession of misery: convoys of
wounded, crowds of refugees penned up like cattle, waiting for hospitality
or comfort. Judith simply pointed to a father and mother and their child.
'Follow us,' she said. 'We will try to make you happy.' Without the least
concern for her increasing material difficulties, she took in the Belgian
couple and their little boy. One day, on a sudden impulse, they left
Saint-Enogat. There seemed no valid reason, unless it was that somebody
had offered them lucrative work. Long afterwards they wrote to Judith,
begged her to forgive them, and told her that they had exchanged paradise
for hell. Then they vanished into oblivion. Their stay at Le Pré des
Oiseaux had, however, led her to write a children's book, *Un Général de
Cinq Ans*. The hero was little Joseph.

The summer of 1914 brought Judith not only the miseries of war but the
death of her sister. It is clear from her memoirs that once, in their
childhood, she and Estelle had been close to each other. It seems, from
Goncourt's comments and those of Mme Daudet, that – at least after
Judith's marriage – they had grown apart. It was not only the marriage
which had divided them: it was also, one suspects, the rivalry between
sisters, one of whom was patently more beautiful and more intelligent, and
her father's unchallenged favourite. Judith had been a turbulent Grisi,
Estelle a solid Gautier, with all the bourgeois qualities of her father's
family. Judith had known fame, but Estelle had led a tranquil married life
with husband and children. Both of them, perhaps, had cause for regret,
even for envy. No doubt Estelle had been a visitor to the rue Washington,
and had asked her sister to the rue Laugier; no doubt she had helped to
choose the summer retreat at Saint-Lunaire, so near Saint-Enogat, where

the family had spent their summers for at least thirty years. Yet there is almost no mention of Estelle in Judith's surviving correspondence.

Only in one undated letter to Charles Clermont-Ganneau did she suggest the relationship between them:

> The Bergerats [she wrote] have been with me for more than a month; they find the countryside so beautiful that they are buying some land in the neighbourhood. This living under the same roof has not brought me any closer at all to Estelle. As far as feelings are concerned, it's probably the opposite; there is a chasm of indifference – perhaps more on her side – between us. This does not prevent us from being on excellent terms. It's extraordinary! How different from the warm affection which I always feel for a certain person whom you know; my real brother isn't the one that people think! And here I give you a big hug . . .[3]

Estelle remained throughout her life a secondary figure. Among the voluminous papers of Robert de Montesquiou there is a photograph taken of her in her latter years: 'Madame Émile Bergerat, daughter of Théophile Gautier and sister of Judith Gautier'.[4] She did not exist, it seems, in her own right. Hard-faced and unsmiling, she faced the camera. In the corner of some cluttered room, among her books and pictures, she sat in a shabby, fraying chair, holding a Siamese cat, with a dog beside her.

It is possible that she had been ill for some time before her death. In a letter to Robert de Montesquiou, in 1896, Bergerat had reported on the health of one of his family. The doctor 'hoped that diabetes was not constitutional with us. We shall see what a visit to the country, rest and sea-bathing can do to put things right again.'[5]

Whatever her relationship with her sister, Judith remained on affectionate terms with Bergerat. Towards the autumn of 1914, when he returned, as a widower, to Paris, he entrusted her with his son, Théo, and with Théo's wife. 'I dare not tell you all the burdens I've taken on my shoulders, which aren't in the least strong,' Judith confessed to a friend. 'Not to mention the three Belgians whom I sheltered for fifteen months and completely supported, my nephew with his delightful wife, whom my brother-in-law thought proper to entrust to me the day after my sister's death.'[6] Judith was for a moment vexed; but she was fond of Théo – in fact they had much in common – and she appreciated Alice. Elegant and vivacious, Alice was also artistic, and illustrated *Un Général de Cinq Ans*. Judith welcomed the young couple at Le Pré des Oiseaux, and they stayed with her for two years.

Judith's relationship with Wagner, her admiration for the god of Bayreuth whose cause she had espoused with such passion, had created bonds between her and Germany. She was profoundly sad to see France once again at war with Wagner's native country. She wanted only to retreat until the storm had passed. For her, wrote Léo Larguier, 'everything was tarnished, the altar profaned; the sun, whose wonderful princess she was, now lit up only ruins'. At Saint-Enogat all she had before her was 'a vast expanse of sea fringed with foam, and, in her ears, the unending song of the waves'.[7]

There were still moments of pleasure. One stormy day,

> four wild ducks fell from heaven, and landed exhausted with fatigue . . . It was in fact [recalled Suzanne] our terrace which they had chosen. They allowed themselves to be caught, without fear or resistance. They were fed. They were spoilt. So much so that they no longer thought of any other skies, and they remained attached to Le Pré des Oiseaux. Judith had a pond made especially for their frolics. As they adored their vermicelli and milk, my Friend of course decided that – although times were hard – they must only be fed in this way. The greatest pleasure one could give her was not to forget her ducks.[8]

In her garden, in her Chinese robe, continued Bergerat, she fed all the animals in the commune. 'When I teased her about this zoolatry, which she had inherited from her family: "What can I do?" she said to me, "animals don't deceive you in love or friendship: they're the only honest creatures that there are."'[9]

Now, as Mathilde Camacho wrote, Judith still found a certain peace at Le Pré des Oiseaux. The trees in the garden had been bent by the Channel winds. Some of them had been planted as saplings by her friends; here was one from Jerusalem, and there one could see bamboos and pines, their branches describing Japanese arabesques; under the trees were shrubs and aromatic plants, eucalyptus, rosemary and mint. On the left, just by the entrance, was the small pavilion, varnished like a ship's cabin, where Robert de Montesquiou had stayed and Pierre Louÿs had written *Aphrodite*; on one of the walls, the names of her favourite animals were engraved in Chinese characters. Further to the left, you could see the semi-circular summer house, perched on piles which made it look like an Indo-Chinese cabin. You reached it by a little wooden staircase. It was there that she liked to work, stretched out on a chaise-longue, admiring the view of the sea and the islands. At the end of the main path stood the house. Over the door, one day, they would set a marble plaque inscribed: 'In this house, Judith Gautier dreamed, laughed, and wept.'[10]

This was Judith's retreat; yet the echoes of the war still reached her. She was president of the Dinard section of the Oeuvre des blessés au travail.

During the day, she and Suzanne paid visits to the wounded, and took them sweets and books and cigarettes. When evening came, they made dolls, arranged in groups with topical themes; these were to be exhibited in Paris in aid of the wounded and prisoners-of-war. 'I was interrupted by my sister's death, but I've set to work again.'[11] So Judith told Henriette Poincaré early in 1915. Mme Poincaré opened the exhibition.

There were also charity shows in aid of other war work, and Judith revived her marionnette theatre to stage a topical play, *L'Héroïque laboureur*, which she had improvised for the occasion. The theatre itself had to be constructed. Then there was scenery to paint, there were characters to model. These days of comparative peace would have been quite happy without the haunting reminders of the war. 'We live as best we can,' Judith explained to Henriette Poincaré, 'consoling the wounded, giving hospitality to Belgians, and living, as everyone does, waiting and hoping to see one another again. It will be a wonderful day.' [12] To Robert de Montesquiou she wrote:

> . . . I have not left my Breton retreat since the beginning of the war; Suzanne is with me, and it is not solitude. I have filled my time in the most bizarre ways, and I continue to do so; the culminating points of my labours were an exhibition of groups of patriotic dolls, in the avenue du Bois, in Paris (I wasn't there, but Mme Poincaré opened it), and an extraordinary performance, in a new puppet theatre, of a drama, *L'Héroïque laboureur*, which is a very special work of literature; the takings, in aid of the wounded, were magnificent. At the moment, I am making a small-scale version of the theatre, which doesn't prevent me from writing my memoirs, too!!! I am beginning the fourth rope of the necklace [*sic*], and it's going to keep close to the war . . .[13]

She began, again, to string her pearls of recollection. 'You may rejoice,' she announced to an admirer. 'Suzanne is spurring me on, like you, and I've promised to settle down to my memoirs again, and to re-awaken the concierge! . . .'[14] And again: 'The fourth string of the *Collier* is already begun. I am not skipping anything, all the gossip will be there . . . I am taking it up again almost where I left off. There will be a sub-title: *Pendant les Jours sanglants*, and at times 1870 will touch 1914–1915.'[15]

It was now nearly half a century since she and Mendès and Villiers had gone to pay tribute to Wagner at Lucerne:

> How far away it is, the day when my companions and I, at once sad and delighted, left the retreat of Tribschen, where Wagner still remained our idol, but he had become our friend! The dream had been realized, and it had not been disappointing; we departed rich in memories.
> Nothing has changed in my own convictions, but how many things have changed around me! . . .

However, I want to summon up my memories again, at the point where I had interrupted them, to try to re-create those days when nothing had yet changed: to find again, in their serenity, their faith, their youthful enthusiasm, the impressions of that time.[16]

In the spring of 1915, Alice Bergerat 'had to undergo a rather serious operation, complicated by appendicitis; and suddenly,' recalled Suzanne, 'there was anxiety, torment and agitation.'[17] Emotions were never less than febrile at Le Pré des Oiseaux. Alice recovered, but on 3 September Suzanne herself was obliged to have her appendix removed. Judith, she said, 'was much affected, and emotionally more ill than I was'.[18]

> Sans toi, je deviens manchote et boiteuse.
> Un oeil m'est ravi, le coeur par moitié,
> Zéro sans le chiffre et voix sans chanteuse
> Ainsi nous fait un la vraie amitié.
> Nous n'avons qu'une âme et mieux que l'amour
> Nous gardons l'accord sans ruse menteuse,
> Et sans redouter qu'il se fausse un jour.[19]

These lines, by Judith, were more than an admission of trust and sympathy. They were a declaration of love.

Exactly a year after Judith's death, Suzanne was to spend the night in her bed.

> Je passais cette nuit dans ce lit vénéré.
> Miracle! Son amour venait de faire naître,
> En moi, la vision du poète inspiré! . . .[20]

For the next year and more, it seems, she wrote the lamentable verse which she sent to Robert de Montesquiou, the verse which she published in 1920 as *La Gloire de l'Illusion*.[21] She herself referred to her 'liaison' with Judith, and to the spark which had been struck between them. It was, she recalled, her mother who had made the relationship possible:

> O bienfaisante mère! De nous trois n'es-tu pas
> De ce lien si profond, la cause tutélaire?
> Tu fis la liaison en dirigeant mes pas
> En ce pays breton. Comme en un reliquaire
>
> Dorment en toi depuis, mes plus chers souvenirs.
> La plus exquise mère, aimante, douce celle,

Qui me donna le jour, accomplit mes désirs
Grâce à qui pût jaillir entre nous l'étincelle . . .[22]

At Le Pré des Oiseaux, she and Judith had shared a bedroom:

Des deux lits, à présent, qui meublaient notre chambre
L'un, seul, est occupé, l'autre devient jaloux!
J'ai la sensation que mon corps se démembre . . .[23]

Such lines would have been a curious tribute to a platonic friendship;
and possibly they help to explain the disaster of the Mendès marriage. It
could be that, despite the impassioned references to heterosexual love
which are found in her novels and short stories, and suggested in her
letters to Victor Hugo, Judith had always been bisexual. It could also be –
and this seems more probable – that her unhappy experience with men
had finally drawn her into a relationship with another woman. Perhaps, at
last, her love for Suzanne had found physical expression.

Whatever its nature, this relationship did not preclude a number of warm
friendships. It was in 1915 that Judith and Suzanne came to know André
and Renée Davids: a husband and wife who were both artists, both
warmly sympathetic. They saw each other almost daily. Judith also
remained acutely aware of the hardship suffered by Fanelli and his family.
In June that year she wrote to him: 'You sent a rather curious answer to
my suggestion that you should come here for a few days. I quite
understand what that meant. But, if we can answer for the cost of this
journey, four is a lot in these testing times! Anyway, the *status quo*
remains; decide as you like.'[24]

In December 1916, she renewed her invitation:

The nightmare continues, and it is more and more dark. How do you bear life?
. . . Everything is getting worse, the meagre resources are almost spent,
otherwise I should have tried to make you come here for a few days . . . But
how can I pay for four journeys? Two, perhaps. Could you come with [your
daughter] Estelle? Think about it. What holidays do they have for Christmas
and the New Year?[25]

The cold was now intense, the cost of living had increased, and the funds
at Le Pré des Oiseaux were nearly exhausted. Judith was no longer able to
support the Fanellis from a distance. Generous as ever, she decided to
offer them board and lodging.

Dear Fano [this on 2 February 1917], it's not a question of anything final, just of giving you shelter during the worst days by bringing you close to the fire to warm yourself and perhaps round the table to share my pittance. Who knows what will happen, and, if Switzerland is invaded, what we shall be able, or rather shan't be able, to do? . . . Dear quartet, come soon if you like.[26]

Fanelli, his wife and two children, descended on Le Pré des Oiseaux. 'I still have a family of four with no resources at all whom I am keeping above water,' so Judith wrote to a lawyer friend. 'Do you remember a musician of genius, and the festival for which you so kindly took a box? I think that he has written a masterpiece, to the sound of the falling shells. And so, by not letting him founder, I have helped to save the future glory of France.'[27]

At Le Pré des Oiseaux Fanelli found the peace that he needed to finish *Séraphitus-Séraphita*, the musical drama which was to be his swan-song. Judith herself, untiringly, continued to promote his claims. She wrote to Jacques Rouché, the director of the Opéra. This theatre was the largest in France, and therefore the only one where Fanelli's grandiose conceptions could be realized. 'Madame,' answered Rouché, 'would you ask M. Fanelli what he could give me for my matinées? An excerpt? As for thinking of new works for 1919 or 1920, . . . this is not perhaps the moment.'[28] Judith decided to have a private performance of the piano version of *Séraphitus*. It was given for her friends at Le Pré des Oiseaux. Fanelli himself was at the piano, and the Marquis de Casa Fuerta assured him that the work was a masterpiece.

The Marquis had recently been introduced to Le Pré des Oiseaux by Joseph Salmon, the cellist, and his wife: herself a pianist. The Salmons had almost reached the end of their stay at Dinard; but the sympathy between them and Judith and Suzanne was immediate, and so strong that, on leaving Dinard, Salmon sent them a telegram: 'I have left the best of myself between the two of you; there is something indefinable inside me, I have seen you five times and it is more than a whole life.'[29]

Judith had looked after Fanelli at some cost to her own inadequate means, and also to her professional commitments. On 16 February 1917, Octave Mirbeau, the novelist, had died. His death had left a vacant chair at the Académie-Goncourt, and the chair was vigorously contested. On 20 June, she wrote to Gustave Geffroy:

Very dear Friend,
    I thought that the election was going to be in October. And now it's going to be immediately. How can I get to you? I am really blockaded in my little house, which is a raft for the shipwrecked. At the moment I am giving shelter to

Fanelli, his wife and son and daughter. It was no longer possible to look after them from a distance. I hope that you understand my situation and that you will forgive me for being absent for the vote. You know that I should choose Péladan. He is a great stirrer of ideas, and they are always lofty, always noble. He would do us honour.[30]

Léon Daudet and Léon Hennique supported Courteline, and expected Judith to vote for him. She herself had suggested Péladan as a candidate; she supported him wholeheartedly, and would not abandon the idea until all hope had gone. Jean Ajalbert was desperately anxious to be elected. He was not only a novelist, he had adapted *La Fille Élisa* for the theatre – a link with Edmond de Goncourt, the founder of the Académie. He had been curator of La Malmaison, and he was now director of the Beauvais factory. Years later, he recorded that, 'after Frédéric Masson, Alfred Droin, and Fasquelle, the publisher, had pleaded my cause, Judith Gautier gave me her vote.'[31] There was another account of events. In 1925, Dumur told the diarist, Paul Léautaud,

> something Ajalbert had done to ensure his election to the Académie-Goncourt. He only had four votes, and not the President's vote (as you know, this vote can create the majority). Judith Gautier was in Normandy [*sic*], ill, and almost at the point of death. Ajalbert made the journey, arrived at her house, cornered her, pleaded with her, tormented her so much that he managed to leave with her signature, which was equivalent to the fifth vote he needed.[32]

He was elected on 26 July 1917. Lucien Descaves refused to attend the Académie's luncheons – there were luncheons, now, not dinners – as a protest. Hennique and Daudet did not go so far, 'but they continued to bear a grudge against Mme Judith Gautier'.[33]

There were still others who remained jealous of her achievement. Cécile Vincens, who wrote under the pen-name of Arvède Barrine, dismissed her as 'an old lady with manias'. Laurent Tailhade, repeating the remark, added that,

> at times of the greatest gravity, she was tortured with anxiety about the health of her four-footed friends. Not long before she died, she lost Pé-Pé, her favourite cat. There were tears, hysterics, an absolute crisis of despair. 'That must be the three hundred and fourteenth she is burying,' said a friend of the household, in a discreet tone of voice, 'and the lamentation is just the same!'[34]

She was still incapable of complying with the slightest ordinary idea, she had no sense of time and no conception of money. She still lived in a dream, like the princess in the fairy-tale.

Nobody was, or will be [wrote Bergerat], more openly idealistic than the beautiful dreamer . . . who only felt herself alive in oriental legends. In this she was like Gérard de Nerval, who 'was never there' and, when you spoke to him, answered from Constantinople, Bagdad or India, as if by wireless telegraphy. At evening parties, at the theatre, or at home, Judith was travelling in Asia. 'Where are you at the moment?' one asked, 'while I am speaking to you? I imagine you believe yourself at the Odéon. Well, you are in Peking, in the Red City, in the presence of *Le Dragon impérial* . . . When are you coming back to Paris to take up *Le Collier des jours* again?' One counted by titles not only her books, but her avatars.[35]

Now, in 1917, Judith found herself in ever-increasing financial straits.

As for my debts, my dear friend [this to Rosny, on 20 July], I must ask you to give me credit for a few weeks. At the moment I am going through a difficult time. You know perhaps that five years ago, now, . . . five years! I decided to support a great composer (and his family) to allow him to write his masterpiece. Only the poor have these fits of madness. And the war? . . . Suzanne has helped me, with her limited means, but her income depends on Alsace and Russia. And then? . . . Six months ago, since I couldn't do any more from a distance, I invited these four refugees to come here! . . . And now their dragon-landlord has risen up. They are driven out of their lodgings. One may be able to save the furniture. But there will be journeys, removals and rentings. Let me get out of this fix, won't you?[36]

It was August, and the Davids had come back to spend the summer in Dinard. Judith had steadfastly refused to pose for Renée; like her father, she was unwilling to leave posterity an image which was not that of her splendid youth – or, at least, her handsome maturity. On Suzanne's insistence, she finally agreed to sit. Renée painted two portraits of her; she also did one of Péladan, who had come to spend the summer at Saint-Enogat. Judith had much admired Péladan. Now she welcomed him when he came to her, a dying man. It almost seemed as if by some presentiment he wanted to spend that summer near her. It was to be the last for both of them.

Fanelli and his family returned to Paris. At Saint-Enogat, Judith lived, now, with her dreams. She had been ill for a long time, and she was increasingly tired; but she was helped by the devotion of Suzanne, the persistent adoration of Benedictus, and the unremitting care of Bergerat. He had seen the constant deterioration of her health, and he had returned to Saint-Lunaire in order to be near her. To him, repeatedly, she expressed her wish to be buried among the cypresses, in the little cemetery near her garden.

In November, suddenly, a telegram arrived to tell her of the death of

Fanelli. He had died of a thrombosis on 26 November. It was a violent
shock for her, and she did not recover from it.

20 November, 1917

Poor Fanella, poor children!
    Your despair is added to our own, and it overwhelms us! What strength one
needs to endure such misfortune! But you must have it, you owe yourselves to
one another. Your children are still him . . . As for you, you keep the thought
of him. A great duty is laid upon you, and you will not fail in it. You alone
know everything about his work, and you must be vigilant so that its integrity is
religiously respected. He is spared all the bitterness of life; henceforward he is
only a spirit, but what a spirit! You must find new strength to defend the finest
part of him . . .
    I embrace you very sadly.

Judith Gautier

As I have vertigo, it is almost impossible for me to write – forgive me for not
saying more about it.[37]

She seems, now, to have suffered from arterio-sclerosis. She found it
difficult to form the letters when she wrote, but she still continued to
write. 'I hear there has been no article about Fanelli's death [this to her
nephew, Théo Bergerat]. That can't be so . . . And I shall have to write
one. Try to find out where, and how long, it should be.'[38] She found the
strength to write about Fanelli in *Le Figaro*. In her article she recalled his
first visit to the rue Washington, his triumph with *Le Roman de la momie*.
'Fanelli survived his advent by a bare six years. But the work has been
created.' It was a work which, 'when life has ceased to be a nightmare of
bloodshed, the future will be happy to acclaim'.
    This tribute to Fanelli was published on 23 December. 'So it was,'
explained *Le Figaro*, 'that the daughter of Théophile Gautier bore
worthily, to the very limits of her strength, the paternal inheritance of
affectionate warmth and generous devotion to art and artists.'[39]
    On 3 December, before the article appeared, a romantic, wholly
unexpected event lit up the solitude of Saint-Enogat. A hydroplane was
stranded on the beach opposite Judith's terrace.

Caught by the ebbing tide, the plane sank in the sand, and could not take off
again until the evening. Suddenly [recalled Suzanne] we had the idea that, as
there was no inn in the town, we would offer hospitality to the whole crew . . .
They accepted our invitation with enthusiasm. With the kind help of the
local people, who were all stirred by the event, we improvised . . . a passable
déjeuner . . .
    The commander chanced to be a friend of Pierre Loti's, and he knew Judith
quite well. Since he had travelled very widely, he had immediately noticed the

Torier [the Chinese door], which seemed to bid him welcome. The crew were soon put at ease by the kindly welcome which they received, and all four of them seemed as happy as princes . . . The news of the adventure had spread, like a trail of gunpowder, through Dinard. In a trice, a crowd of onlookers – led by the mayor – had poured on to the beach at Saint-Enogat. There was the providential help! Everyone harnessed themselves to the hydroplane, and, with a common effort, they gradually managed to get it out of its unfortunate rut and to push it well into the water. This fine gesture from the population won the aviators precious time, and allowed them to leave again that evening.[40]

Late that night, from the naval air station at Tréguier, a grateful squadron leader reported to Judith:

Madame,
We have just come down from heaven to live among the human race again. We arrived after nightfall, having flown for half an hour in obscurity. My heart was beating very hard up there, because flying by night in hydroplanes has generally caused the death of the bold pilots who attempted it . . . .
Allow me, Madame, with my comrades, to thank you for the charming welcome which you gave us. We are all the more touched by it since we rarely receive it. People who do not know the wretched profession are apt to misjudge us . . . .

I kiss your hands respectfully.
G. Guierse.[41]

Very dear friend [replied Judith],
We heard you with anguish, the other night, and, if your heart was beating up above, ours were heavy under our eiderdowns! This flowering friendship with the seraphim is very splendid, and terrible, too, and it is going to give us many torments.
How can you think that you are misjudged? On the contrary, everyone has a fanatical admiration for you. I do hope that henceforward you will consider the little house on which the four angels descended as your own, and that you will often come here.

Most cordially,
Judith Gautier[42]

The incident of the hydroplane had its effect on the Académie-Goncourt, who were soon to decide on their prize.

Very dear friend [wrote Judith to Gustave Geffroy],
Since I have no news about my colleagues' preferences, and time is short, I'm deciding all by myself. My vote will go to the book, or rather the three books by Marcel Nadaud, the wounded aviator. I was in the process of reading them when chance brought down on our beach, just in front of my house, four aviators who could not leave because it was low tide. They readily accepted my invitation to *déjeuner*. They had read these books, and thought very highly indeed of them. And so I am assured of their authenticity.[43]

Judith had not recovered her health. Yet in the last few months she had
worked at her memoirs; she had written newspaper articles and other
work which still remains unpublished. People had never knocked at her
door in vain. Her heart was open to all who were in distress. 'Everyone
comes to me,' she said. 'I don't know why. They think it interests me. But
if I can console them, do them good, I am ready to listen to them.' To
them, as to Fanelli, she was 'visible Providence'.[44]

Christmas was now approaching. André Davids, well aware of the
scarcity of food, sent her some sugar.

> The sweetness of sugar seems [she wrote] more suave and more precious in
> these bitter days! Thank you, thank you, the nice box came this morning, at the
> end of our *déjeuner,* and its arrival was celebrated at once. The weather is
> ridiculously fine . . . . The cats are sprawling round the stove. We gather round
> it with rather more decorum; we hardly leave it except for long walks or drives.
> Today we went to Dinard under a pink and blue sky and came back in limpid
> moonlight. The garden is still pretty. There are still some flowers, and cabbages
> of every colour! The mimosas are beginning, the gold of the gorse is already in
> the fields.
>   Let's try to forget all these horrors, and all of us wish that the coming year
> will end them at last. My very dear friends, I embrace all three of you with
> much affection.
>   Judith Gautier[45]

'She was working on a Bethlehem crib,' Bergerat remembered, 'in which
she grouped round the heavenly Child, and between the legs of the Magi
Kings, gilded, empurpled and mitred, more blessed animals than legend
allows. It was not so much a Holy Manger as a Noah's Ark – "or a Noel's
Ark", I said to her, laughing.'[46] Judith usually decorated a Christmas tree
for her cats: Lilith and Bébé, Iblis and Crevette; this year she made a crib
instead – to celebrate Christmas, and the news that the Allied troops had
just entered Jerusalem.

> The poet of *Le Livre de Jade,* the magician of *Iskender* and *Le Dragon impérial*
> still [wrote the Tharauds] had enchanted fingers. In a few days, she modelled
> the little figures of each legend in clay, dressed them with multicoloured scraps
> of material, and gave each of them his place in the heavenly manger. Overhead,
> in the fir branches, she hooked an angel dressed in sky-blue silk, holding a
> Union Jack aloft. The heavenly Child could be born, the crib was finished.[47]

It was 23 December, and that day Judith received a telegram from
Joseph Salmon. It was soon followed by a letter: 'My dear, great Friend, I
think that the moment has come . . . to go and embrace you at
Dinard . . .'[48] Judith told Suzanne to send a telegram at once: 'Let us

exult!' Suzanne was surprised by such delight. 'At the very moment his telegram arrived,' Judith explained, 'I was wishing ardently that he would come back soon.' It seemed as if the intuitive friend had answered the appeal of her soul.[49]

Meanwhile, she asked Suzanne to arrange a tea party for their local friends. When the crib had been admired, the seasonal wishes and compliments exchanged, and the guests had gone, Judith felt very tired and went to bed. Suzanne spent all night at her bedside. Judith slept fitfully, she was preoccupied with Joseph's arrival. Long before dawn, in her half-sleep, she reminded Suzanne to go and meet him. Day came, and her weariness continued.

Half-way to the station, Suzanne met Joseph. He turned pale, and asked if Judith were ill. He reached Le Pré des Oiseaux, ran upstairs, and threw himself on his knees beside her bed. He grasped her hands, which he kissed, and held for a long while in his own. He was wearing a black cloak; his pallor emphasized his noble features and penetrating gaze. Judith was moved. 'But it is the Archangel Michael!' She had been haunted by this type of masculine beauty, and she had always sought it, but – apart from the vision at Fécamp, more than forty years before – she had always sought it in vain. Perhaps, Suzanne reflected, some dark foreboding said to her: 'Destiny has always prevented me from seeing it, but, now that I am dying, it has come.'[50]

She had been, recorded J.-H. Rosny, 'terribly afraid of a violent death at the hands of a soldier . . . Fate was ironic, and kept watch over her for a different end.'[51] That night, there was a raging storm. The snow whirled round in gusts; the sea crashed on the beach. Judith had once bought a ship's bell: it came from the wreckage of a fishing boat, *La Thérèse.* She had hung it by the gate at the bottom of her garden. Tonight the tempest rang it with increasing violence. Her musical spirit, which had found such delight in Wagner, abandoned itself to the storm, and to the sound of the bronze bell, which seemed to toll for a ship in distress. Suzanne, who was reading aloud to her, suddenly saw her half rise from her pillow, open-mouthed, her eyes wide open, so it seemed, at some strange vision; then, suddenly, her head fell on to the pillow.

Judith Gautier died of a coronary thrombosis, at the age of seventy-two, just before ten o'clock that night, Wednesday, 26 December. The hall clock suddenly stopped. The bell continued to toll in the storm.[52]

Cette beauté des morts, lumière souveraine,
Qui rajeunit leur face et qui la rassérène,
Qu'est-elle? . . . Le reflet de l'immortalité?

Ou bien l'apaisement de la chair torturée,
La paix de la matière à jamais délivrée
De l'âme, et que reprend l'insensibilité? . . . [53]

In *Suprême beauté*, the sonnet which she had written for Henri Monod,
Judith had taken a bitter view of life: a Parnassian view which seemed to
echo Leconte de Lisle. But, whatever her relief at escaping her existence at
last, whatever her thoughts on the prospect of immortality, she died
fortified by the rites of the Catholic Church.[54]

Next day all the foliage which had been cut for the crib, and the crib
itself, which she had set in a corner of the salon, served Judith as her
chapelle ardente. 'The pious little figures, made of oakum, clay, and scraps
of material, surrounded the coffin with joined hands and astonished faces,
and in the fir-tree branches, over her head, the little sky-blue angel waved
his star and his little flag in honour of Jerusalem.'[55]

Although, according to Descaves, Judith had died in the odour of sanctity,
there was some contention about her funeral. Suzanne recalled how 'a
number of nuns were discussing the impropriety of a religious service at
the church, which Judith, Catholic though she was, had not been
accustomed to attend. The blessed Mother Gabriel, Mother Superior of
the Sisters of Mercy, intervened, and, with her usual benevolence and
charity of soul, she decided the matter like this: "Are we sure that we have
practised Charity as She did?"'[56]

> According to her wish [wrote Bergerat], many times expressed, we committed
> her remains to the little Breton cemetery adjoining her garden, a hundred yards
> away from the terrace where she came to watch the children building cities of
> sand, destroyed, too, by the ebbing of the tide. And so she realized the same
> wish as Chateaubriand, her neighbour on the cliffs, to sleep the great sleep in
> the arms of the eternal rocker, and in the unceasing Wagnerian symphony with
> which it envelops the dead.[57]

She lay there among the old sea captains and fishermen, the old country
folk of Brittany. In time a palm tree grew beside her grave. An oriental
motto was painted, in blue letters, on her granite tombstone: 'The light of
heaven has come.' The Chinese inscription had been sent, as a final
homage, by the Emperor of Annam.[58]

Judith Gautier had lived in a dream, wrote Laurent Tailhade,

> like the princess of the fairy-tales. She had loved music, she had loved lands
> which were distant, bizarre and decorative. No doubt her spirit, evaporated like
> a scent, gone from its terrestrial dwelling, has been borne away on the wing of a

black and gold dragon, and it has flown away, among the Immortals . . . ; [no doubt] she is quietly talking, under the flowering trees of some eternal spring, with the gentle Li-Tai-pei.[59]

Émile Bergerat blamed the war for Judith's early death.

It will [he wrote] have taken the total disintegration of our social system, and the immense disorder in which we live, for the death of Judith Gautier not to have aroused the lamentations of all the literary men in the Press. She was, certainly, without any question, a noble figure in our French Parnassus. She had made an illustrious name illustrious once again, and duly prolonged the paternal glory. And now she disappears 'discreetly', as the epitaphs say in village churches, silently, like a bird of paradise under the snow. It is a triumph for Germany and its pan-Germanic culture. This had already killed the father in 1870, it has just, in turn, destroyed the child, for Judith, too, succumbed to the consequences of the war . . .
We sent no announcement of her death and funeral to M. Siegfried Wagner. He is a German; he would have come.[60]

Whatever Bergerat maintained, the Press was well aware that Judith had died, and she was lamented by men of letters. On 28 December – though her age was given as sixty-seven – her death was reported in *La Presse*. On 29 December it was announced in *The Times*. That day *Le Temps* reported: 'The cannonade remains very intense to the north of Verdun.' It also found space to speak of her and to maintain that her election to the Académie-Goncourt had been an act of literary justice. That same day, Mme Alphonse Daudet declared her conviction that Judith had been 'a true writer, an artist in every sense of the word'.[61]
That day, too, Jean-Jacques Brousson wrote:

By one of those brilliant romantic contrasts dear to the school of *le bon Théo*, Judith Gautier, his daughter, died with the year, sensitive to the cold. This princess of the sun, this sensualist, closes her eyes for ever, her eyes enthralled by oriental fantasmagoria, in the mystic mists of Brittany, beside the wild sea . . .
Was she the most brilliant work of the master-jeweller of *Émaux et Camées*? She was, at least, the most loved, the most cherished, the most Théophilesque . . .[62]

On 8 January, in *Le Figaro*, Bergerat himself paid tribute to her:

I am the last person is the world to discuss the artistic value of the work of Judith Gautier, though I am not the only one to believe that it is considerable. She had a powerful reputation among the poets. The greatest of them, and Victor Hugo first and foremost, accorded her the sceptre which had fallen from the hands of George Sand with the feminine mastery of the corporation of letters. If the Cardinal's Académie were open to women writers, the realists of the Académie-Goncourt would not have had the honour of doing justice to this triumphant idealist. 'She would have been one of us long ago,' declared Gaston Boissier, permanent secretary of the Forty, 'because (he added, smiling) she is perhaps her father's masterpiece.'[63]

'The death of Mme Judith Gautier,' continued Paul Souday in *Le Temps*, 'has been deeply felt by all those who love literature . . . In losing her, it seems as if we were losing her father a second time'.[64]

There remained the comments of the Académie-Goncourt. Ravon, taking a narrow view of the event, decided that 'she had been, all things considered, a good Academician'.[65] Some people believed that a woman would succeed to her chair. They recalled Edmond de Goncourt's comment: 'There are only two women who write French, Mme Judith Gautier and Mme Alphonse Daudet.'[66] There was also talk of electing Rachilde, Séverine or Colette. In fact Henry Céard was elected to the vacant chair on 29 April 1918. A year and more later, on 21 May 1919, Émile Bergerat succeeded to the chair of Paul Margueritte. It was a consolation prize for his repeated failure to enter the Académie-Française. As he explained to Adolphe Brisson: 'Well, my dear colleague, there comes a time when one needs some glory!'[67]

In the rue Washington the may tree given, once, by Robert de Montesquiou, wilted and died on Judith's death. At Saint-Enogat, Lilith, the cat, wandered like a soul in torment, and never ceased to prowl round Judith's tomb. She let herself die of starvation. In Judith's grave, fifty-four years later, Suzanne Meyer-Zundel was buried.[68]

Notes

ABBREVIATIONS

Arsenal	=	Bibliothèque de l'Arsenal, Paris
BN	=	Bibliothèque Nationale, Paris
Chantilly	=	Bibliothèque Spoelberch de Lovenjoul, Chantilly
JG	=	Judith Gautier
MVH	=	Maison de Victor Hugo, Paris
Ormond	=	Ormond Papers

CHAPTER ONE

1. For the Grisis, see Richardson: *Théophile Gautier: his life and times*, 48–9 and passim; Lifar: *Carlotta Grisi*, 25 seqq.; and JG: *Le Roman d'un grand chanteur*, passim
2. Guest: *Jules Perrot*, 83
3. [Août 1845.] Chantilly: C 475 f 5
4. JG: *Le Collier des jours*, 1–2
5. Ibid, 9
6. Ibid, 17
7. Ibid, 13
8. Ibid, 20
9. Ibid, 22
10. Ibid, 40–1
11. Ibid, 40
12. Ibid, 44–5
13. Ibid, 52
14. 10 juin 1854. Chantilly: C 476 f 25
15. JG: op. cit., 84
16. Ibid, 88
17. Ibid, 107
18. Ibid, 121–2
19. Ibid, 126, 127, 130
20. Ibid, 132–3
21. Ibid, 173
22. Ibid, 174
23. Ibid, 181–2
24. Undated. Chantilly: C 502 *quater* f 6
25. JG: op. cit., 143, 228
26. Ibid, 230, 236
27. Ibid, 239

CHAPTER TWO

1. JG: *Le Collier des jours*, 243 seqq.
2. Antoine Étex, sculptor, artist and architect, 1808–88
3. JG: op. cit., 268
4. Ibid, 269–70, 273
5. Diary of Eugénie Fort (Pierre

Théophile Gautier)
6. 17 février 1852. Chantilly: C 476 f 14
7. 27 février 1852. Chantilly: C 476 f 18
8. 7 mai 1852. Chantilly: C 476 f 21
9. Bergerat Papers
10. 27 May 1859. Ibid.
11. Bergerat Papers
12. JG: *Le Second Rang du Collier*, 9
13. Ibid, 38
14. Ibid, 42
15. Ibid, 81 seqq.
16. Ibid, 106 seqq.
17. Ibid, 189
18. Larguier: *Théophile Gautier*, 162
19. *Paris-Guide*, II, 999

20. [Fin janvier 1865.] Chantilly: C 479 f
    50
21. JG: *Le Second Rang du Collier*, 169–
    70
22. Guichard: *Lettres à Judith Gautier par
    Richard et Cosima Wagner*, 325–6
23. Diary of Eugénie Fort (Pierre
    Théophile Gautier)
24. *Le Moniteur universel*, 5 août 1861
25. 7/19 août 1861. Bergerat Papers
26. 22 août/3 septembre 1861. Chantilly:
    C 472 ff 205–6
27. [Septembre 1861.] Chantilly: C 472 f
    210
28. Bergerat Papers

CHAPTER THREE

1. Dreyfous: *Ce que je tiens à dire*, I,
   84–5
2. Goncourt: *Journal*, V, 80–1
3. For Gautier's visit to London, see
   Richardson: *Théophile Gautier: his life
   and times*, 174–5
4. JG: *Le Second Rang du collier*, 124
   seqq.
5. 10 mai 1862. Chantilly: C 474 f 99
6. 27 mai 1862. Chantilly: C 473 f 153
7. Chantilly: C 472 ff 226–7
7. JG: op. cit., 128, 130–1
9. Ibid, 132–5
10. Ibid, 159
11. Grison: 'Tin-Tun-Ling'. (*Le Figaro*,
    29 décembre 1917)
12. Ibid.
13. JG: op. cit., 160, 161–2, 163
14. Silvestre: *Portraits et souvenirs*, 187
15. Bergerat: *Souvenirs d'un Enfant de
    Paris*, 370
16. Grison: loc. cit.
17. Tild: *Théophile Gautier et ses amis*,
    170–1

18. Grison: loc. cit.
19. Meyer-Zundel: *Quinze Ans auprès de
    Judith Gautier*, 159
20. Larguier: op. cit., 159
21. JG: *Le Second Rang du Collier*, 68
22. *L'Artiste*, 15 avril 1864
23. Meyer–Zundel: op. cit., 244, 245
24. BN: Théophile Gautier catalogue,
    no. 138. It is dated here early
    February 1866
25. Ibid, no. 139
26. Ibid, no. 140; it is dated here 11
    February 1866
27. Goncourt: *Journal*, VI, 95–6
28. Adam: *Mes premières armes*, 308
29. Bonnières: *Mémoires d'aujourd'hui*,
    217
30. Calmettes: *Leconte de Lisle et ses amis*,
    223–4
31. 18 [?] août 1865, Chantilly: C 476 ff
    77–8
32. Meyer-Zundel: op. cit., 84–7
33. Ibid, 84

CHAPTER FOUR

1. Le Goffic: 'Catulle Mendès et le
   Parnasse contemporain'. (*La Revue
   hebdomadaire*, 20 février 1909, 356–
   7). According to Herlihy: *Catulle
   Mendès*, 8, Catulle was born on 20
   May 1841. The *faire-part* of Suzanne
   Mendès' death records that she died
   on 29 June 1885, at the age of
   seventy-two; her husband died at 18,
   rue Berlioz, on 30 November 1887, at

the age of seventy-three (Arsenal)
2. Mendès: *La Légende du Parnasse
   contemporain*, 32–3
3. C. 1865. Coppée: *Souvenirs d'un
   Parisien*, 75 seqq.
4. Mendès: op. cit., 48
5. C. 1865. Coppée: loc. cit.
6. Guichard: *La Musique et les Lettres en
   France au temps du Wagnérisme*, 28
   and passim

7. 25 mars 1861. Tiersot: *Lettres françaises de Richard Wagner*, 250–1
8. Adam: *Mes sentiments et nos idées avant 1870*, 54
9. Rosny: *Torches et Lumignons*, 194–5
10. Fouquier: *Profils et Portraits*, 110
11. Claretie: *La Vie à Paris, 1909*, 59
12. Hoche: *Les Parisiens chez eux*, 30–1
13. Talmeyr: *Souvenirs d'avant le déluge*, 113–4
14. [1864.] Glatigny: *Lettres inédites*, 58
15. Guichard: *Lettres à Judith Gautier . . .*, 370–1
16. Cazals to Mallarmé. *Documents Stéphane Mallarmé*, VI, 169
17. Guichard: op. cit., 375
18. Ibid, 376
19. Meyer-Zundel: op. cit., 73
20. Ibid, 76
21. Guichard: op. cit., 378
22. Meyer-Zundel: op. cit., 75
23. Guichard: op. cit., 375
24. Ibid, 375–6
25. Ibid, 377
26. Meyer-Zundel: op. cit., 74
27. Ibid, 71
28. Ibid, 72–3
29. Ibid, 74
30. Ibid, 75
31. Ibid, 79
32. Ibid, 73
33. Ibid, 79
34. Ibid, 70
35. Coppée: loc. cit.
36. Paraf: 'Augusta Holmès a-t-elle été la fille de Vigny?' (*Les Nouvelles littéraires*, 12 septembre 1957). Mackworth: 'Stéphane Mallarmé et Augusta Holmès: une amitié de jeunesse' (*Documents Stéphane Mallarmé*, VII, 335 seqq.)
37. Dreyfous: op. cit., 87
38. C. 1860. Imbert: *Nouveaux profils de musiciens*, 137
39. Theuriet: *Jours d'été*, 180–2
40. Jean-Aubry: 'Villiers de l'Isle-Adam et la musique' (*Mercure de France*, 15 novembre 1938, 45–6)
41. Mallarmé: *Correspondance*, I, 323, note
42. Guichard: op. cit., 376
43. Ibid.
44. Meyer-Zundel: op. cit., 70
45. Ibid.
46. Ibid.
47. Ibid.
48. Ibid, 71
49. Ibid.
50. Ibid, 75
51. Ibid, 74
52. Ibid.
53. [Geneva, between 2 and 8 August 1865.] BN N.A.Fr. 14038, ff 3–4
54. 31 December 1864. Diary of Eugénie Fort (Pierre Théophile Gautier)
55. Guichard: op. cit., 370–1
56. Dreyfous: op. cit., 91
57. Talmeyr: op. cit., 116
58. Barrès: *Cahiers*, IV, 65–6
59. [29 juillet [?] 1865.] Chantilly: C 473 ff 160–2
60. [Août 1865.] Chantilly: C 474 ff 105–6
61. Mme Alphonse Daudet: *Journal de Famille et de Guerre, 1914–1919*, 89
62. Ibrovac: op. cit., 99
63. 1er novembre 1865. Mallarmé: *Correspondance*, I, 202, note
64. Guichard: op. cit., 378

CHAPTER FIVE

1. 5 janvier 1866 (Bergerat Papers)
2. Meyer-Zundel: op. cit., 71
3. Diary of Eugénie Fort (Pierre Théophile Gautier)
4. Guichard: op. cit., 371–3
5. Diary of Eugénie Fort (Pierre Théophile Gautier)
6. [16 mars 1866.] Chantilly: C 479 ff 108 seqq.
7. Diary of Eugénie Fort (Pierre Théophile Gautier)
8. Ibid.
9. [Mars 1866.] Chantilly: C 477 ff 74–5
10. Diary of Eugénie Fort (Pierre Théophile Gautier)
11. [21 mars 1866.] Chantilly: C 479 f 110
12. Diary of Eugénie Fort (Pierre Théophile Gautier)
13. Undated. Mallarmé: *Correspondance*, I, 213, note
14. BN N.A. Fr. 16978. Archives Hetzel XLVII ff 428–9, 433–4
15. Monval: 'Catulle Mendès et François Coppée'. (*La Revue de Paris*, 1er mars 1909, 76–7)

16. 25 mars 1866 (Pierre Théophile Gautier)
17. 29 mars 1866 (Pierre Théophile Gautier)
18. Diary of Eugénie Fort (Pierre Théophile Gautier)
19. Ibid
20. 1er avril 1866. *Documents Stéphane Mallarmé*, VI, 304
21. [Fin mars 1866.] Chantilly: C 479 ff 118–9
22. 3 avril 1866 (Pierre Théophile Gautier)
23. Diary of Eugénie Fort (Pierre Théophile Gautier)
24. Ibid.
25. Ibid.
26. [Début d'avril 1866.] Chantilly: C 479 ff 121–2
27. 10 avril 1866. (Pierre Théophile

Gautier)
28. Diary of Eugénie Fort (Pierre Théophile Gautier)
29. Ibid.
30. Ibid.
31. Ibid.
32. Undated. Chantilly: H 1364 f 439
33. Diary of Eugénie Fort (Pierre Théophile Gautier)
34. Chantilly: C 479 ff 123–5
35. Diary of Eugénie Fort (Pierre Théophile Gautier)
36. *La Gazette des Étrangers*, 17 mai 1866
37. Flaubert: *Correspondance*, V, 209
38. 21 [?] avril 1866. Chantilly: C 479 f 126
39. Guichard: op. cit., 373
40. Chantilly: C 479 f 131
41. Bergerat: op. cit., 418

CHAPTER SIX

1. Dreyfous: *Ce que je tiens à dire*, 93
2. Diary of Eugénie Fort (Pierre Théophile Gautier)
3. Ibid.
4. Bergerat: loc. cit.
5. Diary of Eugénie Fort (Pierre Théophile Gautier)
6. Ibid.
7. 23 juin 1866. Chantilly: C 479 ff 148–9
8. 2 juillet 1866. Chantilly: C 479 f 151
9. Goncourt: *Journal*, VII, 187
10. Chantilly: C 479 f 144
11. *La Gazette des Étrangers*, 17 mai 1866
12. Richardson: op. cit., 311–2
13. [Between 20 and 24 September 1866.] BN N.A. Fr. 14038 ff 5–6
14. Diary of Eugénie Fort (Pierre Théophile Gautier)
15. Rude: *Confidences d'un journaliste*, 160
16. Richardson: *Verlaine*, 233
17. Joseph: *Henri Cazalis*, 121
18. [Mai 1866.] Mallarmé: *Correspondance*, I, 218–9, note
19. [1866.] Ibid, I, 224, note
20. Ibid.
21. [Septembre–octobre 1866.] *Documents Stéphane Mallarmé*, VI, 334–5
22. Institut de France. Papiers Heredia.

MS 5688 f 138
23. Tailhade: *Quelques fantômes de jadis*, 169
24. Vedel: Article in unspecified paper of 5 November 1910. (Arsenal: RF 59973 ff 13 seqq.)
25. Tailhade: loc. cit.
26. Undated. Chantilly: C 502 *quater* ff 19–20
27. Meyer-Zundel: op. cit., 245
28. Ibid, 161
29. Ibid, 163
30. Institut de France. Papiers Heredia. MS 5688 f 139
31. 7 juin 1867. Institut de France. Papiers Heredia. MS 5688 f 140
32. Hugo: *Correspondance*, III, 46
33. Escholier: *Victor Hugo, l'homme*, 140–1
34. 16 juin 1867. Hugo: *Correspondence*, III, 48
35. Escholier: loc. cit.
36. Meyer-Zundel: op. cit., 246
37. France: loc. cit.
38. Silvestre: *Portraits et souvenirs*, 185 seqq.
39. JG: *Le Livre de Jade*, 26
40. Ibid, 91
41. *Le Gaulois*, 29 décembre 1917
42. JG: *Le Livre de Jade*, 59
43. France: op. cit., 135–7

44. Monval: op. cit., 77
45. Ibid, 79
46. Ibid, 79–80
47. *Le Moniteur universel*, 5 octobre 1867
48. Sainte-Beuve: *Lettres à la Princesse*, 311
49. Ibid, 314
50. Sainte-Beuve: *Correspondance générale*, XVI, 316, note
51. Ibid, XVI, 562
52. Sainte-Beuve: *Lettres à la Princesse*, 316–7
53. [Late November 1867.] Primoli Papers
54. Undated. Chantilly: C 502 *quater* ff 15–16
55. Sainte-Beuve: *Correspondance générale*, XVI, 593
56. Primoli diary, 1867, 125–6 (Primoli Papers)
57. Undated. Chantilly: C 502 *quater* ff 21–22
58. Undated. Chantilly: C 502 *quater* ff 9–10
59. Judith Mendès' contributions appeared in *Le Moniteur universel* on 7 December 1867, 4 January, 4, 22 March, 8 April 1868. Her brother published an article in the paper on 12 April 1868. In *Les Salons de Paris en 1889*, Claude Vento wrote that 'M. and Mme Théophile Gautier succeeded their father in the Princess's affections.' Toto Gautier had his literary ambitions. In *L'Année litteraire, 1885*, p 238, Paul Ginisty dismissed his novel, *La Baronne Véra*, as 'an account which is complex to the point of obscurity, of the platonic liaison between a woman of the world and a young diplomat who has black humours'.
60. Undated. BN N.A. Fr. 24271 f 209. Judith uses the word 'roman', which can mean a work of fiction or a novel. Among the Collection d'autographes de Félix et Paul Nadar, in the Bibliothèque Nationale (N.A. Fr. 24271), are a number of notes from Judith Gautier. They emphasize that the Nadars were family friends of long standing.
61. *La Liberté*, 23 mars 1868
62. Ibid, 12 avril 1868
63. Goncourt: *Journal*, VIII, 102
64. Dreyfous: *Ce que je tiens à dire*, I, 83
65. Chantilly: C 497 ff 247–8
66. *La Liberté*, 27 mai 1868
67. Undated. BN N.A. Fr. 16978. Archives Hetzel XLVII f 435
68. '*Le Dragon impérial*, par Mme Judith Mendès'. *La Vogue Parisienne*, 13 août 1869; reprinted in *Mercure de France*, 1er novembre 1939.
69. France: op. cit., 136–7
70. [Mardi. Juillet 1869.] Mallarmé: *Correspondance*, I, 307
71. Pouvourville: loc. cit.
72. Silvestre: *Portraits et souvenirs*, 189
73. Mondor: op. cit., 286
74. Meyer-Zundel: op. cit., 75
75. Ibid, 254·5
76. Mendès: op. cit., 228, 224–5
77. Calmettes: op. cit., 310
78. Ibrovac: op. cit., 96–7
79. *La Gazette des Étrangers*, 16 décembre 1866
80. Seillière: *Un poète parnassien*, 51

CHAPTER SEVEN

1. Reyer: *Notes de Musique*, 413
2. Tailhade, op. cit., 165–9; but Guichard observes that Judith was sixteen in 1861, and did not attend the first performance of *Tannhäuser* in Paris (op. cit., 264). See also JG: *Le Second Rang du Collier*, 172–3
3. Bibliothèque de l'Institut de France. Papiers Heredia. MS 5688 f 143
4. *La Presse*, 8 septembre 1868
5. Reyer: op. cit., 229
6. Servières: *Richard Wagner jugé en France*, 137–9
7. *La Presse*, 20 octobre 1868
8. *Paris-Artiste*, 12 décembre 1868. Régamey took a particular interest in the oriental: he later wrote a skit on Loti's *Madame Chrysanthème*, and illustrated books with Japanese themes.
9. *La Vogue Parisienne*, 29 juin 1869. Anatole France wrote under the pseudonym of Camille d'Ivry.
10. Guichard: op. cit., 39, 41
11. Chantilly: C 402 *quater*, ff 7–8, where it is improbably dated May 1869. On

14 April 1869, Gautier wrote to Carlotta Grisi: 'Je vous ai envoyé mon feuilleton de lundi sous enveloppe; l'avez-vous reçu? Il parle de *Rienzi* et de Wagner.' (Chantilly: C 480 ff 11–13)

12. Maison de Victor Hugo. Early in 1869, Mendès had invited Coppée to stay with him and Judith at Neuilly; but among Villiers' correspondence is a letter from Mendès to Garcias which is tentatively dated the same year. Garcias seems to have threatened to write to Émile de Girardin, the editor of *La Liberté*, about his financial problems with Mendès, his tenant in the rue Royale. Girardin was powerful; he could be irascible and ruthless. Mendès saw his future compromised. 'It would be very cruel,' he wrote, 'to get me on bad terms with *La Liberté*, especially when Mme Mendès is just about to publish her novel there, and I am going to publish a long poem. If Monsieur de Girardin were displeased, it would be the ruin of us.' (Villiers de l'Isle-Adam: *Correspondance*, I, 127.) For the invitation to Coppée, see Monval: op. cit., 83. A copy of *Le Livre de Jade*, inscribed 'À mon petit ami William Garcias. Judith Mendès', was listed in the Hôtel Drouot sale, 28–30 April 1981.

13. JG: *Le Troisième Rang du Collier*, 7
14. Guichard: op. cit., 46–7
15. Bibliothèque de l'Institut de France. Papiers Heredia. MS 5688 f 145
16. Mendès: op. cit., 103
17. Ibid, 102
18. JG: op. cit., 14–15
19. Ibid, 19
20. Villiers de l'Isle-Adam: op. cit., I, 132
21. JG: op. cit., 72–3
22. Ibid, 77
23. Ibid, 87–90
24. Guichard: *La Musique et les Lettres en France au temps du Wagnérisme*, 274
25. Villiers de l'Isle-Adam: op. cit., I, 138–9
26. Undated. MVH
27. Guichard: *Lettres à Judith Gautier . . .*, 103, 105
28. Ibid, 106–7
29. Ibid, 119–20
30. Servières: op. cit., 156
31. Guichard: *Lettres à Judith Gautier . . .*, 281, 282
32. Guichard: *La Musique . . .*, 54
33. Imbert: *Nouveaux profils de musiciens*, 157
34. Villiers de l'Isle-Adam: *Chez les passants*, 74
35. Theuriet: op. cit., 180–2
36. Raitt: *The Life of Villiers de l'Isle-Adam*, 153
37. Ibid, 149–50
38. Guichard: *Lettres à Judith Gautier . . .*, 121–2, 124
39. Meyer-Zundel: op. cit., 238
40. Ibid, 241, 242
41. Hugo: *Correspondance*, III, 213
42. Meyer-Zundel: op. cit., 244
43. Ibid, 247, 248
44. Escholier: *Un Amant de génie*, 441–2
45. Undated. Chantilly: C 502 *quater*, ff 23–4
46. Undated. Chantilly: C 502 *quater*, ff 13–14
47. *L'Artiste*, 1er novembre 1869, 242
48. Villiers de l'Isle-Adam: *Correspondance*, I, 148
49. JG: *Iskender*, 126–7
50. Ibid, 203–4
51. Adam: *Mes Sentiments et nos Idées avant 1870*, 424
52. Maison de Victor Hugo, Paris
53. Guichard: *Lettres à Judith Gautier . . .*, 141, 142
54. [January or February 1870.] Ibid, 143–4
55. Mallarmé: *Correspondance*, I, 324–5, note
56. Ibid, I, 326–7
57. Ibid.
58. *Le Rappel*, 24 juin 1870
59. Mallarmé: *Correspondance*, I, 327–8, note
60. JG: *Auprès de Richard Wagner*, 225
61. Mallarmé: *Correspondance*, I, 332, note; Jean-Aubry: op. cit., 48
62. Mallarmé: *Correspondance*, I, loc. cit.
63. Ibid.
64. Guichard: *Lettres à Judith Gautier . . .*, 50 seqq.
65. Ibid, 147
66. JG: *Auprès de Richard Wagner*, loc. cit.

CHAPTER EIGHT

1. Escholier: *Victor Hugo, l'homme*, 134–5
2. Richardson: *Victor Hugo*, 216
3. Undated. Maison de Victor Hugo, Paris
4. Meyer-Zundel: op. cit., 234–5
5. Ibrovac: op. cit., 116; Villiers de l'Isle-Adam: *Chez le passants*, 71–2, 73
6. Un Bourgeois de Paris: *Journal du Siège, 1870–1871*, 880–1
7. Richardson: *Théophile Gautier: his Life and Times*, 256
8. Mallarmé: *Correspondance*, I, 341, note
9. Guichard: op. cit., 148
10. Ibid, 149, 150
11. 3 May 1871. Meyer-Zundel: op. cit., 94–5
12. Du Moulin-Eckart: *Cosima Wagner*, II, 488–9
13. Lepelletier: *Histoire de la Commune de 1871*, II, 243
14. Guichard: op. cit., 151
15. Richardson: *Paris under Siege*, 198
16. Mackworth: loc. cit.
17. Mallarmé: op. cit., II, 19–20
18. 15 août 1871. Ibid, II, 22–3
19. Guichard: op. cit., 301–2
20. *Livres anciens romantiques et modernes. Manuscrits musicaux et Partitions avec dédicaces. 23–24 février 1978. Drouot Rive Gauche.*
21. Guichard: op. cit., 302
22. Mallarmé: op. cit., II, 23–4

CHAPTER NINE

1. Hugo: *Choses vues*, 277
2. Robida: *Le Salon Charpentier et les impressionistes*, 32
3. Goncourt: *Journal*, X, 67
4. Mallarmé to Mendès [19 février 1872]. Mallarmé: *Correspondance*, II, 25, 26
5. In the archives at Chantilly (C 502 *quater* ff 149–50) is an undated letter from Mendès.

Dimanche

Mon cher Maître,
   Vous verrez aujourd'hui Théophile Gautier? Vous pourriez me rendre un vrai service. Voici ce dont il s'agit. – Victor Hugo est venu hier nous inviter à dîner, – pour demain lundi – Naturellement nous avons grande envie d'aller dîner chez Victor Hugo. Mais Gautier, précisément, est attendu ce jour là. À aucun prix et sous n'importe quel prétexte je ne voudrais désobliger un homme que j'admire – et si ma présence chez Hugo pouvait le fâcher en rien, je me hâterais de rester chez moi. – Voulez-vous consulter Gautier sur ce point? Vous seriez cent fois bon. – Merci de tout mon coeur.

Votre
Catulle Mendès

Ma femme vous embrasse.

The letter was addressed to Flaubert, who added a postscript:

Mon cher vieux Théo
   Voici une lettre à laquelle je ne puis répondre pertinemment.
   Fais-moi le plaisir de m'éclairer.
Dis-moi *oui* ou *non*.
à toi
ton
G^{ve} Flaubert

The result of the correspondence is not known.

6. Escholier: op. cit., 528–9
7. Goncourt: *Journal*, X, 82
8. Mme Alphonse Daudet: loc. cit.
9. Drouet: *Mille et une lettres d'amour à Victor Hugo*, 685
10. Brisson: op. cit., III, 37. Bergerat died in 1923.
11. Kahn: *Silhouettes littéraires*, 74, 76
12. Bergerat: op. cit., 420
13. Diary of Eugénie Fort (Pierre Théophile Gautier)
14. Escholier: op. cit., 533; Hugo: *Choses vues*, 284

15. Hugo: op. cit., 285
16. Ibid.
17. Goncourt: *Journal*, X, 102
18. Undated. Théophile Gautier.
    Lettres. BN N.A. Fr. 14038 f 19
19. Escholier: *Victor Hugo, l'homme*, 139;
    Escholier: *Un Amant de génie*, 534.
    Among Judith's letters to Victor
    Hugo is a note dated tentatively July
    1872:

    Mon Maître
       sous vos pieds dans l'ombre un
    homme est là.
       il attend – j'ai réfléchi et je suis
    décidée
                  Merci
                  Judith M
    est-ce la fleur bleue d'Allemagne?

    (Maison de Victor Hugo)

20. Hugo: *Poésies*, III, 567
21. Escholier: *Victor Hugo, l'homme*, 138
22. Meyer-Zundel: op. cit., 112
23. Escholier: *Un Amant de génie*, 543–4
24. Guillemin: *Hugo et la sexualité*, 108–9
25. Escholier: *Un amant de génie*, loc. cit.
26. Hugo: *Correspondance*, III, 319–20
27. Maison de Victor Hugo. The letter is
    addressed simply to 'Monsieur Victor
    Hugo à Guernesay' [*sic*].
28. Hugo: *Correspondance*, III, 322
29. The letter is dated by Escholier: op.
    cit., 535–6; the original letter, in the
    Maison de Victor Hugo, from which
    the present translation is taken, is
    dated tentatively summer, 1872.
    Judith does not indicate which of her
    aunts had been afflicted; but a letter
    from Carlotta Grisi to Gautier, at
    Chantilly, expresses the hope that
    Lili is better. Among the Clermont-
    Ganneau papers is a *faire-part* of the
    death of Lili Gautier: 'Mlle
    Henriette-Adélaïde-Émilie Gautier,
    décédée le 16 novembre 1880, à l'âge
    de 63 ans, dans sa maison, 22, rue du
    Petit Parc, au Grand-Montrouge'.
    (Institut de France. MS 4109 f 263
    bis.)
30. Bergerat: *Souvenirs d'un Enfant de
    Paris*, II, 85–6
31. 23 octobre 1872. Hugo:
    Correspondance, III, 330
32. Flaubert: *Correspondance*, VI, 451–2
33. Billy: *La Présidente et ses amis*, 234–5

34. Escholier: *Un Amant de génie*, 536–7
35. Maison de Victor Hugo. The letter,
    dated provisionally November or
    December 1872, is written on black-
    edged paper.
36. Hugo: *Correspondance*, III, 335
37. Escholier: op. cit., 538
38. 23 or 28 December 1872. Maison de
    Victor Hugo. This letter, again, is
    written on mourning paper.
39. Maison de Victor Hugo
40. Escholier: op. cit., 539
41. Hugo: *Correspondance*, III, 357
42. Reymond: *Albert Glatigny*, 224
43. Guichard: op. cit., 167
44. Meyer-Zundel: op. cit., 68
45. According to Meyer-Zundel (op. cit.,
    68), the incident occurred 'at the
    beginning' of her marriage; but see
    Guichard: op. cit., 369. Possibly this
    was the origin of the anecdote
    recorded and altered by Edmond de
    Goncourt on 25 August 1895
    (*Journal*, XXI, 101)
46. Meyer-Zundel: op. cit., 101
47. Institut de France. Papiers Clermont-
    Ganneau. MS 4109 f 236
48. Meyer-Zundel: op. cit., 102–3
49. Ibid, 103–5
50. Mallarmé: *Correspondance*, II, 45,
    note. It was perhaps now that Jean
    Lorrain, the fervent young
    Symbolist, saw her at Fécamp, where
    she used to go for the bathing. 'As
    she was painting in those days, he
    used to carry her easel for her, and
    pay her all sorts of little attentions.
    By way of thanks to the young man
    who only knew and loved Musset,
    Judith made him read Victor Hugo
    and Leconte de Lisle.' (4 septembre
    1892. Goncourt: *Journal*, XIX, 19.)
51. [August?] 1873. Maison de Victor
    Hugo.
52. [Autumn 1873.] Maison de Victor
    Hugo
53. Escholier: op. cit., 540. On 30 July
    1872 Hugo had reported: 'Mme
    Judith Mendès came to see me with
    Grimace. Grimace is her dog. This
    dog plays the piano, lies down when
    you say PONSARD and gets up
    when you say VICTOR HUGO'
    (Hugo: *Choses vues*, 287, 288)
54. Drouet: op. cit., 738

CHAPTER TEN

1. Undated, but written on mourning paper (Maison de Victor Hugo)
2. Hugo: *Choses vues*, 320
3. Goncourt: *Journal*; X, 154
4. For accounts of the *salon*, see Calmettes: op. cit.; Ibrovac: op. cit., and Mendès: *La Légende du Parnasse contemporain.*
5. Wright: *The Life of John Payne*, 167
6. Calmettes: op. cit., 320
7. Guichard: op. cit., 54, 55, 56
8. Dujardin: op. cit., 137, 138
9. Hugo: *Poésie*, III, 587
10. Escholier: *Un Amant de génie*, 542–3
11. Hugo: *Poésie*, loc. cit.
12. Calmettes: op. cit., 226–7
13. Meyer-Zundel: op. cit., 68
14. BN N.A. Fr. 16264 ff 193–4
15. Mallarmé: *Correspondance*, II, 45–6
16. 20 mai 1874. Ibid, II, 46–7
17. Undated. (Maison de Victor Hugo)
18. Among Flaubert's papers at Chantilly is an undated letter from Mendès, presumably written at about the time of his marriage:

Dear Monsieur Flaubert,
    Judith is most anxious to see you, and I shall be very happy myself to shake you by the hand. But the situation is so disturbed and so abnormal that we hesitate to pay you a visit which is sudden and unannounced. Would it really worry you if one of these mornings we were to come and say good-day to you, and thank you for the trouble you have taken? If it doesn't worry you, we are on our way . . .
                    Yours ever,
                    Catulle Mendès
                    25, rue de Villiers

(Chantilly: H 1364 ff 456–7)

19. My dear Master,
    . . . Your most encouraging consent, and the hope of making no modification to your wonderful poem which you disapprove of, have decided me.
    I am ready to work vigorously . . .

(Chantilly: H 1364 ff 446–7)

20. Undated. Chantilly: H 1364 ff 458–9
21. Henry: *Hours with Famous Parisians*, 55–6
22. Meyer-Zundel: op. cit., 69

CHAPTER ELEVEN

1. 'La Plus Belle'. JG: *Le Livre de Jade*, 53–4
2. Guichard: *Lettres à Judith Gautier*, 168–9
3. Ibid, 170
4. Meyer-Zundel: op. cit., 61
5. Ibid. In *Ravel. Life and Works* (Duckworth. 1960, p 32), Rollo H. Myers records among the composer's friends 'Édouard Benedictus, artist, dandy and inventor – one of his inventions being safety glass'. He was the nephew of Louis Benedictus.
6. *Collection de précieux autographes* . . . Catalogue of Drouot sale, 19 April 1985. Information from Michael Pakenham.
7. France: op. cit., 137
8. BN N.A. Fr. 15434 f 184
9. Riotor: *Les Arts et les Lettres*, 1ʳᵉ série, 451
10. Meyer-Zundel: op. cit., 165
11. Billy: op. cit., 235
12. Camacho: op. cit., 117; see also Gualdo to Coppée: 'Quand je pense que la divine Judith, malgré sa paresse olympienne, noircit dix grandes pages par jour, la rougeur me monte au front.' (Jeudi [1875]. Montera, op. cit., 199–200)
13. 'Les Âges préhistoriques'. (*Le Journal officiel*, 20 février 1875)
14. 'Une Ville retrouvée'. (Ibid, 14 octobre 1875)
15. *Le Journal officiel*, 14 octobre 1875, 8655
16. *Revue des deux Mondes*, 1er février 1918, 695
17. *Le Journal officiel*, 28 août 1876, 6651
18. Ibid, 1er Mars 1876, 1470
19. Ibid, 27 mars 1875, 2311
20. Ibid, 2312

21. Ibid, 12 septembre 1875, 7815; see also the issue for 26 septembre 1875
22. Richardson: *Théophile Gautier*, 42
23. *Le Rappel*, 2 mai 1876
24. Ibid, 6 mai 1876
25. Ibid.
26. To Robert de Montesquiou. Dated only 'Mardi'. BN N.A.Fr. 15116 ff 31–2
27. *Le Rappel*, 23 mai 1876
28. Ibid, 15 juin 1876. In June 1877 *L'Artiste* published Judith's

appreciation of the Diaz exhibition at the École des Beaux-Arts. It was an elegant article, in her father's style. Writing of Diaz' landscape, *Le Parc aux Boeufs*, she said: 'It is hard to tear oneself away from such a marvel. It is so bushy and so full of shade; the thick grass is so soft that one would like to sink one's feet in it, lose oneself in the undergrowth, and it seems as if the delicious smell of the wood freshens your face.'

CHAPTER TWELVE

1. A detailed description of the theatre is given by Édouard Dujardin in the *Revue Wagnérienne*, 8 juin 1885.
2. *La République des Lettres*, 27 août 1876, 212
3. Ibid, 3 septembre 1876, 236
4. D'Indy: *Richard Wagner et son influence sur l'art musical français*, 56
5. Mauclair: *Servitude et grandeur littéraires*, 222, 223
6. JG: *Auprès de Richard Wagner*, 230, 231
7. 1 March 1870. Meyer-Zundel: op. cit., 223
8. Meyer-Zundel: op. cit., 115–6
9. Ibid, 117; Benedictus is said to have kept the scarf in a glass case (Guichard: op. cit., 317)
10. Meyer-Zundel: op. cit., 117–8
11. Guichard: *Lettres à Judith Gautier*, 57
12. Meyer-Zundel: op. cit., 118
13. Pourtalès: *Wagner: histoire d'un artiste*, 391, 392
14. Guichard: op. cit., 57–8
15. [September 1876.] Ibid, 58
16. [Between 25 and 29 September 1876.] Ibid, 59
17. Ibid, 171 seqq.
18. Ibid, 381
19. BN N.A. Fr. 15297 f 106
20. Yamamoto was clearly recommended to Montesquiou by JG. Among the Montesquiou papers is an undated letter from JG about the illustration of a manuscript:

Mardi

Cher ami
    Yamamoto ira vous voir demain Mercredi vers deux heures. Je crois que 20 francs par feuille serait un prix, ou moins si vous voulez . . .
    Vous verrai-je encore un moment avant mon départ?
    J'ai été voir aujourd'hui Gustave Moreau, qui est absolument délicieux.
    'Je bavarde, adieu, – vos Mains' (comme dit Mallarmé).
                        Judith Gautier

(BN N.A. fr. 15116 ff 31–2)

    The same archives also include a letter from S. Yamamoto to Montesquiou, dated 25 June 1884: '. . . Je croyais que votre commande était à peu près de même nature que celle que j'ai reçue de Mme Gauthier [*sic*], c'est-à-dire aquarelle simple et *purement* japonaise . . .' (BN N.A. Fr. 15113 f 225)

21. Meyer-Zundel: op. cit., 7–8
22. Guichard: op. cit., 191, 197
23. Anon: *A Handbook for France*, I, 176–7, 427
24. Muirhead: *Brittany*, 20
25. Bergerat: 'Judith Gautier'. (*Le Figaro*, 8 janvier 1918.)
26. [1er octobre 1877.] Guichard: op.

cit., 59–60

27. JG: *Auprès de Richard Wagner*, 241 seqq.
28. Guichard: op. cit., 61, 62
29. Ibid, 63
30. Pourtalès: op. cit., 391
31. Ibid.
32. *Nouvelles littéraires*, 16 août 1930
33. Guichard: op. cit., 64–5
34. Ibid, 65–6
35. Ibid, 69
36. Ibid, 71, 73
37. Ibid, 76–7
38. Ibid, 78, 79–80
39. Ibid, 82, 83
40. Ibid, 183. Years later, in his *Notes et Réflexions inédites*, Robert de Montesquiou recorded that Judith had shown him a letter from Cosima which he had copied: 'We are moved to tears, my dear Judith, by the surprise which you have just given our children. What a beautiful theatre! . . .' The letter was dated from Bayreuth in 1877. It does not appear in Guichard's edition of the correspondence. One wonders, however, how much trust to put in Montesquiou's comments. Since 1877, or so he maintained, relations between the two women had deteriorated sharply on both sides:
     'Judith thought for a long time that she was Siegfried's godmother. In fact it was Madame de Wolkenstein. And then, I really think that there was some little intrigue with Wagner which was discovered by the widow (letters, perhaps), and that must finally have spoilt everything. Anyway, all relations ended a long time ago. The last contact, a few years back, consisted in banning our poor friend from giving some astonishing performances of *Parsifal*, which she was preparing to give, in her own salon, still with these same wonderfully ingenious marionnettes . . . Truth to tell, it was doing them an honour to attach such significance to them . . .'

(BN N.A. Fr. 15116 f 103)

For this performance of *Parsifal*, see pp.170–1
41. Guichard: op. cit., 183–4, 185
42. Ibid, 84, 86
43. Ibid, 86, 87
44. Ibid, 88
45. Ibid, 89–90
46. Ibid, 189
47. Ibid, 91, 93
48. Ibid, 93, 94
49. Ibid, 190, 191
50. Ibid, 94, 95, 95–6
51. Ibid, 96–7

CHAPTER THIRTEEN

1. Guichard: op. cit., 195, 196–7
2. Mars 1919. BN N.A. Fr. 15152 ff 104 seqq. See also JG to Féli Gautier, 3 janvier 1907: 'Excusez-moi d'être si peu écriveuse de lettres' (Taylor Institution, Oxford).
3. Guichard: op. cit., 198, 199–200
4. According to her school report (BN N.A. Fr. 16538 f1), Hélyonne Mendès (later Mme Henri Barbusse) was born on 12 September 1879.
5. Flaubert: *Correspondance, 1877–80* (Club de l'Honnête Homme), 65. Flaubert had remained in touch with Judith. In September 1876 he had asked her for the address of Clermont-Ganneau, who helped him with research for *Hérodias*. *Correspondance, 1871–1877*. (Club de l'Honnête Homme, 489.)
6. Meyer-Zundel: op. cit., 69
7. Ibid, 101
8. Vendredi 9 août [1879]. BN N.A. Fr. 24510 f 108
9. Huysmans: *Lettres inédites à Émile Zola*, 14
10. [6 avril 1879.] Flaubert: *Correspondance*, VIII, 245. Judith also wrote literary criticism for *Le Rappel* (see Clerget: *Émile Blémont*,

180, 188)
11. Guichard: op. cit., 202–3
12. Ibid, 336
13. Meyer-Zundel: op. cit., 162
14. Guichard: op. cit., 202–3
15. 27 mai 1879. Ibid, 205
16. Ibid, 208
17. Ibid, 211

18. 22 mars 1879. BN N.A. Fr. 15297 f
    50
19. Escholier: *Un Amant de génie*, 543–4
20. Undated. Maison de Victor Hugo.
    See also Escholier: *Victor Hugo,
    l'homme*, 153
21. Drouet: op. cit., 808

CHAPTER FOURTEEN

1. Prinet et Dilasser: *Nadar*, 193, 197,
   199
2. Servières: op. cit., 226–7
3. Guichard: op. cit., 212, 213
4. Vento: *Les Salons de Paris en 1889*,
   205. Among the papers of Robert de
   Montesquiou are two notes from the
   Baronne Annette de Poilly. In the
   first, which is dated simply 'Brides
   les bains, Savoie, 12 juillet,' she
   announces: 'J'ai reçu une lettre de
   Judith, elle passe sa vie sous son
   parasol japonais et s'inquiétait de ne
   pas avoir eu un mot de vous . . .' In
   the second, undated, note, Mme de
   Poilly urges Montesquiou: 'Venez
   donc mercredi dîner rue du Colisée
   avec Judith, qui passe à Paris comme
   un éclair.' (BN N.A. Fr. 15297 ff
   92–3, 94.)
5. Vento: op. cit., 212
6. Guichard: op. cit., 217
7. JG: *Auprès de Richard Wagner*, 231–2
8. Ibid, 234–5

9. Meyer-Zundel: *Quinze ans auprès de
   Judith Gautier*, 116
10. Hugo: *Correspondance*, IV, 79 and
    note. Hugo's letter to Jules Ferry is
    dated simply '13 juillet'. Since Ferry
    was Minister of Public Instruction in
    1881, then again from 30 June to 6
    August 1882, this letter may be
    placed in either year.
11. JG: *Isoline*, 21–2
12. Ibid, 200
13. Ibid, 204
14. Ibid, 213
15. BN N.A. Fr. 15297 f 50
16. Guichard: op. cit., 231
17. JG: *Richard Wagner et son oeuvre
    poétique*. Avant-propos, 7
18. Ibid, 8–9, 10–11
19. Reyer: *Quarante ans de musique*; 71–2
20. JG: op. cit., 11–12
21. Camacho: op. cit., 136–7
22. Meyer-Zundel: op. cit., 118
23. Guichard: op. cit., 232

CHAPTER FIFTEEN

1. Richardson: *Victor Hugo*, 273
2. Ibid, 275
3. Mabel de Courcy Duncan to David
   McKibbin, 16 April 1948 (Ormond)
4. Mount: 'John Singer Sargent and
   Judith Gautier' (*The Art Quarterly*,
   summer 1955, 136)
5. Ibid, 137–43
6. Ibid. Mount reproduces five pictures
   of Judith by Sargent. 'The six
   portraits Sargent did of Judith
   Gautier can all,' he maintains, 'be

established as the work of one
summer . . . Until recently, when the
Detroit Institute of Arts purchased its
portrait of Judith Gautier by
lamplight, only one of the series had
ever been seen by the American
public. Four of them were found in
France by the author while doing
research for a biography of the artist'
(Mount: op. cit., 136). The fifth
portrait was shown at the Sargent
loan exhibition, at Copley Hall,

Boston, in 1899, but it seems since that time to have disappeared.

7. Ormond: *John Singer Sargent*, 240
8. Mount: loc. cit.
9. Duncan to McKibbin, 26 September 1948 (Ormond)
10. Ibid. In the first volume of *The Work of John Singer Sargent, R.A.*, published in 1903, Alice Meynell reproduces the portrait sketch of Judith owned by the Ormond family. She also reproduces a rough 'study for a portrait', which might possibly be another likeness of her.
11. Undated. BN N.A. Fr. 15248 ff 41–2
12. 'Brides les bains, Savoie, 12 juillet'. BN N.A. Fr. 15297 ff 92–3. See also Chapter 14, note 4.
13. This letter, at the Maison de Victor Hugo, in Paris, is tentatively dated 'fin avril 1877', but the reference to Hugo's book sets it firmly in the autumn of 1883.
14. Gautier: *Le Capitaine Fracasse*. Avant-propos par Mme Judith Gautier: I, vi
15. In JG's *Iseult* (1885), Lacroix announced that seventeen other books by the same author would be published in succession:
   La belle Aude
   Cléopatre
   Damajanti
   La Reine de Saba
   Hérodiate [sic]
   Femme de Putiphar[sic]

Leïla
Les Filles de Loth
Marie Stuart
Mélusine
Rosamonde
Sainte Thérèse
Sémiramis
Sophonisbé
Théodora
Vénus
La femme de l'âge de pierre

16. Undated. BN N.A. Fr. 15237 f 90
17. In another undated letter to Robert de Montesquiou, Judith wrote:

Cher ami,
   . . . Ma tante Zoë se meurt au Grand Montrouge et moi pour y aller je me trouve mal en chemin de fer . . .
   Merci de tous vos soins et à bientôt. J'ai fait une petite cire de Victor Hugo mort, je voudrais vous le montrer.
                    Judith Gautier

(BN N.A. Fr. 15306 ff 17–18)

18. Fouquier: op. cit., 12, 18
19. Pringué: op. cit., 221
20. Institut de France. Papiers Heredia. MS 5688 f 181
21. Ducray: 'Leconte de Lisle à l'Académie'. (*La Revue hebdomadaire*, 11 octobre 1919, 242, 243)
22. 25 juillet 1891. (Arsenal. 15096 f 46)

CHAPTER SIXTEEN

1. France: op. cit., 133–4
2. JG: *Le Japon*, 18–19
3. Ibrovac: op. cit., 284–5
4. Ibid, 285
5. Burty: *Catalogue*, 204, 211. *Les Trois Baisers du Serpent* appears to have escaped Camacho's bibliography. The library of Louis Barthou included an *Album de Poèmes* taken from *Le Livre de Jade*, with illustrations and decorations by Lucien Pissarro, engraved on wood, in colour, by Lucien and Esther Pissarro. This limited edition of 125

copies was published by the Eragny Press, in London, in 1911. Théodore de Banville had copies of *La Conquête du paradis* and *Le Lion de la victoire*, the second inscribed 'Hommage à mon cher Maître' (Hôtel Drouot sale, 28–30 April 1981).
6. Huysmans: op. cit., 17, note
7. 31 août 1886. *L'Année littéraire, 1886*.
8. Butter: *La dernière illusion de Leconte de Lisle*, 101 and note
9. On an undated card to Jean Marras, Judith wrote: 'Vous n'étiez pas à l'Apollonide, vous n'avez pas

entendu le sieur Lemaître tomber Leconte de Lisle? Quelle journée et quelle trahison!' (BN N.A.Fr.16264 f 66)

10. *Le Figaro*, 21 avril 1888
11. Vento: *Les Salons de Paris en 1889*, 205
12. Régnier: loc. cit.
13. Meyer-Zundel: op. cit., 158
14. Henry: *French Essays and Profiles*, 250
15. 30 juin 1916. Brody: 'Letters from Judith Gautier to Chalmers Clifton'. (*The French Review*, April 1985, p. 673)
16. Lorrain: *68 Lettres à Edmond Magnier (1887–1890)*, 45
17. Camacho: op. cit., 159
18. *La Revue indépendante*, May 1888, 363; Lemaître: *Impressions de Théâtre*, 3ᵉ série, 39
19. Séché et Bertaut: *L'Évolution du Théâtre contemporain*, 285–6
20. Bergerat: 'Judith Gautier'. (*Le Figaro*, 8 janvier 1918)
21. Undated, but stamped 'Reçu le 2 mai 1888'. BN N.A. Fr. 24271 f 224
22. JG: 'Le Prince Bojidar Karageorgevitch'. (*La Revue de Paris*, 1er juin 1908; p 672)
23. Guillemot: loc. cit. The plaque

outside 30, rue Washington mistakenly records that Judith Gautier lived there from 1872 to 1917
24. *Album Mariani*, juillet 1891
25. Guillemot: loc. cit.
26. Meyer-Zundel: op. cit., 41
27. Morice: *La Littérature de tout à l'heure*, 231, 232
28. France: loc. cit.
29. Haraucourt: 'Judith Gautier' (*Information*, 20 décembre 1922)
30. Tiersot: *Musiques pittoresques*, 1
31. JG: *Les Musiques bizarres*, 5–6. Judith was not listed among the contributors to *Le Journal officiel* in 1889.
32. France: op. cit., 138 seqq.
33. Bonnières: *Mémoires d'aujourd'hui*, 303 seqq.
34. Bell: *The Capitals of the World*, I, 37–9
35. Ibid, 46
36. Ibid, 58
37. An abridged version appeared in England, as a school text, in 1925, and a tenth French edition was published in 1931.
38. *Revue bleue*, 30 décembre 1893, 853
39. JG: 'Le Resplendissement d'Atenn' (*La Revue de Paris*, 15 août 1894, 804)
40. Meyer-Zundel: op. cit., 83

CHAPTER SEVENTEEN

1. Meyer-Zundel: op. cit., 153
2. Aubry: 'Un début chez les Goncourt'. (*Le Temps*, 25 novembre 1910)
3. Bergerat: op. cit., 390
4. Daudet: *Journal* . . ., 189
5. Louÿs: 'Marionnettes'. (*La Revue blanche*, juin 1894, 573–4)
6. Fontainas: *Mes Souvenirs du Symbolisme*, 84
7. Bouhélier: *Le Printemps d'une génération*, 234–5
8. Ibid, 235–6
9. *Journal des Débats*, 19 juillet 1894. Judith does not seem to have attended his funeral, which was held in Paris.
10. Coppée: *Mon Franc Parler*, 4ᵉ série,

160–1. On 24 January 1902, a banquet was held in honour of Alphonse Lemerre, to mark his promotion to Officier de la Légion-d'honneur. The cakes were in the shape of books which he had published, complete with their titles.
11. Jourdain: *Les Décorés. Ceux qui ne le sont pas*, 75
12. Lazare: *Figures contemporaines*, 31, 33–4
13. Mackworth: 'Stéphane Mallarmé et Augusta Holmès: une amitié de jeunesse'. (*Documents Stéphane Mallarmé*, VII, 344); see also Montera: *Luigi Gualdo*, 227–8, note. 'Depuis la fin de 1883, . . . "ce n'était plus charmant entre eux." La

séparation n'aura lieu toutefois que le 5 novembre 1885.'

14. *Le Petit Bleu de Paris*, 29 janvier 1903
15. BN N.A. Fr. 16263. Papiers Augusta Holmès, VI, f 1
16. Mackworth: op. cit., 345
17. Undated, but c. 1889. Gheusi: *Cinquante ans de Paris*, I, 38, 41
18. Ibid, 42
19. Samain: *Des Lettres*, 40–1, 42
20. Larguier: *Avant le déluge*, 199–200
21. Massenet: *Mes Souvenirs*, 238–9
22. Régnier, op. cit., 46–8
23. Undated diary entry. Charavay: *Bulletin d'autographes*, juin 1962, 46–7
24. Bloy: *Le Désespéré*, 394
25. Albalat: *Les Samedis de J.-M. de Heredia*, 45, 46
26. Henry: *Hours with famous Parisians*, 64, 66–7
27. Meyer-Zundel: op. cit., 69
28. Ibid.
29. Ibid.
30. Larguier: *Théophile Gautier*, 244, 245
31. Anon: *Mme Jane Catulle-Mendès* (*Ève*, 26 août 1923). Arsenal: Rf 66. 640 (6); Aghion: *Ce Catulle Mendès qu'on avait oublié* (*Journal de Genève*, 21–22 juillet 1962). Jane Catulle-Mendès was the author of *Les Trois amies* (*La Revue blanche*, 15 juin 1898), and another poem, *Notre Soeur* (*La Revue blanche*, No. 18, 1899), both of which Camacho attributes to Judith Gautier. In the twelfth volume of *Figures contemporaines tirées de l'Album Mariani* (1910), she is described as poet, dramatic critic of *La Presse*, and lecturer. Among her published works were two books of poems: *Le Coeur magnifique* (1909), and *France, ma bien-aimée* (1925), and a biography, *Sampiero Corso* (1938). She founded the Prix Catulle Mendès and the Prix Primice Catulle-Mendès.

32. Primice Catulle-Mendès was, presumably, buried in a military cemetery. After the War, he was re-interred in the Paris cemetery where his father lay. The *faire-part* of his funeral is kept in the Bibliothèque de l'Arsenal (Rf 66. 620 (3)):

> Mme Jane Catulle-Mendès
> vous prie d'assister à l'Inhumation de son fils,
> Jean-Primice Catulle-Mendès
> Brigadier au 103e Régiment d'Artillerie Lourde
> Décoré de la Médaille Militaire et de la Croix de Guerre,
> Mort pour la France, au Bois Noir, en Champagne, le 23 avril 1917, à 20 ans;
> Qui aura lieu le mercredi 7 juin 1922, à 4h.½ précises, au Cimetière Montparnasse.

33. Badesco: *La génération poétique de 1860*, II, 1011, note; and Goncourt: *Journal*, XX, 99
34. Meyer-Zundel: op. cit., 82, 83
35. Ibid, 83
36. Ibid, 81–2
37. Ibid, 89

CHAPTER EIGHTEEN

1. *Le Gaulois*, 28 mai 1898
2. 22 mai 1898. Guichard: op. cit., 235–6
3. *Le Gaulois*: loc. cit.
4. Borgeaud: *Correspondance de Claude Debussy et Pierre Louÿs (1893–1904)*, 126
5. Arsenal. 15060/167
6. Huddleston: op. cit., 424
7. Duncan to David McKibbin, 16 April 1948 (Ormond Papers)
8. Henry: *French Essays and Profiles*, 250
9. Ibid, 251 seqq.
10. JG: 'Le Prince à la tête sanglante'. (*La Revue de Paris*, 15 décembre 1897, 745–6)
11. JG: 'L'Oiseau-fleur lisse ses plumes'. (*La Revue blanche*, 1er avril 1900, 523)
12. Ibid, 525
13. JG: *Les Musiques bizarres*, 9
14. JG: *Les Musiques bizarres: La Musique chinoise*, 10
15. JG: *Les Musiques bizarres: La Musique japonaise*, 5

16. Meyer-Zundel: op. cit., 146
17. JG: *Poésies*, 85
18. 'À Feu Son Excellence Yu-Keng, Ministre de la Chine, pour le remercier d'un poème'. JG: *Poésies*, 85–6
19. *Le Gaulois*, 29 décembre 1917
20. Karageorgevitch: *Notes sur l'Inde*. Préface, iv–v; the book, translated as *Enchanted India*, was published in London by Harper & Bros. in 1899
21. Camacho: op. cit., 178
22. Note to an unnamed correspondent. The Taylor Institution, Oxford
23. *Mercure de France*, février 1903, 481
24. Reprinted in Rémy de Gourmont: *Portraits littéraires*, 3e edition, 136 seqq.
25. Aubry: 'Un début chez les Goncourt'. (*Le Temps*, 25 novembre 1910)
26. Undated copy. Arsenal. MS 13016/49
27. Camacho: op. cit., 160
28. Ibid.
29. Ibid.
30. Ibid.
31. Ibid.
32. 6 juin 1903. Arsenal. MS 13016 f 15
33. Undated. BN N.A. Fr. 15299 ff 130–1
34. Camacho: op. cit., 161
35. Ibid, 161–2
36. Arsenal. MS 13016 f 37. It is tentatively dated 2 juillet 1906, but the year seems improbable.
37. Camacho: op. cit., 162
38. Ibid, 163
39. Arsenal. MS 13016 f 49
40. Camacho: op. cit., 164
41. Ibid.
42. *Bibliothèque de Mme Sarah Bernhardt*, 108
43. Camacho: op. cit., 164
44. Farrère: *Souvenirs*, 36
45. Richardson: *Sarah Bernhardt*, 128
46. Reynier: *Les Premières . . .* Unidentified press-cutting, October 1912. (Arsenal. Rf 59963 f 5)

CHAPTER NINETEEN

1. Her dates – 1882–1971 – are given on her tombstone at Saint-Enogat.
2. BN N.A. Fr. 15311 f 174
3. Meyer-Zundel: op. cit., 130
4. Bac: loc. cit.
5. Meyer-Zundel: op. cit., 11–14
6. Ibid, 21
7. Ibid, 21–4
8. Ibid, 24
9. Ibid, 25
10. Ibid.
11. Ibid, 25–6
12. Ibid, 26
13. Ibid, 27–8
14. Ibid, 31
15. Ibid, 34
16. Ibid, 35
17. Ibid, 36
18. Ibid, 39–40
19. Ibid, 40
20. Bac: loc. cit.
21. 'Judith Gautier'. (*Le Figaro*, 8 janvier 1918)
22. Meyer-Zundel: op. cit., 89
23. Ibid, 98. In the verses which she wrote after Judith's death, Suzanne recorded Judith's possessions, and added:

Parmi tous ces trésors, j'élis un souvenir.
C'est ainsi qu'entre tous, je préfère sa montre,
Dont le vivant tic-tac, me fait me souvenir,
De son coeur qui sut battre après notre rencontre.
(BN N.A. Fr. 15311 f 31.)
In an undated letter to Robert de Montesquiou, Suzanne explained: 'Pour moi, rien ne vaut en effet ces liaisons *pures* et fraternelles *vraies* – par lesquelles, seul, l'on doit pouvoir atteindre au sublime.' (BN N.A. Fr. 15311 f 125)
24. Meyer-Zundel: op. cit., 92–3
25. *La Revue Blanche*, 1er mars 1902, 369 seqq.
26. Ibid, 373
27. Undated. BN N.A. Fr. 15113, ff 45–6
28. Meyer-Zundel: op. cit., 97
29. Ibid, 49–50
30. Ibid, 83
31. Ibid, 87–8
32. Ibid, 107
33. Ibid, 108–112. see also Waleffe:

Quand Paris était un paradis, 82–3
34. Meyer-Zundel: op. cit., 114
35. Ibid, 121
36. Ibid, 101
37. Ibid, 54–5, 56
38. Ibid, 56
39. JG: *Poésies*, 77–8
40. Meyer-Zundel: op. cit., 57, 59
41. Ibid, 62

42. Ibid, 60
43. Ibid, 142
44. Ibid, 132
45. Ibid, 135, 136
46. Ibid, 131
47. Bac: loc. cit.
48. Meyer-Zundel: op. cit., 97
49. Quoted by Souday: *Les Livres du temps*. 3ᵉ série, 76

CHAPTER TWENTY

1. Harry: *Réveil d'ombres*, 222–3; Billy: *L'Époque 1900*, 232–3
2. Melchior-Bonnet: "À la mémoire de Judith Gautier." (*Le Gaulois*, 6 janvier 1923)
3. Meyer-Zundel: op. cit., 88
4. Daudet: *Journal*, 189
5. Billy: op. cit., 217; Harry: op. cit., 214
6. Meyer-Zundel: op. cit., 164
7. France: op. cit., 143–4
8. *Le Temps*, 19 janvier 1918
9. These are the opening lines of *Le Livre de la foi nouvelle*. The pages are un-numbered.
10. *Le Livre de la foi nouvelle*, nos. xi–xv
11. Meyer-Zundel: op. cit., 36–7. After Judith's death, Suzanne Meyer-Zundel returned to the question of communication. On 20 February 1919 she wrote to Robert de Montesquiou:

   > Peut-être étiez-vous au courant de l'idée qu'avait la grande Maya, quand elle était encore de ce monde: 'Si l'on pouvait, disait-elle, transfuser son savoir à un être assez jeune encore, pour qu'il puisse vous continuer sur terre, quand on la quitte'. C'est ce qui m'arrive.

   (BN N.A. Fr. 15311 ff 100 seqq.)

   Writing again in March 1919 (the letter is not more precisely dated), Suzanne Meyer-Zundel continued:

   > . . . Je n'ai pas cessé dès le début, quant j'eus fait connaissance avec elles, d'avoir la plus entière confiance dans les communications. Et cette foi inébranlable ne m'a pas abandonnée un instant.
   > J'avais raison, puisque l'Amie devait se manifester en moi, depuis, d'une façon éclatante . . .
   > *Le Livre de la foi nouvelle* (qui n'est pas écrit en chinois) – C'est précisément au sujet de cet ouvrage qui se compose de pensées philosophiques excessivement serrées qu'Elle vient de se servir de moi pour m'en dicter les Commentaires . . .
   > Si cela ne vous effraye pas, dites-le moi – Alors je vous enverrai un passage de mes Commentaires qui, j'en suis sûre, en vous ouvrant de nouveaux horizons, vous fera peut-être entrevoir 'la Vérité' . . .

   (BN N.A. Fr. 15152 ff 104 seqq.)

12. Meyer-Zundel: op. cit., 37
13. Camacho: op. cit., 186
14. Péladan: *L'Art idéaliste et mystique*, 33
15. Camacho: op. cit., 185
16. Tharaud: *En Bretagne*, 36
17. Meyer-Zundel: op. cit., 170
18. Haraucourt: loc. cit.
19. Tailhade: op. cit., 173
20. *Le Temps*, 25 novembre 1910; in a letter to Clermont-Ganneau, tentatively dated August 1896, Judith writes: 'Je me mets au drame annamite . . .' (Institut de France. Papiers Clermont-Ganneau. MS 4109 f 241)
21. To Robert de Montesquiou. 'Lundi soir'. BN N.A. Fr. 15311 ff 122 seqq.
22. Meyer-Zundel: op. cit., 105
23. Press-cutting from unspecified paper. Arsenal: RF 59973 ff 13 seqq.

24. Press-cutting from unspecified paper, 7 January 1918. Arsenal: RF 59973 ff 42 seqq.
25. Imbert: op. cit., 31 seqq.
26. Uzanne: *Figures contemporaines tirées de l'Album Mariani* (1894)
27. Daudet: loc. cit.
28. Ibid.
29. *Les Nouvelles littéraires*, 16 août 1930
30. Meyer-Zundel: op. cit., 184–5
31. Riese: *Les salons littéraires parisiens*, 155
32. Willy: *Souvenirs littéraires . . . et autres*, 100 seqq.
33. Ibid.
34. Camacho: op. cit., 172
35. 'Judith Gautier'. (*Le Gaulois*, 29 décembre 1917)
36. Tharaud: *En Bretagne*, 36
37. Régnier: loc. cit.
38. 'Judith Gautier'. (*Le Figaro*, 8 janvier 1918)
39. *Le Temps*, 19 janvier 1918
40. Letter of 1890. Camacho: op. cit., 177

CHAPTER TWENTY-ONE

1. Thompson: *French Portraits*, 75, 84
2. Montfort: 'Catulle Mendès'. (*Candide*, 31 juillet 1930)
3. For an account of the funeral, see Mondor: *Vie de Mallarmé*, 802–3
4. Régnier: loc. cit.
5. Rosny: *Torches et Lumignons*, 194–5
6. Fouquier: *Profils et Portraits*, 107
7. Lemaître: *Impressions de Théâtre*, 3ᵉ série, 174
8. Montfort: loc. cit.
9. Ibid.
10. Ibid.
11. Undated. Porel: *Fils de Réjane*, II, 201–2
12. Gheusi: op. cit., II, 97
13. Cocteau: *Portraits–Souvenir. 1900–1914*, 170, 171–2
14. Waleffe: op. cit., 41
15. *Le Figaro*, 9 février 1909
16. Anon: 'Mort tragique de Catulle Mendès'. (*Le Petit Figaro*, 9 février 1909)
17. Cocteau: op. cit., 176
18. Rateau: 'Catulle Mendès: ses premières années et ses dernières heures'. (*Gil Blas*, 9 février 1909)
19. *Le Figaro*, loc. cit.; see also Léautaud: *Journal littéraire*, II, 370
20. *Le Figaro*, loc. cit.
21. Cocteau: op. cit., 178
22. Talmeyr: op. cit., 117–8
23. Waleffe: loc. cit.
24. Le Goffic: 'Catulle Mendès et le Parnasse contemporain'. (*La Revue hebdomadaire*, 20 février 1909, 355)
25. Gheusi: op. cit., I, 43
26. *Le Figaro*, 9 février 1909
27. Beaunier: *Éloges*, 273
28. Clarietie: *La Vie à Paris, 1909*, 49, 51
29. Renard: *Journal. 1887–1910*, 1223
30. Ernest-Charles: *Le Théâtre des Poètes*, 131, 147
31. Dubeux: *La curieuse vie de Georges Courteline*, 57
32. Bac: op. cit., 269 seqq.
33. Ibid.

CHAPTER TWENTY-TWO

1. Rostand: *Confession d'un demi-siècle*, 136–7
2. Meyer-Zundel: op. cit., 168
3. Pringué: *Trente ans de dîners en ville*, 120–1
4. Ibid.
5. Undated. BN N.A. Fr. 15297 f 84
6. Montesquiou: *Majeurs et mineurs*, 218
7. Ibid, 209 seqq.
8. BN N.A. Fr. 15297 ff 54 seqq.
9. Undated. BN N.A. Fr. 15189 f 110
10. Montesquiou: *Les paroles diaprées*, 142. See also BN N.A. Fr. 15116 f 30
11. Undated. BN N.A. Fr. 15116 ff 27–8
12. Montesquiou: *Les Quarante Bergères*, 14
13. BN N.A. Fr. 15116 f 109
14. Bac: *Intimités de la Troisième République*, 269 seqq.
15. Melchior-Bonnet: loc. cit.

16. Bac: loc. cit.
17. 'Ode au Champagne'. JG: *Poésies*, 107
18. Bac: loc. cit.
19. Ibid.
20. Meyer-Zundel: op. cit., 43
21. Vizetelly: *Paris and her People*, 227
22. Rosny: *Mémoires de la vie littéraire*, 56 seqq.
23. Deffoux: *Chronique de l'Académie-Goncourt*, 66 seqq.
24. Rosny: loc. cit.
25. Rosny: op. cit., 63–4
26. *Le Temps*, 30 octobre 1910
27. *Le Figaro*, 8 janvier 1918; Judith Gautier had been awarded the Prix Née in 1898.
28. *Le Temps*, 25 novembre 1910
29. Vizetelly: loc. cit.
30. Meyer-Zundel: op. cit., 94, 35
31. *Le Temps*, 25 novembre 1910
32. Ibid; and Montera: op. cit., 199, note
33. Unidentified press cutting, 29 octobre 1910. Arsenal. RF 59973 ff 25–6
34. Vedel: loc. cit.
35. Unidentified press-cutting. Arsenal. RF 59973 f 18
36. 29 octobre 1910. Unidentified press-cutting. Arsenal. RF 59973 ff 25–6
37. Rosny: loc. cit.
38. Billy: *Paris littéraire en 1910*, 52
39. Sherard: *Modern Paris*, 192–3
40. Deffoux: op. cit., 68
41. Ravon: op. cit., 63–4
42. Descaves: op. cit., 251–2
43. Ibid.
44. Daudet: *Vers le roi*, 156–7

CHAPTER TWENTY-THREE

1. Meyer-Zundel: op. cit., 154
2. Ibid.
3. Ibid, 155
4. Ibid.
5. Ibid, 156
6. Ibid, 157
7. Ibid; and Riese: op. cit., 155
8. Undated. To Robert de Montesquiou. BN N.A. Fr. 15298
9. In his *Confession d'un demi-siècle*, p. 145, Maurice Rostand wrote of d'Annunzio: 'On devinait certes qu'il nourrissait une ambition démesurée, l'orgueil peut-être d'égaler les personnages les plus fabuleux de l'histoire, mais il était exempt de cette morgue concentrée que l'on observe chez tant de littérateurs.'
10. Pringué: op. cit., 222; Meyer-Zundel: op. cit., 167–8
11. *Excelsior*, 9 décembre 1910
12. Meyer-Zundel: op. cit., 168
13. Undated. BN N.A. Fr. 15149 f 170
14. Undated. BN N.A. Fr. 15189 f 112. After Judith's death, Suzanne continued to correspond with Robert de Montesquiou. In a letter dated 'Mardi 1919', from 2, rue Thiers, Mulhouse, she sent him a poem on the may tree: 'Emblème d'Amitié'. It began:

    De votre part nous vint une

    rouge aubépine
    L'Amie vit en elle, un symbole touchant:
    Celui du lien sacré, par le sang et l'épine
    De notre liaison . . .
    (BN N.A. Fr. 15311 f 106)
15. Undated. BN N.A. Fr. 15189 f 110
16. Undated. BN N.A. Fr. 15035 f 84; see also BN N.A. Fr. 15042 f 153
17. Meyer-Zundel: op. cit., 168–9
18. Collonges: 'Madame Judith Gautier à l'Académie-Goncourt' (*Le Figaro*, 20 octobre 1910)
19. Poiteau: *Quelques Écrivains de ce temps*, 189–90
20. *Excelsior*, 27 janvier 1911
21. Ibid.
22. Ibid, 13 février 1911
23. Photographs of two scenes from the play appeared in *Excelsior*, 22 février 1911
24. *Excelsior*, 4 mai 1911
25. Ibid, 7 mai 1911
26. Ibid, 11 juin 1911
27. Ibid, 14 juin 1911
28. Ibid, 28 juin 1911
29. Ibid, 30 juin 1911
30. Ernest-Charles: 'Les Livres dont on parle'. (*Excelsior*, 21 juillet 1911)
31. Ibid.
32. Judith sent a copy of the book 'to my

dear friend Robert de Montesquiou, who is sulking, so that he does not sulk any more' (BN N.A. Fr. 15297 f 50)

33. JG: *Poésies*, 82–3
34. *Excelsior*, 26 juin 1911
35. *Centenaire Théophile Gautier*, 9, 13
36. Larguier: *Théophile Gautier*, 13 seqq.
37. Tailhade: op. cit., 169–70
38. Waleffe: *Quand Paris était un paradis*, 84, 85–6
39. JG: *Le Roman d'un grand chanteur*. Avant-propos. Un-numbered page.
40. Barrès. *Cahiers*, III, 57
41. JG: *Lettre inédites de Madame de Sévigné*, 17–18
42. Poiteau: op. cit., 193
43. Ibid, 197
44. Thompson: op. cit., 82
45. Bonnières: *Mémoires d'aujourd'hui*, loc. cit.
46. Ibid.
47. Fouquières: *Cinquante ans de*

panache, 126
48. Waleffe: op. cit., 86, 88
49. Tailhade: op. cit., 165–9
50. JG: 'Fanelli' (*Le Figaro*, 23 décembre 1917)
51. Ibid.
52. Calvocoressi: 'An Unknown Composer of Today'. (*Musical Times*, 1 April 1912, 225)
53. Meyer-Zundel: op. cit., 172
54. Calvocoressi: op. cit., 226
55. Meyer-Zundel: op. cit., 173
56. Papiers Poincaré. Lettres adressées à Mme Poincaré, tome XXIX. BN N.A. Fr. 16020 f 263
57. Ibid, f 249
58. Ibid, f 255
59. 22 décembre 1911. BN N.A. Fr. 15239 ff 192 seqq.
60. Undated. BN N.A. Fr. 15116 f 106
61. Mars 1919. BN N.A. Fr. 15152 ff 104 seqq.
62. Meyer-Zundel: op. cit., 169

CHAPTER TWENTY-FOUR

1. Meyer-Zundel: op. cit., 229–30. Judith was not always accurate about dates. In fact it was on 2 August that general mobilization was announced in France; the following day, Germany declared war.
2. Meyer-Zundel: op. cit., 232, 235–6
3. Institut de France. Papiers Charles Clermont-Ganneau. MS 4109 f 257
4. BN N.A. Fr. 15239 f 187
5. [14 juin 1896.] BN N.A. Fr. 15239 ff 188–9
6. Meyer-Zundel: op. cit., 188
7. Larguier: *Théophile Gautier*, 247
8. Meyer-Zundel: loc. cit.
9. Bergerat: 'Judith Gautier'. (*Le Figaro*, 8 janvier 1918.)
10. Camacho: op. cit., 183, 184, note
11. BN N.A. Fr. 16020, tome XXIX, ff 240–1
12. Meyer-Zundel: op. cit., 190. The Taylor Institution, Oxford, has a copy of Judith Gautier's *Poésies*, inscribed: 'À Madame Raymond Poincaré, en toute sympathie'. Among the Poincaré papers in the Bibliothèque Nationale is a note from Judith dated 19 October 1914:

'Suzanne est ici avec moi, et, par bonheur, sa mère est auprès d'elle. Quelle angoisse si elle était restée en Alsace!' (N.A. Fr. 16020. Papiers Poincaré. Lettres adressées à Mme Poincaré, tome XXIX, f 239.)
13. Meyer-Zundel: op. cit., 189
14. Ibid, 198
15. Ibid, 205
16. Ibid, 238
17. Ibid, 191
18. Ibid.
19. Ibid, 192
20. Meyer-Zundel: *La Gloire de l'Illusion*, 6
21. The verse was dated 26 December 1918 to 5 February 1920
22. BN N.A. Fr. 15311 f 46
23. BN N.A. Fr. 15311 f 50
24. Meyer-Zundel: *Quinze Ans auprès de Judith Gautier*, 192
25. Ibid, 193
26. Ibid.
27. To Maître L. Ibid, 188
28. Ibid, 196
29. Ibid, 199
30. Ibid, 194
31. Ajalbert: *Les Mystères de l'Académie*

Goncourt, 251, note

32. 18 août 1925. Léautaud: op. cit., V, 77
33. Deffoux: op. cit., 70
34. Tailhade: loc. cit.
35. Bergerat: loc. cit.
36. Meyer-Zundel: op. cit., 194
37. Ibid, 205–6
38. Ibid, 209
39. Anon: 'Mort de Mme Judith Gautier'. (*Le Figaro*, 28 décembre 1917.)
40. Meyer-Zundel: op. cit., 212–3
41. Ibid, 213
42. 6 décembre 1917. Ibid, 214
43. 7 décembre 1917. Ibid.
44. Ibid, 214
45. 22 décembre 1917. Ibid, 211
46. Bergerat: loc. cit.
47. Tharaud: *En Bretagne*, 34
48. Meyer-Zundel: op. cit., 215
49. Ibid, 216
50. Ibid.
51. Rosny: *Mémoires de la vie littéraire*, loc. cit.
52. Meyer-Zundel: op. cit., 217–8. Among the papers of Robert de Montesquiou (N.A. Fr. 15311 ff 72 seqq.) is a letter from Suzanne Meyer-Zundel, dated 9 November, and clearly written in 1918.

> Vous saviez, n'est-ce pas, combien nous nous intéressions à Fanelli, le grand compositeur, et à son oeuvre?
> Ne pouvant plus le soutenir de loin, lui et sa famille, nous avions mis le pavillon (ou boîte à cigare) à leur disposition . . .
> Au mois de novembre dernier, mourait notre grand musicien d'une ambolie cardiaque.
> *Un mois* plus tard, Maya (morte aussi d'une amoblie cardiaque) me quittait pour accomplir à son tour le grand voyage à travers l'espace . . . Nul doute pour moi que Fanelli ait rappelé Maya . . .
> Le 26 décembre dernier, à mon tour, j'aurais *dû* partir, si j'avais été *toute seule* avec l'Amie; j'avais même déjà passé [*sic*] de l'autre côté'. – Étant tombée sans connaissance et

étant restée plus de 2h ½ inanimée. – Mais je n'étais *pas seule*. Un ami, le Marquis de Casa Fuerte, venu – poussé par je ne sais quel étrange concours de circonstances – le 26 au Matin, s'est trouvé là, pour cueillir le soir du même jour, à 10h ½ [*sic*], le dernier soupir de l'incomparable Amie. C'est par *lui*, que je fus pour ainsi dire, arrachée à la Mort . . .

53. JG: *Póesies*, 30–1. A copy of this poem, in her hand, is among the correspondence of Anatole France. (BN N.A. Fr. 15434 f 183)
54. Descaves: op. cit., 252
55. Meyer-Zundel: op. cit., 217
56. Ibid, 217–8
57. Bergerat: loc. cit.
58. Ravon: op. cit., 65–6; Meyer-Zundel: op. cit., 218. Among Robert de Montesquiou's papers is a note from Suzanne Meyer-Zundel (BN N.A. Fr. 15192 ff 95–9). It is dated 26 November 1918, and refers to Judith, and to 'la pensée qu'elle avait écrite en caractères chinois, dans sa chambre et dont le Prince d'Annam vient de m'envoyer la traduction: "La lumière du Ciel arrive" . . .'
59. Tailhade: op. cit., 173
60. Bergerat: loc. cit.
61. Daudet: loc. cit.
62. Brousson: 'Judith Gautier'. (*Excelsiur*, 29 décembre 1917)
63. Bergerat: loc. cit.
64. Souday: 'Les Livres. Judith Gautier'. (*Le Temps*, 19 janvier 1918)
65. Ravon: loc. cit.
66. Writing to JG on 18 July 1905, Maurice de Waleffe acclaimed her as 'la seule femme de lettres purement artiste qui existe in France'. (Meyer-Zundel: op. cit., 141)
67. Brisson: op. cit., III, 43. In 1889, Bergerat had been appointed Chevalier de la Légion-d'honneur. It is clear from Bergerat's *Notes quotidiennes, 1919–1920*, that after Judith's death he had problems with Suzanne Meyer-Zundel:

> 29 avril 1919
> . . . Le jeune musicien Marcel Rousseau est venu hier avec ma fille me demander de mettre

pour l'Opéra la Momie de
Gautier en drame lyrique . . . Il
y faut l'autorisation de
Benedictus, qui dépend de celle
de Melle Mayer!!! [*sic*] C'est à
ne pas raconter ni croire.

                                    3 mai 1919
Hennique me dit que jamais on
ne lui a parlé de se charger des
intérêts littéraires de la
succession de Judith. C'est un
mensonge de Benedictus et de
Melle Mayer, qui, paraît-il, fait
des vers, comme elle faisait de
la musique!

                                1er juin 1919
Hennique . . . croit à la
réincarnation possible de Judith
en Melle Mayer. C'est un
adepte de l'occultisme . . ..

(BN N.A. Fr. 14604 ff 21, 29, 54)

68. Meyer-Zundel: op. cit., 47; and
    Pakenham: information to the
    author. In the deplorable 'poem'
    which she wrote in memory of
    Judith, Suzanne Meyer-Zundel
    explained why she had had the palm
    tree planted by the grave:

            Ce qui fut, ici-bas, je le
                veux sur sa tombe
            Puisqu'elle doit de même
                accueillir mes lambeaux

À dessein, j'ai planté cet
    arbre qui retombe
Avec beaucoup de grâce en
    formant des arceaux.

Je voudrais arriver sur
    notre sépulture
À fixer à jamais, notre belle
    amitié
Sans parole, sans phrase un
    arbre en la nature,
Parlerait seulement, au seul
    initié.

Celui-ci comprendrait que
    de cet amalgame
(Nos deux corps réunis)
    l'arbre s'est sustenté,
Réalisant ainsi, pour le
    mieux le programme
Qu'avait voulu tracer ma
    simple volonté . . .

(N.A. Fr. 15311 f 31).

In *La Gloire de l'Illusion*, p 34,
Suzanne Meyer-Zundel also recorded
her jealousy of Lilith, Judith's cat:

        . . . Je nourrissais pour elle un
            sentiment de haine
        Quand ma Judith en pleurs
            courait à demi nue,
        Pour rechercher Lilith,
            risquant de perdre haleine
            . . .

Select Bibliography

I
— WORKS BY JUDITH GAUTIER —
NOVELS, SHORT STORIES, POETRY, NON-FICTION

1. *Le Livre de Jade*. (Lemerre, 1867.)
    Published under the name of Judith Walter.
    Chinesische Lieder aus dem Livre de Jade von Judith Mendès, in das deutsche übertragen von G. Böhm. (München. Theodor Akermann. 1873.)
    Il Libro di Giada. Echi dell' estremo Oriente recati in versi Italiani secondo la lezione di Mme J. Walter da Tullo Massarani. (Firenze. Successori Le Monnier. 1882.)
    Poèmes traduits du Chinois par Judith Gautier. (Juven. 1902.) Illustrated with vignettes after Chinese artists. De luxe editions contain an engraved frontispiece. New corrected and enlarged edition, 1908.
    Album de Poèmes tirés du Livre de Jade. (The Eragny Press. The Brook, Hammersmith, London, W. 1911.)
    Chinese Lyrics from the Book of Jade. Translated from the French of Judith Gautier by James Whitall. (Erskine Macdonald, Ltd. 1919.)
    Le Livre de Jade. (Les Belles Œuvres littéraires. Éditions Jules Tallandier. 1928.)
    Le Livre de Jade. (Les Beaux Textes illustrés. Librairie Plon. 1933.) Seven heliogravure illustrations.
2. *Le Dragon impérial*. (Lemerre, 1869.)
    Published under the name of Judith Mendès. This novel was serialized in *La Liberté* from 23 March–27 May 1868.
    Le Dragon impérial. (Bibliothèque de Romans Historiques. Armand Colin. 1893.) Published under the name of Judith Gautier.
    The Imperial Dragon. Translated by M.H. Bourchier. (Brentano's. 1928.) Published under the name of Judith Gautier.
3. *L'Usurpateur*. (Librairie Internationale. Albert Lacroix. 1875.) 2 volumes. With two frontispieces by the author. Published under the name of Judith Mendès. This work was crowned by the Académie-Française.
    L'Usurpateur. (Marpon & Flammarion. 1883.) Two volumes.

La Soeur du Soleil (L'Usurpateur). (Dentu. 1887.) New edition, with variants.
La Soeur du Soleil. (Colin & Cie. 1891.) A further edition was published by Colin in 1897, in the Bibliothèque de Romans Historiques.

4. *Lucienne*. (Calmann-Lévy. 1877.) This work was serialized in *Le Rappel* under the title *Jeux de l'Amour et de la Mort*. 1876.
5. *Les Cruautés de l'Amour*. Nouvelles. (Dentu. 1879.) Reprinted by Marpon & Flammarion, 1890. Volume 139 of the Collection des Auteurs célèbres.
6. *Les Peuples étranges*. (Charpentier. 1879.)
7. *Isoline*. Avec 12 eaux-fortes par Auguste Constantin. (Charavay. 1882.)
8. *Isoline, et la Fleur-Serpent*, et autres nouvelles. Trois gravures de F. Régamey et de A. Constantin. (Charavay frères. 1882.)
9. *Richard Wagner et son oeuvre poétique depuis* **Rienzi** *jusqu'à* **Parsifal**. (Charavay frères. 1882.)
10. *La Femme de Putiphar*. (Les Grandes Amoureuses. C. Marpon & E. Flammarion, Libraires. A. Lacroix, Éditeur. 1884.)
11. *Iseult*. Avec illustrations par P. Morel, D. Vierge et A. Bertrand. (Les Grandes Amoureuses. C. Marpon & E. Flammarion, Libraires. A. Lacroix, Éditeur. 1885.)
12. *Poèmes de la Libellule*. Traduits du japonais d'après la version littérale de M. Saionzi, Conseiller d'État de S.M. l'Empereur du Japon, par Judith Gautier. Illustrés par Yamamoto. (Gillot, imprimeur. 1885.) Chez Mme Judith Gautier, 108, avenue des Champs-Élysées. (Hors commerce.)
13. *Iskender*, histoire persane. (Frinzine & Cie. 1886.) This work had been serialized in *La Liberté* from 10 November–17 December 1869.
    Iskender. Histoire persane. Avec un sonnet liminaire de Leconte de Lisle. (Bibliothèque de Romans Historiques. Armand Colin. 1894.)
14. *La Conquête du Paradis; Le Lion de la victoire*. (Frinzine. 1887.) 2e volume: *La Reine de Bangalore*. (Frinzine. 1887.) The two volumes were reprinted, but condensed, in the series Bibliothèque de Romans Historiques, published by Armand Colin, in 1890. *La Conquête du Paradis* was republished, with illustrations by Alex. Lagé, by Ollendorff in 1909. It was republished, under the title *L'Inde éblouie*, by Armand Colin in 1913.
15. *Les Noces de Fingal:* poème en trois parties, écrit pour le concours Rossini. (Imprimerie Firmin-Didot. 1888.) This work was reprinted in *Poésies*, 1911.
16. *Les Musiques bizarres à l'Exposition (1889)* recueillies et transcrites par Louis Benedictus, dessins de A. Gorgnet. (G. Hartmann & Cie. 1889.) The exotic songs in this work were translated by Judith Gautier, but they are unsigned.
17. *Les Capitales du Monde. Tokio.* (Hachette. 1892.) These illustrated monographs, edited by Nancy Bell and H.D. Traill, and translated by Nancy Bell, were published this year by Sampson Low, Marston, in two volumes, as *The Capitals of the World. Tokio* appears in Vol. I, Division II, pp. 35 sqq.
18. *Fleurs d'Orient*: nouvelles historiques. (Bibliothèque de Romans historiques. Armand Colin. 1893.)
19. *Le Vieux de la montagne*. (Bibliothèque de Romans historiques. Armand Colin. 1893.)
20. *Parsifal*. Poème de Richard Wagner, traduction littérale de Judith Gautier. Dessin de Paul Baudry et autographe de Wagner. (Armand Colin & Cie. 1893.)
    Traduction nouvelle s'adaptant à la musique. (Société française d'Éditions d'Art. 1898.) There are copies with the imprint of Fasquelle, 1900.
    Nouvelle édition, suivie de la correspondance de Mme Judith Gautier avec Wagner à propos de la traduction de *Parsifal*. (Armand Colin. 1914.)
    Traduction nouvelle s'adaptant à la musique. (Société française d'éditions artistiques. 1898.)

Version française de Judith Gautier et Maurice Kufferath de *Parsifal*, drame sacré en trois actes de Richard Wagner. Livret seul. (Imprimerie de L'ILLUSTRATION, 1914.)

21. *Mémoires d'un éléphant blanc.* (Armand Colin & Cie. 1983.)
   Mémoires d'un éléphant blanc. Illustrations par M. Mucha. (Armand Colin. 1894.)
   Mémoires d'un éléphant blanc. Illustrations par A. Mucha. Ornementations par M. Ruty. (Librairie Armand Colin. 1900.)
   Mémoires d'un éléphant blanc. Édition abrégée, avec une introduction et des notes par Emily A. Crosby. (London. Sidgwick & Jackson. 1925.) This is a slightly abridged text of the first half of the work.
   10th edition by Armand Colin. 1931.

22. *Khou-n-ato-nou* (fragments d'un papyrus) et diverses nouvelles. (Armand Colin. 1898.)

23. *Les Musiques bizarres à l'Exposition de 1900*, transcrites par Louis Benedictus. (Ollendorff. 1900.) This work consists of six brochures published separately:
   La Musique chinoise. Transcrite par Benedictus. (Société d'Éditions littéraires et artistiques. Librairie Paul Ollendorff. 1900.)
   Danse javanaise – danse du diable. Transcrites par Benedictus. (Société d'Éditions littéraires et artistiques. Librairie Paul Ollendorff. 1900.)
   La Musique Indo-Chinoise. Transcrite par Benedictus. (Société d'Éditions littéraires et artistiques. Librairie Paul Ollendorff. 1900.)
   La Musique Japonaise. Transcrite par Benedictus. Les Danses de Sada-Yacco. (Société d'Éditions littéraires et artistiques. Librairie Paul Ollendorff. 1900.) The introduction contains the play *La Gheisha et le Samouraï* re-worked and re-presented at the Théâtre des Mathurins in 1901. Published in this new form in *Les Parfums de la pagode* (Charpentier & Fasquelle. 1919.)
   La Musique égyptienne. Chant Khédivial – Danse de l'Abeille – Danse des Verres. Transcrits par Benedictus. (Société d'Éditions littéraires et artistiques. Librairie Paul Ollendorff. 1900.)
   Les Chants de Madagascar. Transcrits par Benedictus. (Société d'Éditions littéraires et artistiques. Librairie Paul Ollendorff. 1900.)

24. *Le Livre de la foi nouvelle.* (1900.) No author or publisher is given for this pamphlet, which may be found in the Bibliothèque Nationale. (Reference: Pièce 4o R 1287)

25. *Les Princesses d'amour* (Courtisanes japonaises). Roman. (Ollendorff. 1900.) This work appeared in *La Grande Revue* in 1900.
   Princesas de amor. Versión castellana de Carlos de Battle. Prólogo de Luis Bonafoux. (Ollendorff. 1907.)

26. *Le Collier des jours.* (*Souvenirs de ma vie*). (Félix Juven. 1902.) A sixth edition of this work appeared in 1910.

27. *Le Second Rang du Collier.* (*Souvenirs littéraires*). (Félix Juven. 1903.) Serialized in *La Revue de Paris*, No. 6, in 1902, and in Nos. 1, 2, 3 and 4 in 1903.

28. *Le Paravent de soie et d'or.* (Fasquelle. 1904.)

29. *Le Troisième Rang du Collier.* (Félix Juven. 1909.) This work, which went into a fifth edition in the year of publication, had been serialized in *La Revue de Paris*, Nos. 1, 2 and 3, in the same year. It was published as *Wagner at Home.* Fully translated by Effie Dunreith Massie. (Mills & Boon. 1910.)

30. *En Chine.* (*Merveilleuses histoires*). Préface de Jean Aicard. Illustré de 12 planches en couleurs et d'une carte. (Vincennes. Les Arts Graphiques. 1911.)

31. *Poésies.* Les Rites Divins – Au Gré du rêve – Badinages – Pour la Lyre. (Bibliothèque Charpentier. Eugène Fasquelle. 1911.)

32. *Le Japon.* (*Merveilleuses histoires*). Préface de Jean Aicard. (London: A. & C. Black. Paris: Les Arts Graphiques. 1912.)

33. *Le Roman d'un grand chanteur*. (Mario de Candia). D'après les 'Souvenirs' de sa fille Madame Cecilia Pearse et la version française de Mademoiselle Ethel Duncan. (Bibliothèque Charpentier. 1912.)
34. *Dupleix*. Pages d'histoire. (Vincennes. Les Arts Graphiques. 1912.) An illustrated edition was published in London, by T.C. & E.C. Jack, in 1913.
35. *Lettres inédites de Madame de Sévigné*. Recueillies par Judith Gautier, et illustrées par Madeleine Lemaire. (À la Marquise de Sévigné. 1913.) These letters were in fact written by Judith Gautier. Twelve hundred numbered copies of this work were printed, and were not for sale.
36. *Les Parfums de la pagode*. (Charpentier & Fasquelle. 1919.)
37. *Auprès de Richard Wagner*. Souvenirs (1861–1882). Avant-propos par Gustave Samazeuilh. (Mercure de France. 1943.)

PLAYS

1. *Le Ramier blanc*. This Chinese play, with music by Benedictus, was performed on 3 June 1880, at the hôtel de Poilly (see p. 139).
2. *La Marchande de sourires*. A Japanese play in five acts and two parts. Prologue by Armand Silvestre. Music by Benedictus. First performed at the Théâtre de l'Odéon on 21 April 1888. (Charpentier. 1888.)
3. *La Camargo*. Ballet-pantomime in two acts and three tableaux, written in collaboration with Armand Tonnery. (Armand Colin. 1893.)
4. *La Sonate du clair de lune*. One-act opera. Libretto by Judith Gautier, music by Benedictus. (Armand Colin. 1894.)
5. *La Barynia*. Russian drama, written in collaboration with Joseph Gayda, performed at the Théâtre de l'Odéon on 20 September 1894. This play is based on the short story of the same title published in *Les Cruautés de l'amour*. (Dentu. 1879.)
6. *La Tunique merveilleuse*. Chinese play, in one act, performed at the Odéon on 14 January 1899. Published in the collection *Le Paravent de soie et d'or*. (Fasquelle. 1904.)
7. *Le Gheisha et le Chevalier*. Translation of a Japanese play in the repertoire of Sada-Yacco. The original was performed in Paris in 1900. The translation was performed at the Théâtre de Mathurins in 1901. Published in *Les Parfums de la pagode* (Charpentier & Fasquelle. 1919.)
8. *Une Fausse Conversion*. One-act play based on a work by Théophile Gautier, performed at the Odéon on 24 April 1899.
9. *Princesses d'amour*. Play based on the book of the same title, and performed at the Vaudeville in 1908.
10. *L'Avare chinois*. Performed at the Odéon on 30 January 1908, and published in *Les Parfums de la pagode*.
11. *Tristiane*. (*La Revue de Paris*, 15 novembre 1910.)
12. *Embûche fleurie*. This one-act Japanese play was performed at the Théâtre-Michel in February 1911 (see pp. 233, 281).
13. *La Fille du ciel*. Chinese drama written in collaboration with Pierre Loti. (Calmann-Lévy. 1911.) The eleventh edition was published in 1923.
    The Daughter of Heaven. Translated by Ruth Helen Davis. (Constable. 1913.)
14. *L'Apsara*. A Hindu play, listed by Camacho.
15. *Les Portes rouges*. An Annamite play, also listed by Camacho. Judith Gautier mentions writing this in a letter to Charles Clermont-Ganneau (see p. 279).
16. *Mademoiselle de Maupin*. A play based on the novel by Théophile Gautier, and written in collaboration with Ernest Fanelli.

NEWPAPERS AND PERIODICALS

Judith Gautier contributed to newspapers and periodicals, under various names, for some forty years. A list of her contributions would probably fill a substantial volume, and there would be no way of knowing that it was complete. The following list has no pretensions to completeness; it is intended to supplement the inadequate and sometimes inaccurate bibliography given by Mathilde Camacho in her thesis.

I
JUDITH WALTER

Variations sur des thèmes chinois. (L'ARTISTE, 15 janvier 1864, 37–8)
Exposition de la Société nationale des beaux-arts. (L'ARTISTE, 15 mars 1864, 129–30)
EUREKA d'Edgar Poë. (LE MONITEUR UNIVERSEL, 29 mars 1864)
Collection chinoise de M. Négroni. (L'ARTISTE, 15 avril 1864, 188–9)
Salon de 1864. Sculpture. (L'ARTISTE, 15 juin 1864, 265–7)
Variations sur des thèmes chinois. (L'ARTISTE, 1er juin 1865, 261)
Salon de 1866. M. Ribot. (GAZETTE DES ÉTRANGERS, 7 mai 1866)
Salon de 1866. M. Gustave Moreau – M. Gustave Courbet. (GAZETTE DES ÉTRANGERS, 17 mai 1866)
Salon de 1866. M. Gérôme. – M. Bonnat. – M. Horovitz. (GAZETTE DES ÉTRANGERS, 1er juin 1866)
Salon de 1866. M.H. Madarasz. – M. Hamon – M. Puvis de Chavannes – M. Schryer – M. Robert-Fleury – M. Monet – M. Tavernier – M. Oudry – M. Roybet. (GAZETTE DES ÉTRANGERS, 14 juin 1866)
Salon de 1866. (Dernier article.) MM. Chintreuil, Gustave Doré, Daubigny fils, Auguste Herst; Mlle Louisa Rochat; MM. Ernest Hébert, Jalabert, Pérignon, Lazarus Will, Carpeaux, Aimé Millet, Carrier-Belleuse, Jacquemart, Klagman, Godebski, Moulin, Claudius Popelin, Jules Crosnier. (GAZETTE DES ÉTRANGERS, 1er juillet–7 juillet 1866)
Comptes rendus de l'Exposition Universelle. Chine-Japon-Siam. I. (LE MONITEUR UNIVERSEL, 12 novembre 1867)
Comptes rendus de l'Exposition Universelle. Chine-Japon-Siam. I. (Suite.) (LE MONITEUR UNIVERSEL, 16 novembre 1867)
Comptes rendus de l'Exposition Universelle. Chine-Japon-Siam. II. (LE MONITEUR UNIVERSEL, 1er décembre 1867)
Comptes rendus de l'Exposition Universelle. Chine-Japon-Siam. II. (Suite). (LE MONITEUR UNIVERSEL, 25 décembre 1867)
L'Art siamois. (L'ARTISTE, 1er novembre 1869, 240–6)

II
JUDITH MENDÈS

Théâtre de Bade: **Lohengrin**, *opéra en 3 actes, de Richard Wagner.* (LA PRESSE, 8 septembre 1868)
Richard Wagner et la critique. (LA PRESSE, 17 octobre 1868)
Richard Wagner et la critique. (Suite et fin). (LA PRESSE, 30 octobre 1868)
Richard Wagner chez lui. (LE RAPPEL, 3 août 1869)
Théâtre de Munich. **L'or du Rhin**. (LE RAPPEL, 7 septembre 1869)
Lohengrin *par Richard Wagner.* (LA LIBERTÉ, 26 mars 1870)
Le Festival Richard Wagner à Weimar. (LE RAPPEL, 24 juin 1870)

III
F. CHAULNES

Les Poètes persans. (JOURNAL OFFICIEL, 17 janvier 1875, 434–6)
Les Poètes persans. (*Deuxième article*). (JOURNAL OFFICIEL, 30 janvier 1875, 815–6)
Les Âges préhistoriques. (JOURNAL OFFICIEL, 20 février 1875, 1327–8)
La Loi des Tempêtes. (JOURNAL OFFICIEL, 5 mars 1875, 1686–7)
Une journée dans le royaume de Siam. (JOURNAL OFFICIEL, 21 mars 1875, 2167–8)
Une journée dans le royaume de Siam. (*2e et dernier article*). (JOURNAL OFFICIEL, 27 mars 1875, 2311–2)
Notes sur la Chine. Les Comédiens et la Comédie. (JOURNAL OFFICIEL, 31 juillet 1875, 6143–4)
Notes sur la Chine. Les Comédiens et la Comédie. (JOURNAL OFFICIEL, 25 août 1875, 7208–10)
Douze heures dans la baie de Tourane en Cochinchine. (JOURNAL OFFICIEL, 12 septembre 1875, 7815–6)
Douze heures dans la baie de Tourane en Cochinchine. (*Suite*). (JOURNAL OFFICIEL, 26 septembre 1875, 8363–5)
Une Ville retrouvée. (JOURNAL OFFICIEL, 14 octobre 1875, 8654–5)
Notes sur la Chine. La Médecine et les médecins. (JOURNAL OFFICIEL, 29 octobre 1875, 8908–10)
Notes sur la Chine. La Médecine et les médecins. (JOURNAL OFFICIEL, 13 novembre 1875, 9279–80)
Notes sur la Chine. La Médecine et les médecins. (JOURNAL OFFICIEL, 8 décembre 1875, 10125–7)
Notes sur la Chine. La Médecine légale. (JOURNAL OFFICIEL, 30 décembre 1875, 10926–7)
Notes sur la Chine. Un Mariage à Péking. (JOURNAL OFFICIEL, 15 janvier 1876, 431–2)
Notes sur la Chine. Cérémonies funèbres. (JOURNAL OFFICIEL, 27 janvier 1876, 812–4)
Notes sur la Chine. La Peinture. (JOURNAL OFFICIEL, 16 février 1876, 1245–7)
Notes sur la Chine. La Poésie et les Poètes. I. (JOURNAL OFFICIEL, 1er mars 1876, 1470–1)
Notes sur la Chine. La Poésie et les Poètes. (*Suite.*) *II.* (JOURNAL OFFICIEL, 2 avril 1876, 2367–8)
Notes sur la Chine. La Poésie et les Poètes. II. (*Suite.*) (JOURNAL OFFICIEL, 22 avril 1876, 2863–4)
Notes sur la Chine. Les Dieux et les Pou-sahs. I. La déesse de la Miséricorde. (JOURNAL OFFICIEL, 24–25 mai 1876, 3599–3600)
Notes sur la Chine. La Musique. (JOURNAL OFFICIEL, 9 juillet 1876, 4983–4)
Le Trésor de Curium. (JOURNAL OFFICIEL, 28 août 1876, 6650–1)
Notes sur la Chine. La Musique. (*Suite.*) (JOURNAL OFFICIEL, 3 septembre 1876, 6751–2)
Notes sur la Chine. La Musique. (*Suite*). (JOURNAL OFFICIEL, 22 septembre 1876, 7100–2)
Les Muses de l'Orient. I. Les Quatre Sages de l'Arabie antique. (JOURNAL OFFICIEL, 24 mai 1877)
Les Muses de l'Orient. II. La Reine Bilkis et la Reine Kaïdafa. (JOURNAL OFFICIEL, 6 août 1877)
Les Muses de l'Orient. III. La Reine Kaïdafa. (JOURNAL OFFICIEL, 28 septembre 1877)
Les Muses de l'Orient. IV. Toumadir la Solamide. (JOURNAL OFFICIEL, 14 octobre 1877)
Les Muses de l'Orient. V. Leïla. (JOURNAL OFFICIEL, 3 novembre 1877)
Les Muses de l'Orient. VI. Aïchah. (JOURNAL OFFICIEL, 8 décembre 1877)
Les Muses de l'Orient. VII. Avyar l'indienne. (JOURNAL OFFICIEL, 16 janvier 1878)
Les Muses de l'Orient. VIII. Mira. (JOURNAL OFFICIEL, 8 février 1878)
Exposition Internationale Universelle de 1878. (JOURNAL OFFICIEL, 28 février 1878)

Exposition Universelle. La Chine. (JOURNAL OFFICIEL, 12 mai 1878)
Exposition Universelle. La Chine. Les Sculpteurs sur bois. (JOURNAL OFFICIEL, 21 mai 1878)
Exposition Universelle de 1878. La Chine (1). Les Costumes. (JOURNAL OFFICIEL, 1er juin 1878)
Exposition Universelle de 1878. La Chine (1). Les émaux, le jade, l'ivoire, les potiches. (JOURNAL OFFICIEL, 9 juin 1878)
Exposition Universelle de 1878. Le Japon. (JOURNAL OFFICIEL, 27 juin 1878)
Exposition Universelle de 1878. Le Japon. 2e et dernier article. (JOURNAL OFFICIEL, 7 juillet 1878)
Exposition Universelle de 1878. La Perse. (JOURNAL OFFICIEL, 18 juillet 1878)
Exposition Universelle de 1878. Le Mobilier. France. (JOURNAL OFFICIEL, 31 juillet 1878)
Exposition Universelle de 1878. Le Mobilier. Russie, Autriche, Belgique, Italie. (JOURNAL OFFICIEL, 25 août 1878)
Exposition Universelle. Le Mobilier. Angleterre. (JOURNAL OFFICIEL, 5 septembre 1878)
Exposition Universelle. Le Mobilier. La Hollande. La Suisse. Le Portugal. Le Pérou. (JOURNAL OFFICIEL, 14 septembre 1878)
Exposition Universelle. Les Tissus d'ameublement. Cristallerie et verrerie: Venise. (JOURNAL OFFICIEL, 19 septembre 1878)
Exposition Universelle. Cristallerie et Verrerie (Suite). La France. Autriche-Hongrie. Angleterre. (JOURNAL OFFICIEL, 20 septembre 1878)
Exposition Universelle. La Parure. Colonies françaises. (JOURNAL OFFICIEL, 5 octobre 1878)
Exposition Universelle. La Parure. L'Inde Britannique. (JOURNAL OFFICIEL, 23 novembre 1878)

IV
JUDITH GAUTIER

Le Salon. I. Première impression. (LE RAPPEL, 2 mai 1876)
Le Salon. II. Gustave Moreau. (LE RAPPEL, 6 mai 1876)
Le Salon. III. Les Grandes Toiles. Mahomet II, par Benjamin Constant. (LE RAPPEL, 7 mai 1876)
Le Salon. IV. Les Grandes Toiles. Puvis de Chavannes (&c.) Sculpture. (LE RAPPEL, 10 mai 1876.)
Le Salon. V. Les Grandes Toiles . . . Sculpture. (LE RAPPEL, 14 mai 1876)
Le Salon. VI. Le Boudoir et la rue. (LE RAPPEL, 23 mai 1876)
Les Refusés. (LE RAPPEL, 27 mai 1876)
Histoire et Genre. (LE RAPPEL, 2 juin 1876)
L'Orient. Sculpture. (LE RAPPEL, 15 juin 1876)
Le Salon. Les Champs, les bois et la mer. (LE RAPPEL, 21 juin 1876)
Le Salon (dernier article). Les Portraits. Dessins, porcelaines, gravures, sculpture. (LE RAPPEL, 26 juin 1876)
Les Envois de Rome. Sculpture. Peinture. (LE RAPPEL, 2 juillet 1876)
Exposition des oeuvres de Diaz. (L'ARTISTE, juin 1877, 463–4)
Les Sévérités du Calife. Conte oriental. (REVUE BLEUE, 4 février 1888, 137–40)
Villiers de l'Isle-Adam, Fragment inédit d'un Roman. Première Lettre, précédée d'une note de Mme Judith Gautier. (MERCURE DE FRANCE, avril 1893, 289 sqq.)
Le Resplendissement d'Atenn. (Fragments d'un papyrus). (LA REVUE DE PARIS, 15 août 1894, 769–806)
Poésies. (LA REVUE DE PARIS, 1er septembre 1896, 116–8)
Le Prince à la tête sanglante. (LA REVUE DE PARIS, 15 décembre 1897, 744–62)

L'Oiseau-Fleur lisse ses plumes. (LA REVUE BLANCHE, 1er avril 1900, 523–6)
L'Oiseau-Fleur conte une histoire. (LA REVUE BLANCHE, 15 avril 1900, 578–80)
Poèmes chinois de tous les temps. (LA REVUE DE PARIS, 15 juin 1901, 805–20)
Le Prince Bojidar Karageorgevitch. (LA REVUE DE PARIS, 1er juin 1908, 664–72)
L'Empereur de Chine. Kouang-Siu. (LA REVUE DE PARIS, 1er décembre 1908, 514–22)
Le Collier des jours. Le Troisième Rang du collier. (LA REVUE DE PARIS, 1er, 15 février, 1er mars, 1er, 15 avril, 1er mai 1909)
L'académicienne est heureuse. Remerciements d'une solitaire. (Undated cutting, presumably of 1910, from unspecified newspaper. Bibliothèque de l'Arsenal. RF 59973 f 18)
Le Conflit des Compositeurs. (EXCELSIOR, 16 novembre 1910)
Une première à l'Apollo. 'Malbrouk s'en va-t-en guerre'. Opérette en 3 actes, de MM. Maurice Vaucaire et A. Nessi. Musique de R. Léoncavallo. (EXCELSIOR, 17 novembre 1910)
Une première à l'Opéra-Comique. 'Macbeth'. Drame lyrique en 7 tableaux . . . Adaptation d'Edmond Fleg. Musique d'Ernest Bloch. (EXCELSIOR, 1er décembre 1910)
Les Virtuoses du bâton. Siegfried Wagner conduira, dimanche, un concert à Paris. – Mme Judith Gautier expose, à ce propos, le rôle des chefs d'orchestre. (EXCELSIOR, 9 décembre 1910)
Concert Lamoureux. Siegfried Wagner dirige des oeuvres de Liszt, de Richard Wagner et de lui-même. (EXCELSIOR, 12 décembre 1910)
Théâtre Lyrique Municipal de la Gaîté. 'Don Quichotte'. Comédie héroïque en 5 actes; poème de Henri Cain (d'après Le Lorrain). Musique de Massenet. (EXCELSIOR, 30 décembre 1910)
Académie Nationale de Musique. 'Le Miracle'. Drame lyrique en 5 actes de MM. P–B. Gheusi et A. Mérane. Musique de M. Georges Hue. (EXCELSIOR, 31 décembre 1910)
Théâtre de l'Opéra-Comique. 'L'Ancêtre'. Drame lyrique en 3 actes par Camille Saint-Saëns; poème de A. de Lassus. (EXCELSIOR, 24 janvier 1911)
Une grande première à Dresde. 'Le Chevalier à la Rose.' . . . La nouvelle comédie musicale de Richard Strauss et d'Hugo von Hoffmannsthal. (EXCELSIOR, 27 janvier 1911)
Les Grands Concerts. Concert Lamoureux. (EXCELSIOR, 6 février 1911)
Une première au Théâtre Déjazet. 'Les Camelots du 201e'. Vaudeville en 3 actes, de MM. Jacques Nayral et Henri Clerc. (EXCELSIOR, 9 février 1911)
Les Grands Concerts, Au Conservatoire. Concerts-Colonne. Concerts-Lamoureux. (EXCELSIOR, 13 février 1911)
Une première au Trianon-Lyrique. 'Zaza'. Comédie Lyrique en 4 actes de M.R. Léoncavallo, tirés de la pièce de MM. Pierre Berton et Ch. Simon. (EXCELSIOR, 17 février 1911)
Reprise des 'Maîtres Chanteurs' à l'Opéra. (EXCELSIOR, 19 février 1911)
Les Grands Concerts. Concerts-Colonne. Concerts-Lamoureux. Concerts-Sechiari. (EXCELSIOR, 20 février 1911)
Les Grands Concerts. Concerts-Lamoureux. (EXCELSIOR, 27 février 1911)
Opéra-Comique. 'Le Voile du Bonheur'. Comédie musicale en 2 actes, d'après la comédie de Georges Clemenceau, par Paul Ferrier, musique de M. Charles Pons. 'La Jota'. Conte lyrique en 2 actes, paroles et musique de M. Raoul Laparra. (EXCELSIOR, 27 avril 1911)
'Gwendoline'. Opéra en 2 actes. Musique d'Emmanuel Chabrier. Paroles de Catulle Mendès: 'España'. Ballet en un acte de Mme Jane Catulle-Mendès. Musique de Chabrier. Inauguration de la Grande Saison au Châtelet. Festival Beethoven. (EXCELSIOR, 4 mai 1911)
Théâtre du Châtelet. Festival Beethoven (Deuxième Concert). (EXCELSIOR, 7 mai 1911)
Le Festival Beethoven. Troisième Concert. (EXCELSIOR, 10 mai 1911)
Théâtre de l'Opéra-Comique. 'Thérèse'. Drame lyrique en 2 actes, de MM. Jules Claretie et Jules Massenet. 'L'Heure Espagnole'. Comédie musicale on 1 acte, de Franc-Nohain. Musique de Maurice Ravel. (EXCELSIOR, 18 mai 1911)

La Tétralogie à l'Opéra. 'L'Or du Rhin'. Prologue. Une anecdote sur Charles Garnier. (EXCELSIOR, 11 juin 1911)

La Tétralogie à l'Opéra. 'La Valkyrie'. (EXCELSIOR, 12 juin 1911)

La Tétralogie à l'Opéra. 'Siegfried'. (EXCELSIOR, 14 juin 1911)

La Tétralogie à l'Opéra. 'Le Crépuscule des Dieux'. (EXCELSIOR, 16 juin 1911)

Le 2eme cycle de la Tétralogie à l'Opéra. (EXCELSIOR, 25 juin 1911)

Le 2eme cycle de la Tétralogie à l'Opéra. 'La Valkyrie'. (EXCELSIOR, 26 juin 1911)

'La Fille du Ciel'. Une préface de Mme Judith Gautier et de Pierre Loti pour la pièce chinoise qu'ils ont écrite en collaboration. (EXCELSIOR, 27 juin 1911)

À l'Opéra. Le 2eme cycle de la Tétralogie. 'Siegfried'. (EXCELSIOR, 28 juin 1911)

À l'Opéra. Le 2eme cycle de la Tétralogie. 'Le Crépuscule des Dieux'. (EXCELSIOR, 30 juin 1911)

Fanelli. (LE FIGARO, 23 décembre 1917)

II
GENERAL

BOOKS

The following are among the books consulted. English books are published in London, French books in Paris, unless otherwise stated.

ADAM, Mme Juliette (Juliette Lamber) *Mes Premières Armes littéraires et politiques.* (Lemerre. 1904.)
 Mes Sentiments et nos Idées avant 1870. (Lemerre. 1905.)
AJALBERT, Jean *Les Mystères de l'Académie Goncourt.* (Ferenczi & Fils. 1929.)
ANON *Album Mariani.* Juillet 1891. 1re série. (G. Richard. 1891.)
 Album Mariani. Août 1892. 2e série. (G. Richard. 1892.)
 A Handbook for Travellers in France. 2 vols. (Murray. 1892.)
ARDITI, Luigi *My Reminiscences.* (Skeffington & Son. 1896.)
ARMORY *Cinquante ans de vie parisienne.* (Jean-Renard. 1943.)
AUBRY, Raoul *Une Enquête sur les trois livres préférés.* Préface de M. Jules Lemaître. (Ollendorff. n.d.)
BAC, Ferdinand *Intimités de la IIIe République. La fin des 'temps délicieux'. Souvenirs parisiens.* (Hachette. 1935.)
 Intimités de la IIIe République. De Monsieur Thiers au Président Carnot. Souvenirs de Jeunesse. (Hachette. 1935.)
BADESCO, Luc *La Génération poétique de 1860. La Jeunesse des deux rives.* 2 tomes. (A.–G. Nizet. 1971.)
BAEDEKER, Karl *Northern France.* Handbook for travellers. 5th edition. (Leipzig. Karl Baedeker. 1909.)
BANVILLE, Théodore de *Les Camées parisiens.* (Pincebourde. 1873.)
BARRÈS, Maurice *Mes Cahiers.* 14 tomes. (Plon. 1929–57.)
BEAUNIER, André *Éloges.* (Roger & Chernoviz. 1909.)
BERGERAT, Émile *Théophile Gautier. Entretiens, Souvenirs et Correspondance.* Avec une préface de. Edmond de Goncourt. 4e édition. (Charpentier-Fasquelle. 1911.)
 Souvenirs d'un enfant de Paris. Les Années de Bohème. (Charpentier. 1911.)
 La Chasse au Mouflon, ou petit voyage philosophique en Corse. Avec 43 gravures hors texte d'après des photographes et 55 dessins de Madame Émile Bergerat. (Ch. Delagrave. n.d.)
BERSAUCOURT, A. de *Au temps des Parnassiens. Nina de Villard et ses Amis.* (La Renaissance du Livre. 1922.)
BILLY, André *La Présidente et ses amis.* (Flammarion. 1945.)

L'Époque 1900. 1885–1905. (Tallandier. 1951.)

BLOY, Léon *Le Désespéré*. (Tresse & Stock. 1887.)

BONNIÈRES, Robert *Mémoires d'aujourd'hui*. 2e série. (Ollendorff. 1885.)

BORGEAUD, Henri (ed.) *Correspondance de Claude Debussy et Pierre Louÿs (1893–1904)*. (Corti. 1945.)

[BOUCHOR, Maurice] *Figures contemporaines. Tirées de l'Album Mariani*. Causerie préliminaire par Maurice Bouchor. 6e volume. (Floury. 1901.)

BOUHÉLIER, Saint-Georges de *Le Printemps d'une génération*. (Nagel. 1946.)

BOURGEOIS DE PARIS, Un *Journal du Siège, 1870–1871*. (Dentu. 1872.)

BRISSON, Adolphe *Portraits intimes*. 5 tomes. (Armand Colin. 1894–1901.)

[BURTY, Philippe] *Catalogue de Peintures et Estampes japonaises, . . . et de livres relatifs à l'Orient et au Japon*. (Ernest Leroux. 1891.)

CALMETTES, Fernand *Leconte de Lisle et ses amis*. (Librairies-Imprimeries réunies. n.d.)

CAMACHO, M. Dita *Judith Gautier. Sa Vie et son Œuvre*. (Droz. 1939.)

CHAMPSAUR, Félicien *Les Hommes d'aujourd'hui*. 5 tomes. (Vanier. 1878 —)

CLARETIE, Jules *La Vie à Paris, 1908*. (Charpentier-Fasquelle. 1909.)
La Vie à Paris, 1909. (Charpentier-Fasquelle. 1910.)

COCTEAU, Jean *Portraits-Souvenir, 1900–1914*. (Éditions Grasset. 1935.)

COPPÉE, François *Mon Franc-parler*. 4e série. (Mars 1895–Janvier 1896.) (Lemerre. 1896.)
Souvenirs d'un Parisien. (Lemerre. 1910.)

DAUDET, Mme Alphonse *Journal de Famille et de Guerre, 1914–1919*. (Charpentier. 1920.)

DAUDET, Léon *Vers le roi*. (Nouvelle Librairie Nationale. 1921.)

DEFFOUX, Léon *Chronique de l'Académie Goncourt*. (Librairie de Paris. Firmin Didot. 1929.)

DESCAVES, Lucien *Souvenirs d'un ours*. (Les Éditions de Paris. 1946.)

DESCHAMPS, Gaston *La Vie et les Livres*. 6 tomes. (Armand Colin. 1894–1903.)

DREYFOUS, Maurice *Ce que je tiens à dire. I. 1862–1872*. (Ollendorff. n.d.)

DROUET, Juliette *Mille et une lettres d'amour à Victor Hugo*. Choix, préface et notes par Paul Souchon. (N.R.F. Gallimard. 1951.)

DUBEUX, Albert *La curieuse vie de Georges Courteline*. (Pierre Horay. 1958.)

DU MOULIN-ECKART, Richard, Count *Cosima Wagner*. Translated from the German by C.A. Phillips. And with an Introduction by Ernest Newman. 2 vols. (New York. Knopf. 1930.)

ERNEST-CHARLES, J. *Le Théâtre des Poètes, 1850–1910*. (Société d'Éditions littéraires et artistiques. n.d.)

ESCHOLIER, Raymond *Un amant de génie. Victor Hugo. Lettres d'amour et carnets intimes*. (Fayard. 1953.)

FARRÈRE, Claude *Souvenirs*. (Fayard. 1953.)

FÉVAL, Paul (et al.) *Paris-Guide. II. La Vie*. (Librairie Internationale. 1867.)

FLAUBERT, Gustave *Correspondance*. Nouvelle edition augmentée. (Conard. 1926–1933.)
Correspondance, 1871–1877. (Club de l'Honnête Homme. 1975.)
Correspondance, 1877–1880. (Club de l'Honnête Homme. 1975.)

FONTAINAS, André *Mes Souvenirs du Symbolisme*. (Éditions de la Nouvelle Revue Critique. 1928.)

FOUQUIER, Marcel *Profils et Portraits*. (Lemerre. 1891.)

FOUQUIÈRES, André de *Cinquante ans de panache*. (Horay – Flore. 1951.)

FRANCE, Anatole *La Vie littéraire*. 4e série. (Calmann-Lévy. n.d.)

GAUTIER, Théophile *Le Capitaine Fracasse*. Publié en trois volumes avec un avant-propos par Mme Judith Gautier. (Librairie des Bibliophiles. 1884.)

GHEUSI, P.–B. *Cinquante ans de Paris. Mémoires d'un témoin. 1889–1938.* 2 tomes. (Plon. 1939, 1940.)

GINISTY, Paul *L'Année littéraire, 1886.* (Charpentier. 1887.)
    L'Année littéraire, 1887. (Charpentier. 1888.)
    L'Année littéraire, 1893. (Charpentier, 1894.)

GLATIGNY, Albert *Lettres inédites.* Publiées par Victor Sanson. (Rouen. No publisher given. 1932.)

GONCOURT, Edmond et Jules de *Journal. Mémoires de la vie littéraire.* (Monaco. Les Éditions de l'Imprimerie Nationale. 1956.)

GOURMONT, Rémy de *Judith Gautier.* (Les Celébrités d'aujourd'hui. Bibliothèque internationale d'édition. 1904.)
    Promenades littéraires. 3e édition. (Mercure de France. 1904.)

GREGH, Fernand *L'Âge d'airain.* (Grasset. 1951.)

GUICHARD, Léon *La Musique et les Lettres en France au temps du Wagnérisme.* (Presses universitaires de France. 1963.)
    (ed.) *Lettres à Judith Gautier par Richard et Cosima Wagner.* (Gallimard. 1964.)

GUILLEMIN, Henri *Hugo et la sexualité.* 6e édition. (N.R.F. 1954.)

HENRY, Stuart *Hours with Famous Parisians.* (Chicago. Way & Williams. 1897.)
    French Essays and Profiles. (Dent. 1922.)

HERLIHY, James F. *Catulle Mendès. Critique dramatique et musical.* (Lipschutz. 1936.)

HOCHE, Jules *Les Parisiens chez eux.* (Dentu. 1883.)

HUDDLESTON, Sisley *Bohemian Literary and Social Life in Paris.* (Harrap. 1928.)

HUGO, Victor *Correspondance.* 4 tomes. (Albin-Michel. 1947–52.)
    Choses vues. Souvenirs, journaux, cahiers, 1870–1885. Édition établie, présentée et annotée par Hubert Juin. (Gallimard. 1972.)
    Poésie. Préface de Jean Gaulnier. Présentation et notes de Bernard Leuilliot. III. (Éditions du Seuil. 1972.)

HUYSMANS, J.–K. *Lettres inédites à Émile Zola.* Publiées et annotées par Pierre Lambert, avec une introduction de Pierre Cogny. (Genève. Librairie Droz. 1953.)

IBROVAC, Miodrag *José-Maria de Heredia, Sa vie – son oeuvre.* (Les Presses Françaises. 1923.)

IMBERT, Hugues *Nouveaux profils de musiciens.* (Fischbacher. 1892.)
    Portraits et Études. (Fischbacher. 1894.)

INDY, Vincent d' *Richard Wagner et son influence sur l'art musical français.* (Librairie Delagrave. 1930.)

JOSEPH, Lawrence A. *Henri Cazalis. Sa vie, son oeuvre, son amitié avec Mallarmé.* (Nizet. 1972.)

JOURDAIN, Frantz *Les Décorés. Ceux qui ne le sont pas.* (H. Simonis Empis. 1895.)

KAHN, Gustave *Silhouettes littéraires.* (Éditions Montaigne. 1925.)

KARAGEORGEVITCH, Prince Bojidar *Notes sur l'Inde.* (Calmann Lévy. 1899.)

LARGUIER, Léo *Avant le déluge. Souvenirs.* (Grasset. 1928.)
    Théophile Gautier. (Tallandier. 1948.)

LAZARE, Bernard *Figures contemporaines.* (Perrin. 1895.)

LÉAUTAUD, Paul *Journal littéraire.* (Mercure de France. 1954–1966.)

LE GOFFIC, Charles *Les Romanciers d'aujourd'hui.* (Vanier. 1890.)

LEMAÎTRE, Jules *Impressions de Théâtre.* 2e série. (Lecène & Oudin. 1888.)
    Impressions de Théâtre. 3e série. (Lecène & Oudin. 1889.)

LEPAGE, Auguste *Les Cafés artistiques et littéraires de Paris.* (Martin-Boursin. 1882.)

LEPELLETIER, Edmond *Histoire de la Commune de 1871.* 3 tomes. (Mercure de France. 1911–13.)

LORRAIN, Jean *68 Lettres à Edmond Magnier (1887–1890).* Préface de Henri Chapoutot. (No publisher given. 1909.)

MALLARMÉ, Stéphane *Correspondance, 1862–1871*. Recueillie, classée et annotée par Henri Mondor avec la collaboration de J.–P. Richard. (N.R.F. Gaillimard. 1959.)
Correspondance. II. 1871–1885. Recueillie, classée et annotée par Henri Mondor et Lloyd James Austin. (N.R.F. Gallimard. 1965.)
Documents Stéphane Mallarmé. VI. Présentés par Carl Paul Barbier. Correspondance avec Henri Cazalis 1862–1897 recueillie, classée et annotée avec la collaboration de Lawrence A. Joseph. (Nizet. 1977.)
MASSENET, Jules *Mes Souvenirs (1848–1912)*. (Pierre Lafitte. 1912.)
MAUCLAIR, Camille *Servitude et Grandeur littéraires*. (Ollendorff. 1922.)
MENDÈS, Catulle *Poésies*. 1re série. (Sandoz et Fischbacher. 1976.)
La Légende du Parnasse contemporain. (Bruxelles. Auguste Brancart. 1884.)
Richard Wagner. (Charpentier. 1886.)
Le Mouvement poétique français de 1867 à 1900. (Imprimerie Nationale. 1903.)
MEYER-ZUNDEL, S. *La Gloire de l'Illusion*. (Éditions Hispano-Françaises. Librairie Cervantès. 1920.)
Quinze Ans auprès de Judith Gautier. (No place of publication, or publisher, given. 1969.)
MEYSENBUG, Malwida von *Rebel in a Crinoline*. Memoirs of Malwida von Meysenbug. Edited by Mildred Adams from the translation of Elsa von Meysenbug Lyons. (Allen & Unwin. 1937.)
MIOMANDRE, Francis de *Figures d'hier et d'aujourd'hui*. (Dorbon-Aîné. 1910.)
MONDOR, Henri *Vie de Mallarmé*. (N.R.F. Gallimard. 1941.)
Eugène Lefebure. Sa Vie – ses lettres à Mallarmé. (N.R.F. Gallimard. 1951.)
MONTERA, Pierre de *Luigi Gualdo (1844–1898)*. Son milieu et ses amitiés milanaises et parisiennes. Lettres inédites à François Coppée. Pages oubliées. (Rome. Edizioni di Storia e Letteratura. 1983.)
MONTESQUIOU, Robert de *Les Perles rouges. Les Paroles diaprées*. (n.p. 1910.)
Majeurs et mineurs. (Sansot. 1917.)
Les Quarante Bergères.(Librairie de France. 1925.)
MOORE, George *Confessions of a Young Man*. (Heinemann. 1917.)
MORICE, Charles *La Littérature de tout à l'heure*. (Perrin. 1889.)
MUIRHEAD, Findlay, and MONMARCHÉ, Marcel (ed.) *Brittany*. (The Blue Guides Macmillan. 1925.)
ORMOND, Richard *John Singer Sargent*. (Phaidon. 1970.)
[PAKENHAM, Michael] Anatole France: *Croquis féminins*; Catulle Mendès: *Figurines de poètes*; Adolphe Racot: *Portraits-cartes*, Texte établi et présenté par Michael Pakenham. (Exeter. University of Exeter. 1979.)
PEARSE, Mrs G., and HIRD, Frank *L'Art idéaliste et mystique. Doctrine de l'ordre et du salon annuel des rose + croix*. 2e édition. (Chamuel. 1894.)
POITEAU, Émile *Quelques écrivains de ce temps*. (Grasset. 1918.)
POREL, Jacques *Fils de Réjane. Souvenirs*. 2 tomes. (Plon. 1951, 1952.)
POURTALÈS, Guy de *Wagner. Histoire d'un artiste*. (N.R.F. Gallimard. 1932.)
PRINET, J. et DILASSER, A. *Nadar*. (Armand Colin. 1966.)
PRINGUÉ, Gabriel-Louis *Trente ans de dîners en ville*. (Édition Revue Adam. 1950.)
PUTTER, Irving *La dernière illusion de Leconte de Lisle. Lettres inédites à Émilie Leforestier*. (Genève. Droz. 1968.)
RACOT, Adolphe *Portraits d'aujourd'hui*. (Librairie illustrée. 1887.)
RAITT, A.W. *The Life of Villiers de l'Isle-Adam*. (Oxford. The Clarendon Press. 1981.)
RAVON, Georges *L'Académie Goncourt en dix couverts*. (Aubanel. 1946.)
RÉGNIER, Henri de *De mon Temps . . .* (Mercure de France. 1933.)
Figures et Caractères. 2e édition. (Mercure de France. 1901.)
RENARD, Jules *Journal. 1887–1910*. Texte établi par Léon Guichard et Gilbert

Sigaux. (N.R.F. Bibliothèque de la Pléïade. 1960.)

REYER, Ernest *Notes de Musique*. (Charpentier. 1875.)

Quarante ans de musique. (Calmann-Lévy. 1909.)

REYMOND, Jean *Albert Glatigny. La vie – l'homme – le poète. Les origines de l'École Parnassienne*. (Droz. 1936.)

RICARD, L.-X. de *Petites mémoires d'un Parnassien*. RACOT, Adolphe: *Les Parnassiens*. Introductions et commentaires de M. Pakenham. (Minard. 1967.)

RICHARDSON, Joanna *Théophile Gautier: his Life and Times*. (Reinhardt. 1958.)

Princess Mathilde. (Weidenfeld & Nicolson. 1969.)

Verlaine. (Weidenfeld & Nicolson. 1971.)

Victor Hugo. (Weidenfeld & Nicolson. 1976.)

Paris under Siege. (The Folio Society. 1982.)

RIÈSE, Laure *Les Salons littéraires parisiens du Second Empire jusqu'à nos jours*. (Toulouse. Éditions Privat. 1962.)

RICTOR, Léon *Les Arts et les Lettres*. 1re série. (Lemerre. 1901.)

Les Arts et les Lettres. 3e série. (Lemerre. 1908.)

ROBIDA, Michel *Le Salon Charpentier et les impressionistes*. (La Bibliothèque des Arts. 1958.)

ROSNY, J.-H. (aîné) *Mémoires de la vie littéraire. Académie Goncourt. Les Salons. Quelques Éditeurs*. (Crès & Cie. 1927.)

Torches et Lumignons. Souvenirs de la vie littéraire. (Éditions de La Force française. 1921.)

ROSTAND, Maurice *Confession d'un demi-siècle*. (La Jeune Parque. 1948.)

RUDE, Maxime *Confidences d'un journaliste*. (André Sagnier. 1876.)

SAINTE-BEUVE, C.-A. *Lettres à la Princesse*. 4e édition. (Michel Lévy frères. 1873.)

Correspondance générale. Recueillie, classée et annotée par Jean Bonnerot (et par son fils Alain Bonnerot). 18 tomes. (Stock; Privat; Didier. 1935–1977.)

SAMAIN, Albert *Des Lettres, 1887–1900*. (Mercure de France. 1933.)

SÉCHÉ, Alphonse, et BERTAUT, Jules *L'Évolution du Théâtre Contemporain*. Avec une préface par Émile Faguet. (Mercure de France. 1908.)

SEILLIÈRE, Baron Ernest de *Un poète parnassien. André de Guerne: 1853–1912*. (J. de Gigord. 1930.)

SERVIÈRES, Georges *Richard Wagner jugé en France*. (Librairie Henry du Parc. n.d.)

SHERARD, R.H. *Modern Paris. Some sidelights on its inner life*. (T. Werner Laurie. 1911.)

SILVESTRE, Armand *Portraits et Souvenirs, 1886–1891*. (Charpentier. 1891.)

Figures contemporaines, tirées de l'Album Mariani. 2e volume. Causerie préliminaire par Armand Silvestre. (Henry Floury. 1896.)

Au Pays des Souvenirs. Mes Maîtres et mes maîtresses. (Librairie illustrée. n.d.)

SOUDAY, Paul *Les Livres du temps*. 3e série. (Éditions Émile–Paul Frères. 1930.)

SOURIAU, Maurice *Histoire du Parnasse*. (Éditions Spès. 1929.)

TAILHADE, Laurent *Quelques fantômes de jadis*. (L'Édition Française illustrée. 1920.)

TALMEYR, Maurice *Souvenirs d'avant le déluge. 1870–1914*. (Perrin. 1927.)

THARAUD, Jérôme et Jean *En Bretagne. Essais*. (Éditions de la Chronique des Lettres Françaises. Aux Horizons de France. 1927.)

THEURIET, André *Jours d'été*. (Ollendorff. 1901.)

THOMPSON, Vance *French Portraits. Being Appreciations of the Writers of Young France*. (Boston. Richard G. Badger & Co. 1900.)

TIERSOT, Julien *Lettres françaises de Richard Wagner*. Recueillies et publiées par Julien Tiersot. (Éditions Bernard Grasset. 1935.)

Musiques pittoresques. Promenades à l'Exposition de 1889. (Librairie Fischbacher. 1889.)

TILD, Jean *Théophile Gautier et ses amis.* (Albin Michel. 1951.)

UZANNE, Joseph *Figures contemporaines, tirées de l'Album Mariani.* Rédigées par Joseph Uzanne, 10e volume. (Henry Floury. 1906.)

UZANNE, Octave *Le Miroir du Monde. Notes et sensations de la vie pittoresque.* (Quantin. 1888.)

Figures contemporaines, tirées de l'Album Mariani. 1er volume. Prélude Iconographique par Octave Uzanne. (Flammarion. 1894.)

VENTO, Claude *Les Salons de Paris en 1889.* (E. Dentu. 1891.)

VERLAINE, Paul *Œuvres complètes.* Tomes IV, V. (Éditions Messein. 1949.)

VILLIERS DE L'ISLE-ADAM, J.–M.–N.–P.–A. de *Chez les passants.* (Comptoir d'édition. 1890.)

Correspondance générale et documents inedits. Édition recueillie, classée et présentée par Joseph Bollery. 2 tomes. (Mercure de France. 1952.)

VIZETELLY, E.A. *Paris and Her People Under the Third Republic.* (Chatto & Windus. 1919.)

WAGNER, Richard *Une Capitulation. Comédie à la manière antique.* (Alphonse Leduc. 1920.)

WALEFFE, Maurice de *Quand Paris était un paradis. Mémoires, 1900–1939.* (Société des Éditions Denoël. 1947.)

WILLY *Souvenirs littéraires . . . et autres.* (Éditions Montaigne. 1925.)

WRIGHT, Thomas *The Life of John Payne.* (T. Fisher Unwin. 1919.)

ARTICLES, PAMPHLETS AND CATALOGUES

AGHION, Max *Ce Catulle Mendès qu'on avait oublié.* (JOURNAL DE GENÈVE, 21–22 juillet 1962)

ALBALAT, Antoine *Les 'Samedis' de José-Maria de Heredia.* (LA REVUE HEBDOMADAIRE, 4 octobre 1919, 34 sqq.)

ANON *Le Duel Catulle Mendès – Vanor.* (LE FIGARO, 24 mai 1899)

Une princesse. (MERCURE DE FRANCE, janvier 1900, 184–5)

Mort tragique de M. Catulle Mendès. (LE PETIT JOURNAL, 9 février 1909)

Mme Judith Gautier est élue membre de l'Académie-Goncourt. (Unspecified newspaper cutting, 29 octobre 1910. Bibliothèque de l'Arsenal. RF 59973 ff 25–6)

Mort de Mme Judith Gautier. (LE FIGARO, 28 décembre 1917)

Mort de Mme Judith Gautier. (LA PRESSE, 28 décembre 1917)

Mort de Judith Gautier. (MERCURE DE FRANCE, 16 janvier 1918, 376–7)

Nécrologie. Mme Judith Gautier. (JOURNAL DES DÉBATS, 29 décembre 1917)

Les Lettres. (L'INTRANSIGEANT, 28 décembre 1917.)

Mme Jane Catulle-Mendès. (ÈVE, 26 août 1923)

AUBRY, Raoul *Un début chez les Goncourt.* (LE TEMPS, 25 novembre 1910)

BARRACAND, Léon *Souvenirs des Lettres: Heredia, Leconte de Lisle.* (LA REVUE DE PARIS, 1er mars 1914, 183 sqq.)

BARTHOU, Louis *Richard Wagner et Judith Gautier (documents inédits). I, II.* (LA REVUE DE PARIS, 1er août 1932, 481 sqq.; 15 août 1932, 721 sqq.)

BASTARD, Georges *Leconte de Lisle. Souvenirs de jeunesse.* (REVUE BLEUE, 14 décembre 1895, 742 sqq.)

BEAUNIER, André *Catulle Mendès.* (LE FIGARO, 9 février 1909.)

Judith Gautier. (REVUE DES DEUX MONDES, 1er février 1918, 692 sqq.)

BERGERAT, Émile *Catulle Mendès.* (LE FIGARO, 9 février 1909.)

Judith Gautier. (LE FIGARO, 8 janvier 1918.)

[BERNHARDT, Sarah] *Bibliothèque de Mme Sarah Bernhardt*. (Leclerc. 1923.)

BILLY, André *Paris littéraire en 1910*. (LES ŒUVRES LIBRES, 1945.)

BOUCHER, Henri *Lettres familières de Théophile Gautier. I, II*. (MERCURE DE FRANCE, 15 mai 1929, 108 sqq.; 1er juin 1929, 319 sqq.)

BRODY, Elaine *Letters from Judith Gautier to Chalmers Clifton*. (Champaign, Illinois. THE FRENCH REVIEW, Vol. LVIII, No. 5, April 1985, 670 sqq.)

BROUSSON, Jean-Jacques *Judith Gautier*. (EXCELSIOR. 29 décembre 1917.)

BUFFENOIR, Hippolyte *Grandes Dames contemporaines. La Duchesse de Rohan*. (Librairie Henri Leclerc. 1904.)

BURTY, Philippe *Poèmes de la Libellule*. (LA RÉPUBLIQUE FRANÇAISE, 22 mai 1885.)

CALVOCORESSI, M.–D. *An Unknown Composer of To-day. M. Ernest Fanelli*. (MUSICAL TIMES, 1 April 1912, 225–6)

[CHARAVAY, J., E., & N.] *Bulletin d'autographes*, juin 1962. (Charavay. 1962.)

COLLONGES *Mme Judith Gautier à l'Académie Goncourt*. (LE FIGARO, 29 octobre 1910.)

COPPÉE, François **Le Livre de Jade**, par *Mme Judith Walter*. (LE MONITEUR UNIVERSEL, 5 octobre 1867.)

DAVENAY, G. *Catulle Mendès. Notes biographiques*. (LE FIGARO, 9 février 1909.)

DESCHAMPS, Gaston *La Vie littéraire. Mme Judith Gautier à l'Académie Goncourt*. (LE TEMPS, 30 octobre 1910.)

Nécrologie. Judith Gautier. (LE TEMPS, 29 décembre 1917.)

DIVOIRE, F. *Quand Mendès était dans la salle*. (L'ORDRE, 3 septembre 1938.)

DUCRAY, Camille *Leconte de Lisle à l'Académie*. (LA REVUE HEBDOMADAIRE, 11 octobre 1919, 236 sqq.)

DUJARDIN, Édouard *Bayreuth. Histoire du théâtre de Richard Wagner*. (REVUE WAGNÉRIENNE, 8 juin 1885, 136 sqq.)

DUQUESNEL, Félix *Catulle Mendès*. (LE GAULOIS. 9 février 1909.)

ERNEST-CHARLES, J. *Les Livres dont on parle*. **Poésies** *par Judith Gautier*. (EXCELSIOR, 21 juillet 1911.)

ESCHOLIER, Raymond *Victor Hugo, l'homme* . . . (LES ŒUVRES LIBRES, mai 1952, 105 sqq.)

FOURCAUD *Les Concerts. Galerie Nadar: L'Oeuvre de Richard Wagner expliqué et commenté en six soirées. Première soiré;* **Rienzi** *et* **Le Vaisseau Fantôme**. (LE GAULOIS, 6 mars 1880.)

GANDERAX, Louis *Revue dramatique* . . . **La Marchande de Sourires**, *drame en 5 actes, de Mme Judith Gautier*. (REVUE DES DEUX MONDES, 15 mai 1888, 454 sqq.)

[GAUTIER, Théophile] *Centenaire Théophile Gautier. Fête organisée à Tarbes le 2 juillet 1911. Conférence de M. Laurent Tailhade. Discours de M. S.–C. Leconte et de M. Tristan Dérème*. (Tarbes. Dussèque. 1911.)

Théophile Gautier (1811–1872). (Bibliothèque Nationale 1961.)

GOURMONT, Jean de *Littérature . . . Judith Gautier:* **Le Collier des Jours: Le Second Rang du Collier. Souvenirs Literatures**. *(Félix Juven.) Rémy de Gourmont:* **Judith Gautier**. (MERCURE DE FRANCE, mars 1904, 748 sqq.)

GOURMONT, Rémy de *Littérature. . . Judith Gautier:* **Le Collier des Jours**. *(Juven.)* (MERCURE DE FRANCE, février 1903, 748 sqq.)

GRISON, Georges *L'accident mortel*. (LE FIGARO, 9 février 1909.)

Tin-Tun-Ling. (LE FIGARO, 29 décembre 1917.)

GUILLEMOT, Maurice **La Marchande de sourires**. (LE FIGARO, 21 avril 1888.)

HARAUCOURT, Edmond *Le Petit Théâtre*. (LE GAULOIS, 28 mai 1898.)

Judith Gautier. (INFORMATION, 20 décembre 1922)

HARRY, Myriam *Réveil d'ombres*. (LES ŒUVRES LIBRES, novembre 1950, 191 sqq.)

HENRIOT, Émile *Des lettres de Wagner à Judith Gautier*. (LE TEMPS, 30 juin 1925.)

HIRSCH, Charles-Henry *Les Revues . . . REVUE DE PARIS: Mme Judith Gautier, sur*

Théophile Gautier et les Goncourt. (MERCURE DE FRANCE, janvier 1903, 209 sqq.)

JEAN-AUBRY, G. *Villiers de l'Isle-Adam et la musique.* (MERCURE DE FRANCE, 15 novembre 1938, 40 sqq.)

KAHN, Gustave *Théâtre:* **La Marchande de Sourires** . . . (LA REVUE INDÉPENDANTE, mai 1888, 362–3)

LE GOFFIC, Charles *Catulle Mendès et le Parnasse contemporain.* (LA REVUE HEBDOMADAIRE, 20 février 1909, 355 sqq.)

LE SENNE, C. *Judith Gautier est morte.* (Unspecified press-cutting of 29 December 1917. Bibliothèque de l'Arsenal, RF 59973 f 41)

LOUŸS, Pierre *Marionnettes.* (LA REVUE BLANCHE, juin 1894, 573–4.)

MACKWORTH, Cecily *Stéphane Mallarmé et Augusta Holmès: une amitié de jeunesse.* (*Documents Stéphane Mallarmé*, VI, 335 sqq. Nizet. 1980.)
Correspondance de Mallarmé et Marras. (*Documents Stéphane Mallarmé*, VII, 231 sqq. Nizet. 1980.)

MAURCELAY, Baude de *La vérité sur le salon de Nina de Villard.* (LE FIGARO, 2–8 avril 1929.)

MAURICE-VERNE *La fille de Théophile Gautier vient de mourir.* (Unspecified press-cutting of 7 January 1918. Bibliothèque de l'Arsenal. RF 59973 ff 42 sqq.)

MELCHIOR-BONNET, Christian *À la mémoire de Judith Gautier.* (LE GAULOIS, 6 janvier 1923.)

MENDÈS, Catulle *Le salon universel de Munich.* (L'ARTISTE, 1er septembre 1869, 400–406.)

MEYER-ZUNDEL, S. *Requiem pour Judith.* (LES NOUVELLES LITTÉRAIRES, 25 janvier 1968.)

MONSIEUR DE L'ORCHESTRE, Un *La Soirée théâtrale. Un Quartier aux abois.* (LE FIGARO, 28 février 1880.)

MONTFORT, Eugène *Catulle Mendès.* (CANDIDE, 31 juillet 1930.)

MONVAL, Jean *Catulle Mendès et François Coppée.* (LA REVUE DE PARIS, 1er mars 1909, 73 sqq.)

MOUNT, Charles *John Singer Sargent and Judith Gautier.* (Detroit. THE ART QUARTERLY, summer 1955, 136 sqq.)

PARAF, Pierre *Augusta Holmès, a-t-elle été la fille de Vigny?* (LES NOUVELLES LITTÉRAIRES, 12 septembre 1957.)

POUVOURVILLE, Albert de *Judith Gautier.* (LE GAULOIS, 29 décembre 1917.)

RACHILDE *Revue du Mois. Les Romans. Judith Gautier:* **Princesses d'Amour.** (MERCURE DE FRANCE, septembre 1900, 758–60.)

RATEAU, Jules *Catulle Mendès: ses premières années et ses dernières heures.* (GIL BLAS, 9 février 1909.)

RÉGNIER, Henri de *Faces et Profils. Judith Gautier.* (LES NOUVELLES LITTÉRAIRES, 16 août 1930.)

REYER, Ernest *À propos de* **Lohengrin** *et de Richard Wagner. I, II.* (JOURNAL DES DÉBATS, 30 septembre, 7 octobre 1868.)

REYNIER, R. *Les Premières. À New-York le Century-Theater de New-York représente la 'Fille du Ciel', de Pierre Loti.* (Unidentified press-cutting, 15 octobre 1912. Bibliothèque de l'Arsenal. Rf 59963 f 5.)

ROUZIER-DORCIÈRES, E. *Comment est mort Catulle Mendès.* (COMOEDIA, 9 février 1909.)

SOUDAY, Paul *Les Livres. Judith Gautier.* (LE TEMPS, 19 janvier 1918.)

VEDEL, Émile *Judith Gautier.* (Press-cutting from an unspecified paper, 5 November 1910. Bibliothèque de l'Arsenal. RF 59973 ff 13 sqq.)

VILLIERS DE L'ISLE-ADAM, J.–M.–N.–P.–A. de *Le Dragon Impérial, par Mme Judith Mendès.* (LA VOGUE PARISIENNE, 13 août 1869. Reprinted in MERCURE DE FRANCE, 1er novembre 1939, 230–2.)

WOLFF, Albert *Gazette de Partout*. (LE FIGARO, 15 septembre 1869.)

WYZEWA, T. de *Les Livres nouveaux* . . . *Judith Gautier:Le Dragon Impérial. La Soeur du Soleil ou l'Usurpateur. Fleurs d'Orient. Le Vieux de la Montagne. Les Mémoires d'un Éléphant Blanc*. *(Colin)* . . . (REVUE BLEUE, 30 décembre 1893, 853.)

Index